THE
SS

Also by Adrian Weale

Patriot Traitors
Green-Eyed Boys
Secret Warfare
The Real SAS
Fighting Fit
Eyewitness Hiroshima
Renegades: Hitler's Englishmen
Science and the Swastika

THE
SS

A NEW HISTORY

ADRIAN WEALE

Little, Brown

LITTLE, BROWN

First published in Great Britain in 2010 by Little, Brown
Reprinted 2010

A CIP catalogue record for this book
is available from the British Library.

ISBN HB 978-0-316-72723-5
ISBN CF 978-1-4087-0304-5

Typeset in Sabon by M Rules
Printed and bound in Great Britain by
Clays Ltd, St Ives plc

Papers used by Little, Brown are natural, renewable and
recyclable products sourced from well-managed forests and certified
in accordance with the rules of the Forest Stewardship Council.

Little, Brown
An imprint of
Little, Brown Book Group
100 Victoria Embankment
London EC4Y 0DY

An Hachette UK Company
www.hachette.co.uk

www.littlebrown.co.uk

Contents

Acknowledgements

I am extremely grateful for the help I have received from a number of organisations during the writing of this book. These include:

The UK National Archives at Kew
The US National Archives at College Park, Maryland
The Imperial War Museum Library, London
The Defence Academy Library, Shrivenham
The German Federal Archives in Koblenz, Freiburg and Berlin
The United States Holocaust Memorial Museum, Washington DC
Yad Vashem, Jerusalem
The Auschwitz State Museum, Poland

Over the years I have spoken to and corresponded with a large number of individuals on this and related subjects and I hope they will forgive me for not listing them all here. Nevertheless, all of them have contributed in some way and I would like to offer my thanks.

Work on this book was interrupted when I was called up and sent to Iraq with the British Army in 2003. Resuming work after a high-stress combat tour proved somewhat difficult and I am extremely grateful for the patience of everyone at Little, Brown, particularly including Tim Whiting, Iain Hunt and Steve Guise, who bore with me as I readjusted! As always, my friend and agent Andrew Lownie has been a tower of strength.

On a personal level, I'm very grateful for the help and advice of my friends Guy Walters and Michael Burleigh; and finally I must thank my wife Mary and my children Robert, Ivo and Dido for putting up with the general grouchiness of a writer working on a long and involved project!

Preface

Thirty or so years ago, when I first studied the history of the Third Reich as a schoolboy, I began to read about the SS. In the material we were using, they were often described as 'Hitler's Bodyguards', but this struck me as odd. I could understand the sense in a wartime head of state having a bodyguard unit, but as I read more I came to understand that the SS had played a central role in the attempted murder of the Jewish population of Europe; it had key responsibilities in policing National Socialist Germany; and it had fielded a substantial military force. How, I wondered, had this come about?

This book is my answer to that question. The reason why I wanted to write about the SS – apart from the fact that it had always fascinated me – was because there seemed to be an increasing disconnection between what the organisation actually was and how it is now portrayed, more than sixty years since it was dissolved. A generation of casual readers of military history is likely to believe that the Holocaust was perpetrated by a gang of psychopathic sadists, while the Waffen-SS was an elite force of military supermen whose reputation has been tainted simply because of the uniform they wore.

I did not want to write a combat history of the Waffen-SS: there are plenty of those already, dealing with units at all levels from company to 'Panzer Army'. And I did not want to write a comprehensive history of the Holocaust: some of the most compelling historical writing of recent years – by Christopher Browning, Saul Friedlander, David Cesarani, Michael Wildt, Götz Aly and Michael Burleigh, among others – has done that job. Instead, I have attempted to write a book for the general reader rather than the academic, in order that they may understand the links between the SS's background and formation, the ideology it adopted, its decision-making processes and its strategies 'on the ground', while also gaining an insight into how the various parts of the organisation fitted together. This is not a comprehensive history of the activities of the SS, but it deals in some depth with the organisation's key roles during the Third Reich.

About a month after I signed the contract to write this book, I received a call-up notice from the British Ministry of Defence, requiring me to rejoin the regular army, travel to Iraq and serve six months as a member of the occupation forces there. In one respect this was frustrating, because I had been researching and planning this book for some time, but it was also extremely instructive. I had originally trained as an army intelligence officer, and was expecting to be employed in a liaison role in Iraq. Instead, I was appointed chief of staff (or deputy governor) of the Coalition Provisional Authority that was running the province of Dhi Qar, centred on the ancient city of Nasariyah (the biblical Ur of the Chaldees). I therefore found myself in the distinctly odd position – for an author, at least – of possessing almost absolute authority over a population of some two million people.

Occasionally I had time to reflect on how I would have behaved in that situation if I had come up through a system that had indoctrinated me with the Nazi principles of Aryan supremacy, eugenics, *Lebensraum* and the *Führerprinzip*, rather than through my own system of British grammar school, university and the army. I'm not sure I ever found an answer. To this day, the crimes committed by the SS almost – but not quite – defy imagination. I cannot believe that I, or indeed any soldier with whom I served, would willingly participate in the mass murder of men, women and children, or take part in a continental war of conquest. Yet one group of people did precisely that just over sixty years ago. It is important to try to understand why.

Adrian Weale
London

Author's Note

Books written in English about the Third Reich inevitably use some German vocabulary, simply because some German words and concepts do not translate conveniently into English. As far as possible, I have rendered all German words into English, with the exception of the proper names of a few organisations that defy translation (such as the paramilitary group the *Frontbann*) and words that have effectively passed into English, like 'Reich', 'Gestapo' and so on. German military ranks have been given as their nearest English equivalent. SS ranks are somewhat more complicated. As a political organisation, SS ranks had no meaningful military equivalence until after 1933, when some members of the SS acquired rank equivalence, firstly with the police and later with the army. For these people, I have used an approximate military equivalent rank in English, prefixed with 'SS-'. A detailed comparative table is included as an appendix to the main text.

Introduction

The SS has exerted a powerful hold on the popular imagination for more than six decades. The most compelling reason for this is the central role that the SS and its leadership played in the German state's attempt to exterminate the Jewish population of Europe and enslave many other people who found themselves under German control. But the enormity of the crimes committed by members of the SS has, in some ways, distorted our view of the organisation.

The SS (an abbreviation of *Schutzstaffeln* – protection squads) was created in 1925 as a small, local bodyguard for Adolf Hitler and other senior leaders of the National Socialist German Workers' Party (NSDAP) as they tried to re-establish themselves as an effective force in German politics following the disaster of the Munich *Putsch*. Over the next few years, its membership fluctuated from the low hundreds to a thousand or so, but the character of the SS remained much the same. Its members were a slightly more reliable and trustworthy brand of part-time political thug than the bullies and bruisers of the National Socialists' main paramilitary force, the brown-shirted 'Stormtroopers' of the *Sturmabteilung* (SA). Thereafter though, the SS changed radically. The catalyst for this transformation was Heinrich Himmler, who became Deputy National Leader of the organisation in 1928 and took over as National Leader in January 1929. First, Himmler developed a national structure and role for the SS within the whole

National Socialist movement. Second, he created a distinct ideology for the organisation, with the intention of making it attractive to the 'best' members of the National Socialist movement and subsequently the German 'race-community'. They would then be moved to join the SS, and Himmler would be at the head of an elite group in German society. Third, after the NSDAP came to power, Himmler assumed control of the policing and security apparatus of the German state, which enabled him to place many of the SS's activities outside the realm of traditional legal structures. Finally, he developed a significant armed force that was independent of the traditional military structures of the state. All of this enabled the SS to function as an instrument of Hitler's will – through Himmler – largely unfettered by traditional constitutional and moral constraints.

In the early years of the SS, the majority of its members were drawn from the generation that had recently fought in the First World War. Although the popular media have traditionally stereotyped SS personnel as either brutal, sadistic thugs or colourless bureaucrats, in reality many of the middle-ranking and senior officers were highly educated, creative, technically accomplished members of Germany's intellectual elite. Just as Himmler had hoped, the organisation attracted many talented young men into its officer corps. They saw the SS as a vehicle for their professional and political ambitions in the new, National Socialist Germany, and embraced the organisation and its elitist outlook with enthusiasm. In all likelihood, they would have struggled to achieve similar success in the German Army, given its traditional social prejudice.

Since his suicide in British custody in 1945, Himmler has been portrayed as a homicidal monster, a hypocrite, a fussy pedant and a ditherer.[1] He was all of these things, but also one of the most energetic, ferociously ambitious, sure-footed and successful political operators in the Third Reich. At school, he was an unusually bright student. Despite his somewhat weak physique and poor eyesight, he passed his training as an infantry officer with few problems (although he was too young to serve as a frontline soldier in the First World War). He sailed through both the practical and academic elements of his agriculture studies in Munich after the war. As a young political activist, he was well regarded and rose quickly through the ranks. He set himself realistic targets and worked diligently and creatively to achieve them. In short, he was well read, well educated and highly organised.

He was also an excellent selector of personnel. Much of the business of government in the Third Reich was hampered by cronyism: long-serving or well-connected party members were often given jobs that were well beyond the scope of their talents. This was much less the case in the SS: 'old fighters' might be given something to do, but they rarely had roles of crucial importance to the functioning of the organisation and its operations unless they also possessed the talent to see it through.

As an intelligent and effective leader supported by high-quality subordinates, Himmler adopted the German military doctrine of *Auftragstaktik* (mission command). In this system, orders are given only in the form of broad directives, with authority delegated to the lowest appropriate level, so that actions can be carried out in a streamlined, timely and effective manner. This proved to be an ideal system for the SS as its mission developed. The organisation's ideology gave its personnel a common doctrinal framework in which to operate, but mission command allowed them to use initiative to achieve specific objectives. Good examples of this can be seen in the activities of the *Einsatzgruppen* (special task groups) that followed the German Army into Russia in 1941. Each adopted a different approach to their overall mission of murdering Jews – with some fomenting anti-Semitic pogroms by local pro-German militias while others carried out the killing themselves – but all achieved comparable results. Meanwhile, the local SS commander in Lublin, SS-*Obergruppenführer* (General) Odilo Globocnik, set up static camps in which the majority of the Jews of south-eastern Poland – at least 1.5 million people – were murdered by a group of no more than 125 members of the SS, assisted by relatively small units of Ukrainian auxiliaries.[2] The effectiveness of Zyklon B gas as an instrument of mass slaughter was discovered as a result of this sort of local experimentation at the Auschwitz concentration camp complex in Silesia.

Himmler advanced in the National Socialist hierarchy by making himself and his organisation available to carry out every order, no matter how distasteful. When Hitler wanted to eliminate one of his oldest collaborators, Himmler and the SS agreed to do it. When Hitler decided that the sick and the handicapped should be subjected to euthanasia, Himmler provided the men to staff the gas chambers and dispose of the bodies.[*] Hitler was no closer to Himmler than he was to any of his other senior collaborators, but Himmler's determination to fulfil the dictator's wishes earned him the nickname 'Faithful Heinrich'. This was not simply slavish devotion. Himmler accepted the crude principles of National Socialist ideology and developed a specific ideological framework for the SS. He positioned the members of his organisation – whom he saw as a kind of chivalric order – as the vanguard of a new 'breed' of German who would lead the people out of their racial, cultural, political and economic chaos by any means possible.[3] Within this framework, the ferocious savagery that the SS visited upon the Jews and other supposed racial enemies of the German people became a political and biological imperative. This was the nature of the SS.

---

[*] While the SS provided most of the ancillary personnel in the euthanasia programme, the actual killing was largely done by doctors and nurses.

1

The Defeat of Wilhelmine Germany and the Origins of the National Socialist Party

Like the National Socialist Party itself, the SS owed its existence to the wave of revolution that swept through Germany in the autumn of 1918, when it finally became clear that the First World War was lost. Many German civilians, as well as members of the armed forces, had been blithely convinced that they were on the brink of victory, despite the miserable conditions and endemic shortages that had increasingly blighted their lives as the war dragged on. However, despite defeating Russia the previous year, the German High Command had recognised their precarious situation at the beginning of 1918 and had gambled everything on a last great offensive in the West against the British and French, before too many US troops arrived.

The offensive began in March 1918 and achieved startling initial success: within a week, the Germans were within 120 kilometres of Paris, and subsequent operations pushed the British back towards the Channel ports. But without tanks and motorised artillery they were unable to consolidate their gains, and an Allied counter-offensive launched in July soon pushed the German armies back to their spring start-lines. Then, under the supreme command of the French Marshal Foch, but spearheaded by Haig's British Expeditionary Force and Pershing's newly arrived American divisions, the Allies started to force the Germans out of France and Belgium. By the beginning of September, the German armies were on the Hindenburg Line, where they had begun the war in 1914. On the 26th, the Allies started their attack on the Line. Before long, General Erich Ludendorff, Germany's commander-in-chief on the Western Front, recommended seeking an immediate armistice. The alternative, he said, was complete annihilation. Secret exploratory peace contacts were made to the administration of President Woodrow Wilson, who responded with a series of demands, including the 'democratisation' of the German government, the withdrawal of German armies from all occupied lands and the cessation of the U-boat war. The German leadership agreed, and on 3 October Kaiser Wilhelm II appointed his cousin, Prince Max of Baden, as Chancellor and gave up his own supreme command of the armed forces. The next day, Germany formally requested an armistice.

Defeat brought political turmoil to Germany as a power struggle between left and right developed, with armed, mutinous and disaffected servicemen joining one side or the other. Across Germany, liberals and moderate leftists sought to preserve some aspects of the old order as the state started to collapse into total chaos. On 7 November, Kurt Eisner, a leading member of the Independent Socialists, declared Bavaria a 'free state', effectively overthrowing the Wittelsbach dynasty, who had been the hereditary rulers of the southern German kingdom for seven hundred years. The last of the line, Ludwig III, fled to Austria the following day, probably thinking he would soon return and resume his rule. However, he was persuaded to sign the 'Anif Declaration', which absolved officers, soldiers and officials of the Kingdom of Bavaria of their oath of loyalty to him, and this was treated by Eisner as a statement of abdication.

Meanwhile, the Kaiser's abdication had become a sticking point in armistice negotiations with the Allies. He hoped that he could at least remain King of Prussia, if not Kaiser, but Prince Max finally put an end to the matter by announcing Wilhelm's abdication from both roles on 9 November. Wilhelm looked to the army for support, but none was forthcoming: Ludendorff had already resigned and fled to Sweden at the end of October; and, in any case, the High Command had little control over its own forces.* The German soldiers were prepared to return home in relatively good order, but Germany could count on no more than that. The Kaiser confirmed his abdication and left for exile in the Netherlands on 10 November. Prince Max had brought some moderate members of the German Socialist Party (SPD) – the largest single party in the Reichstag – into his government as soon as he was appointed. Now, they were anxious to try to establish some order, so that Germany should not follow Russia into Bolshevism. With the Kaiser gone, though, Prince Max had no authority or mandate to remain as Chancellor, so he resigned in favour of the SPD leader, Friedrich Ebert, the same day.

That was the catalyst for a power struggle between several leftist groups. In addition to the SPD, there were the USPD, independent socialists who had opposed the war, and the *Spartakusbund* (Spartacus League), a communist group led by Karl Liebknecht and Rosa Luxemburg. The USPD were prepared to work with the SPD; the Spartacists were not. Throughout November and December, Germany effectively had two parallel governments: the 'constitutional' provisional government under Ebert; and the radical 'workers' and soldiers' councils', of which there soon more than ten thousand across the country. Crucially, the armed forces, under Ludendorff's successor, General Groener, pledged support to Ebert's government. On 16 December 1918,

---

* The author's grandfather was an infantry officer in the British Army between 1915 and 1918. He realised the retreating Germans were finally beaten when he saw their weapons and equipment abandoned by the roadside – the first time they had exhibited such lack of resolve on the Western Front.

the councils held a congress in Berlin and agreed to the formation of a constituent assembly that would be tasked with drawing up a new constitution. By this time, it was clear that the SPD and its allies were in the majority in most of the councils. The Spartacists, acknowledging that they would not be able to take power by democratic means, decided to follow the Russian model and seize power through armed rebellion, using various republican militias.

This political turmoil, together with external threats from the newly independent Poland and Czechoslovakia, led to a spontaneous upsurge of nationalist and patriotic sentiment among many recently returned German officers, NCOs and soldiers. In part, this was fostered by the High Command's creation of semi-official militias staffed by loyal volunteers, in the hope that they would preserve order among the rest of the soldiery. But the end result was the birth of the *Freikorps* (Free Corps) movement – bands of freebooting ex-soldiers who would haunt German politics and threaten the nascent German democracy for years to come.

On 23 December 1918, the Spartacists, together with renegade sailors of the *Volksmarine* Division, attempted to seize power in Berlin. Units of the regular army were summoned to help but refused to fire on civilian defenders supporting the revolutionaries, and the best that could be managed was the rescue of the provisional government. So the Spartacists remained in occupation of the seat of government. On 30 December, they formally renamed themselves the German Communist Party (KPD), and on 5 January 1919 they summoned seven hundred thousand demonstrators onto the streets of Berlin, effectively seizing control of the capital.

The provisional government's response was to turn to the Free Corps. The previous month, General Maercker, a divisional commander in the army, had created a volunteer corps from several thousand of his men, and his example had been followed by a number of commanders in the area around Berlin. The forces they led were not necessarily very large or well equipped, but they were well disciplined and had a sense that they were fulfilling their patriotic duty. On 10 January, they began to move towards Berlin, where they proved more than a match for the larger but poorly organised and badly led revolutionary forces of the KPD. Just two days later, the Free Corps were in control of much of the city. On 15 January, Liebknecht and Luxemburg were arrested by members of the *Garde-Kavellerie-Schützen-Division* (Guards Cavalry Soldiers' Division). Luxemburg was beaten with rifle butts, then shot. Her body was thrown into the Landwehr Canal, which runs through the centre of the city. Liebknecht was shot and dumped in the Tiergarten, next to the government quarter of the city. Hundreds of their supporters were also killed, both in the fighting and after their surrender.

While the Free Corps were mopping up in the capital, elections for the National Assembly were held. The SPD emerged victorious, and it was decided to move the seat of government from Berlin to Weimar in Thuringia, where the Constituent Assembly could begin its work. Over the next eight months, the so-called Weimar Constitution was drafted, amended and finally passed into law, establishing the German Reich as a federal parliamentary republic.

It was under this constitution that the SS was established and the National Socialist Party found a route to power. In 1919, though, it was widely regarded as a model of liberalism. It contained a number of devices that many people assumed would guarantee the long-term flourishing of a flawless and equitable democracy. With the benefit of hindsight, much has been made of its 'weaknesses', and how they allowed Hitler to come to power, but the reality at the time was not so clear cut. It may not have been a perfect document, but it was fit for purpose and contained no more flaws than other parliamentary democracies' constitutions. In effect, it was a modified version of the constitution created by Bismarck for the newly unified Germany in 1871,[1] with the Kaiser replaced by an elected Reich President, and a federal parliament – the Reichstag – elected by universal adult (over twenty years of age) suffrage in an electoral system of direct proportionality. The problems that beset Germany in the inter-war period and ultimately led to the collapse of democracy were not so much due to this constitution as to the perceived lack of legitimacy of the state it defined. For most of the lifetime of the Weimar Republic, fewer than half of the deputies sitting in the Reichstag represented parties that supported the democratic republican system. Even the Social Democrats – who were widely perceived as the party that had created the republic – were ambivalent, with many of them clinging to their Marxist heritage. The institutions of state – the civil service and the military – were equally ambivalent, when not actively hostile. For many, the republic was an undesirable and temporary system that had been forced upon Germany because of its defeat in the war.

The chaos of the immediate post-war period was the backdrop for the political awakening of a Bavarian infantryman of Austrian birth named Adolf Hitler, who had spent the previous four years serving at the front as a messenger in the headquarters of the List Regiment. He was awarded the Iron Cross (second and first class), and finished the war as an *Obergefreiter* (lance corporal). The final military defeat of the German Army was inexplicable to Hitler. He was caught in a British gas attack at the beginning of October that left him temporarily blind, so he did not see the final collapse of his comrades, literally or metaphorically. But while in hospital, he later claimed, he had vowed to reverse the personal and national humiliation of defeat.[2] On his discharge, after the armistice, he made his way through a country he no longer recognised. The old order was being violently swept away: the Kaiser had abdicated; the Social Democrats were in power; communist and socialist revolutionaries were establishing their councils. In Munich, Hitler found the barracks of his regiment under the authority of a committee of junior soldiers. Unwilling to serve in such a system, he volunteered instead as a guard at a POW camp, where he stayed until February 1919.[3]

Under Eisner, Bavaria had been pursuing a policy of confrontation with the central provisional government. But that

February, Eisner was murdered by a right-wing extremist, Count Arco-Valley. This provoked a violent backlash from the left. On 7 April, a group of extreme leftists seized power and proclaimed a *Räterepublik* (councils' – or soviet – republic) in Bavaria. SPD militias attempted to overthrow this, but they were defeated. In response, the KPD founded a 'Red Army' for the republic, and initiated a reign of terror against their political opponents. Communists rampaged through the streets of Munich, looting and plundering, while schools, businesses and newspapers were shut down.

The provisional government's response was to mobilise about thirty thousand members of the Free Corps, with whom they surrounded Munich at the end of April. While this was happening, the KPD struck at nationalists within the city, arresting seven members of the extreme right-wing Thule Society – an occultist, anti-Semitic group that was organising nationalist agitation against the communist regime. Among the seven were Countess Heila von Westarp and Prince Gustav von Thurn und Taxis, who were both shot dead in the cellars of the Luitpold Gymnasium on 30 April. The next day, the Free Corps attacked, and gained control of the city forty-eight hours later. A rightist reign of terror then replaced the leftist one: some 650 people were shot by the Free Corps, more than half of them 'civilians'. But the net effect was the restoration of central government control over Bavaria.

For all his later hostility to communism, the 'November criminals'* and the Bavarian Soviet Republic, Hitler's role in all of this was curiously ambiguous. He acted as a company and battalion representative on one of the soldiers' councils,[4] and as far as he made any public comment on the situation at the time, he was generally supportive of the SPD-led provisional government. Certainly, he played no part in the Free Corps' attack on the leftists.

---

* The SPD politicians who supposedly 'stabbed the German Army in the back' in November 1918.

It was at this point that Hitler's fortunes changed. Although he was scheduled to be demobilised from the army, he had come to the attention of Captain Karl Mayr, an officer who had been assigned to organise courses of political instruction to guide the soldiery away from radical, revolutionary views. Mayr seems to have met Hitler in the aftermath of the suppression of the communists in Munich and recognised some hitherto unseen talent in him. He booked Hitler on to a short political indoctrination course at Munich University – in which the students were both indoctrinated themselves and taught how to indoctrinate others – and then assigned him to a camp for returning soldiers as part of an 'enlightenment squad'. The idea was that the soldiers would be given the 'correct' perspective on recent events in Germany. Having impressed his superiors in this task, in the late summer Hitler assumed the role of liaison officer between the army and the bewildering number of intensely right-wing parties and factions that had sprung up across Bavaria. It was a fateful appointment. On 12 September, he was commissioned to visit and write a report on a group calling itself the German Workers' Party, which had formed around a former locksmith, Anton Drexler, and a sports journalist, Karl Harrer. During the course of discussions among the group's members, someone suggested that Bavaria should secede from Germany and seek union with Austria. Unable to contain himself, Hitler jumped in, angrily denounced the idea and railed against the proposer of the motion. Impressed by his eloquence, the leaders of the group invited him to come to their next meeting. Two days after his second visit, Hitler accepted the party's invitation to join as member responsible for propaganda and recruitment.

He threw himself into the role with enthusiasm, and within a month had organised a public meeting attended by over a hundred people. Spurred on by this success, in February 1920 he persuaded nearly two thousand people to pack into the Hofbräuhaus in Munich. There he faced down some noisy opposition from a rowdy audience, changed the name of the organisation to the

National Socialist German Workers' Party,* and presented a twenty-five-point plan to solve Germany's ills. Hitler remembered this meeting as the moment when he realised where his destiny lay: as a politician and orator. A few months later, he was discharged from the army and set off down the path that would lead, less than thirteen years later, to the chancellorship of Germany and the subsequent horrors of the Third Reich.

Hitler rapidly struck a chord in post-First World War Bavaria, appealing not only to the ex-servicemen and street-corner toughs who comprised the early membership of the NSDAP, but to a much wider audience. Many of his fellow ex-soldiers firmly agreed that they had not been defeated in the war, but 'stabbed in the back' by socialists, Bolsheviks, Jews, capitalists and speculators, who had then tried to take over the country while the heroes of the armed forces were stuck at the front. (Of course, this ignored the reality that many of the revolutionaries were themselves soldiers.) The population of Germany endured great deprivation during the war but was continuously misled by its leaders into thinking that the military and strategic situation was much better than it actually was. That partly explains why the final defeat of the German Army came as such a shock to soldiers and civilians alike, most of whom were convinced that victory was near at hand.

From the late nineteenth century onwards, a division had started to widen in the German middle class. At the upper end, professionals, successful businessmen and high-ranking civil servants had become almost indistinguishable, both financially and socially, from the aristocracy and traditional 'ruling' class. After all, their activities had given the emerging Reich the industrial and intellectual muscle to take its place on the world stage. Meanwhile, the lower middle class of small farmers and businessmen, shopkeepers and, above all, the great army of white-collar clerks, low-level officials, teachers, civil servants and junior managers had

---

* The name was probably chosen to appeal across the spectrum of political views, from right-wing nationalists to left-wing socialists.

come under the twin pressures of large-scale corporate capitalism from above and organised labour from below. This had produced a move towards right-wing radicalism with undertones of nationalism and anti-Semitism even before the outbreak of the First World War. But Germany's defeat, and the subsequent upheavals as the old order collapsed, greatly exacerbated the lower middle class's dislocation: small businesses failed and hard-earned savings were wiped out by rampant inflation. The National Socialist message was that this was the work of the Jews and the communists – as far as Hitler was concerned, the two were virtually synonymous – not the inevitable result of German expansionist nationalism. This perspective resonated as much with the struggling lower middle class as it did with the bewildered ex-soldiers.

Hitler was the outstanding personality within the party, and he assumed leadership as early as 1921. Under his guidance, over the next couple of years the NSDAP steadily built its strength as a local party. The atmosphere in Bavaria – as in much of the rest of the country – remained violent and edgy, but it was also tinged with a strong separatist element: the largely Catholic population saw itself as different from the Protestant north, and many Bavarians resented rule from Berlin. Anger between left and right remained fierce, too, with the communists' short-lived republic widely remembered as a 'reign of horror'.[5] The factions that had faced off against each other back then now disrupted each other's political meetings, with violence often the end result.

Many of the Free Corps had entered into border skirmishes with Germany's eastern neighbours, initially with the tacit approval of the central government. But pressure from the victorious Allies eventually forced the government to disband and attempt to disarm the Free Corps and other militias in the summer of 1921. Some weapons were surrendered or seized as a result of this campaign, but many remained in circulation, in the hands of both left- and right-wing groups. The German government and High Command were prepared to tolerate this volatile situation for one very good reason. Under the terms of the Versailles Treaty, Germany's standing army had been limited to just one hundred thousand men, which obviously left the country vulnerable to attack. However, the militias could potentially provide tens of thousands more well-armed, well-trained men to defend Germany at a moment's notice, so it was hardly surprising that the country's leaders were far from enthusiastic about disarming them.

Around this time, Hitler formed an alliance with a serving army officer – *Hauptmann* (Captain) Ernst Röhm – a Bavarian career soldier who had fought as a company commander during the war. A staunch monarchist, Röhm had participated in the suppression of the revolutionary government in Bavaria. In its aftermath, he had organised an anti-communist *Einwohnerwehr* (Citizens' Militia), and armed it with a vast quantity of weapons collected from various sources. This militia was subsequently banned when the central government clamped down on the Free Corps, but Röhm retained control of its large arsenal. He also maintained connections with various right-wing groups which had provided the militia's manpower.

Röhm's political ambitions were fairly straightforward: he wished to see Germany return to a position of military strength with a reformed army; and he viewed Adolf Hitler as the man to achieve this. He joined the NSDAP and soon set about training the strong-arm men who were employed by the party to keep order at their meetings and protect their speakers. This was done in the party's euphemistically titled 'Gymnastic and Sport Section',[6] with the thugs taught by a group of ex-army officers – many with experience in the Free Corps – whom Röhm recruited specifically for the purpose. In August 1921, the unit was officially named the *Sturmabteilung Hitler* (SA – Assault Detachment Hitler), which was coined to bring to mind the elite 'stormtroops' that had fought in the trenches.

However, Hitler and Röhm had different ideas about the unit's role. The party leader saw its members as political soldiers: 'a force to stick up election posters, use its knuckle-dusters in meeting-hall fights and impress the discipline-loving Germans by propaganda marches'.[7] By contrast, Röhm and his subordinates viewed themselves as a genuine military force. They knew that they had been included in the army's secret mobilisation plans and had received military training from the Munich garrison. Hitler's response to this was to bring in his own man as leader of the SA in early 1923, leaving Röhm to organise yet another militia outside of the party (although he remained a close associate of Hitler). Captain Hermann Goering had won the 'Blue Max'* as commander of the Richthofen fighter squadron during the war and he possessed an air of glamour, as well as considerable military ability. Goering organised a headquarters to coordinate the activities of the various groupings that made up the SA,† but Hitler remained suspicious of its members' motives. Consequently, he placed his and his close associates' personal protection in the hands of a new group that was christened the *Stabswache* (Headquarters Guard). The members of this small group were all close associates of Hitler: working-class ex-soldiers and toughs like Emil Maurice (a former watchmaker and a gunner during the war, born in 1897), Ulrich Graf (who had organised the first *Saalschutz* (Hall Protection) squad – a small, informal band of toughs who had acted as an escort for National Socialist speakers) and Christian Weber. All of these men were fiercely devoted to Hitler both as a person and as their political leader.[8]

The Headquarters Guard lasted just a few months before it was superseded in May 1923 by a slightly larger and more organised body, named the *Stosstrupp* (Raiding Squad) Adolf Hitler. This was run by another SA member and companion of Hitler, Julius Schreck, and a former army officer turned stationery salesman, Joseph Berchtold. However, Weber, Maurice, Graf and other 'Old Fighters' from the Headquarters Guard still comprised the inner

---

* The official name of the award was Pour le Mérite. It was the highest Prussian distinction for bravery and leadership in the First World War.
† The SA did not, at this stage have a formal, coherent organisational structure. Rather, it consisted of a number of units and sub-units, loyal primarily to their own commanders rather than the party.

cadre.[9] Other members included the future diplomat Walther Hewel, who eventually became the German Foreign Office's liaison with Hitler's headquarters during the war.[10]

The first major test for the SA and the Raiding Squad came in November 1923. The conspiratorial Röhm had allied the SA with several other right-wing paramilitary groups to form the *Kampfbund* (Combat League), which could call on the services of approximately fifteen thousand well-armed men. Meanwhile, General Ludendorff, who had returned from exile in 1920, had begun to involve himself in the politics of the extreme right, seeing groups like the NSDAP as the means to begin national renewal. All of these parties were furious about the French occupation of the Ruhr, which had taken place in response to German non-payment of war reparations in January 1923. The Ruhr was the heart of German heavy industry, so the occupation had a paralysing effect on an already struggling economy. Chancellor Gustav Stresemann's government encouraged a policy of passive resistance – through strikes, minor sabotage and non-cooperation – but this led to economic collapse and consequent civil disturbance and unrest. Hyperinflation, caused by Germany's massive war indebtedness and reparations obligations, only added to this. The NSDAP, among many other groups, advocated radical opposition to the French occupation, and Hitler sought to turn the situation to his advantage by launching the NSDAP on the national stage. In his analysis, if he could mobilise the masses, the state would be unable – and the army unwilling – to oppose them.

With the German economy in ruins, the passive resistance campaign was called off on 26 September. Then, to forestall any trouble with the radical right, which was now operating under the broad patronage of Ludendorff, a state of emergency was declared in Bavaria and power put in the hands of a triumvirate: Gustav Ritter von Kahr as State Commissar; Colonel Hans Ritter von Seisser as Chief of Police; and General Otto von Lossow as head of the Bavarian army. These triumvirs had a similar agenda to Hitler's – the installation of a military-backed government in Berlin by coup – but they did not share his view that he should play a leading part in it. Throughout October, the Combat League negotiated with the triumvirate to little avail, basically because neither side trusted the other. Frustrated by the impasse, at the beginning of November Hitler and the Combat League decided to act.

On the evening of 8 November, a force of NSDAP supporters with Hitler at their head surrounded the Bürgerbräukeller in Munich, where von Kahr was addressing a meeting commemorating the fifth anniversary of the November revolution. Von Seisser and von Lossow were also in attendance. Berchtold's Raiding Squad aimed a machine gun at the front door and Hitler entered the hall, waving a pistol and shouting noisily. Then he jumped onto a chair and fired his weapon into the ceiling to gain attention. With all eyes focused on him, he declared that a national revolution had started and that the hall was surrounded by six hundred armed men. Then, ushering the triumvirs into a nearby room, he left it to Goering to quieten the mob.

The intention of this *Putsch* was to inspire something akin to Mussolini's 'March on Rome', with the radical, patriotic right following the Bavarians' lead throughout the country and eventually deposing the democratic regime. However, the plan soon started to unravel. The triumvirs reneged on promises they had made at pistol point as soon as they had extricated themselves from National Socialist custody. Then, as Hitler and his followers floundered through the streets, attempting to grab control of the levers of state power in Bavaria, the government, police and army organised their defences. By the next morning, the initiative was firmly back in the hands of the authorities, but in a last, desperate effort, Hitler organised a march through Munich in the hope of attracting popular support. As the rebels reached the central Odeonsplatz via the Residenzstrasse, they were confronted by a police cordon and gunfire broke out, leaving sixteen of the marchers dead and many more wounded. As the blood ran across the cobblestones and into the gutters, Hitler fled, his dream of a national revolution exposed, for now at least, as a puny farce.[11]

2

The Rebirth of National Socialism and the Creation of the SS

By rights, the ultimate outcome of the *Putsch* should have been oblivion for both Hitler and the NSDAP. Four policemen had been killed in the fighting, and the revolt was an undeniable act of treason, which was supposedly punishable by death. It also clearly demonstrated Hitler's lack of genuine support among the Bavarian military circles that had been encouraging the militarist nationalist groups and secretly arming the militias. They were certainly contemplating a *coup d'état* themselves, but it was now clear that it would be launched only on their terms, not Hitler's.

In the immediate aftermath of the shooting in the Residenzstrasse, Hitler was treated for a dislocated shoulder by Walter Schultze, an SA doctor, and then bundled into a car that took him to the country house of a wealthy associate, the half-American socialite Ernst 'Putzi' Hanfstängl, at Uffing on the Staffelsee, south of Munich. Police found him there two days later and took him to the prison fortress of Landsberg. The prisoner was 'depressed but calm, dressed in a white nightgown, his injured left arm in a sling'.[1] There was some residual support for the *Putsch* in Bavaria,[2] manifested in the form of demonstrations against the triumvirs, but these did not continue for long. In short, the revolution had failed, its leader was in custody and there was little popular support for a renewal of hostilities. That should have been the end of the matter, and the end of Hitler as a political force.

That was not to be the case because of the close links between the Bavarian government and army and the *Putsch* attempt. The attempted revolution was typically Hitlerite, characterised by 'half-baked planning, dilettante improvisation [and] lack of care to detail',[3] but senior figures within the Bavarian establishment had been closely involved with it, too. Once it failed, they had to find a 'fall guy', and Hitler – for his own purposes – was happy to fill that role. A trial for high treason would provide a great propaganda opportunity at the national level and allow him to present himself as the potential saviour of Germany. Furthermore, his knowledge of the triumvirs' antipathy towards Berlin and the role the local military had played in arming the paramilitaries virtually guaranteed lenient punishment.[4]

And so it proved. Some sort of deal seems to have been offered by von Kahr to ensure the defendants' discretion. Certainly, the Bavarian government lobbied hard to move the trial from the Reich Court in Leipzig to the People's Court in Munich, where the presiding judge, Georg Neithardt, showed extraordinary bias towards Hitler and his co-defendants.[5] The trial was a piece of political theatre. Ludendorff, Hitler's senior co-defendant, who had acted as 'patron' of the *Putsch* but had not been intimately involved in its planning or execution (although he had marched on 9 November), arrived every day in a limousine dressed in full uniform with his decorations. Hitler was permitted to wear his own clothes, including his Iron Cross, rather than a prison uniform, and he was given unprecedented latitude to interrogate witnesses and harangue the court.[6]

Given these circumstances, the final result was hardly unexpected, although 'the judgement was scandalous, even by the biased standards of the Weimar judiciary'.[7] Ludendorff, much to his annoyance, was acquitted. Hitler and three others received five years' 'fortress incarceration' – a lenient form of imprisonment usually reserved for those who had acted with supposedly 'honourable' motives.[8] This verdict caused nearly as much outrage on the conservative right as it did on the left. It was not difficult to see through the court's claim that the defendants had been moved to act by 'a pure patriotic spirit and the most noble will'.[9] It was an obvious fix.

Hitler was returned to Landsberg, where he lived in a bright, comfortable and airy cell, hitherto occupied by Count Arco-Valley, the murderer of Eisner. He had the company of some forty fellow inmates, some of whom had volunteered to share his incarceration. All enjoyed 'almost all the comforts of normal daily life',[10] as well as many gifts and messages of goodwill.

Hitler's conviction drew a line under the first phase of National Socialism. In some respects, the movement appeared shattered: the party had been suppressed, the SA banned and largely disarmed, and the nationalist–racist coalition was in a state of disintegration. But incarceration gave Hitler a chance to concentrate on his future and crystallise his political views. He was already an extreme anti-Semite with a passionate desire to overturn the terms of the Versailles Treaty, but the rest of his political outlook was far from focused. In Landsberg, at the urging of Max Amann, his platoon sergeant in the war, and with the assistance of Rudolf Hess and Emil Maurice, he set down his thoughts in detail for the first time. These writings would eventually be published under the title *Mein Kampf (My Struggle)*. Although in no sense a manifesto or blueprint for his future actions as German dictator, this provided a basic framework of the philosophy that lay behind them.[11] It is a turgid, almost unreadable tract with no literary merit, but it is useful in revealing an author obsessed with race and imbued with a startlingly visceral, murderous anti-Semitism, combined with a strong desire to acquire 'living space' for the German race in the East. Of course, SS activity would later be dictated by these obsessions.

Imprisonment also gave Hitler the opportunity to plot his ascent to power. It was abundantly clear that the paramilitary route was no longer a realistic option for a relatively small movement whose centre of gravity was still in Bavaria. While the NSDAP would continue to position itself as the political party of the combat veterans of the Great War, Hitler began to realise that he would need to mobilise the wider masses to gain power, so a tighter and more disciplined organisation would be needed. He concluded that he should take on the full mantle of leadership of the National Socialist movement, rather than merely acting as its propagandist, or 'drummer', as he had previously described himself.[12] His destiny was no longer to place a figure like Ludendorff in power, but to rule Germany himself.

Prior to his arrest, Hitler had passed control of the now banned NSDAP to Alfred Rosenberg, an Estonian German who had served in the Tsar's army in the First World War. Rosenberg had been educated in Estonia, Latvia and Russia, but emigrated to Germany following the Bolshevik coup of 1917. There was undoubtedly a Machiavellian element in Hitler's appointment of the uncharismatic and unpopular Rosenberg – he did not want to be challenged for leadership of the party when he was eventually released, so he picked an interim leader who was detested by everybody. However, there were also few other candidates who were not in prison themselves.[13]

Rosenberg's leadership proved to be catastrophic. With both the NSDAP and the SA now temporarily illegal, in January 1924 he created the *Grossdeutsche Volksgemeinschaft* (GVG – Greater German Racial Community) as a rallying point for former members. However, Walter Buch, acting head of the SA at this time, refused to accept either Rosenberg's or the GVG's authority over the SA, while a number of significant former NSDAP members, including the charismatic Gregor Strasser, joined alternative splinter groups. Schism and rivalry continued throughout the first half of the year. Despite this, though, the Reichstag elections on 4 May saw the nationalist–racist parties gain 6.5 per cent of the vote nationwide, with particularly good results in Bavaria and Mecklenburg, in northern Germany. This threw into sharp relief the argument between those elements in the *völkisch* (literally 'folk-ish', but implying a Germanic nationalist–racist outlook) groups who favoured a legal parliamentary strategy and those who wanted to seize power by force.

The remnants of the NSDAP comprised a minority group among the thirty-two folkish deputies elected to the Reichstag, and shortly afterwards they agreed to merge, for parliamentary purposes, with their rivals. For many NSDAP supporters, this reeked of compromise and parliamentarianism, so bickering continued through the summer. This was exacerbated by Hitler's equivocation over which route he favoured; by Ludendorff's apparent interest in assuming the overall leadership of the folkish groups; by Hermann Esser and Julius Streicher, who ousted Rosenberg from the leadership of the GVG; and by Röhm, who attempted to unite the folkish and nationalist paramilitary groups under the title *Frontbann*.

Hitler himself withdrew from politics in June 1924 to concentrate on writing *Mein Kampf*. This was probably motivated in part by an acceptance of his inability to control events from inside the fortress, and in part by his hope for parole and an early release. Such was his self-confidence that he assumed he would be able to rejoin the cut and thrust of nationalist politics later, when he was in a better position to do so.[14]

In December, there were more elections to Reichstag. This time, the 'united' folkish groups secured only 3 per cent of the vote, which meant their representation in the parliament dropped to just fourteen seats. This electoral disaster pleased Hitler greatly. As far as he was concerned, the near collapse of the nationalist–racist groups in his absence strengthened his claims for overall leadership. He may also have calculated that the Bavarian government would now view the extreme right as a spent force, which would leave him free to rebuild the movement on his release from Landsberg.[15]

Hitler was freed on parole on 20 December 1924, meaning that he served just over thirteen months of his five-year sentence.

Suggestions that he should be deported to Austria were quickly quashed by the Austrian government's refusal to accept him, which allowed him to return immediately to the political fray in Bavaria. Hitler's parole conditions meant that, in theory, he was not permitted to speak in public in most parts of Germany until 1927 (in Prussia until 1928), but he still had sufficient influence among sympathetic officials within the Bavarian government for the NSDAP and its newspaper to be unbanned in February 1925.[16]

Apart from the disintegration of the NSDAP and its blurring with the folkish groups, one of the key problems that Hitler faced was the issue of the SA, which had also been banned and had fragmented under various leaders. Prior to the *Putsch*, Hitler and Röhm had shared similar ideas about the purpose of the organisation and its allied paramilitaries: they were the armed force that would be needed to overcome both the state and political opponents and push through a National Socialist seizure of power. The failure of 9 November 1923, however, convinced Hitler that this was a ludicrous notion: the SA and the other paramilitaries had not even been able to take Munich, let alone Germany, and they had been outfought by the local police. He acknowledged that the SA, or something similar, might still be useful, but now he viewed it as only one of many tools that might bring him to power. Röhm, on the other hand, continued to insist on the primacy of the military element and lobbied for another coup. His involvement in the *Putsch* had finally led to him being cashiered from the army and placed on probation, but this had left him free to create a new organisation from the remnants of the SA and the other paramilitary groups. As Hitler had languished in Landsberg through the spring and summer of 1924, Röhm's *Frontbann* had increased in strength to some thirty thousand members,[17] drawn from former members of the SA as well as the *Reichskriegsflagge* (Imperial War Flag), the *Stahlhelm* (Steel Helmets – a First World War veterans' group) and other Free Corps and combat leagues. The groups in this loose coalition usually maintained loyalty to their old leaders, mostly charismatic junior officers from the war such as Edmund Heines, Gerd Rossbach and Graf Wolf von Helldorf. They did not see either Röhm or the ostensible patron of the organisation, Ludendorff, as their new chief, but the *Frontbann* still seemed to be a significant and potentially threatening force.

Röhm and Hitler were personally close – Röhm was almost unique in addressing Hitler with the familiar *du* – but he did not appreciate that Hitler now saw himself as the overall leader and strategist of the movement, rather than as an equal, ally and associate. When Hitler was released from Landsberg, he asked Röhm to re-form the SA as 'propaganda troops at the beck and call of party leaders',[18] but Röhm demurred and the issue was still not resolved by February 1925 when the SA was unbanned with the rest of the party and could be organised openly. Hitler had grasped, with a clarity that Röhm did not possess, that the route to power in Germany had to be largely legal, so the party and its peripheral groups needed to reflect this. Their reorganisation had to begin immediately, whether Röhm wanted to implement it or not.

Hitler and his associates had hoped the Munich *Putsch* would succeed given the collapse of the German economy, hyperinflation and consequent civil unrest precipitated by the French occupation of the Ruhr in January 1923. They had been proved wrong, but the occupation had still generated a great deal of international sympathy for Germany and parallel condemnation of France. Before long, an international committee was established to re-examine the question of war reparations. This resulted in the Dawes Plan of August 1924, in which it was agreed that Germany's reparations payments would be reduced, the German central bank would be reorganised, and US loans would be made available to Germany. Foreign troops were also ordered to leave German soil, and the last French soldiers left the Ruhr almost a year later.

The Dawes Plan gave an immediate short-term boost to the

German economy. Hyperinflation ended, foreign investment increased and exports began to flow, all of which ushered in a period of relative political stability. Nevertheless, violence remained a significant part of the political scene in Bavaria and many other parts of Germany. Hitler and other senior leaders of the NSDAP were potential targets for attack, both from the left and from rivals on the far right. Consequently, in March 1925, he ordered Julius Schreck to organise a new personal security detail. As Hitler later remarked: 'When I came out of Landsberg, everything was broken up and scattered in sometimes rival bands. I told myself then I needed a bodyguard, even a very restricted one, but made up of men who would be enlisted without restriction, even to march against their own brothers. Only twenty men to a city (on condition that one could count on them absolutely) rather than a suspect mass.'[19] Schreck, a stocky, coarse-featured man who wore a moustache like Hitler's, had joined the NSDAP in 1921 via the Free Corps, having been a member of a 'revolutionary' unit in 1919.[20] He had been an early member of the SA and was in the small circle of tough ex-soldiers who formed Hitler's personal entourage, acting as chauffeurs, bodyguards and even audiences for his monologues. He was also in the Headquarters Guard and was an organiser of the Raiding Squad Adolf Hitler, which had been in the vanguard during the *Putsch*. Now, in response to Hitler's order, he mustered up to twelve of his close associates and formed the new bodyguard team.

The team – labelled the *Schutzstaffel* (Protection Squad, or SS) – included several of the 'usual suspects' who had formed Hitler's close personal entourage since the early days of the movement: Maurice, currently Hitler's first-choice dogsbody, chauffeur and factotum; Graf; Julius Schaub, who would later become Hitler's personal adjutant* and bore SS number 7;[21] and Erhard Heiden.

---

* In the last days of the war, Schaub, by then an *SS-Obergruppenführer* (general), was tasked with destroying Hitler's personal papers in Berlin, Munich and at the Obersalzburg.

Christian Weber and Rudolf Hess may have been members, too. In April 1925, eight members of the new force made their first public appearance, acting as torchbearers at the funeral of Ernst Pöhner, the former Munich Chief of Police and a National Socialist supporter, who had been killed in a car accident.[22] In 1942, Hitler would remark: 'It was Maurice, Schreck and Heyden [sic] who formed in Munich the first group of "tough 'uns", and were thus the origin of the SS.'[23]

However, soon the organisation had to look beyond Hitler's existing inner circle for its recruits, and personnel records give an indication of the type of person who was favoured. A typical example was Robert Bednarek,[24] who joined the SS on 20 May 1925 and was given membership number 467. Born in 1899 in Gleiwitz, Silesia, Bednarek completed just one year of secondary school and then served as an infantryman from May 1917 to August 1919. He was never promoted to NCO rank. After demobilisation, he joined a local Free Corps – the *Jägerschar von Heydebreck* – with whom he served for two years before moving into a succession of low-paid, unskilled jobs. Like many Germans, he had received no professional training before or after his military service, so he turned his hand to whatever work he could find: he was a bus conductor when he joined the SS. It is difficult to tell what motivated him to join the organisation, but political zealotry seems unlikely as he did not join the party for another year. Most likely he was simply led into it by a former army or Free Corps comrade, but he probably shared the opinions of thousands of other right-wing paramilitaries: their politics were shaped by an ignorant resentment of the German state in the post-war era; and, on a personal level, they missed the discipline and the certainties of military life. Although one of its longest-serving members, Bednarek – who eventually became an SS officer – was expelled from the organisation in 1939 because of persistent drunkenness.

In later years, SS leaders liked to cite the Raiding Squad Adolf Hitler as its precursor, and certainly some of its earliest members had previously been in that group, but in reality the SS was something new. The Raiding Squad, like the SA, was a combat group, designed to be in the vanguard in a National Socialist revolution. The SS's full title indicates that it was conceived for a totally different purpose.

Hitler had his first serious breach with Röhm in April 1925. By then, it was clear that Röhm did not want to reorganise the SA on Hitler's terms; while Hitler would not support the continuation of Röhm's alliance of right-wing militias as an independent organisation. In a conversation between the two men on the 16th, Hitler made his feelings clear to Röhm,[25] and the next day Röhm resigned as leader of both the alliance and the SA. Soon afterwards, he got a job as a military adviser to the government of Bolivia and left Germany. Although the SA remained intact under new leadership, Schreck seized the opportunity to bolster his new, rival organisation.

Hitler wanted the SS to abandon the pseudo-military structure of the SA. Instead, he proposed that each local party group should form a squad of about ten men, drawn from its most reliable elements, to protect the local leadership and their meetings, and reinforce the party leaders' escort whenever they visited. This was formalised in a circular issued by Schreck on 21 September 1925 to all '*Gau**' leaderships and independent local groups',[26] which outlined the guidelines under which leaders of the squads, labelled *Schutzstaffeln*, were to operate. The key was controllability: 'the protection squads were not to become muddled up with the SA'; names of proposed leaders were to be approved by the central leadership of the squads; and membership application forms and membership cards were available only from the central leadership. Subscriptions were set at one mark per month (soon reduced to

---

* *Gaue* were the regional organisations of the National Socialist Party. These were headed by *Gauleiters* (regional leaders), who were among the most important and influential of National Socialist Party officials acting, in effect, as local representatives for Hitler himself.

fifty pfennigs), which were to be forwarded promptly to the central leadership. Uniform items – initially a brown, SA-type shirt, a black kepi with a skull-and-crossbones badge and an imperial cockade, and a black necktie – were to be obtained from the SS's headquarters in Munich.

There was not an overwhelming rush to join the new squads, but this is hardly surprising, as so many other paramilitary and combat groups were already associated with the NSDAP. It seems that local party members simply did not understand the need for the protection squads. Koehl points out that, by the time of Schreck's circular, the Hamburg NSDAP was using teenagers from the nationalist *Blücherbund* group; Berlin was employing members of Röhm's alliance; Cuxhaven was using the *Stahlhelm* nationalist war veterans' group; while the Ruhr had created its own SA under a former Free Corps commander, Franz Pfeffer von Salomon.[27] All of these were ill-disciplined mobs of bouncers and brawlers from the ranks of the SA, Free Corps and other troublemaking groups, who might very well attract the attention of regional and national authorities. That was specifically what Hitler and his immediate circle wanted to avoid – hence the need to put their personal security in the hands of a tight-knit, well-led, disciplined new organisation.

The SS was officially founded – or at least proclaimed as an organisation of the NSDAP – on 9 November 1925, the second anniversary of the *Putsch*. But there was certainly some form of SS administration several months before this date. Schreck's file lists him as joining on 1 November,[28] but, as we have seen, Bednarek's dates his enrolment to May (and presumably 466 men had joined before him). More remarkably, Ulrich Graf supposedly signed up on '1.1.25'.[29] This early membership – some months before the SS was even mooted – is doubtless the result of some sort of creative backdating, but it should not disguise the fact that Schreck wasted no time in implementing Hitler's orders, and that local groups had begun to organise their protection squads long before his formal directives were issued.

The SS leadership was 'directed to take over the "Hall Control" for the [party anniversary meeting] on 25 February 1926',[30] but it is indicative of the somewhat ad hoc nature of the organisation at this time that it was also 'absolutely essential that members of the appointed "hall protection" receive a pass in order to ensure free entry'.[31] SS groups continued to organise sporadically in March, but there was little impetus until the return to Munich of the diminutive Josef Berchtold, who had fled to Austria after the *Putsch*. In April, he took over from Schreck,* styling himself *Reichsführer der Schutzstaffeln* (National Leader of the Protection Squads), in contrast to his predecessor's old title, *Führer der Oberleitung* (Leader of the Headquarters Staff). Berchtold soon installed Erhard Heiden as his deputy and issued a new set of rules – apparently drafted by Schreck – in order to establish the SS's position vis-à-vis the SA. He specified that the 'SS is neither a (para-)military organisation nor a group of hangers-on, but a small squad of men that our movement and our Führer can rely on. They must be people who can protect our meetings against troublemakers and professional stirrers. There are no "ifs" and "buts" in the SS, only party discipline.'[32] He also suggested that the strength of a standard SS squad should be one officer and ten men, but stressed that bigger party districts might need more. A subsequent instruction forbade 'district SS leaders to give their men military training, to allow them to be members of other

---

* Schreck resumed his role as Hitler's chauffeur and ceased to take an active part in the SS, although he was subsequently given the rank of *SS-Standartenführer* (colonel). He died on 15 May 1936 of meningitis. At his funeral, Heinrich Himmler gave a graveside eulogy which ended: 'We have now taken our leave of you. But you live in our ranks still, as when you were actually there. And now I have an honour for you, dear Comrade Schreck, that your Führer has given you. When you founded the squad, you were a tiny group of ten men. From today the Führer has ordered that the 1st SS Regiment in Munich should bear the name "Julius Schreck". We will all strive to ensure that this regiment which carries this name – of a man who was a hero in our ranks – does so with honour!' (USNA: SSO100B)

"combat organisations" or to participate in military training with them'.[33]

Berchtold's efforts were rewarded on 4 July 1926, when Hitler placed the 'Blood Banner', a swastika flag allegedly stained with the blood of the fallen National Socialist 'martyr' Andreas Bauriedel during the *Putsch*, into the SS's safekeeping as a kind of holy relic of the movement. However, the SS still had a rival: the SA. Following Röhm's departure, this had been reorganised as a mass, uniformed formation that would be tolerated by the authorities. At the end of July, Franz Pfeffer von Salomon was named as its leader.[34]

Around this time, there was something of a rupture between the southern and northern factions of the NSDAP. The latter, led by Gregor Strasser, recognised Hitler's overall leadership but were less enthusiastic about the Bavarian cliques that surrounded him. To some extent, the problem was ideological: Strasser was extremely anti-Semitic, but he focused on the 'socialist' rather than the 'nationalist' elements of the NSDAP's programme. Hitler knew that he had to bring the northerners back onside, and the way to achieve this was to allow the revival of the SA, whose non-southern branches had been largely untainted by the *Putsch*. On 1 November, Franz Pfeffer von Salomon was named leader of the SA, and shortly thereafter – despite Berchtold's best efforts – the SS was subordinated to the SA as a 'special formation'.

Part of Pfeffer von Salomon's task was to bring the SA back under political control. Many of the organisation's units were still directly descended from – indeed, in some cases, were one and the same as – the lawless Free Corps. In the relatively peaceful Germany of 1926, these groups were unlikely to appeal to the kind of people who were being targeted as potential supporters by the NSDAP. Hitler wanted the reformed SA simply to create the conditions in which the party's propagandists could do their work, so Pfeffer von Salomon introduced drill, parades and other straightforward military techniques to instil some discipline into his units.

By contrast, members of the SS, when not acting as personal bodyguards, were typical political activists: they collected donations, canvassed potential supporters and sold the party newspaper, the *Völkische Beobachter* (*Folkish Observer*). An SS newsletter, published in December 1926, gives somewhat breathless accounts of these relatively mundane tasks. However, it also offers to sell SS members 'knock-out gas pistols' for a few marks each, under the legal warning that they should 'only be used in case of "danger"; unprovoked or unwarned use may result in legal punishment. Knock-out guns are not toys, but primarily handy defence weapons.'[35]

The subordination of the SS to the SA appears to have disenchanted Berchtold, and he handed over leadership to his colourless deputy, Heiden, in March 1927. But Heinz Höhne notes that Heiden also 'found it difficult to compete with the growing size and influence of the SA; Pfeffer von Salomon, for instance, forbade the SS to form units in towns where the SA was still under strength'.[36] Even so, Heiden continued to enforce a far stricter code upon his SS members than would have been tolerated in the SA. He demanded that his men should not get involved in party matters that did not concern them; insisted on strict discipline during party meetings; and – notwithstanding the sale of 'knock-out guns' – ordered commanders to search for and confiscate any illegal weapons prior to SS men going on duty. The intention was to create a self-conscious elite that would take pride in its difference from the SA and attract a better class of recruit. Höhne repeatedly refers to the SS as a kind of party 'aristocracy', even at this early stage in its development. This may seem slightly odd, given the radical working- and lower-middle-class nature of the organisation, but it gives an indication of how members of the SS regarded themselves. It was always intended to be a small, elite group with a pronounced *esprit de corps*.

Nevertheless, outside Munich, it struggled in the early years to maintain any organisational momentum. At Christmas 1925, it had claimed a membership of 'about a thousand men',[37] but shortly thereafter this had declined to 'about 200'.[38] And there it languished for the next three years, throughout the reigns of Berchtold and Heiden. The latter was finally dismissed at the beginning of 1929, probably because of his lacklustre perform-ance, although a rumour suggested that he had been exposed as a police spy. There would be no such doubts about his replacement.

3

Heinrich Himmler

The most significant date in the early history of the SS was 20 January 1929,* because that was when Heinrich Himmler, hitherto Heiden's deputy, took over as National Leader of the tiny organisation. It would soon prove to be an appointment of enormous significance. At the time of his promotion, Himmler was only twenty-eight years old, but he was already a salaried activist within the NSDAP, enjoyed a growing reputation as an outstanding organiser, and had been instrumental in the party's recent rise to prominence in southern German politics.

Unlike many of his contemporaries amongst the party's 'old fighters', no great trauma led Himmler into the ranks of the NSDAP: he had not fought at the front during the war and his involvement in the early post-war power struggles had been minimal. Instead, it appears that he was attracted to the movement because it offered him an opportunity to identify with a class of men he greatly admired and was desperate to join: soldiers. Himmler's own background was comfortable and stolidly middle class. His paternal grandfather, Johann Himmler, was born in

* His appointment was later officially backdated to 6 January for reasons which remain unclear.

1809 in the Ansbach region of northern Bavaria, where he was raised by his mother. He trained as a weaver before leaving home at eighteen to join the Royal Bavarian Regiment, where he was noted for his brawling and 'immoral behaviour with a low woman'.[1] Later, he joined the Munich Police and then transferred into the Bavarian Police. At the age of fifty-three he became a *Gendarmerie Brigadier* (senior sergeant[2]) in the district of Lindau, and around the same time he married Agathe Kiene, the twenty-nine-year-old daughter of a local watchmaker. Although of no special significance, Johann's rise in social status – from illegitimate peasant, via military and police service, to government official and member of the middle classes – is curiously reminiscent of Hitler's father's ascent in Austria.

Johann and Agathe's only son was born in Lindau in 1865 and christened Joseph Gebhard (although he was known by his second name). He was just seven years old when his father died, and Agathe struggled to make ends meet. However, as the son of a deceased civil servant, Gebhard had access to scholarships, and these, combined with his evident academic talent, ensured that he received a top-class education at a classical high school and then at the Royal Bavarian Maximilian University in Munich, where he read philosophy and later philology.[3] He finished his studies in 1894 and became a teacher at a Munich high school as well as tutor to Prince Heinrich, the son of Prince Arnulf of Bavaria. Peter Padfield has suggested that Gebhard Himmler was 'a member of the educated middle class, with the credentials to rise further in the social scale, and a powerful desire to do so'.[4] Providing service to the Bavarian royal family was an excellent way to achieve this end.

In July 1897, Gebhard married Anna Heyder, a quiet, mousy Munich woman a year his junior, and they set up home in a comfortable apartment in the centre of the city. The following summer, their first son, also called Gebhard, was born. He was followed on 7 October 1900 by Heinrich Luitpold. He was given the name after Gebhard Senior had written to the sixteen-year-old Prince Heinrich to request permission to name his new son after his former pupil. This was duly granted, and the prince also agreed to be the baby's godfather.

Heinrich Himmler's childhood seems to have been happy and reasonably normal, given the circumstances (war broke out when he was thirteen). His father, by all accounts, was a pedantic and fussy man, but both he and Anna lavished a great deal of attention and affection on their sons (a third, Ernst, was born in 1905) and this was returned by all three boys. Professor Himmler would read them tales of the old Germans, accounts of famous battles and stories of their grandfather's exploits as a soldier of fortune in Greece and elsewhere. Heinrich received his primary education at the Cathedral School in Munich and then, at the age of ten, followed his elder brother to the Royal Wilhelm High School. Former classmates recalled him being at or near the top of the class in all of the academic subjects. The only area where he was lacking was in sport and physical education. One former classmate described him as: 'of scarcely average size, but downright plump, with an uncommonly milk-white complexion, fairly short hair, and already wearing gold-rimmed glasses on his rather sharp nose; not infrequently he showed a half embarrassed, half sardonic smile either to excuse his short-sightedness or to stress a certain superiority'.[5] He suffered a number of illnesses, and his health was never particularly robust. The plumpness can be explained by his great love of cakes and sweets. Consequently, PE became a terror to him, not least because the gym instructor sometimes dealt with him harshly.

In 1913, Professor Himmler was appointed deputy headmaster at the high school in Landshut, north-east of Munich. Once the family had relocated there, they lived in a comfortable house in the old town. Young Gebhard and Heinrich were both enrolled in their father's new school, and Heinrich formed a great friendship with another boy who had moved there from Munich, Falk Zipperer.

The family were on holiday in Titmoning near the Austrian border when war broke out between Austria and Serbia on 29 July 1914. Heinrich, a young boy brought up on tales of martial glory, was intensely excited by this development. Since the age of ten, at the instigation of his father, he had been keeping a diary, and now he recorded his thoughts on the war. Naturally, he was fully in support of it, and frequently he revealed his contempt for those who were not: 'Whenever there is talk of our troops retreating, they wet themselves.'[6] He played games of war with his friend Zipperer, and expressed his longing to prove himself as a soldier.

Before long, he joined a youth cadet force – the *Jugendwehr* – for pre-military training, and began a programme of exercises to toughen himself up. But his family life continued largely as before. Then, in 1916, his elder brother left school to begin officer training, and in 1917 Zipperer did the same. Professor Himmler was keen that Heinrich should finish his schooling and gain his leaving certificate, but Heinrich prevailed on him to pull some strings (via the Bavarian royal family) and at Christmas 1917 he received orders to report at the start of January to the 11th Bavarian Infantry Regiment to begin his training as a *Fahnenjunker* (officer cadet). This would eventually qualify him as an officer of the reserve.

Much has been made of Himmler's 'failure' as a soldier, but in reality he was no such thing. Although he suffered from homesickness during his first few weeks in the army, he was an entirely satisfactory recruit. He did his basic infantry training in Regensburg between January and June 1918; officer training between June and September; and a machine-gun course in September and October.[7] Had the war continued, he would have joined his regiment at the front and, in due course, would almost certainly have been commissioned. However, once the armistice was declared, there was no point in his leaving Regensburg. Once the regiment returned, he learned that he and his fellow cadets were to be demobilised, which duly happened shortly before Christmas 1918.

There is no doubt that Himmler was bitterly disappointed that he did not get to serve as a frontline soldier and earn his commission – later in life, he would lie that he had done both – but his 'failure' was merely due to his age, not to any inadequacy or lack of ability. At this point, poised on the brink of manhood, achieving officer's rank was the summit of his ambition, and he clung to the hope that he might be able to resume his military training at some stage.[8] He would be disappointed in that, too, but it is worth considering the degree to which he developed during his relatively short military period. Before joining the army, he had essentially been a spoiled, fussy, naïve, middle-class mother's boy who had rarely been outside the bosom of his family. In the first few months of his military service, his letters home contained endless requests for sweets and cakes to supplement his rations. However, as time went by, he toughened up and grew to enjoy the disciplined routine. He never shook off the pedantry that he inherited from his father, but by the time he was demobilised he was considerably more independent, was starting to formulate his own opinions and was finding his own path through the world. He had been forced to rely for the first time on his own instincts and intellect, and he had thrived. He was probably physically tougher, too. Above all, though, military service increased Himmler's self-confidence. He would have gained experience in commanding and leading soldiers, even at the very basic, cadet level. The effect of such experience is considerable: military leadership carries with it the obligation to balance the needs of subordinates against the requirements of the hierarchy; to understand basic operational, logistical and administrative planning; and to act decisively when required. Himmler surely developed at least some of these attributes.

However, with a military career snatched away from him, Himmler returned to education. He had missed a year of school, so in early 1919 he returned to Landshut High School to take a special course for ex-servicemen – led by his father – which would take him through the last two years of secondary schooling in just two terms. However, this was interrupted in April by political events as the Free Corps mobilised to suppress the revolutionary government in Munich. Himmler first joined a small Free Corps unit in Landshut and subsequently the reserve company of the *Oberland* Free Corps, in which he served as an adjutant to the commander. But neither group was needed by the regular army forces and they remained in reserve. Around this time, there was some speculation that the *Oberland* might be absorbed into the regular army, but it was disbanded instead, and Himmler returned to his studies.

His second choice for a career after the army was agriculture. In the summer of 1919, Professor Himmler was appointed head-master of the high school at Ingolstadt, and he arranged for Heinrich to spend a year working on a nearby farm, in prepara-tion for an agronomy course at the *Technische Hochschule* (Technical University) in Munich. He began work on the farm on 1 August, in time for the harvest, and Peter Padfield remarks: 'the work was hard and it must have been especially so for Himmler after the desk-work at school'.[9] Possibly, although it is important not to confuse the current ex-soldier with the adolescent mother's boy. Nevertheless, little more than a month after he started, he was hospitalised after catching paratyphus and was then under doctor's orders to study rather than remain on the farm. Consequently, in October, he moved into a rented room in Munich and began his course at the university.

What followed was probably as formative for Himmler as his year in the army. As in everything else he did, he applied himself to student life assiduously: he fell in (unrequited) love; he joined a duelling fraternity; and overall he was 'friendly, helpful, studious and something of a bore'.[10] Politically, his views were unremark-able: he adopted the conservative nationalism of the Munich bourgeoisie and appears to have been no more than convention-ally anti-Semitic: there were no Jews in his social circle at this time and as a typical middle-class Catholic he regarded them as 'aliens', but his diaries betray no trace of his later ferocious hatred.[11]

A year of academic study was followed by his deferred year of practical study on another farm. This time he found a place at Fridolfing, near the Austrian border, and he seems to have been far happier here than he was at Ingolstadt. The farmer and his wife treated him as a member of their family and he appears to have had plenty of free time, during which he read widely in politics, history and literature, often transcribing passages from books that appealed to him.

Throughout his three years as a student, Himmler kept in touch with the military. In November 1919, he and his brother Gebhard had joined the 14th Alarm Company of the Munich Protection Brigade, an official army reserve unit. When this was disbanded at Allied insistence in the spring of 1920, he enrolled as a member of the Munich Citizens' Militia, a semi-official group that was sponsored and equipped by the army. Joining these groups put him in touch with some of the radicalised army officers who were prominent in political circles within Munich. He eventually became a *Fähnrich* (senior officer cadet – in effect, a cadet NCO), which was just one step away from being a commissioned officer.

In the autumn of 1921, Himmler returned to Munich for the final year of his academic studies. It was around this time that he first met Ernst Röhm. In his diary entry for 26 January 1922, Himmler noted that he had encountered Röhm as well as his former company commander at a meeting at the Arzberger Keller in Munich. But the tone of the entry – 'Captain Röhm and Major Angerer were there; both very friendly. Röhm pessimistic about bolshevism'[12] – suggests that he knew him, or at least of him, before this meeting. Himmler admired and respected Röhm as a decorated frontline soldier, despite the latter's open homosexuality.

Himmler passed his final exams in August 1922 and quickly found a job as an agricultural assistant at a fertiliser factory in Schleissheim. At Röhm's suggestion, he also joined an unofficial nationalist paramilitary group called the *Reichsflagge* (Imperial Flag), with which he did more military training. By now, he was more radical in his views, which was hardly surprising, given that he associated almost exclusively with right-wing ex-servicemen. In the year he worked at Schleissheim he became increasingly convinced that Germany's republican constitution needed to be replaced, perhaps by force. This was the year of hyperinflation, an economic catastrophe that weighed particularly heavily on financially prudent, middle-class families like his own. Furthermore, he was already nationalistic and martial in outlook, so Röhm must have had little trouble persuading his young friend to join the NSDAP, which Himmler did on 1 August 1923. He became party member 14,303.[13]

He also resigned from his job. With Germany seemingly on the brink of civil meltdown, semi-official volunteer units were being created from the various paramilitary groups and fragments of the Free Corps. The Imperial Flag had split, and Himmler followed Röhm into the Imperial War Flag faction. From there, he applied to and was accepted by the Werner Company, a volunteer unit sponsored by the German Army. This group was soon disbanded, but Himmler was back in the Imperial War Flag when Röhm took it into the folkish–nationalist combat league at the end of September 1923.

Consequently, Himmler had a small, walk-on role in the *Putsch*. On the evening of 8 November, Röhm led his group to the Bavarian War Ministry building, and Himmler carried the banner (which, of course, was the old imperial war flag). There is some confusion about whether they gained access to the building,* but they certainly surrounded it: Himmler was photographed outside, clutching the flag atop a barricade. Before long, they themselves were surrounded by the police, who approached carefully in armoured vehicles and set up their own machine guns and light artillery.

It was to Röhm's besieged group that Hitler and his cohorts were marching when the shooting broke out on the Residenzstrasse on 9 November. The Imperial War Flag was attacked on

---

* Padfield, for example, says, 'Röhm could not gain access' (p. 65), while Höhne has him 'in possession of the War Ministry . . . the muzzles of their machine guns poked menacingly out of the windows' (p. 36).

the same day, but after two men had been killed, and Röhm and a few other leaders had been arrested, the remainder, including Himmler, were disarmed and allowed to go home.[14]

This was a defining event in Himmler's life. It made him an active comrade of men whom he greatly admired; it gave him a cause; and it satisfied a deep urge to be at the centre of conspiratorial events and 'in the know'. He was an assiduous organiser of his own and, to some extent, his family and friends' lives, to such an extent that some thought him an interfering busybody, and he carried this trait into his membership of the Imperial War Flag.

In the aftermath, his worried parents hoped that he would settle down and resume his career. Instead, he devoted his energies to keeping alive the flame of the Imperial War Flag and acting as a courier between folkish groups and leaders who were trying to revive the movement. He also joined the National Socialist Freedom Movement – Gregor Strasser's successor group to the NSDAP – and gave several public speeches during the 1924 election campaign. He travelled from town to town on his motorbike, lecturing small crowds, proselytising the message of National Socialism, which meant he had now embraced the extreme anti-Semitism of the movement. He still kept an assiduous record in his diary of what he was reading, and around this time these lists are dominated by anti-Semitic pamphlets, heroic German myths and several spiritualist and occult tracts.[15] He adopted militant anti-Semitism simply because that was the creed of the movement and the milieu he had joined. In his youth, he had been no more than a 'mild' anti-Semite, and his father had several Jewish friends. However, his post-war association with such radical nationalists as Röhm undoubtedly focused his attention on the 'Jewish question'. The anti-Semitic propaganda he read, especially when combined with the romantic German imagery that had been a staple of his life since childhood, evidently had a striking and deepseated effect on him.

There can also be little doubt that Himmler had a powerful

desire to conform to the values of anyone he admired and respected. In his youth, he had submerged himself in the bourgeois Roman Catholic mores of his parents, family and schoolfriends; as a young adult, he wholeheartedly – even fanatically – subscribed to the radical, militarist nationalism of his student circle; and once he entered the National Socialist movement, he eagerly adopted its virulent anti-Semitism.

Himmler's campaigning did not go unnoticed, and in July he was offered the position of Gregor Strasser's secretary. Strasser was a resident of Landshut so probably knew the Himmlers from their time in the town, but it was equally possible that Himmler was recommended by Röhm or another leading National Socialist. Either way, Himmler, at the age of just twenty-three, was now on the National Socialist payroll.[16] At the time, Strasser was regional leader for Lower Bavaria, a deputy in the Bavarian *Landtag* (state parliament) and was also forging links with National Socialist-leaning groups in northern Germany and the Rhineland. It seems that Himmler was tasked with holding together the various threads of the semi-underground National Socialist groupings – both party and SA – in Lower Bavaria. Strasser thought his new secretary was 'incredibly keen . . . he's a perfect arms NCO. He visits all the secret depots.'[17]

In the December general election, Strasser was one of the few National Socialists elected to the Reichstag, which meant he needed Himmler even more and lead to Himmler's appointment as Strasser's deputy regional leader for Lower Bavaria. This was a significant promotion: Lower Bavaria was one of the key strongholds of National Socialism. The fact that a man as young as Himmler was put in effective charge of this region after just over a year in the party speaks volumes for his reputation as an administrator and organiser, if not his personal charisma and popularity among the rest of the membership (Strasser was unlikely to appoint a potential rival in his place).

Himmler was therefore the 'man on the spot' when Schreck's 'protection squad' circular arrived in Lower Bavaria. However, he had already joined the SS on 2 August, when he was given membership number* 168[18] (he had nominally joined the SA on the same day). As Strasser's deputy, Himmler was no doubt privy to the internal workings of party headquarters in Munich, which explains how he had prior knowledge of the new organisation before it was announced to the mass of the party.

There is little record of Himmler's SS activities at this stage, and he may well have devoted as much, if not more, of his time to several other organisations. He was, for example, the Regional Leader in Bavaria for the Artamanen Society, a folkish agricultural society that espoused a 'back to the land' ideology and advocated settling German farmers in the East as a sort of pioneer group. The putative elite status of the SS within the NSDAP, and its focus on intelligence-gathering, probably appealed strongly to Himmler, but there was no reason for him to think that it would ever become anything more than a small bodyguard service. He did take his squad to the 'Party Day' at Weimar in July 1926, when the Blood Banner was placed in the custody of the organisation, but it seems likely that Himmler's role as Strasser's deputy took precedence over any SS activity.

In September 1926, Strasser was appointed National Propaganda Leader, but he was still busy with his Reichstag duties and organising the North German National Socialists, so much of the propaganda work was actually done by Himmler, who deputised for him in this role as well. He is credited with inventing the technique of saturating an area with posters, speakers and canvassers, which became the standard campaign method for the NSDAP. Equally importantly, from September 1926, he was working in the party's headquarters in Munich and so was able to impress the

---

* It isn't entirely clear how SS membership numbers were allocated. Individuals who joined before Himmler have higher numbers (for example, see Bednarek above). It is probably the case that numbers were allocated by the SS HQ in Munich and that, therefore, it was easier for those in close physical proximity to prod them into action.

people who really mattered. At this relatively early stage, the majority of the NSDAP's members and indeed its leadership were still members of the lower middle classes, so the well-educated, bourgeois Himmler would certainly have stood out.

It was also in 1926 that Himmler met the woman he would eventually marry. Margarete ('Marga') Siegroth was the daughter of a Prussian landowner. A qualified nurse, she and a Jewish gynaecologist had opened a private clinic in Berlin,[19] where they practised homoeopathy, hypnosis and a variety of other popular, alternative treatments. Himmler met her while sheltering from a rain shower in a hotel lobby at Bad Reichenhall, and was apparently captivated by her statuesque figure, blond hair and blue eyes. Marga was eight years older than him, a Protestant and a divorcée, but as far as Himmler was concerned, it was love at first sight. According to Otto Strasser,[20] Himmler lost his virginity to her, which is probably true, because he remained extremely socially conservative and prudish.

In September 1927, Himmler became Heiden's deputy in the SS. There was a certain logic to this appointment: in his previous propaganda role, Himmler had made use of intelligence reports compiled by SS groups that detailed the activities of left-wing opponents and right-wing rivals; and, of course, he himself had been an active member of the SS almost since its inception. His enthusiasm and organisational talent were two more points in his favour, and he wasted little time in exerting his influence. In 'SS Order No. 1', which he issued on 13 September 1927,[21] he tightened up regulations to ensure that SS members always appeared in the same uniform, rather than in sportswear and lederhosen, which had apparently been worn at a recent Nuremberg Party Day. Another directive was that local SS units should conduct at least four 'activities' each month, two of which had to involve drill and singing. Finally, the order enjoined local SS commanders to begin forwarding various pieces of information to party headquarters: systematic intelligence reports about opponents' political activities; the names of prominent local Jews and Freemasons;

special community events; secret orders and plans of political opposition groups; and press clippings about the party.[22] This presaged the SS's later role as the Third Reich's primary security organisation.

Himmler soon became the driving force within the organisation. He still fulfilled his propaganda duties – although Strasser handed responsibility for propaganda over to Hitler in the run-up to the spring 1928 elections[*] – but he found the time and the energy gradually to eclipse Heiden. According to Koehl, the latter 'seems to have become a fifth wheel, hanging around the offices of the "[Folkish] Observer" as a survival of an earlier free corps type'.[23] Even so, the SS remained a comparatively small and obscure organisation. By comparison, Pfeffer von Salomon's SA, the party's mass uniformed group, was commanding much of the leadership's attention and was increasingly being used by the younger generation of leaders as the workhorse of the movement.

Although a full-time party official, Himmler's salary at this time was relatively modest. Following his marriage to Marga in 1928, they used the proceeds of the sale of her clinic to fund the purchase of a small farm at Waldtrudering, near Munich, where they intended to supplement their income by raising chickens. However, despite Himmler's enthusiasm for agriculture, by now his party duties were leaving him little time for either the farm or his new wife. Indeed, the couple were soon leading largely separate lives, a pattern that would continue until Himmler's death. Their only child, a daughter named Gudrun (known as Püppi), was born in 1929. By then, her father was busy plotting a path that would make him one of the most powerful men in Germany.

---

* Hitler took control of Party propaganda in the run up to the elections in the spring of 1928 before handing over responsibility to two individuals: Josef Goebbels in Berlin and Fritz Reinhardt in Munich.

4

A New Broom

There is no record of what specific instructions were given to Heinrich Himmler when he took over as National Leader of the SS on 20 January 1929. Following his two predecessors' poor performance, it is likely that he was simply told to rejuvenate the organisation and increase its membership.

The entire strength of the SS at this time was approximately 280 subscription-paying members,[1] who comprised fewer than 75 protection squads. The largest of these was attached to party headquarters in Munich and commanded by Josef 'Sepp' Dietrich, who would later be a key figure in the militarised Waffen-SS. Many of the others consisted of just two or three members, so it is scarcely surprising that few other party members were inspired to join an organisation that was a long way from being a dynamic elite.

Dietrich, an earthy ex-soldier and -policeman, was a relatively recent addition to Hitler's inner circle of gophers, drivers and bodyguards – the so-called *Chauffeureska*. He was born in the village of Hawangen in the Bavarian province of Swabia on 28 May 1892.[2] After some eight years of schooling, he was employed as a farm-worker before travelling a little in Europe, eventually becoming an apprentice in the hotel trade in Switzerland. The Dietrich legend has it that he then served in the Bavarian Army as a cavalry-man and professional NCO, before joining the elite Storm Troops* during the Great War and ending up as a senior NCO in Germany's first tank unit. The truth is somewhat more prosaic: he did indeed join the Bavarian Army, in October 1911, but served in an artillery regiment and was invalided out little more than a month later, after falling from a horse. Thereafter, he worked as an errand boy for a baker. When he rejoined the army on the outbreak of war, he again served in an artillery regiment. He transferred to the Storm Troops only in late 1916. Just over a year later, he became a crewman in captured British Mark IV tanks, and he served in that capacity to the end of the war. He was certainly awarded the Iron Cross (second class) in November 1917, and was wounded several times before the armistice, but aside from that his Great War history is murky. By 1945, he was one of Germany's most highly decorated soldiers, and he claimed to have received several of those decorations during the First World War. However, his biographer could find no record of Dietrich being awarded either the Iron Cross (first class) or the Austrian Bravery decoration.[3]

Similarly, his post-war career was somewhat obscure. He claimed to have served in various Free Corps – including the *Oberland*, during the Munich *Putsch* – but he also spent some time as a regular policeman. In short, it seems that his record was significantly edited in the late twenties and early thirties to paint him in a more politically favourable light. Again, there is no evidence to support his claim that he took part in the *Putsch*, even though he was awarded the Blood Order, instituted by Hitler in 1933 to honour participants. Indeed, there is no evidence that he was politically active at all until he joined the NSDAP in May 1928 at the urging of Christian Weber, who was employing him at a filling station. Dietrich joined the SS a week later. This lack of

---

* These were specialised infantry units who mounted commando-style raids on enemy trenches to facilitate the movement of conventional infantry.

any obvious political hinterland has led Dietrich's biographer to suggest that he was essentially apolitical,[4] but such a claim cannot be supported. Dietrich did not disagree in any meaningful way with the verbose monologues that Hitler tried out on the *Chauffeureska*. Just like the other members of the inner circle, he retained his place at the table in Munich's Café Heck every afternoon because of his soldierly good humour *and* his unquestioning acceptance of the corrosive, racist gibberish that was bandied around.

Dietrich's protection squad was vibrant and healthy, but this was certainly the exception rather than the rule. Outside of Munich, no one could realistically expect such a tiny organisation to fulfil its primary function of protecting the party's leadership. Indeed, many within the NSDAP saw the SS as little more than a group of newspaper salesmen and canvassers, rather than a quasi-military elite. However, at least they could not claim it was a drain on resources, as it was entirely self-funded. Most of the money came from members' subscriptions, but there were also *Fordernde Mitglieder* (FM – sponsoring members), who contributed to SS funds without taking part in its activities. A smattering of Jewish names in this group suggests that becoming an FM was not always voluntary, and that the SS may have followed the custom of the SA and other paramilitary groups in operating shakedowns and protection rackets. Nevertheless, the SS operated on a shoestring budget, which was reflected in its relative lack of administrative and clerical support.

The central organisation and administration of the SS, such as it was, seems to have been almost entirely the responsibility of Himmler himself. He operated from party headquarters at 50 Schellingstrasse, Munich, and was the only member of the SS to receive a salary (albeit just RM200 per month, which was not really a living wage) from central party funds. In his first few months as National Leader, anything emanating from SS 'headquarters' was invariably drafted, edited and typed by Himmler. At first, this was probably not too much of a stretch for him, but as the organisation expanded he began to be overwhelmed. Eventually, although he maintained an intense disdain for bureaucracy, he was forced to sanction the growth of an enormous and complex network of offices and staff.

Within the framework of the NSDAP, the biggest obstacle in the way of expansion of the SS was the SA, of which it was still nominally a subordinate formation. By bringing in a number of former military and Free Corps comrades as regional leaders, Pfeffer von Salomon had given Hitler what he had demanded back in 1926: a more controllable and disciplined SA that was still large enough to project the NSDAP's 'strength' on the streets. However, in return, Pfeffer von Salomon had demanded authority over the nascent SS. When he had still been Heiden's deputy, Himmler had attempted to assert the independence of the SS from the SA, but on 12 April 1929 the following order was issued from SA headquarters: 'The SS is a special formation of the SA. The basic regulations of the SA are thus valid for the SS, provided no special instruction has been enacted.'[5]

The only solution seemed to be to build up the SS's strength through a recruitment drive. By the end of 1929, Himmler, almost single-handedly, had got membership up to the thousand mark; and the following month, he wrote to his old colleague Röhm, with whom he had remained in correspondence during Röhm's absence in South America, to say that he expected to reach two thousand by the end of April.[6]

Running in parallel with this expansion was a process of organisational restructuring that would continue throughout the SS's existence. Up to this point, each individual protection squad had been commanded by an 'officer' who reported directly to the National Leader. With no intermediate ranks or organisational strata, each unit should, in theory, have received equal attention from the National Leader. However, this became impossible as the organisation grew, so, from August 1929, the SS began to ape the organisational model of the SA. The smallest unit became the *Schar* (squad), which comprised approximately eight men and roughly corresponded to a military section. This squad was commanded by a *Scharführer* (squad leader) – equivalent to an NCO. Three squads formed a *Trupp* (troop) of between twenty and sixty men – equivalent to a military platoon. This was commanded by a *Truppführer* (troop leader). Three troops then formed a *Sturm* (company), which was commanded by the lowest 'officer' rank: *Sturmführer* (company leader). Three companies constituted a *Sturmbann* (battalion), which was led by a *Sturmbannführer* (battalion leader). Three or four battalions formed a *Standarte* (regiment), which was commanded by a *Standartenführer* (regimental leader). Two or more regiments formed an *Untergruppe* (sub-group) – later renamed a *Brigade* (brigade) and then an *Abschnitt* (division) – which was commanded by an *Oberführer* (senior leader). Several sub-groups constituted a *Gruppe* (group).*

To help him implement all of this, in 1930 Himmler acquired a business manager, a treasurer and an adjutant in the shape of Josias Erbprinz zu Waldeck-Pyrmont.

Waldeck-Pyrmont was born in 1896 – the son and heir of the ruler of the principality of Waldeck-Pyrmont. He was also a nephew of the Dutch Queen Emma and was related by marriage to the British royal family. He served as an infantry officer in the First World War and then studied agriculture before taking over the management of his family estates. He joined the NSDAP in November 1929 and the SS – as one of Himmler's earliest aristocratic recruits – in March 1930. In some respects, this was a coup for Himmler: he was anxious to promote the notion that the SS constituted an elite within both the movement and the Germanic race as a whole, and what better way to do this, in class-conscious

---

* Although it is tempting to ascribe military equivalence to all of these ranks and groupings, it would be wrong to do so at this stage in the development of the SS. Rank in the SS was of purely political significance until after the National Socialist seizure of power, when the SS set up its own military units and started to penetrate the police and security forces. Even then, it was common for individuals to hold a political rank in the SS and a totally different rank, with genuine military equivalence, in the Waffen-SS or the police.

Germany, than by the recruitment of members of the hereditary nobility? Within a month of joining the SS, Waldeck-Pyrmont was promoted to the rank of battalion leader; and within two months he was a regimental leader and adjutant of the SS-Brigade Bayern.[7] In September, he became Himmler's adjutant and head of the National Leader's personal staff.

In the 1928 general election, the NSDAP had gained 810,000 votes, which meant it secured just 12 out of the 491 Reichstag deputies. In the September 1930 elections, it garnered 6,371,000 votes and 107 seats in the Reichstag, which meant it was now the second-largest party in the parliament after the Social Democrats. Several factors lay behind this extraordinary turnaround in the party's fortunes.

As we have seen, the Dawes Plan of 1924 had helped resolve the hyperinflation crisis and had given a much-needed boost to the country. However, by the end of the decade, Germany's reparations payments were still hobbling the economy, so another attempt to address the issue was made by the American lawyer Owen D. Young. The Young Plan, signed in June 1929, reduced the total reparations bill to thirty-seven billion gold Reichsmarks and extended the payment period to fifty-nine years. Internationally this was widely seen as a good deal for Germany, but the nationalist right, who had never accepted the concept of German war guilt, was outraged. The media magnate Alfred Hugenberg led a campaign against the Young Plan, and he made his considerable newspaper resources available to Hitler. The more radical and anti-capitalist elements within the NSDAP – led by Gregor Strasser's younger brother Otto – expressed their distaste at this alliance, but Hitler exploited it to great political and personal advantage. The militant, radical NSDAP was able to reach a much wider audience, and it also gained an aura of respectability and credibility that had previously eluded it.

In the midst of this right-wing campaign against the Young Plan, two events occurred that had great significance for the future of the NSDAP and Germany. On 3 October, Gustav Stresemann, Germany's foreign minister, died suddenly of a stroke at the age of fifty-one. He had steered Germany's foreign relations throughout most of the 1920s with good sense and moderation, and his death left the country without a statesman of any particular international stature. That might not have been critically important, were it not for what happened three weeks later.

On 24 October, in a wave of panic selling, the value of shares on the New York stock market crashed. Individuals, businesses and banks faced bankruptcy, and the repercussions were severe all around the world, especially in Germany. The fragile German economy depended on loans from the United States, but threatened American bankers now began to call these in. Consequently, Germany was plunged into chaos. The hyperinflation of 1923 had pauperised the non-property-owning classes in Germany by destroying their savings. Now the process began again through unemployment.

This situation was the best possible recruiting sergeant for the NSDAP. It was the third major catastrophe in Germany in eleven years – first defeat in the war, then inflation, now the depression – so the NSDAP's claim that the democratic Weimar system had failed seemed highly credible. Membership of the party and its various organisations soared as Germans looked for a solution to their problems. Moreover, because Hitler had chosen the path of legality rather than revolution after the *Putsch*, ordinary people were not afraid to throw in their lot with the National Socialists.

In reality, much of the NSDAP's programme was old hat. Its anti-capitalism was shared by the Communists and Social Democrats; its nationalism was typical of the parties of the right; and it did not even have a monopoly on anti-Semitism. However, the National Socialists seemed to offer a degree of dynamism, vitality and action that the other parties lacked. They explicitly identified themselves as the movement of the 'front generation' – the men who had taken Germany to the brink of victory only to be cruelly 'stabbed in the back' by Jews, communists and other

'November criminals'. And they offered a break with the failures of the Weimar system by harking back to the values that had supposedly made Germany great.

While the depression pushed the struggling and unemployed towards the NSDAP, the National Socialists' propaganda techniques penetrated areas of German society that had hitherto been out of reach – sporting clubs, churches, businessmen's associations – and this especially benefited the SS. As the praetorian guard of this new, dynamic movement, aloof from the violence and corruption of the SA rabble, Himmler's SS cultivated an image of respectability, exclusivity and discipline. This soon proved very attractive to the educated, middle-class Germans who were now being drawn into the party.

The NSDAP's 1930 election campaign was the first to be centrally coordinated by Josef Goebbels (in accordance with guidelines laid down by Hitler). Goebbels was born in Rheydt, on the edge of the Ruhr district, in 1897 into a lower-middle-class, Catholic family. A childhood illness left him with a deformed right foot and lower leg, which meant he was turned down for military service in the First World War. Instead, he studied literature and philosophy at the universities of Bonn, Freiburg, Würzburg and Heidelberg, gaining a Ph.D. in eighteenth-century romantic literature in 1921. He joined the NSDAP in 1924 in response to the French occupation of the Ruhr, and soon gained a reputation as a highly intelligent, charismatic orator. Initially, he was associated with Strasser's more 'socialist' wing of the party, but Hitler recognised his ability in the mid-1920s and soon made him a key ally.

In 1930, Goebbels' activists blanketed Germany in a blizzard of propaganda, agitation and street violence, forcing themselves onto the front pages of newspapers that had ignored them two years previously. The result of the election was astonishing: the NSDAP's share of the vote rose from 2.6 to 18.3 per cent. As Ian Kershaw has pointed out: 'the NSDAP was [now] no mere middle-class party, as used to be thought. Though not in equal proportions, the

Hitler movement could reasonably claim to have won support from all sections of society. No other party in the Weimar period could claim the same.'[8] That is a little misleading, as the party never gained mass working-class support, but it made significant inroads even in that sector in 1930.

However, in spite of this electoral success, the NSDAP had been lurching from one internal crisis to another. The first problem was precipitated by Otto Strasser, younger brother of Gregor, who questioned whether the party had a meaningful programme beyond its quest for political power. He espoused a variety of National Socialism that emphasised radical anti-capitalism alongside nationalism and anti-Semitism, and he soon gathered a coterie of supporters who propagated their ideas via his Berlin-based publishing house, Kampfverlag. They were dismayed by the NSDAP's increasingly close relationship with the bourgeois establishment and heavy industry, and published ever more critical tracts against this tendency in the first few months of 1930. Hitler and especially Goebbels – who was Regional Leader in Berlin – were infuriated by this lack of loyalty. Goebbels now fully accepted Hitler's argument that the party's first priority was to achieve power – only then could it begin the National Socialist revolution.

The dispute reached a head in April and May 1930. Hitler convened a series of meetings of the party leadership to denounce Kampfverlag, and followed these with a face-to-face meeting with Otto Strasser himself on 21 May. Opinions differ as to whether this was designed to bring Strasser into line or to force him out of the movement. Hitler was probably simply probing Strasser to see whether an accommodation could be reached or more decisive action was needed. Whatever the motive for the meeting, it did not go well. Strasser forcibly argued that 'the idea' was greater than 'the leader'. Leaders, he said, were fallible and temporary, while the idea was eternal. Not surprisingly, Hitler thought this was nonsense: 'For us, the Leader is the Idea, and each party member has only to obey the Leader.'[9] He was equally dismissive of Strasser's claim that the NSDAP's strategy of legality and cooperation with the bourgeois right would hinder the 'Social Revolution' that they both espoused. In Hitler's view, this was 'Nothing but Marxism.'[10]

Despite the frosty nature of this meeting, Hitler typically hesitated before deciding to act against Strasser's clique. In fact, he took so long that he was pre-empted by Strasser and his supporters, who in early July announced that they were leaving the NSDAP to create their own radical National Socialist organisation: the Union of Revolutionary National Socialists, later known as the Black Front. This proved to be political suicide: very few National Socialists followed Strasser, and his departure signalled the end of any serious 'socialist' strand within the NSDAP. It also allowed Goebbels' elevation to National Propaganda Chief.

The second internal party crisis – which also began in 1930, although it only came to a head the following year – had a profound effect on the position of the SS within the movement.

As we have seen, the chief of the SA, Pfeffer von Salomon, recruited a number of ex-officers from the German armed forces, the Free Corps and the *Frontbann* in a bid to instil some military-style discipline into a corrupt and brutal gang. One of these new recruits was a former police captain, Walter Stennes, who became *SA-Oberführer Ost* (SA-Senior Leader East) – responsible for Berlin and eastern Germany. However, this appointment effectively supplanted the man who had created and built up the Berlin SA into a force of over five hundred men: Kurt Daluege – a tall, burly building engineer. Born in Kreuzberg in 1897, Daluege had joined the NSDAP in 1922[11] and had swiftly gained a reputation as a vicious and effective operator in Berlin street politics (where his limited intelligence earned him the nickname 'Dummi-Dummi'[12]). Unsurprisingly, he was far from happy when Stennes was brought in to run 'his' unit.

Stennes, for his part, seems to have been in sympathy with Otto Strasser. Certainly, both he and the men of the Berlin SA shared Strasser's frustration at the slow pace of the National Socialist 'revolution'. Their unrest grew when the party leadership refused to nominate Stennes and several other leading SA officers as candidates for the Reichstag. But this was just the tip of an iceberg of disquiet in Berlin and throughout the SA. Stennes was by no means alone in disagreeing with Hitler's legal route to power, and the economic crisis that followed the Wall Street Crash threw this dispute into sharp focus.

The SA benefited greatly from the crisis, with its membership increasing in 1930 to between '60,000 and 100,000'.[13] But most of these were not hard-core National Socialists; rather, they were unemployed and distressed, and had turned to the SA simply as a source of food and support. Stennes himself reported: 'In some Berlin units 67% of the men are unemployed.'[14] Meanwhile, the central party organisation – administrators who were widely derided within the SA as 'civilians' – kept the SA on a tight financial rein. Resentment grew at the traffic of cash from SA street collections and membership dues to party headquarters, with little coming back the other way. SA commanders wanted to hang on to their new recruits, and felt the need to spend some money on them in order to do so, but all of that money – which they had collected – was being channelled into the election campaign.

Notwithstanding the SA's lack of cash, its huge increase in membership, combined with its increased activity in the run-up to the September election, had the potential to cause a shift in the balance of power within the party. SA members were on the streets, fighting with their Communist and Social Democrat opponents, and this gave Stennes the opportunity to make his move. He demanded that senior SA commanders should be on the party's electoral list for the Reichstag; an increase in funding for the SA, including payment for members who guarded party meetings; and a reduction in the power of the 'civilian' regional leaders. On 23 August, just three weeks before the election, he led a delegation to Munich to put these demands directly to Hitler. The latter refused to see them, which led to a kind of strike by the Berlin SA: Stennes' staff officers resigned and refused to carry out their propaganda or protection duties. Then, on 28 August, a group of SA men raided the Berlin party headquarters and beat up the business manager. In response to this attack, SS guards were posted at the building.

By now, the Berlin SS was under the control of Stennes' predecessor, Daluege. Seething with resentment at Stennes' appointment, he had left the SA and had joined its rival organisation on 25 July (membership number 1119). He gained immediate promotion to senior leader rank and was given command of the Berlin SS* in place of the relatively ineffectual Kurt Wege. Thereafter, Daluege was specifically commissioned by Hitler to keep an eye on the manoeuvrings of Stennes and his clique, and a number of trusted former SA colleagues supplied him with information. Even so, Daluege failed to predict the Berlin SA's next move, which came on the night of 30 August. A large group of SA men again attacked the party headquarters, where they beat up the seven SS guards (two of whom received serious head injuries) and then smashed up the furniture inside. The raid was reported to Goebbels – who had been speaking at a party meeting in Breslau – and he drove through the night to take control of the situation. Humiliatingly, the only way to get Stennes' men out of the headquarters was to enlist the help of the much despised Berlin Police. A riot squad duly arrived and arrested twenty-five SA men.

This in-fighting represented a real crisis for the NSDAP, so Goebbels quickly contacted Hitler, who was in Bayreuth, and asked him to intervene. The next day, Hitler met with Stennes at a hotel near the Anhalter railway station in Berlin. Then he toured Berlin's SA bars and cafés, where he told the disgruntled SA men that they could trust him and that he would soon remedy their complaints.

Hitler's intervention papered over the cracks for the time being. Little news of the dispute reached the press and the election duly passed off successfully. Nevertheless, Hitler was well aware that he

---

* Then referred to as 'SS-Senior Leader Command East', and subsequently as 'SS-Regional Headquarters-Spree'.

would need to address the deep-rooted problems in the SA sooner rather than later. Before long, he dismissed Pfeffer von Salomon and took over the role of *Oberste SA Führer* (SA Commander-in-Chief) himself. He also wrote to Ernst Röhm (who was still in Bolivia) to ask him to return and become SA *Stabschef* (Chief of Staff). Röhm had kept in touch with the situation in Germany and was fully aware of the implications of the NSDAP's success in the general election.[15]

Critically, the SS's loyalty to the party leadership in the face of the SA unrest had not gone unnoticed, and soon it was given a new official function. In a circular sent to senior SA officers at the beginning of October 1930, the SS was described as a police organisation within the movement, with the authority to prevent illegality among party formations. This required the SS to be functionally independent of the SA in recruitment (its membership was supposedly capped at 10 per cent of total SA strength) and to perform its new policing function, even though it remained notionally subordinate to the SA.

At the same time, the overall role of the SA was re-examined. At a meeting of the organisation's leadership in Munich on 30 November 1930, Hitler proposed Röhm as his nominee for Chief of Staff against considerable opposition, especially from the Stennes faction. Röhm was, in his own way, as radical in his views about the future role of the SA as anybody within the organisation. Nevertheless, he was a strict disciplinarian who could be counted on to recognise how high the stakes now were for the National Socialist movement. High on the momentum of the party's recent electoral success and in the expectation that the NSDAP would soon assume power, the organisation's existing leadership (Röhm did not take up his new role until January 1931) began to prepare themselves for their future after the seizure of power. In principle, the SA was to 'turn away from propaganda, guard duty and the solicitation of funds'[16] and start to organise itself into the NSDAP's national military force. In turn, the SS would take over most of the SA's former tasks as the movement's political footsoldiers. On 1 December, Himmler – somewhat prematurely, as it turned out – announced the formal separation of the SS from the SA.[17]

If anything, the NSDAP's success in the election heightened the tension between the party and the Stennes faction within the SA. With power almost within his grasp, Hitler knew he needed to tread carefully in order to avoid provoking the somewhat rattled establishment into a decisive strike against the whole National Socialist movement. But this softly-softly approach frustrated many members of the SA, who clung to their romantic, albeit brutal, notions of seizing power by force. The election campaign had witnessed an upsurge of political violence between right and left, and this had continued largely unabated afterwards, partly because the Communists had also significantly increased their support. This had led Röhm, in his first month as Chief of Staff, to ban SA participation in street battles. Meanwhile, Daluege's Berlin SS continued to keep a wary eye on the Stennes clique, after all attempts to buy off and intimidate its leader had failed. For instance, when Stennes was offered the Interior Ministry of the state government of Brunswick – which had come under NSDAP control in the elections – he not only turned it down but openly criticised the corrupt and cynical party leadership in Munich.

All of this tension finally came to a head on 28 March 1931, when President Hindenburg gave Chancellor Heinrich Brüning's government the power to act against political excesses. The NSDAP leadership viewed this as a possible prelude to a ban on the party – or at least the SA – so Hitler ordered strict compliance with the rule of law. Stennes, seeing this as an attempt to curb his freedom of action, refused. Then, at a meeting in Weimar on 31 March, Hitler announced that Stennes was to leave his role as SA-Senior Leader East and would become Röhm's executive officer in Munich. This transfer could have been seen as a sideways move rather than a demotion, but there is no doubt that Hitler – warned of Stennes' continued plotting by Daluege – fully intended to provoke a strong reaction. He did not have to wait long. The very next day, the SS guards at Berlin's party offices were again beaten up by a mob of Stennes' SA supporters, who then occupied the headquarters as well as the offices of Goebbels' newspaper *Der Angriff* (*The Attack*). Stennes then announced Hitler's 'dismissal' as party leader, and SA leaders throughout northern and eastern Germany publicly declared their support for their man.

Berlin Regional Leader Goebbels had been trying to steer a middle course between Stennes and the Munich party leadership for many months, but now he clearly had to choose one side or the other. He had considerable personal sympathy for Stennes' political views, but after being given plenipotentiary powers by Hitler to resolve the crisis, he came out firmly in support of the leadership. The Berlin Police again cleared the SA men from party headquarters. Then, in the face of a barrage of propaganda and persuasion from Hitler and Goebbels, support for Stennes collapsed. A few hundred of his leading supporters were purged, the dust settled, and the revolt was over.

As an odd postscript to this tale, Stennes managed to survive the Third Reich. Imprisoned in a concentration camp after the NSDAP came to power, he was released after the personal intervention of Hermann Goering. He was smuggled across the Dutch border and then made his way to China, where he served as commander of Chiang Kai-Shek's bodyguard. During that time, he became an agent of Soviet Military Intelligence,[18] but his warnings about the imminent German invasion of the Soviet Union in 1941 went unheeded by Stalin. He left China when the Nationalists were defeated in 1949 and returned to Germany, where he died in 1989.

The SS's unwavering loyalty during the Stennes faction's revolt cemented its *de facto* independent role as the party's police force, even though Hitler had reaffirmed its subordination to the SA as recently as January 1931. In a letter to Daluege, Hitler wrote: '*SS-Mann, Deine Ehre heisst Treue*' ('SS-man, your honour is called loyalty'). Daluege then had the message printed on thank-you cards that were circulated among the Berlin SS on Hitler's behalf.[19] The phrase evidently resonated with Himmler, too. He slightly altered it to '*Meine Ehre heisst Treue*' ('My honour is called loyalty') and then adopted it as the organisation's motto. It was subsequently stamped on the SS's metal belt buckles and various other regalia.

But there were far more important consequences of Stennes' revolt than the coining of a pithy maxim. The SS had been given the opportunity to consolidate its unique role within the NSDAP, and this would enable Himmler to extend his organisation's reach throughout the movement and position it for future power struggles within National Socialism. Less welcome for Himmler was Daluege's continuing meteoric rise. As head of the Berlin SS, he had an independent power base and was now effectively number two in the organisation, even though he had joined less than a year before. Henceforth, Himmler would view Daluege as, at best, a potential rival and, at worst, an enemy.[20]

Despite his worries about his subordinate, Himmler was determined to press ahead with distancing the SS from the SA and building up its power. He decided that one of the best ways to achieve this was by giving the organisation its own distinct ideological framework, which would help to establish it as the elite of the National Socialist movement. To assist him in this endeavour, he turned to an old friend from his days in the Artamanen Society, Richard Walther Darré.

Darré was born in Buenos Aires, Argentina, in 1895, the son of a prosperous German businessman. He was educated at private schools in Argentina, Germany and, briefly, Britain, where he attended King's College School, Wimbledon. He entered the German Colonial School at Witzenhausen in 1914, but completed only one term before volunteering for military service. After a relatively successful war, in which he was commissioned as a reserve officer, he returned to civilian life to study agriculture, specialising in animal breeding.[21]

During the 1920s, as he continued to study, work in agriculture and participate in the Artamanen Society, he developed a theory that would later prove to be ideal for what Himmler had in mind for the SS. In effect, he argued that peoples and races are always led by aristocracies, and that 'It is an undisputed empirical fact of history that the growth and success of a nation is directly related to the health, both physical and moral, of its nobility.'[22] He then went on to say that the old German nobility had been corrupted by the decline in 'Germanic consciousness', which was the direct result of the rise of 'liberalism' since the Enlightenment and the French Revolution. This liberalism had led to 'race defilement, materialism, greed and a disregard for the welfare of society'. Aristocratic selfishness and disinterest in the 'collective' had thus led to an overall decline in the *Volk*. To Darré, the solution was simple: Germany needed a new aristocracy. He even suggested where its members could be found: among the Nordic peasant farmers, 'the true repository of the Germanic spirit and race'. The peasantry comprised the wellspring of the German nation and had 'always formed the only reliable basis for [the German] people from the point of view of the blood'. As a result, the state had a duty to protect and expand this sector of society by promoting settlement schemes and providing incentives to raise the birth-rate and curtail the rural drift to urban areas. All of the great empires, in Darré's view, had been created by men of Nordic blood, but had subsequently decayed because they had succumbed to humanistic ideologies: Freemasonry and Christianity, for example. They had also allowed their blood to become 'diluted and impure'. He particularly bemoaned the ongoing process in Eastern Europe, where Germanic blood was becoming increasingly intermingled with 'inferior' Jewish and Slavic blood.

All of this provided Himmler with the perfect ideological niche into which he could insert his organisation. It also allowed him to put the SS at the forefront of a mission that was a central plank of National Socialism: the reinvigoration and defence of the Germanic race. To achieve this aim, the SS would have to become both a military and a racial elite.

Bizarre (and indeed repugnant) as Darré's theories now appear, they were far from radical at the time. Many German nationalists, as well as innumerable supposedly 'progressive' thinkers in other countries, held similar opinions. In large part, this was due to the widespread acceptance of the pseudo-science of eugenics through-out the Western world.[23] Eugenics fitted the National Socialist world view perfectly. Although it did not promote the hatred and persecution of other races, many of its proponents were happy to accept a racial ranking system with Germanic, Nordic and Aryan peoples at the top, and Mediterraneans, Slavs, Asians, Jews, Africans and so on much lower down. National Socialist supporters usually believed that such a ranking was virtually self-evident. To their minds, human evolution could be characterised scientifically as the struggle for mastery between various races, and the Germanic race had emerged on top.

Himmler's SS was wedded to mainstream eugenic thinking within Germany, so many people would have viewed its ideology as 'science', rather than blind prejudice. Furthermore, he could point to his academic background in agronomy to buttress his own credibility on the subject. His plan was to make the SS selec-tive and exclusive on the basis of racial background and characteristics, and ultimately the biological foundation of a renewed German nation. He had little difficulty in gaining support for this project within the National Socialist movement as a whole, as well as in the SS, and this basic idea underpinned many of his subsequent actions.

As a first step, he introduced physical as well as political crite-ria into SS recruitment. Hitherto, potential SS members had only had to display absolute political loyalty, discipline and obedience, but now that often would not be enough. In a wartime speech, he described how he 'went about it like a nursery gardener trying to reproduce a good old strain which has been adulterated and debased; we started from the principles of plant selection and then proceeded, quite unashamedly, to weed out the men whom we did not think we could use for the build up of the SS'.[24] This, like many of Himmler's later pronouncements on matters of principle, was not entirely true. There was no 'weeding out' because the physical criteria were not – at that time – applied to existing members (if they had been, Himmler would have lost about half his manpower overnight). And they were not even universally enforced among new members: Himmler was always prepared to turn a blind eye to allow politically or socially well-connected individuals to join the SS, no matter what they looked like.

Nevertheless, on the whole, he was serious about his project. In late 1931, he appointed Darré as leader of the SS *Rassenamt* (Race Office) and began to enact measures to turn their ideas into reality. The most important of these was the SS Marriage Law, promulgated by Himmler on 31 December 1931, which read:

> The SS is a band of German men of strictly Nordic descent chosen according to certain principles.
>
> In accordance with National Socialist ideology and in the realisation that the future of our *Volk* rests upon the preservation of the race through selection and the healthy inheritance of good blood, I hereby institute the 'Marriage Certificate' for all unmarried members of the SS, effective 1 January 1932.
>
> The desired aim is to create a hereditarily healthy clan of a strictly Nordic German sort.
>
> The marriage certificate will be awarded or denied solely on the basis of racial health and heredity.
>
> Every SS man who intends to get married must procure for this purpose the marriage certificate of the National Leader of the SS.
>
> SS members who marry despite having been denied marriage certificates will be stricken from the SS; they will be given the choice of withdrawing.
>
> Working out the details of marriage petitions is the task of the Race Office of the SS.
>
> The Race Office of the SS is in charge of the Clan Book of

the SS, in which the families of SS members will be entered after being awarded the marriage certificate or after acquiescing to the petition to enter into marriage.

The National Leader of the SS, the Leader of the Race Office, and the specialists of this office are duty bound to secrecy on their word of honour.

The SS believes that, with this command, it has taken a step of great significance. Derision, scorn and incomprehension do not move us; the future belongs to us![25]

In 1932, Darré recruited two friends, Dr Schultz and Dr Rechenbach (an anthropologist and an army veterinarian, respectively) into the Race Office. These two men introduced the concept of the 'scientific' eugenic racial examiner, who was supposedly able to determine racial origin objectively – through measurement of body parts, eye colour, hair colour and so on. Over the next two years, when there was a massive increase in applications to join the SS, all potential recruits were vetted for these characteristics by racial desk officers – medically trained collaborators and 'experts' who also acted as instructors in SS racial ideology. These officers worked to guidelines drawn up by Schultz that meant all candidates (and existing SS members' proposed spouses) were placed in one of five groups: 'pure Nordic'; 'predominantly Nordic or Phalic'; harmonious bastard with slight 'Alpine, Dinaric or Mediterranean characteristics'; bastards of predominantly East Baltic or Alpine origin; and bastards of extra-European origin. In theory, only those in the first three groups would be allowed to join the SS or marry one of its members.[26]

Auslese (selectivity) thus became the overarching, founding principle of the SS's ideological framework. As guardian of the National Socialist movement and wellspring for the reinvigoration of the Germanic people, it could proceed only on the basis of having the 'correct' racial material. But Himmler added a further five key principles: struggle, honour, loyalty, obedience and *Führerprinzip* (the principle of leadership). The regeneration of the

Germanic race would entail a struggle to eliminate 'impurities', but through that struggle each SS man would gain strength and endurance. In some respects, this was a racist twist on the Marxist doctrine of class struggle. Himmler wrote:

> as long as humans have existed on earth, war between humans and sub-humans has become a rule of history. As far back [in history] as we can see, this Jewish-led battle has become the natural course of life on this planet. However, you may rest assured that this struggle for life and death is as much a law of nature as man's fight against anything else. Such is the fight between the bacillus and a healthy human body.[27]

Thus, the SS was explicitly involved in a racial war to cleanse the Germanic race of the Jewish 'bacillus', and obedience was vital to achieve this. Absolute obedience to the will of Hitler – the authoritative interpreter of National Socialism – would guarantee that the movement's programme would be implemented. In that way the New Order – and consequently freedom for the Germanic people – would be realised.

Complementing struggle and obedience were honour and loyalty. This linked the SS to the romantic ideal of the old German chivalric orders:

> the true SS man, like the true knight, was to be judged by his loyalty to the Cause, and the honour displayed in pursuing it . . . With this, we mean loyalties of every kind, including loyalty to the Führer and consequently to the German people; loyalty to one's conscience and race, blood loyalty; loyalty to one's ancestors and descendants; loyalty to one's 'clan'; loyalty to one's comrades and loyalty to the absolute laws of decency, cleanliness and chivalry.[28]

The principle of leadership was intended to be a binding force. In *Mein Kampf*, Hitler had articulated it as his reason for rejecting democracy.[29] As far as he was concerned, 'The progress of culture and humanity are not a product of the majority, but rest exclusively on the genius and energy of the personality.' In Hitler's view, a leader should hold absolute power while bearing absolute responsibility to the people for his decisions and actions. Democracy, based on a principle of equality, meant that rule was inevitably given to 'inferiors' who were more interested in maintaining power than in wielding it for the good of the people, which meant that leaders could not be held to account for their actions. It was also 'unnatural', because it eliminated the struggle for supremacy between unequals in which the strong would inevitably come to the fore. Consequently, 'inferior' races had inhibited the supremacy of the Germanic people. Hitler believed that absolute authority was the right of a leader who had shown his worth by struggling to the top; it should not be granted (and potentially withdrawn) by the governed in democratic elections.

The SS leadership principle was a refinement of this, with a disciplined, meritocratic hierarchy being formed from the organisation's racial and political elite. An SS man would thus be able to rise to the limit of his abilities within the hierarchy, but would still recognise his absolute subordination to those whose talents had raised them even higher. Ultimately, of course, they would always remain subordinate to Hitler – the *Führer* – himself.

For the most part, National Socialism's 'enemies' had already been identified by Hitler: Jews, Marxists, democrats, liberals, capitalists, the bourgeoisie, Freemasons, internationalists and homosexuals. The SS was quite explicit in adding the Roman Catholic Church to this list. But there were secret enemies too – ostensible National Socialists who were subverting the movement from within. The SS had to be prepared to strike them down. They had already done so in the case of Stennes and his supporters, but soon their attacks on the 'enemy within' would become much more comprehensive.

Taking Control

The Reichstag elections of September 1930 had established the NSDAP as a credible alternative to the traditional German political parties. Subsequently, its new-found prominence amplified the impact of National Socialist propaganda on the middle classes, war veterans and the rural population (although the NSDAP never really gained a foothold amid the urban working classes). The great depression was now exerting a profound influence on Germany, and Chancellor Brüning had been forced to introduce a raft of austerity measures. The NSDAP, never having participated in a national government, was ideally placed to claim that it could offer something different.

Paul von Hindenburg's first presidential term was due to end in March 1932 and he planned to seek re-election. Hitler, wishing to gauge his electoral appeal, decided to stand against him. This was to be one of the first modern, mass-media electoral campaigns. The theme of the National Socialist campaign was 'Hitler over Germany', which combined the idea of Hitler as head of state with footage of him flying from city to city in his personal aircraft, conveying the impression of a young, energetic man of action in contrast to the elderly Hindenburg. It also allowed him to campaign in more than one city every day. Hitler's candidacy provoked panic among the mainstream parties – the Social Democrats, the Catholic Centrum and the Conservatives – who all united behind Hindenburg. The only other candidates were Ernst Thälmann of the Communists and Theodor Düsterberg of the right-wing German National People's Party. In the first round, Hitler came second, polling more than eleven million votes (30.1 per cent of the total). Hindenburg achieved 49.6 per cent, Thälmann 13 per cent and Düsterberg 6.8 per cent.[1] In the second round, in April, it was a foregone conclusion that Hindenburg would win the necessary 50 per cent of the popular vote to gain re-election. Nevertheless, Hitler still managed to increase his support by 6.8 per cent by claiming the votes of almost all of those who had supported Düsterberg in the first round. The election firmly established the NSDAP's leader as a major figure in German national politics.

Upon resuming office, Hindenburg urged the government to pursue a more authoritarian, right-wing stance in a bid to counter the National Socialist threat. Brüning resisted, preferring a more 'parliamentary' approach to government, and he and his cabinet were swiftly dismissed. Hindenburg then handed the chancellorship to Franz von Papen, a Catholic nobleman who was a close adviser to the President and had the support of the right-wing, conservative bloc in the Reichstag. Von Papen called federal elections for July 1932 in the hope that he could secure a parliamentary majority, but the political momentum was now with the NSDAP. At the polls, the National Socialists secured 37 per cent of the popular vote, making them the largest single party in the Reichstag, with 230 seats.

The only hope left for von Papen was to try to persuade the NSDAP to join his government, so he offered Hitler the vice-chancellorship. Hitler refused, saying he would accept nothing less than the chancellorship itself, which he claimed by right as leader of the largest party in the Reichstag. However, Hindenburg was not prepared to make this 'Austrian corporal' his Chancellor.

Throughout the summer of 1932, the government and the

NSDAP manoeuvred against each other, as von Papen sought to 'wear down' the National Socialists. Meanwhile, the SA, the SS and communist paramilitaries fought increasingly violent battles in the streets. In some respects, the NSDAP's electoral successes were starting to count against them: inside the party, there was pessimism that they were no closer to achieving power, in spite of their massive increase in support at the ballot box. Furthermore, the movement was now heavily in debt as a result of almost per-petual campaigning and because vast numbers of SA men effectively lived off the party. Nevertheless, von Papen still could not persuade the National Socialists to work with him; even more ominously, he was also unable to build a coalition against them in the Reichstag.

In September, when the new Reichstag met for the first time under the presidency of Hermann Goering (as representative of the largest party), a motion of no confidence proposed by the Communist Party was passed with a majority of 84 per cent. This meant yet more elections had to be called. The SS and SA were sent into the streets to rattle tins for donations. The elections duly took place in November and, as expected, the National Socialist vote slipped to just over 33 per cent, giving the NSDAP 196 seats in the Reichstag. It remained the largest single party, but von Papen was encouraged by its slight decline and thought Hitler would now be obliged to accept his offer of the vice-chancellorship. However, once again, Hitler refused.

At this point, von Papen's plans began to unravel. He had assumed that he could continue to serve as Chancellor, using dic-tatorial powers given to him by Hindenburg. But now some members of his own government – particularly Minister of Defence General Kurt von Schleicher – began to oppose him. Von Schleicher was a career soldier who had established himself in the late 1920s as the main liaison officer between the armed forces and the civilian government. Between 1930 and 1932, he had served as a principal aide to General Groener, the Minister of Defence, and had also assumed the role of *éminence grise* by forging a close association with Hindenburg, whom he knew through the President's son, Oskar. It was von Schleicher who had been behind the ousting of Brüning and the appointment of von Papen, and now he insisted that the NSDAP must be brought into the government. In fact, von Schleicher had already opened channels of communication with Gregor Strasser, who appeared to represent the moderate wing of the NSDAP, with a view to the National Socialists joining a cabinet headed by himself. All of this manoeuvring came out of fear that the political deadlock was leading Germany towards catastrophe. In November, the Communists had secured some six million votes, which gave them 100 seats in the Reichstag. If something was not done, it surely would not be long before the German state came under attack from both the extreme left and the extreme right, with not enough people remaining in the middle to defend democracy.

At a meeting between Hindenburg, von Papen and von Schleicher on 1 December, von Papen admitted that his attempts to form a coalition government had failed. Nevertheless, he proposed that he should continue in office, with the Reichstag prorogued indefinitely while the constitution was amended and the electoral laws changed in order to break the deadlock. Von Schleicher argued that this suggestion was unconstitutional, likely to provoke civil war and, in any case, unnecessary, because he himself could command a majority in parliament comprising Gregor Strasser's remaining followers in the National Socialist Party, the Social Democrats and the Centrists. Hindenburg was surprised by this claim, but decided to stick by von Papen for the time being.

However, events now moved quickly. At a cabinet meeting held the next day, von Schleicher announced that the army had no confidence in von Papen. He produced a military assessment which stated that if the National Socialists and the Communists launched rebellions, and Poland then took the opportunity to attack in the East, the army would be unable to cope. Stunned, von Papen reported back to Hindenburg, who felt he now had no option but to dismiss von Papen and appoint von Schleicher to the chancellorship.

Von Schleicher then went straight to Strasser. If Hitler were unwilling to accept the vice-chancellorship, perhaps Strasser would take the job, especially if he was also offered the important role of Minister President of Prussia? Strasser wanted to accept, but instead he reported back to Hitler and the rest of the National Socialist leadership and sought advice. Opinion was bitterly divided. As head of party organisation, Strasser was well aware that the NSDAP's electoral support was weakening and that the party was facing a funding crisis. But Hitler, Goering and Goebbels all felt that accepting the offer might cause a split in the movement, so they urged Strasser to turn it down. After a series of acrimonious meetings in Berlin, Strasser resigned his position in the party on 7 December without accepting von Schleicher's offer.

Hitler quickly shored up his support within the party, while von Schleicher looked elsewhere – to the trade unions, the Social Democrats and the Centre Party – for backing. However, none of these groups trusted him, and his social policies – aimed primarily at reducing unemployment – began to stir up violent opposition from industrial and agricultural interests. Nevertheless, he naïvely believed that he would be able to turn the situation around.

At this point, von Papen re-entered the fray. Outraged by von Schleicher's betrayal and keen to exact revenge, he emerged as leader of a cabal of businessmen and bankers intent on bringing down the new Chancellor. On 4 January 1933, he met Hitler secretly at a house in Cologne and the two men discussed how they might work together to remove von Schleicher. It was decided that von Papen would persuade Hindenburg and the conservative right to accept National Socialist involvement in a coalition government, while his rich friends would quietly settle the NSDAP's debts and allow it to resume campaigning.

On 23 January, von Schleicher, finally accepting that he was unable to form a coalition, appealed to Hindenburg to dissolve the

Reichstag and grant him dictatorial powers. Hindenburg refused, repeating the very arguments that von Schleicher had used to bring down von Papen. Five days later, Hindenburg once again rejected von Schleicher's request. By then, he knew that von Papen was on the verge of forming a coalition with the National Socialists and the Nationalists. This time, von Schleicher had little option but to resign, which he duly did.

A day of frantic negotiation followed, as von Papen put the finishing touches to his coalition amid rumours that von Schleicher was stirring the garrison of Potsdam, south-west of Berlin, into rebellion. In fact, Hindenburg had already decided that General von Blomberg was to be Minister of Defence in the new government, and this appointment was seen as giving Hitler the army's imprimatur. The way was now clear for the NSDAP's leader to become Chancellor on 30 January 1933.

In later years, Hitler and the National Socialists would revel in the lie that they 'seized' power in 1933. However, as the events of late 1932 and early 1933 show, in reality they came to power through the kind of political machination Hitler affected to despise: 'he was jobbed into office by a backstairs intrigue',[2] to use the memorable phrase of one of Hitler's biographers.

The SS played a very minor role in this: all they did was intimidate opponents, sell newspapers, solicit donations and canvass voters. And it initially seemed that Himmler would gain little from the recent turn of events. His only tangible reward was his appointment, in March 1933, as acting Police President of Munich. By contrast, his colleague and rival Daluege became head of the Prussian uniformed police service, the *Ordnungspolizei* (Order Police), and was given the rank of Police Lieutenant General by Goering, who himself was now Prussian Minister of the Interior (as well as Ministry without Portfolio) in Hitler's cabinet. Certainly, SS men were co-opted as auxiliary policemen, but far more members of the SA were used in this capacity, and it seemed that the larger organisation was much more likely to benefit from the National Socialists' new position. However, from these inauspicious beginnings, albeit through luck as much as judgement, Himmler soon gained control of the greater part of the police structure throughout the whole country.

Intelligence collection and reporting had been among the SS's principal tasks ever since its foundation, but prior to Himmler's elevation to National Leader it had not been centralised. Instead, the SS had relied on local commanders and their subordinates to collect and forward reports to the leadership on their own initiative. Consequently, the intelligence had usually comprised little more than general information, gossip and rumours about 'enemies' of the movement. This can seldom have been of much practical use to the leadership, and it was certainly not 'intelligence' in the accepted sense of the term.* Recognising this, in his reorganisation of the SS in 1929, Himmler specified that each local unit should include an 'Ic' officer to coordinate the collection of information, analyse it, and only then forward it to headquarters.† Initially, the Ic was also obliged to act as adjutant to the unit commander, which suggests that intelligence collection was by no means seen as a top priority in the organisation.[3]

Then, in the summer of 1931, Himmler made one of the most important decisions of his first three years as National Leader: he recruited Reinhard Tristan Eugen Heydrich as his Chief of Intelligence. At the post-war Nuremberg trials, Heydrich would assume the role of the ghost at the banquet: a Mephistophelean evil genius who escaped Allied justice by being assassinated in June 1942. In many respects, this assessment is perfectly fair, as Heydrich must bear much of the responsibility for one of the greatest crimes in history – the Holocaust. But it has made it difficult to understand what motivated this well-educated, cultured,

---

* Broadly speaking, 'intelligence' is information that is gathered and analysed before informing decisions. Without the crucial analysis step – or at least being put in some kind of context – it is of little or no value.
† This followed the German general staff system, in which 'Ia' was the chief operations officer, 'Ib' the chief logistics officer and 'Ic' the chief intelligence officer.

highly intelligent man to become – along with Himmler – one of the principal architects of the Third Reich's machinery of political repression and, ultimately, genocide.

Heydrich was born on 7 March 1904 in Halle, Saxony, into a respectable, well-off, middle-class family. His father, Bruno, was a composer, opera singer and founder of the Halle conservatoire; his mother, Elisabeth, was an actress and pianist. Bruno was a fan of Wagner and sang at Bayreuth during the Wagner Festival. Later, he become acquainted with the composer's widow, Cosima, who ran the festival. Reinhard inherited his parents' musical talent: he learned the piano and violin from an early age, with his skill on the latter – which he continued to play throughout his life – being particularly notable.[4] He was also a dedicated sportsman. At around six months old he suffered an inflammation of the brain that endangered his life, and this was followed by a succession of other illnesses. To overcome this, his father encouraged him to take up as many sports as possible, including running, horse-riding, football, swimming and fencing. He would eventually represent Germany as a fencer in the 1930s, in parallel with his career as the SS Intelligence Chief.

Heydrich's family seems to have been strict and disciplinarian, but loving. His tall, stout father had a reputation as a joker, but he could also be pompous and overbearing, and he seems to have taken little interest in his children's education. However, like Gebhard Himmler with his sons, he introduced them to German folk myths at an early age. There are many rumours – most of them unsubstantiated – about Heydrich's youth and background. The majority of them seem to have gained momentum because of a supposition that he must have suffered some kind of childhood trauma which would explain – if not excuse – his later monstrosities. The most persistent of these – which caused him some problems even during his lifetime – was that Heydrich himself was of Jewish extraction. But this was not true. The confusion arose because Heydrich's grandmother married a locksmith called Gustav Süss after her first husband, Bruno's father, died. Süss was a common German-Jewish name at the time,[*] although Gustav himself was not Jewish. Nevertheless, as Heydrich's grandmother occasionally referred to herself as Frau Süss-Heydrich, people started to assume that the family, including Bruno, had Jewish blood. This was compounded in 1916 when that year's edition of Riemann's *Musiker-Lexicon*, a directory of German musicians, listed 'Heydrich, Bruno *alias* Süss'.[5] The pro-nationalist Bruno insisted that the error must be corrected in future editions. Notwithstanding the rumours about his heritage, Heydrich satisfied both the NSDAP and the SS about his racial origins as early as 1932, after the matter had been brought to Himmler's attention.

There is some anecdotal evidence that Heydrich was bullied at school because of his father's alleged Jewishness, but it seems highly unlikely that this fuelled his later hatred of the whole Jewish race. In fact, he suffered much more teasing as a child because of his odd, high-pitched voice: he was known as 'Hebbe' (Goat). He was also a solitary, arrogant young man who did not bond with his peers and even appeared to hold them in contempt. So, if he was traumatised by bullying at school, it seems that he largely brought it upon himself.

The family's income declined steadily during the war as the number of students attending the conservatoire dropped off. Then they were caught up in the revolutionary upheaval that followed the armistice. Despite being only fifteen years old (and thus two years underage), Heydrich volunteered for service in the *Maercker* Free Corps in March 1919. He served as a messenger with both the Free Corps and the Halle Citizens' Militia for more than a year while continuing his studies. Later, he joined another armed group, the extreme nationalist *Völkischer Schutz- und Trutzebund* (People's Protection and Retaliation League), which was affiliated

---

[*] In 1940, Hitler's government funded a notorious anti-Semitic propaganda film called *Jud Süss* (*Jew Süss*), which was a remake of a 1933 British film of the same title (although the original film was far more sympathetic to the eponymous character).

to the Thule Society. This affiliation suggests that he leaned towards the extreme right on racial issues long before joining either the NSDAP or the SS.

Having graduated from Halle Grammar School, Heydrich entered the navy as an officer cadet in 1922. Part of his training took place aboard the cruiser *Berlin*, whose first officer at the time was Commander Wilhelm Canaris, who went on to become head of German Military Intelligence in 1935. Heydrich's naval career initially followed a straightforward path. He was promoted to *Fähnrich zur See* (midshipman) in 1926 and *Leutnant zur See* (sub-lieutenant) later the same year. Then, after attending the Naval Signals School, he became a communications officer on board the *Schleswig-Holstein*, one of the few First World War-era battleships that the Allies had allowed Germany to keep. Thereafter, he was stationed in the communications division of the Baltic Naval Station at Kiel, but he may have had some connection with the intelligence branch of naval headquarters as well.[6]

However, his naval career came to an abrupt end because of his private life. According to Walter Schellenberg, who later became head of the SS's Foreign Intelligence Service, 'Heydrich's only weakness was his ungovernable sexual appetite. To this he would surrender himself without inhibition or caution and the calculated control which characterised him in everything he did left him completely.'[7] In December 1930, he became engaged to Lina von Osten, the beautiful, blonde, nineteen-year-old daughter of a schoolteacher from the island of Fehmarn, in the Baltic. Shortly thereafter, though, a previous girlfriend appeared and claimed he had already proposed to her – after they had spent the night together in a hotel. Heydrich vigorously refuted the woman's claims, but her father complained to the Commander-in-Chief of the German Navy, Grand Admiral Erich Raeder, and in early 1931 a Naval Court of Honour was convened to examine Heydrich's behaviour. The standard version is that Heydrich defended himself before the court with a confidence that bordered on arrogance – to the point where he was reprimanded for insubordination – and was subsequently dismissed for 'impropriety'. However, Peter Padfield argues that it would have been highly unlikely for a promising young naval officer to be dismissed merely because he had betrayed one girl for another. Instead, he suggests two alternatives: that Heydrich was planted by Naval Intelligence into the SS in order to monitor the activities of the National Socialist movement from the heart of its new 'police' branch; or that he was genuinely dismissed, but because he was already involved in National Socialist political activities.[8] Unfortunately, neither of these theories is supported by any evidence. The proceedings of the court have not survived, and the spurned girl has never been positively identified. For what it is worth, Lina von Osten, whom Heydrich went on to marry and who lived into the 1980s, subsequently stated: 'He was just a professional naval officer; he was wedded to his naval career. His only other interest was sport. He knew nothing about politics – and had never shown any great interest in them.'[9] This can be taken with a large pinch of salt, though, because von Osten was an enthusiastic National Socialist at the time and it was she who led him into the party. Interestingly, despite the immense power that he wielded later, Heydrich never took action against the members of the court that ejected him from the navy.

Heydrich's dismissal came when he was just a few weeks short of being eligible for a naval pension,[10] and there were few options for gainful employment in the harsh economic climate of May 1931. He explored the possibility of becoming a sailing instructor at a yacht club, then of joining the merchant navy, but neither appealed. Instead, at the prompting of his wife, he joined the naval branch of the SA and used a family contact to secure a paid position within the NSDAP. That contact was Friedrich Karl Freiherr von Eberstein, the son of Heydrich's godmother. Von Eberstein was ten years older than Heydrich and had had a distinguished career as a reserve officer during the First World War before becoming a banker. He had originally joined the NSDAP as early as October 1922, and had rejoined soon after the party became legal again in 1925. In April 1929 he had been recruited by Himmler as one of the first SS officers; and two years later he held the dual ranks of SS-company leader and SA-regimental leader as adjutant to the quartermaster of the SA High Command. Knowing that Himmler was expanding the SS, and perhaps seeing useful qualities in Heydrich, von Eberstein wrote to the National Leader to recommend Heydrich as a potential recruit.

In a speech in 1943, Himmler described how he selected Heydrich to be his chief of intelligence:

> I recruited Lieutenant Heydrich through the recommendation of the then *Gruppenführer* von Eberstein. This recruitment was actually based on an error. Somewhat at least. Heydrich was a 'Nachrichtenoffizier' (information or communication officer). I didn't know much about it in 1930 [*sic* – it was 1931] and I thought a 'Nachrichtenoffizier' was a man who got 'Nachrichten'.[11]

Nachrichten is news, information or intelligence (the current German intelligence service is called the *Bundesnachrichtendienst*), but it is also the military term for communications, and Heydrich had trained as a technical signals officer.

Summoned to an interview at Himmler's farm on 15 June, Himmler asked the younger man to outline how he would organise an intelligence branch for the SS. Despite his lack of practical intelligence experience, this was a straightforward task for a professionally trained naval officer and Himmler gave Heydrich the job more or less on the spot. Heydrich returned home to Hamburg to prepare for his new job. He was appointed to Himmler's personal staff as a company leader on 10 August, then, after relocating to Munich, he set to work on the SS's existing intelligence files. At this stage, he had no role in collecting or directing the intelligence-collection efforts of the local SS units. Rather, he simply collated any material that was passed to him by Himmler's adjutant, Waldeck-Pyrmont.[12]

But Heydrich was an opportunist, and he was quick to see the advantages that his position gave him within a movement that, to some extent, defined itself by its enemies, both real and imagined. According to George Browder, 'Heydrich built his authority upon an ability to paint two pictures convincingly. He depicted first the Movement, then the national community, as surrounded and penetrated by enemies, successfully camouflaging themselves as loyalists.'[13] Heydrich developed a vision of the *Ic-Dienst* (Intelligence Service) as an instrument of surveillance over all aspects of German national life, guaranteeing the total dominance of the National Socialist Party, and he convinced Himmler of the merit of this idea. Nevertheless, it started in a very limited way. The Intelligence Service was no more than a staff branch within the main SS headquarters in Munich, linked to intelligence officers in subordinate SS headquarters.

But Heydrich worked hard over the next two years to develop his organisation, partly by forging an extremely close working relationship with Himmler. There was never any doubt about who was in charge, though: Heydrich was always remarkably formal and deferential towards Himmler. In return, Heydrich's work was highly valued by Himmler, who started to receive ever more information about potential enemies both within and outside the National Socialist movement. Thus, when Himmler was put in charge of the Munich Police, naturally he took Heydrich with him.

As soon as he became Chancellor on 30 January 1933, Hitler prevailed upon President Hindenburg to call new elections. Through these, he hoped to gain enough strength in the Reichstag to pass an Enabling Act, which would allow him to rule by decree. The elections were set for 5 March. During the campaign, the NSDAP fully exploited the fact that they now had some control over the state's machinery of government. On 22 February, Prussian Minister of the Interior Goering established a 50,000-strong auxiliary police force, including 25,000 SA members and 15,000 SS men.[14] This both legitimised National Socialist terror against their political opponents – especially the Social Democrats and the Communists – and shifted the burden for funding a significant section of the NSDAP's paramilitary machine from the party to the state. The National Socialists justified the creation of this auxiliary force by claiming it was needed to forestall an imminent revolt from the left. Of course, this only heightened the atmosphere of hysteria among the electorate, which further boosted support for the NSDAP.

Then, during the evening of 27 February 1933, the Reichstag was set on fire. Arriving at the scene, the Berlin Police managed to apprehend the arsonist, who was running around, shirtless, inside the building. He was a twenty-four-year-old Dutch leftist, Marinus van der Lubbe.* There has been much speculation over the years that the National Socialists themselves orchestrated this attack, but it now seems that it came as a complete surprise to them.[15] They may even have believed that it presaged the start of an actual left-wing revolution. However, van der Lubbe seems to have acted entirely alone, motivated by fury about the National Socialists' rise to power and the subsequent inactivity of the German Communist Party. Unsurprisingly, the National Socialists immediately branded him an agent of a left-wing conspiracy, while the Communists portrayed him as a deranged tool of the NSDAP.[16] Most ordinary people simply did not know what to believe.

Irrespective of what motivated van der Lubbe, his attack had an immediate, ominous consequence: the so-called 'Reichstag Fire Decree', promulgated on 28 February after hurried discussions, which effectively ended civil liberty within Germany. *Habeas corpus* was suspended, as were freedom of the person, freedom of expression, freedom of association and assembly, confidentiality of post and telecommunication, and the right to protect one's home and property.[17] This was originally formulated at the Prussian

---

* Van der Lubbe had been a member of the Dutch Communist Party, but had broken with them and joined the Council Communists, who espoused a form of syndicalism.

Ministry of the Interior and was to be applied only in Prussia, but the national Interior Minister, Wilhelm Frick, soon came up with a version to be enforced nationwide. It was passed by Hitler's cabinet and signed into law the same day by Hindenburg. By now, though, the President was descending into senile dementia, beset by ill-health and largely under the control of his son Oskar.

A wave of anti-opposition terror was legitimised by the decree, and it was a pivotal piece of legislation in facilitating the creation of what later became the National Socialist security state. Critically, it separated the judiciary from the exercise of the power of detention: suspects could now be rounded up by agents of the state, including the newly formed auxiliaries, and detained without any legal scrutiny of the case against them. Consequently, worried friends and relations often had no idea why an individual had been detained, nor even where they were being held.

In Weimar Germany's last free elections, in November 1932, the Social Democrats and the Communists had received a fraction under 38 per cent of the vote, with the Communists accounting for 16.9 per cent of this. Just over four months later, with Hitler and the NSDAP in control of the machinery of government and many elements of state security, the majority of Communist leaders and deputies were either under arrest or had fled the country. In Goering's Prussia, ten thousand Communists and sympathisers were arrested in the week leading up to the 5 March election. By the end of the month, some twenty-five thousand Communists were either in prison or in one of several hastily set-up concentration camps.[18] By the summer, more than a hundred thousand Communists, Social Democrats, trade unionists and other opponents of the NSDAP had been arrested. A conservative official estimate suggests that at least six hundred of them died in captivity.[19]

The National Socialists won the election with 43.9 per cent of the vote, an increase of 10 percentage points since November. This did not give the NSDAP the overall majority that Hitler had wanted and predicted, but it meant it could form a coalition government with just one other party – the conservative-nation-alist German National People's Party. In spite of the oppression that had been directed at the Communist Party, it still managed to poll more than 12 per cent of the vote, which entitled it to eighty-one deputies. But with its leaders in custody, hiding or exile, there were a lot of empty seats in the Reichstag. The scene was now set for the government to seek the votes of the Catholic Centrum Party and gain the necessary two-thirds majority to pass an Enabling Act.[20] This duly happened on 23 March, when the newly elected Reichstag convened. With a series of Hitler's empty promises ringing in their ears, the Centrum deputies voted with the government and brought Weimar democracy to an end.[21] Effectively, Hitler's word was now law. Meanwhile, the increas-ingly frail Hindenburg announced that he would be withdrawing from the day-to-day affairs of government, and would not nor-mally need to be consulted on legislation passed under the Enabling Act.

On 27 March, Hitler appointed Franz Ritter von Epp, one of his longest-serving collaborators, as *Reichskommissar* (Governor) of Bavaria, which opened the way for Himmler to become the new police chief of Munich. Himmler immediately installed Heydrich as head of the force's 'political desk',[22] which effectively put him in charge of surveillance of potential enemies of the Bavarian state.

Himmler's position in Munich was strengthened on 1 April when he became a special adviser to the Bavarian Ministry of the Interior and was appointed Commander of the state-wide Bavarian Political Police. Again, Heydrich rose with him, becoming Himmler's exec-utive deputy, and set about reorganising the Bavarian political police. Hitherto, this had been a branch of the general police serv-ice, but Heydrich made it an entirely separate body, free from any administrative ties to the mainstream police, yet still able to use the latter's resources, if needed. At first, most of the manpower came from the existing Bavarian political police, but this was supple-mented by members of Heydrich's Intelligence Service – now renamed the *Sicherheitsdienst* (SD – Security Service) – which he had been gradually building up over the past two years. Importantly, one of Himmler's new responsibilities was to assume control of the concentration camps that had been set up in the wake of the Reichstag fire. He closed down the existing camps in Bavaria, and replaced them with one, centralised camp in the Munich suburb of Dachau. Command of this camp was put in the hands of SS-Battalion Leader Hilmar Wäckerle, an early National Socialist who had been a student with Himmler in Munich.[23]

Circumstances gave Himmler an ally in his quest to expand and consolidate his power base from the Bavarian political police in the shape of Minister of the Interior Frick. Prior to the National Socialist takeover, many of the powers of government within Germany, including the police forces, were in the hands of the individual *Länder* (states – such as Bavaria and Saxony). But in March and April 1933, Frick introduced a series of decrees that redefined the relationship between central government and the states, established the primacy of central government and vested ultimate local authority in 'Reich Governors' – who were tasked with ensuring that their states observed 'the political principles laid down by the Reich Chancellor'.[24] He also began to work towards converting the provincial police forces into a unified, national force under the Ministry of the Interior. However, these plans were opposed by Frick's National Socialist cabinet colleague, Goering, who exercised *de facto* control over more than half of Germany's police, first in his role as Prussian Interior Minister and then as Minister-President of Prussia.

Somewhat disturbed by the violence that he had unleashed in the wake of the Reichstag fire, Goering called upon the help of a small, obscure section within the Prussian Police headquarters, section IA – the Prussian political police. This was the closest thing Germany had to a national political intelligence clearing house. Goering appointed Dr Rudolf Diels, a lawyer and professional civil servant who had been working as head of the political police in Berlin, to lead IA. Diels was a fellow traveller rather than an ideologically committed National Socialist, but he was prepared to work with Goering to create a Prussian political police force similar to the one being set up by Himmler and Heydrich in Bavaria. It would be used as an executive instrument of the state to suppress the National Socialists' political enemies, both outside and inside the NSDAP. Diels recruited detectives from the criminal branches of the mainstream police, while Goering put in place the legal framework that would enable them to operate unfettered. Primarily, he allowed the force to arrest and detain suspects on their own authority, without any judicial oversight. At the end of April, Diels' section was officially renamed the *Geheime Staatspolizeiamt* (Secret State Police Office) and made an independent police authority responsible only to the Minister-President of Prussia – that is, Goering himself. The new organisation was officially abbreviated to 'Gestapa', but in popular slang it was given the better-known sobriquet 'Gestapo'. Before long, it had set up its offices in a former arts and crafts school on Prinz-Albrecht-Strasse in central Berlin.[25]

Diels began to exercise his new powers to bring order back to Prussia by clamping down on the excesses of the SA. A major part of the problem was that the auxiliaries mobilised by Goering after the Reichstag Fire Decree owed their primary loyalty to their SA (or SS) commanders, not to him, so setting them in motion actually reduced rather than enhanced his power to influence events. Diels used his expanded force to collect intelligence on SA activities and, where necessary, curtail them. In a series of raids, his men swooped on SA-run 'illegal' concentration camps, released the inmates and arrested the gaolers.

Having reasserted his authority in Prussia through the Gestapo, Goering was not inclined to hand control of his police forces over to Frick at the Ministry of the Interior, so a political stand-off developed between the two men. Frick needed an ally to overcome Goring's resistance to a national police force, and the obvious candidate was Himmler. So, between November 1933 and January 1934, Frick helped manoeuvre Himmler into command of every state-level political police force, save for Prussia's.

Initially, Goering fought back by increasing his personal control over the Gestapo, in order to prevent a Himmler takeover there as well. But he soon accepted that this battle was not worth fighting – primarily because he was facing a greater threat. Instead, he decided that a new tactical political alliance was in order. In April 1934, he appointed Himmler as 'Inspector'* of the Prussian Gestapo, which finally sealed Himmler's control over all of Germany's political police forces. Heydrich, as ever following on the coat-tails of his boss, became the operational chief of the Gestapo.

A little later, in November 1934, Daluege, who was still head of the Prussian uniformed police, had his authority extended throughout Germany. This came about when the Prussian Ministry of the Interior was combined with the national Ministry, creating a united police department for the whole country. Meanwhile, Arthur Nebe, a long-time National Socialist and member of the SS who had been serving as executive head of the Gestapo, was appointed chief of the Prussian *Kriminalpolizei* (Kripo – Criminal Detective Branch).

Officially, these men had been appointed by the national Interior Ministry, the Prussian government, or one of the smaller state governments, so in theory they owed allegiance to one of those institutions. In practice, in under two years, the SS had assumed effective control over the entire German police force.[26]

---

* *Inspekteur* – an appointment implying responsibility for the proper conduct of training, administration and operations, without direct operational command.

Consolidation

The threat that caused Goering to throw in his lot with Himmler and give him control over the Gestapo came from Ernst Röhm and the SA. Although individual SA officers had done well out of the National Socialist takeover, tension between the organisation and the German state was increasing. While Himmler was prepared to play a long game to assert SS power over the police, Röhm had more immediate ambitions for the SA. He had been a military radical ever since his days as a company commander in the First World War. During that time, he had come to the conclusion that the great majority of professional career soldiers were hidebound reactionaries, wedded to tactics and concepts that saw their men killed in vast numbers for little gain. His post-war service with the Free Corps and Citizens' Militia had shown him a different and, he believed, more effective way of waging war – a people's army based on egalitarian principles of comradeship, driven by ideological nationalism.

It could be argued that Röhm's radicalism derived, to some extent, from his personal character. He was an active homosexual who was attracted to young, working-class men – a fact that was widely known from the mid-1920s onwards – and he was regarded with considerable disgust and contempt by many of his former army colleagues: Hindenburg, for example, refused to shake his hand. For his part, Röhm returned that contempt with interest, and treated any advice from the military establishment with disdain. Since it had been unbanned in 1925, the SA had grown – particularly after the NSDAP's spectacular success in the 1930 elections – to a strength of some 500,000 members. Röhm could genuinely foresee his organisation fulfilling a long-held ambition: for it to be the foundation of a new type of army, a fact he made no secret of. He also assumed that the whole National Socialist movement would be right behind him: it would be Röhm's reward for all the hard work the SA had put in to facilitate Hitler's rise to power.[1]

By contrast, the army planned to take over the SA. The Versailles Treaty still restricted Germany to an army of just a hundred thousand men, but its leaders were anxious to develop a framework for the future expansion that had been promised by Hitler. In order to broaden the 'national defence base', including creating a Frontier Protection Service for the eastern part of the country, they proposed that the SA should be integrated with and trained by the army as a militia. In May 1933 – with both sides seeing it as a way of furthering their ambitions – the SA and army agreed on a training programme that would prepare up to 250,000 men a year for eventual entry into the army,[2] while the SA would absorb the members of any other right-wing paramilitary groups that were still in existence. The largest of these was a conservative-nationalist ex-servicemen's group called the *Stahlhelm* (Steel Helmet), which boasted more than a million members. The group's leader, Theodor Düsterberg, and the army's General von Reichenau had hatched a plan to outmanoeuvre Röhm. They thought if members of Düsterberg's organisation joined the SA *en masse*, and von Reichenau simultaneously appointed army officers to command positions in the militia and the Frontier Protection Service, Röhm's whole power base would be undermined.

However, Röhm countered this plan by dividing the SA into

three sections and then putting his half a million men into the most important of the three – the 'active' SA. Once he had absorbed all of the right-wing paramilitaries as reserves, Röhm was able to claim a strength for the SA of 4.5 million men. Soon he was demanding that his officers must be given real roles in the new Frontier Protection Service, as well as control over its weapons. Unsurprisingly, the army's leaders baulked at this, and from December 1933 they ceased to cooperate with Röhm's militia training.[3]

All of this tension between the army and the SA was a serious problem for Hitler. He was sympathetic to Röhm's ideas but much more realistic about the practicalities: he knew he needed the support of Germany's professional soldiers to carry his programme forward, and he could not have the SA stirring up trouble with them. So, on 28 February 1934, he called a meeting at the Army Ministry in which he urged the military leaders and the SA to patch up their differences. His proposal was that the army would be the sole bearer of arms in the Third Reich, while the SA would assume responsibility for pre- and post-military training. With the meeting over, the two sides went for lunch at Röhm's headquarters. What followed began the process of Röhm's destruction and the SA's elimination as a serious force in the Third Reich. Once the generals had departed, Röhm began a drunken tirade against Hitler: 'What that ridiculous Corporal says doesn't go for us. Hitler has no loyalty and must at least be sent on leave. If not, then we'll manage the thing without Hitler.'[4] Among those hearing this rant was SA-*Obergruppenführer* (Senior Group Leader) Viktor Lutze, commander of the Hannover SA, who immediately reported it to Rudolf Hess, Hitler's party deputy, then to Hitler himself and finally to von Reichenau. At first, none of them took any action against Röhm. But now he had alienated almost every power group in the Third Reich, and they all had good reasons to want rid of him. For Goering, he was a rival whose network of highly placed SA officers within government and the police represented a threat to his authority in Prussia; for the army, he was a direct threat to their position as traditional bearer of arms for the state; for the NSDAP, he had far too much control over the party's uniformed presence on the streets; and for the SS – which was still nominally subordinate to the SA – he was an obstacle to further expansion. So, once Himmler and Heydrich had sealed their alliance with Goering and assumed control of Germany's political police in April 1934, it was only a matter of time before they turned their attention to eliminating Röhm.

Heydrich's initial tactic was to use his control of the SS intelligence service and the Gestapo to find evidence that Röhm and his clique were plotting a coup against Hitler, but this turned out to be a chimera.[5] He turned up some trivial material regarding arms caches, but, in reality, nothing was further from Röhm's mind than a *Putsch*. In fact, he was trying to force Hitler to support the SA in their struggle with the army, but his tactics were clumsy, crude and open to misinterpretation. As he toured the country making rabble-rousing speeches to his men, he failed to appreciate that even ordinary Germans were becoming afraid of an SA attempt to seize power.[6]

The principal obstacle to the elimination of Röhm was now Hitler himself, who retained a sense of loyalty to his old colleague and the SA. This stayed his hand for some time, but eventually a visit to the moribund Hindenburg's Neudeck estate decided the matter. On 21 June 1934, Hitler met General von Blomberg, the Minister of Defence, there. Von Blomberg forcibly stated that if Hitler wanted the army to support him in the post-Hindenburg era, which was obviously now only weeks away, he had to eliminate the army's main rival. It seems that Hitler made the decision to make a punitive strike against the SA during the flight back to Berlin.

At that point, the SA was somewhat rudderless, as Röhm was two weeks into a spa treatment at Bad Wiessee. Hitler decided to summon the other senior SA staff to a conference there, where the SS would arrest them and 'settle accounts'.[7] A period of intense preparation followed, with secret orders going out to the relevant army headquarters to supply the SS troops with weapons and all the facilities they required. The SS men were drawn from Sepp Dietrich's newly formed, militarised *Leibstandarte* (Life Guards Regiment) Adolf Hitler and concentration camp staff from Dachau under Theodor Eicke, who would make the assault and deal with the prisoners afterwards. Meanwhile, orders were sent to Gestapo and SD offices to keep tabs on other senior SA personnel and ensure that they did not escape the dragnet. Finally, under the supervision of Himmler and Heydrich, a welter of bogus and exaggerated reports of SA insurrectionary activity were produced and fed to the army (and to Hitler) to guarantee that there would be no turning back.[8] On 28 June, Hitler telephoned Röhm at his hotel in Bad Wiessee and ordered him to muster all SA senior group leaders, group leaders and inspectors for a conference in two days' time.[9]

This was the signal to begin final preparations. Heydrich and his staff sent out further orders to regional SS, SD and political police offices. Meanwhile, Hitler set off for Bad Wiessee. However, by now, rumours of the move against Röhm and the SA had started to leak out, and groups of SA men across Germany were taking part in violent, drunken rampages through towns and cities in an outpouring of despair.[10] By doing so, of course, they were playing directly into their enemies' hands.

By contrast, Röhm and his cronies at the spa still suspected nothing. They spent the night indulging in their usual routine of beer-drinking and sex until they were interrupted in the early morning of 30 June by the unexpected arrival of Hitler, revolver in hand, together with a small entourage of bodyguards. Hitler personally banged on Röhm's door and denounced his astonished subordinate as a traitor. Röhm was then led away, protesting his innocence. Edmund Heines, chief of the Breslau SA, was found in bed with a young man and came close to being shot on the spot by a furious Hitler. All the other SA leaders were arrested and locked in a cellar while transport was organised to take them to Munich.

Simultaneously, Dietrich moved two companies of his unit to

Munich to act as the execution detail, while Heydrich dispatched plainclothes SD men and Gestapo detectives to arrest and assassinate a long list of SA chiefs and other opponents of the regime, both real and imagined. Over the next two days, these plainclothes 'death squads' and uniformed firing squads at the Lichterfelde Barracks, Berlin, and Stadelheim Prison, Munich, killed between 85 and 200 victims, the majority of whom were members of the SA. This was an episode of pure political savagery against men who had, for the most part, been comrades in arms of their executioners until just the day before. There could be no better illustration of how the SS defined its mission. Thuggery – towards Jews, communists and other enemies of National Socialism – had been a major part of the SS's *raison d'être* ever since its foundation. But the members of the SS saw themselves as much more than thugs. They craved a special status within the movement, and this mass killing of *internal* opponents demonstrates just how far they and their leaders – Himmler and Heydrich – were prepared to go to achieve it. It also demonstrates how effective they had been in inculcating a specific SS ideology at all levels of the organisation: it seems that no SS men baulked at what they were being asked to do. For instance, Dietrich faithfully carried out his orders to execute six of the most senior members of the SA – most of whom were personal friends. At his trial in 1957, he did claim that he left the scene 'after the fourth or fifth shooting' as he was unable to witness any more.[11] But he made no effort to prevent the rest of the murders.

Hitler took the opportunity to do away with some old political rivals while he was dealing with the SA. So Gregor Strasser was arrested and shot by Gestapo officials in his prison cell in Berlin. And Hitler's predecessor as Chancellor, von Schleicher, who was still considered a dangerous figurehead for conservative opponents, was also gunned down, along with his wife, at their home in Neu-Babelsburg.

However, Hitler's feelings for Röhm remained torn. At midday on 1 July, he was still inclined to let his old friend live, but Goering and Himmler finally persuaded him that the SA's leader had to die with the rest. He was awaiting his fate in Stadelheim Prison, and Eicke was ordered to go there and give Röhm the opportunity to kill himself. If he failed to do so, then Eicke should pull the trigger. Eicke arrived at the prison with his adjutant, SS-Battalion Leader Michael Lippert, and SS-*Brigadeführer* (Brigade Leader) Schmauser, who was Himmler's liaison officer with the army. They found Röhm sitting alone in his cell, stripped to the waist and sweating profusely. Eicke handed over a copy of the *Folkish Observer*, which detailed Röhm's supposed coup attempt, placed a pistol containing one round on the table, and gave the prisoner ten minutes to 'draw the conclusions'.[12] He then left the cell. Ten minutes later, when he returned, he saw that Röhm had not moved. He and Lippert now drew their pistols and opened fire. Röhm fell to the ground, and was then finished off with a bullet to the chest.

The results of the so-called 'Night of the Long Knives' were twofold. First, on 20 July 1934, the ever-loyal SS became a fully independent organisation within the framework of the NSDAP, rather than merely a component of the SA, and this allowed Himmler to tackle something that had been concerning him for some time.[13] In the immediate aftermath of the NSDAP's assumption of power, there had been a rapid increase in applications to join the SS, with the number of members doubling, on paper, from 50,000 to over 100,000 between January and May 1933.[14] There was a freeze on recruitment between the end of April and November 1933, but thereafter the SS had again doubled in size, to around 200,000, by June 1934. Now, Himmler decided it was time to do some pruning. Following the 20 July proclamation, around sixty thousand undesirables were expelled from the SS.[15] Mostly these comprised recent recruits, opportunists who had jumped on the National Socialist bandwagon – or 'March Violets', in National Socialist slang. But a fair few of the old guard were also told their services were no longer required. There was simply no role for them in Himmler's upwardly mobile organisation.

Second, and more importantly, just a month after Hindenburg had finally succumbed to lung cancer on 2 August, the army kept its promise and allowed Hitler to combine the offices of Chancellor and President. In a plebiscite held two weeks later, the German people approved this move with a 90 per cent majority. The way was now clear for a complete National Socialist takeover of the German state, which meant the SS would have total authority over security and policing.[16]

Dachau and the Establishment of the Concentration Camps

As we have seen, the German prison system simply could not accommodate the massive influx of real and imagined enemies of the National Socialist regime arrested in the wake of the Reichstag fire. In consequence, dozens of 'wild' detention camps were created throughout Germany by the SA, the SS, the police and various other agencies of the state and National Socialist Party. These camps were subject to little or no external control, and were often set up in disused buildings, barns or police barracks, with few if any facilities for the detainees. Furthermore, the prisoners were subjected to random beatings and torture by vengeful – and often drunk – National Socialist thugs. Many of the detainees were eventually released, but Himmler remained determined to use his new policing powers to bring order to the system of political detention, and he searched for a member of his organisation to implement this. We have already met the coarse, aggressive, ruthless man he chose for the task, because the pre-war SS concentration camp system was largely the creation of Theodor Eicke.

Born in Alsace – which was then under German rule – in 1892, Eicke was the son of a stationmaster. He had an undistinguished school career before dropping out at the age of seventeen. With little prospect of civilian employment, he joined the army as a clerk and served as a paymaster throughout the First World War. He left in 1919, having gained the rank of career assistant paymaster, equivalent to a senior NCO.[1] He and his wife then moved to the Rhineland, where he tried to find work as a policeman. He applied in several different towns, but every time he was taken on, he was soon dismissed for expressing extremist views or for participating in violent demonstrations against the Weimar Republic. Nevertheless, he earned some money as a paid informer.[2] Eventually, in 1923, he became a security officer for the chemical company IG Farben at their plant in Ludwigshafen am Rhein, where he rose to the position of chief of the internal security team.[3]

In December 1928, he joined the National Socialist Party and the SA, in which he stayed for eighteen months before transferring into the SS.[4] Himmler quickly promoted him to SS-company leader and gave him command of the SS unit in Ludwigshafen. Eicke displayed a talent for both recruitment of new members and organisation, which led to him being promoted again, this time to SS-battalion leader. Now he was tasked with raising a second 'battalion' for the Rhineland-Palatinate, which he had achieved by the summer of 1931. In gratitude, Himmler promoted him to SS-regimental leader and gave him command of the 10th SS Regiment[5] – the SS unit that covered the whole of the Rhineland-Palatinate.

By the end of that year, Eicke's political activities had come to the attention of his employers and he was laid off. On 6 March 1932, he was convicted of being in possession of explosives and conspiring to carry out acts of political violence in Bavaria. This earned him a two-year sentence in July, but the Bavarian Minister of Justice, who was an NSDAP sympathiser, temporarily reprieved him from the sentence so that Eicke could 'recover his health'.[6]

Eicke returned to Ludwigshafen and initially continued much as before, but this was a provocation too far for the local police authorities, and before long he was forced to go into hiding. Fearing political scandal at a critical time, in September 1932 Himmler ordered Eicke to go to Italy, where Mussolini's regime had set up a camp for National Socialist exiles on Lake Garda. However, before Eicke left, Himmler promoted him to SS-*Oberführer* (senior leader) and placed him in command of the SS camp.

While Eicke was in Italy, Josef Bürckel, the NSDAP's regional leader in the Palatinate and one of his enemies, attempted to have him dismissed from the party. Bürckel and Eicke had quarrelled the previous year over Bürckel's plans to coordinate all activities of the SA and SS within his region. Eicke had seen off the threat, but now Bürckel evidently sensed a chance to gain his revenge. Eicke had enough friends among the senior party leadership for Bürckel's attempt to fail, but when he returned to Ludwigshafen in March 1933, Himmler ordered the two men to forget their differences. Eicke, though, was never one to let any perceived slight go unpunished, so he led a squad of armed SS men to the Ludwigshafen party headquarters and detained Bürckel. However, party loyalists came to Bürckel's rescue, and Eicke was arrested and committed to a psychiatric hospital in Würzburg, where he was placed under the care of Dr Werner Heyde.[7]

Himmler was extremely annoyed by Eicke's erratic behaviour, and for a short time he was struck from the SS's seniority lists. However, Heyde, who was a National Socialist sympathiser, befriended his new patient and eventually persuaded Himmler that he should be released and reinstated into the SS. This was duly done in June 1933, and Eicke was immediately handed a new role: commandant of the concentration camp at Dachau.[8] Eicke was not an obvious choice to take over from Hilmar Wäckerle at Dachau: his only experience of prisons had been his time on remand during and after his trial in 1932. However, he had an attribute that Himmler prized greatly in those under his command:

he was personally indebted to the National Leader for freeing him from the psychiatric hospital.*

Eicke arrived at Dachau in the middle of a scandal. Himmler had established the camp in the grounds of a semi-derelict factory back in March, and Wäckerle had been in charge ever since. His first task had been to draw up a set of rules for the camp, which he had done, but his rulebook contained various 'crimes', such as 'incitement to disobedience', which were punishable by a death sentence that was imposed by a tribunal of camp officers. In effect, Wäckerle had given himself the power of life and death over the prisoners within the camp. In the camp's first three months, when it served solely as a detention centre for political opponents of the National Socialists, thirteen prisoners were killed or died as a result of their ill-treatment. The mother of one of the dead prisoners made a formal complaint to the Munich Police, and Wäckerle was charged with four murders.† Himmler, in these early days of the Third Reich, had no option but to remove him from his post.[9]

Eicke's brief was to impose order and discipline on the camp, not to make life any easier for the inmates, and that was precisely what he did. He organised administrative and logistics offices; he hired a doctor; and he drafted suitable prisoners into repair, maintenance and manufacturing roles to ensure that the camp was as self-sufficient as possible.[10] He also organised the prisoners into 'blocks' of 250, commanded by a 'block leader', who was normally a senior NCO. The block leaders were subordinated to a

* A similar case was Odilo Globocnik, whom Himmler shielded from corruption allegations that arose when he was Regional Leader of Vienna. Himmler promoted him to Lieutenant General of the Police and made him his representative in Lublin, where he subsequently oversaw the extermination of the Jewish population of Poland.

† The charges were dropped after intervention by Himmler, and Wäckerle moved sideways into the newly forming militarised SS. He was killed on the Eastern Front in July 1941 when commanding the Westland Regiment of the SS-Wiking Division.

Rapportführer (reporting officer), who was normally an SS-*Hauptscharführer* (sergeant major). He, in turn, was commanded by a *Schutzhaftlagerführer* (protective custody camp leader) of 'officer' rank. However, most of the day-to-day supervision of the inmates was carried out by prisoner trusties, known as 'Kapos'. These were normally recruited from the ranks of professional criminals who, for some reason, had been sent to Dachau rather than to regular prisons. According to Rudolf Höss, who served at Dachau under Eicke,* the SS guards tried to have as little contact with the prisoners as possible.[11]

Rather than Wäckerle's broad guidelines, Eicke drew up a detailed schedule of carefully defined offences with punishments to match. Just as importantly, he began to inculcate the guard force with a strong disciplinary code of conduct, based on blind obedience to orders from their SS superiors and on hatred and contempt for their prisoners: these became the rules on which the concentration camp system was based. The most serious offences were still punishable by death, but beneath that was a sliding scale of punishment: periods of between eight and forty-two days in solitary confinement on bread and water; corporal punishment in the form of whippings inflicted by SS men; periods of particularly hard labour; special exercises that were 'usually performed with accompanying kicks and blows from the SS guards';[12] and tying the prisoner to a stake or a tree for a specified period of time. In addition to these formal punishments, the Kapos ruled over their fellow prisoners through informal bullying and brutality, to which the guards would turn a blind eye.

In the early years at Dachau, prisoners were subjected to hard labour of a particularly nugatory type: digging ditches and filling them back in; quarrying stones for aggregates; levelling ground. This was not designed to be productive in any sense, but simply to add to the burden of the prisoners' lives and 'educate' them to

---

* Höss, subsequently commandant of Auschwitz, learned his trade as a 'block leader' at Dachau in 1935.

forget their opposition to the National Socialist regime. As time passed, however, the SS decided that better use could be made of their captives, and they were rented out as slave labour in factories and plants controlled by both the SS and private industry.

Even more appallingly – particularly during the war – camp inmates were used for SS-sponsored medical experiments, being treated like human guinea pigs. For the most part, these experiments originated outside the SS and simply exploited the supply of prisoners within the SS system. Researchers would apply to the chief SS doctor, Ernst-Robert Grawitz, who would forward the requests to Himmler for approval.

One example of this was a series of experiments conducted on behalf of the Luftwaffe at Dachau by Sigmund Rascher to investigate the effects of low pressure and high altitude on the human body.[13] Rascher was a thirty-year-old physician working in a Munich hospital when the war broke out, and he was conscripted into the Luftwaffe as a medical officer. His wife had worked as Himmler's secretary at one time (she may also have had an affair with him), and Rascher was a member of the SS, having transferred from the SA in June 1939. At the beginning of 1942, after an introduction from his wife, he asked Himmler for permission to begin high-altitude experiments on inmates from Dachau. How far Rascher was acting on his initiative or under orders from the Institute of Aviation Medicine in Berlin remains unclear. Himmler approved his proposal, provided him with an assistant and a special low-pressure chamber, and gave him access to as many prisoners as he needed. The experiments began in April 1942. A report survives of the effects they had on those unfortunate enough to be selected:

> The third experiment of this type took such an extraordinary course that I called an SS physician of the camp as a witness, since I had worked on these experiments all by myself. It was a continuous experiment without oxygen at a height of 12 kilometres on a 37 year old Jew in good general condition.

Breathing continued up to 30 minutes. After 4 minutes the experimental subject began to perspire, and wiggle his head; after 5 minutes cramps occurred; between 6 and 10 minutes breathing increased in speed and the experimental subject became unconscious; from 11 to 30 minutes breathing slowed down to three breaths per minute, finally stopping altogether.

Severest cyanosis developed in between and foam appeared at the mouth.

At 5 minute intervals electrocardiograms from three leads were written. After breathing had stopped the ECG was continuously written until the action of the heart had come to a complete standstill. About half an hour after breathing had stopped, dissection was started . . .

When the cavity of the chest was opened the pericardium was filled tightly (heart tamponade). Upon opening the pericardium, 80cc of clear yellowish liquid gushed forth. The moment the tamponade had stopped, the right auricle of the heart began to beat heavily, at first at the rate of 60 actions per minute, then progressively slower. Twenty minutes after the pericardium had been opened, the right auricle was stopped by puncturing it. For about 15 minutes, a thin stream of blood spurted forth. Thereafter, clogging of the puncture wound in the auricle by coagulation of the blood and renewed acceleration of the action of the right auricle occurred.

One hour after breathing had stopped, the spinal marrow was completely severed and the brain removed. Thereupon, the action of the auricle of the heart stopped for 40 seconds. It then renewed its action, coming to a complete standstill 8 minutes later. A heavy subarachnoid oedema was found in the brain. In the veins and arteries of the brain, a considerable quantity of air was discovered. Furthermore, the blood vessels in the heart and liver were enormously obstructed by embolism.[14]

It is significant that a good proportion of the post-mortem section of the report dwells on the effects of the damage that Rascher himself had inflicted during his dissection. His qualifications to conduct medical research were dubious at best, and he is believed to have faked evidence to obtain 'correct' results during pre-war cancer research. In later experiments, he simulated parachute descents. For example, a former delicatessen worker was given an oxygen mask and raised to a simulated height of 47,000 feet in the pressure chamber, at which point the mask was removed and freefall simulated. The prisoner's reactions were described in detail in Rascher's report: 'spasmodic convulsions', 'agonal convulsive breathing', 'groaning', 'yells aloud', 'convulses arms and legs', 'grimaces, bites his tongue', 'does not respond to speech', 'gives the impression of someone who is completely out of his mind'.

Altogether, about a hundred Dachau inmates were killed in under five months of high-altitude experiments. The Institute of Aviation Medicine in Berlin was kept informed of Rascher's results throughout.

Rascher's second series of human experiments began almost as soon as the first set ended. This time, he wanted to test the effects of extremely low temperatures on the human body, and to investigate how to warm up patients who had been subjected to extreme chilling. The intention was to find treatments for Luftwaffe pilots who had crash-landed in the sea and become hypothermic.

One survivor of these experiments, a Polish priest, gave evidence during the post-war Nuremberg trials:

On 7 October, 1942, a prisoner came and told me that I was to report to the hospital immediately. I thought I was going to be examined once more, and I was taken through the malaria station to block 5 in Dachau, to the fourth floor of block 5. There, the so-called aviation room, the aviation experimental station, was located there, and there was a fence, a wooden fence so that nobody could see what was inside, and I was led there, and there was a basin with water and ice which floated on the water . . .

Now I was told to undress. I undressed and I was examined. The physician then remarked that everything was in order. Now wires had been taped to my back, also in the lower rectum. Afterwards I had to wear my shirt, my drawers, but then afterwards I had to wear one of the uniforms which were lying there. Then I had also to wear a long pair of boots with cat's fur and one aviator's combination. And afterwards a tube was put around my neck and was filled with air. And afterwards the wires which had been connected with me – they were connected to the apparatus, and then I was thrown into the water. All of a sudden I became very cold, and I began to tremble. I immediately turned to those two men and asked them to pull me out of the water because I would be unable to stand it much longer. However, they told me laughingly, 'Well, this will only last a very short time.' I sat in this water, and I had – and I was conscious for one hour and a half. I do not know exactly because I did not have a watch, but that is the approximate time I spent there.

During this time the temperature was lowered very slowly in the beginning and afterwards more rapidly. When I was thrown into the water my temperature was 37.6. Then the temperature became lower. Then I only had 33 and then as low as 30, but then I already became somewhat unconscious and every fifteen minutes some blood was taken from my ear. After having sat in the water for about half an hour, I was offered a cigarette, which, however, I did not want to smoke. However, one of those men approached me and gave me the cigarette, and the nurse who stood near the basin continued to put this cigarette into my mouth and pulled it out again. I managed to smoke about half of this cigarette. Later on I was given a little glass with Schnapps, and then I was asked how I was feeling. Somewhat later still I was given one cup of Grog. This Grog was not very hot. It was rather lukewarm.

I was freezing very much in this water. Now my feet were becoming as rigid as iron, and the same thing applied to my hands, and later on my breathing became very short. I once again began to tremble, and afterwards cold sweat appeared on my forehead. I felt as if I was just about to die, and then I was still asking them to pull me out because I could not stand this much longer.

Then Dr Prachtol came and he had a little bottle, and he gave me a few drops of some liquid out of this bottle, and I did not know anything about this liquid. It had a somewhat sweetish taste. Then I lost my consciousness. I do not know how much longer I remained in the water because I was unconscious. When I again regained consciousness, it was approximately between 8 and 8:30 in the evening. I was lying on a stretcher covered with blankets, and above me there was some kind of an appliance with lamps which were warming me . . . [15]

The low-temperature experiments concluded in the spring of 1943 amid disagreements between the SS and the Luftwaffe. Some of Rascher's data had proved useful to the Luftwaffe, but the experiments had become increasingly strange. In order to test whether human body heat could be used to warm up subjects, Rascher had used pairs of prisoner-prostitutes from the Dachau camp brothel. These women would be ordered to sandwich the frozen subject in a sleeping bag; then, once he had warmed up a little, on Rascher's command, they would attempt to have sexual intercourse with him. However, Rascher sufficiently impressed Himmler for the National Leader to find him an academic post at the University of Strasbourg. While there, Rascher worked on projects for the *Ahnenerbe* (see Chapter 9).[16]

In the mid-1930s, these medical experiments lay in the future, but Dachau was still a brutally harsh environment, especially for Jewish inmates. Eicke was an ardent anti-Semite, and he ensured that copies of Julius Streicher's virulently anti-Semitic newspaper *Der Stürmer* (*The Stormer*) were readily available for both guards and non-Jewish prisoners. He also imposed collective punishment for Jewish inmates whenever articles that were critical of the concentration camps appeared in the foreign press.

During the first year of his command at Dachau, both Eicke and the camp itself were subordinated to SS-Regional Command South, based in Munich (just as other concentration camps were subordinated to their local SS regional headquarters). From Eicke's point of view, this was far from ideal. He had a deep, obsessive hatred towards those he regarded as rivals, and he resented anyone placed in authority over him. Consequently, he complained to Himmler that he did not have sufficient supplies and that the men sent to him as guards were not up to the task.[17] Himmler took these criticisms seriously, and started to contemplate a wholesale reorganisation of the existing camp system. In the 30 January 1934 promotion round,[*] Eicke was promoted to senior rank as an SS-brigade leader, indicating that he was now firmly back in favour with Himmler. By May, the National Leader had decided to centralise control of the SS camps within an 'Inspectorate of Concentration Camps', based near the Berlin satellite town of Oranienburg, with Eicke as the Inspector. Then, on 20 June, Eicke was appointed to Himmler's personal staff, pending the formal announcement of his new role. This came on 5 July, four days after Eicke had murdered Ernst Röhm in his prison cell in Munich. A week later, Himmler promoted him to SS-group leader,[†] at that time the second-highest rank in the SS.[18] Eicke was now in a position to expand the concentration camp system and run each camp strictly on his organisational model.

---

[*] SS promotions had traditionally taken place on 9 November, the anniversary of the Munich *Putsch*. But from 1934 they also took place on 30 January, the anniversary of the 'seizure of power'.

[†] Ranks in the General-SS – which remained a party formation – were not formally equivalent to military ranks; ranks in the Waffen-SS and police were.

In the early part of 1934, members of the SS were involved in making plans to take over a number of camps that were still being run to hold 'protective custody' inmates on behalf of the provincial authorities, the police and the SA. In April 1934, the Reich Ministry of the Interior had established national rules for imposing protective custody, confirming the Gestapo's key role in the detention process.[19] This was accelerated following the 'Night of the Long Knives' in July 1934, when SS units seized control of three camps from the SA. A fourth came under SS control in August.

By the summer of 1935, the number of active concentration camps across Germany had fallen to five (of which Dachau was the largest), holding about 4000 prisoners between them. (By contrast, the regular German prison system at the time held more than 100,000 prisoners, including some 23,000 political prisoners). Further consolidation of SS control over existing camps in the summer of 1936 increased this number to six, but by the end of the following year, just two of these – Dachau and Lichtenberg – were still operational. The rest had been closed and superseded by a new wave of 'model' concentration camps purpose built under Eicke's guidance.[20]

The first of the model concentration camps was Sachsenhausen, built alongside the Inspectorate headquarters itself, in September 1936. It became the specialist training centre for SS personnel assigned to the concentration camp system. Some 200,000 prisoners are believed to have passed through the camp in the course of its existence, with approximately 30,000 of them dying – by execution, casual brutality, untreated disease or overwork; many of them in and around the nearby brickworks, established by the SS to exploit prisoner labour. Sachsenhausen was the first camp to use the motto *Arbeit macht Frei* ('Work Will Free You') at its entrance, later copied by Rudolf Höss above the main gate at Auschwitz.

Buchenwald, located close to Weimar in Thuringia, opened in July 1937. More than 250,000 prisoners are estimated to have passed through its gates, with more than 56,000 of them dying. It is particularly notorious as the fiefdom of SS-Colonel Karl Koch, the camp's first commandant. Koch was arrested by the Gestapo in August 1943 – by which time he was commandant of the Majdanek camp in Lublin, Poland – on charges of forgery, embezzlement, mismanagement and insubordination. He was executed at Buchenwald in April 1945, shortly before the arrival of US troops. Koch and his wife, who was chief women's overseer, had brazenly looted Buchenwald throughout their tenure there, and had organised the murder of at least one inconvenient witness. The camp's motto, inscribed above the gates in wrought ironwork, was '*Jeden das Seine*' (colloquially, 'Everyone Gets What They Deserve').

The prisoners incarcerated in these camps were a heterogeneous group. Alongside political prisoners, in March 1937, Dachau and Sachsenhausen received some 2000 'habitual criminals' rounded up by the civil police after a trawl through criminal records. The next year, the much wider category of 'Asocials' was added to those being identified, arrested and detained within the system. Between April and June 1938, 12,000 men with irregular work records, beggars, vagrants and itinerant labourers were rounded up and detained. These groups were joined, from 1938 onwards, by Jews. Hitherto, they had largely been arrested as political opponents, not simply because of their religion or ethnicity; now this became a basic reason. In the wake of *Kristallnacht* (Night of the Broken Glass), some 26,000 Jews were incarcerated in the camps.

The fourth major concentration camp was Flossenbürg, in the Oberpfalz, Bavaria, which opened in May 1938. From then until April 1945, 96,000 prisoners are believed to have been incarcerated there, of whom approximately 30,000 died. It was here that some of the last survivors of 1944's bomb plot against Hitler, including Admiral Canaris, were executed in April 1945.

Mauthausen was the first concentration camp to be opened by the SS on Austrian soil following the *Anschluss*. Located approximately fifteen miles east of Linz, it was built by prisoners from

Dachau. Conditions here were among the harshest in the whole concentration camp system, and at least 150,000 prisoners are believed to have died in either the main camp – where prisoner labour centred on a stone-quarrying operation – or its network of more than fifty sub-camps.

The last of the pre-war camps was the women's camp at Ravensbrück. It opened in May 1939 to replace Lichtenberg, which had previously acted as the camp for women. Overall, it incarcerated some 130,000 women, more than half of whom are believed to have died either there or elsewhere within the system. The majority of the SS's uniforms were assembled at an SS economic 'enterprise' at Ravensbrück. It was also here that women employed by the SS (they were not allowed to be *members* of the organisation) were trained to be guards and overseers of female prisoners for the rest of the camps.

As the population subject to German control expanded during the early part of the war, so the requirement for concentration camp space grew and with it the number of camps. Neuengamme, near Hamburg, opened in early 1940; Auschwitz, near Krakow, in June 1940; Gross-Rosen, also in Silesia, opened in May 1941, as did Natzweiler in Alsace. These were followed in October 1941 by the camp at Lublin/Majdanek and, shortly afterwards, by the conversion of the existing detention facility at Stutthof, near Danzig, into a main concentration camp. These were supplemented by a huge network of sub-sites: smaller camps and labour groups administered by the main camps that also supplied their guards.[21]

The rise in numbers of those detained in the camps is instructive. In November 1936, the figure was 4761; in December 1937, 7750; in June 1938, 24,000; in November 1938, 50,000; in September 1939, 21,400; in December 1940, 53,000; in September 1942, 110,000; in August 1943, 224,000; in August 1944, 524,286; in January 1945, 714,211.[22]

This huge expansion in the concentration camp system is indicative of the scale on which the SS's ideological and racial war was being fought, at least in the minds of the SS itself. The majority of those who were detained within the system – whether Jews, Freemasons, Jehovah's Witnesses or the homeless – were not in any sense active opponents of the regime that imprisoned them, but simply its nominated targets. Real opponents of National Socialism, domestically at least, had almost all been dealt with within a few months of the beginning of the National Socialist regime.

8

The Central Organisation of the SS

In the first few years of his leadership, Himmler experimented with and soon abandoned several administrative formats for SS headquarters.[1] Between 1929 and 1931, the SS-*Oberstab* (Higher Staff), which was personally headed by Himmler himself, comprised five branches: I Administration, II Personnel, III Finance, IV Security and V Race. This was partially replaced in 1932 by the SS-*Amt* (Office), originally headed by SS-Colonel Ernst Bach, which was given responsibility for administration, personnel, reserves and medical services. Meanwhile, security was put in the hands of Heydrich's fledgling intelligence service, and racial issues were entrusted to Darré's Race Office. The expansion of both the NSDAP and the SS itself in the run-up to 1933 increased the funding available to Himmler, so he started to recruit full-time 'technical' experts to replace the part-time 'old fighters' who had formed the bulk of his staff hitherto. Around this time, Himmler's adjutant, Waldeck-Pyrmont, also took on the role of executive officer and chief of his personal staff. He was succeeded in 1934 by Karl Wolff, a dapper, well-spoken banker and ex-army officer who would go on to hold the position until the end of the war.

After January 1933, as Himmler and Heydrich began to take control of the German police system and Himmler began the creation of the first militarised SS units, the organisation became a hybrid: part party formation, part state agency. Reflecting this, Himmler created the *Führungsstab* (Leadership Staff) as a liaison office between the SS and various state and party agencies. Siegfried Seidel-Dittmarsch, a Prussian ex-army officer, was put in charge, but he died suddenly at the beginning of 1934 and his liaison function was passed on to Waldeck-Pyrmont as leader of the so-called 'Special Duties Staff'.

However, none of these arrangements proved satisfactory for Himmler, so at the beginning of 1935 he began the process of creating the twelve *Hauptämter* (Main Offices) that would ultimately form the bureaucratic core of the SS. The first and initially most important of these was the SS-*Hauptamt* (Main Office), led by SS-Major General Kurt Wittje, a former general staff officer. It was formed on 30 January 1935 as part of a general reorganisation which also saw the creation of an SD-Main Office under Heydrich and the *Rasse und Siedlungs Hauptamt* (Race and Settlement Main Office – RuSHA) under Darré. There were six staff branches within the SS-Main Office: the Command Staff, responsible for militarised units; the Personnel Office; the Recruiting Office; the Administrative Office for Military Courts; the Administration and Supply Office; and the Medical Office. Additionally, the Main Office itself housed a press department, a welfare office and the Inspectorate of Concentration Camps.

Wittje was dismissed from the SS in May 1935 amid rumours about his homosexuality, to be replaced by SS-Brigade Leader August Heissmeyer, a lawyer who had served as a pilot in the First World War. Heissmeyer reorganised the Command Staff, separating functions that supported the General-SS from those linked to the SS-*Verfügungstruppe* (Special Purpose Troops), the newly formed, full-time military SS units that were the forerunners of the Waffen-SS.

A key figure within the Main Office at this time was Oswald Pohl, who had been appointed to the Administration and Supply Branch. Born in 1892, his father was a foreman in a steelworks in the Ruhr. Pohl graduated from his local high school in 1912, enlisted in the navy's administrative branch, and spent the First World War as a paymaster.[2] After his demobilisation, he began legal studies at the University of Kiel, but he gave these up when the navy asked him to rejoin and continue his administrative career. He first joined the NSDAP as early as 1922, and remained an activist even when the party was banned after the Munich *Putsch*. Unlike most commissioned officers in the German armed forces, he was officially classified as a naval civil servant, which meant he was allowed to join a political party, and he duly rejoined the 'reformed' NSDAP in August 1926.[3]

Pohl came to the attention of Himmler in 1933 because of a letter he wrote to Hitler concerning the naval career of Heydrich. Pohl reported that some of his fellow officers at the Kiel Naval Base had joked that Heydrich had been forced to leave the navy because of his immoral conduct, and that was the only reason why he was now following a career in the SS. According to Pohl: 'I wrote to Hitler that if all the things rumoured about Heydrich were true, I couldn't understand why he was permitted to wear an SS uniform.'[4] In May, Himmler visited the naval base and met Pohl – who was by now a *Kapitänleutnant* (Commander) – during a reception in the officers' mess. Doubtless Himmler recalled Pohl's letter, but he had also received a recommendation from Wilhelm Canaris, Heydrich's old first officer and now commander of the battleship *Schlesien*. Canaris, who had been deeply involved in the nationalist political scene in the 1920s, pointed out that Pohl was a loyal National Socialist and a 'first rate man in every way'.[5]

Himmler was looking for an officer to take over the administrative and financial side of the SS, and he evidently took a shine to Pohl. He explained that the rumours about Heydrich were untrue and asked whether Pohl might be interested in joining the SS. By now, Pohl had a secure, successful career – he headed a staff of over five hundred men at Kiel – but as an enthusiastic National Socialist, he was interested. And clearly the National Leader thought he was the right man for the job:

Himmler became very insistent and wrote me one letter after another urging that I take over the administrative organisation of the SS. In December 1933 and January 1934, he invited me to Berlin and Munich, and showed me the whole SS administrative set-up and the many complex problems that were involved. It was only in February 1934, after I saw what a big job was in store for me, that I finally accepted.[6]

Pohl initially joined Himmler's personal staff as chief of the administrative section with the rank of SS-*Obersturmbannführer* (senior battalion leader). He remembered:

When I took over my office, the SS was a comparatively small organisation, like a union, with a group here and there in various towns and cities. I started by installing administrative commands in various key cities, and I selected personnel who would be fit for their jobs. I inaugurated schools that taught these administrative officials for a few weeks before they were dispatched to take over my branch offices all over Germany. I achieved a sound administration in the SS, with orderly bookkeeping and financial sections.[7]

With the creation of the Main Office the following year, Pohl became head of the Administrative Branch and also retained his role as chief of administration on Himmler's staff.

Before January 1933, much of the SS's funding had come from membership dues, with occasional subsidies from party headquarters for special projects, but as it began to take over state functions, it increasingly became eligible for state funding. It was in this area that Pohl really made his mark. Despite the supposedly revolutionary nature of the National Socialist government, expenditure still had to be justified, budgets formulated and fiscal probity maintained to the satisfaction of both the civil service and the party. Pohl, drawing on his long experience in naval administration, succeeded in achieving all of this. In addition, he established relationships between his office and the various departments and ministries on whom the SS depended for its budget: the party treasury, the Finance Ministry, the Ministry of the Interior, the Army Ministry and so forth. Among the first SS recipients of state funding were the Special Purpose Troops being formed at various locations around Germany. Later, following Himmler's appointment as Chief of the German Police in 1936, a much wider range of SS activities was brought under the umbrella of state support, including running the concentration camps.[8]

In the last months of 1934, Himmler had launched the SS's first 'corporate venture' when he founded a publishing house – the Nordland Verlag – which went on to produce a wide range of ideological tracts, training manuals, propaganda texts and novels.[9] This was followed by a porcelain factory – Allach Industries – which produced commemorative plates and figurines as well as symbolic items, like 'Yule candlesticks', that were presented to SS families; a photographic studio; and even a company that produced electric bicycle lights. None of these ventures was intended to be profitable; instead, they were founded to demonstrate the superiority of the SS order and to act as cultural showcases.[10]

Meanwhile, the Inspectorate of Concentration Camps determined to make the camps economically productive. Part of the motivation for this was the shortage of materials and workers for the reconstruction projects that Hitler and his favourite architect, Albert Speer, were developing. An obvious answer seemed to be to force concentration camp prisoners to quarry stone and make bricks, cement and other materials.[11] However, the SS had no experience in managing building projects or indeed any other type of business. This was highlighted by the large financial losses incurred by several of the businesses, particularly the German Earth and Stone Works, which operated brick-making plants and stone quarries at Buchenwald, Neuengamme, Sachsenhausen, Flössenberg and Mauthausen. This failure was a source of acute embarrassment to Himmler. His solution was to create a new

Main Office that would allow Pohl to control all of the businesses and then develop them to generate profits for the SS. Accordingly, in April 1939, the *Verwaltung und Wirtschaft Hauptamt* (VuWHA – Administration and Business Main Office) was set up, with Pohl combining his former tasks of chief administrator and treasurer with two new roles: control over all of the SS's construction projects and business enterprises. However, the Interior Ministry was concerned that state funds might now be diverted towards SS businesses, so another new Main Office – 'Budget and Buildings' – was established to deal with funding and administration, while the VuWHA concentrated on the business side.[12] Pohl recruited young, idealistic, professional managers and engineers to turn around the businesses. They did this by welding the large pool of available, cheap (effectively slave) labour to modern management techniques.

Inevitably, utilising manpower from the camps required ever-closer relations between the VuWHA and the Inspectorate of Concentration Camps, which was now led by Richard Glücks. Between 1939 and 1942, a new hierarchy of administrators was created within the camps to manage SS production and the outsourcing of prisoner labour to private industry. The logical conclusion of this came in February 1942, when the VuWHA, the Household and Budget Main Office and the Inspectorate of Concentration Camps were merged to create the *Wirtschafts und Verwaltung Hauptamt* (WVHA – Business Administration Main Office). This gave Pohl and his staff direct control over the concentration camps and the exploitation of their prisoners.

By now, SS businesses had expanded considerably. Among its interests were: land and forestry; brick-making; stone quarrying; fine porcelain and pottery; building materials; cement; mineral water extraction and bottling; meat processing; bakeries; small-arms manufacture and repair; wooden furniture design and production; military clothing and accessories; herbal medicine; fish processing; book and magazine publishing; art acquisition and restoration; and production of ceremonial swords, knives and daggers.

Unsurprisingly, the concentration camps supplied a significant amount of the clothing, weapons, equipment and insignia for the Waffen-SS.

In addition to exploiting prisoners as labour, the WVHA profited through the confiscation of inmates' clothing, property and goods, all of which could be recycled or sold; the confiscation of their cash and investments; and, most gruesomely, the exploitation of their bodies if they died within the system. Specifically, prisoners' hair was used in the manufacture of felt insulation and gold fillings were routinely extracted, melted down and deposited in the Reichsbank or converted into cash. This continued until late 1944, when control of prison labour was transferred to Speer's Armaments Ministry in a last, desperate bid to keep the German military machine working.

As the Special Purpose Troops, the camp guard force of *Totenkopfverbände* (Death's Head units) and the General-SS all continued to expand in the run-up to the Second World War, the Main Office under Heissmeyer accrued ever more responsibility and power. By September 1938, it was responsible for the inspectorates of all the militarised SS formations, including the concentration camps; the military formations; the officer-training schools; border guards; riding schools; all SS garrison commands; the SS command staff; the SS personnel office; the SS courts system; the SS administrative office; the SS medical office; the SS recruiting office; SS records and archives; procurement for the General-SS; and a range of minor offices.[13] In April 1939, Pohl's administrative office was hived off from the Main Office to become a main office in its own right, but it was only after the outbreak of war that a major reduction in the scale of the Main Office took place.[14]

The Main Office was primarily structured to administer a 'civilian' political organisation, and even though several of its sections had catered for the SS's military formations, these arrangements had worked poorly. Consequently, when the formations went to war in 1939, they often exhibited serious deficiencies in organisation, equipment and training. Heissmeyer paid for these failings with his job at the beginning of April 1940. He was replaced by SS-Major General Gottlob Berger, who had hitherto been head of recruitment within the Main Office.[15] Then, in the summer of 1940, the Main Office's military supervisory functions were transferred to the Commander-in-Chief of the Army. The heavily trimmed Main Office continued primarily as a recruitment agency.

Nevertheless, Berger became one of the most significant figures within the Waffen-SS, even though he was broadly disliked by many of the field commanders.[16] Born in Gerstetten, near Ulm, in 1896, he was a shrewd, forceful, dynamic man. He served as an infantry officer during the First World War but was wounded four times and classified as 70 per cent disabled. Despite this, he later trained and worked as a physical education teacher. He first joined the NSDAP in 1922 and was briefly arrested after the Munich *Putsch*, but he then drifted away from politics. However, he rejoined the party and the SA in January 1931. He was recruited into the SS by Himmler in 1936 as the officer responsible for sports and physical training in SS-Regional Headquarters South West, and subsequently joined the National Leader's personal staff as head of the sport office.[17]

From 1940, Berger* reorganised the Main Office to reflect its more limited – but still critical – role. In place of the previous multiple staff branches, he set up just four *Amtsgruppen* (business groups). Business Group A dealt with the administration of the Main Office itself. Business Group B was the Waffen-SS recruitment headquarters for Germans, and as such controlled regional Waffen-SS recruiting '*kommandos*' throughout Germany. It also ran the records office for the General-SS. Business Group C dealt with non-military training and political indoctrination for all

---

* Berger was promoted to SS-*Brigadeführer* (major general) on 20 April 1940, to SS-*Gruppenführer* (lieutenant general) on 20 April 1942 and to SS-*Obergruppenführer und General der Waffen-SS* in June 1943.

German members of the Waffen-SS. And Business Group D over-saw the recruitment and welfare of all 'Germanic' volunteers from Western Europe and the Baltic States, which meant it controlled the recruiting offices in Brussels, Liege, Oslo, Copenhagen, the Hague, Riga and Tallinn.[18]

Berger, then, more than anyone else, was responsible for the recruitment of large numbers of foreigners into Waffen-SS field units. Consequently, he was one of very few high-level SS men to retain Himmler's confidence throughout the war. He would have preferred a field command, but Himmler always resisted appoint-ing him to one, although he did serve for a few weeks as Senior SS and Police Leader in Slovakia in the autumn of 1944, when there was an attempted uprising against the German occupiers.[19]

Once Berger had recruited men into the Waffen-SS, it was the job of the *Führungshauptamt* (FHA – Command Main Office) to organise, train and equip them. The FHA also had responsibility for the General-SS,* but, unlike the German Army High Command, it did not have command authority over Waffen-SS units in the combat zone. So it functioned in much the same way as the *Ersatzheer* (Replacement Army) – as a home command.

Relationships between the Berger's Main Office and the Command Main Office were fraught. The latter was headed by an ex-army officer, Hans Jüttner, and he and his staff of professional soldiers wanted the Waffen-SS to be a relatively small, highly pro-fessional elite. By contrast, Berger, supported by Himmler, knew that Hitler was desperate for as much combat power as possible, even if that meant many Waffen-SS units would be second- or third-rate.

---

* The outbreak of war reduced the part-time, unpaid, political General-SS to a rump. Members of military age were called up into *all* branches of the armed forces, not just the Waffen-SS. Consequently, the General-SS's wartime mission was primarily to provide pre- and post-military training for SS men.

9

The Race and Settlement Office

As we have seen, the Race and Settlement Main Office began life in 1931 as the SS Race Office. Although small, it exercised a disproportionately large influence in the pre-war SS largely because it was led by Richard Darré, Himmler's friend and adviser. In its first few years of operation, the Race Office had a primarily advisory function: setting basic racial criteria for recruitment into the SS, for officer commissions and for engagements and marriages of SS men. In practice, new recruits were admitted to the organisation, commissioned and given permission to marry by their local commanders, who then simply notified the Race Office.

Darré was also highly active in agricultural policy. Before he joined the SS, he had been central in setting up the NSDAP's 'Farm Policy Apparatus', and it was his idea that the SS should become an agricultural aristocracy,[1] with SS families settled in farms, smallholdings and 'garden cities'. The 'settlement' branch of the Race Office was created to implement this. Darré assiduously cultivated middle- and upper-class farmers – often influential local community leaders – and persuaded many of them to join the SS or, at least, the National Socialist Party. He was installed as Minister of Agriculture at the end of June 1933, replacing Alfred

Hugenberg, the Nationalist press baron, who had originally held the agriculture portfolio in the NSDAP-Nationalist coalition cabinet of January 1933.[2] The Farm Policy Apparatus effectively became a branch of the state, with Darré's contacts installed as regional and local 'farm leaders'. In subsequent years, Darré would often utilise these men as his regional race and settlement 'experts' within the Race and Settlement Office.

On 30 January 1935, the Race and Settlement Office gained equal status to the SS-Main Office. It now had four main responsibilities: the ideological training of SS members; racial selection and filtering of members and their spouses; agricultural settlement and training for members; and family welfare.[3] The settlement branch was notably active, particularly once Curt von Gottberg – a minor East Prussian aristocrat who had joined the SS a few weeks before the National Socialists assumed power – became its leader in 1936. Von Gottberg started to use Agricultural Settlement Companies, wholly or partly owned by the SS, to gain control of large estates that could then be divided into small farms for SS members, and he imposed central control over all SS housing projects.[4]

Another particularly active branch was the *Sippenamt* (Office for Family Affairs), which assumed responsibility for the racial vetting of all SS applicants, and for checking the racial background of members' spouses. Any SS man who wished to marry had to produce a detailed family tree going back to at least 1750 for both himself and his fiancée, proving that neither had Jewish or any other 'undesirable' antecedents,* together with medical reports, political references and other background information, accompanied by portrait and full-length photographs. In theory, all of this information would be checked in detail by local representatives of the Race and Settlement Office, by SS units and, in 'difficult' cases, by the central office in Berlin; Himmler continued to take a close interest in the racial exclusivity of the SS until

---

* In reality, though, only Jewish antecedents were ever seriously problematic.

1945, and he was frequently called upon to act as final arbiter in problematic cases.*

The Office for Family Affairs also oversaw the activities of one of the more controversial SS organisations: the *Lebensborn e. V.* (Well of Life Society), which was founded in 1935.[5] Post-war sensationalism has obscured this society's true role – to increase Germany's birth rate. (The rate had declined dramatically in the early 1930s because young men were reluctant to take on the financial burden of providing for a family in the midst of a depression.[6]) In 1936, Himmler wrote to SS members ordering them to support the society and explaining why it had been established:

> The organisation 'Lebensborn e. V.' serves the SS leaders in the selection and adoption of qualified children. The organisation 'Lebensborn e. V.' is under my personal direction, is part of the Race and Settlement Main Office of the SS, and has the following obligations:
>
> 1. Aid for racially and biologically hereditarily valuable families.
> 2. The accommodation of racially and biologically hereditarily valuable mothers in appropriate homes, etc.
> 3. Care of the children of such families.
> 4. Care of the mothers.[7]

The society built a number of maternity homes, where SS men's wives could give birth and receive advice, help and medical treatment. The homes also cared for other 'racially suitable' women,

---

* However, the thoroughness of this checking is open to question. In early 1945, a British SS volunteer, Eric Pleasants, obtained permission to marry a secretary from the SS-Main Office. Among the many untruths in his application were the claims that he had been a sergeant in the British Army and that he had been born in Ireland. Permission to marry was granted with neither of these falsehoods being questioned.

even if they were unmarried, particularly when the father was in the SS. They were eventually built throughout Germany, in occupied North-West Europe (there were at least nine in Norway alone), and in Poland. Between 20,000 and 25,000 children were born within the system.

Post-war accounts of the society suggested that it was also involved in the forced adoption and relocation of supposedly 'Germanic' children from occupied countries; and that the homes provided SS men to impregnate women whose husbands were infertile. However, neither of these claims is true. The society *did* arrange the adoption of children born to unmarried mothers, but this was always done with the consent of the mother (although some of the women might not have realised that their children would subsequently be taken to Germany). The confusion probably arose because up to 200,000 children were kidnapped in occupied territories and relocated to Germany, for adoption or fostering by German families, but this was never done by Well of Life personnel. Furthermore, there is no evidence whatsoever that SS men were ever 'put out to stud'.

In keeping with the racial 'mission' of the SS, the Well of Life was funded by substantial compulsory deductions from SS officers' pay. This was highly unpopular and many sought to avoid it. (For example, the personnel file of the homosexual Waffen-SS General Felix Steiner indicates that he strongly resented the tax.[8]) Even so, the Well of Life was one of the few SS organisations that played a generally positive and beneficial role in German society, notwithstanding the fact that it worked within the framework of National Socialist racist ideology. In 1938, administration of the society was transferred from the Race and Settlement Office to Himmler's personal staff.

From 1931 through to 1938, Darré was one of the leading personalities in the SS, acting, in effect, as Himmler's ideological mentor. However, his relationship with the National Leader began to deteriorate, and in September 1938 he was replaced as chief of the Race and Settlement Office by Günther Pancke.[9] The ostensible reason for this was a dispute over ideological training. Himmler complained that much of the training material being produced by the *Schulungsamt* (Education Office) of the Race and Settlement Office was too theoretical and had little practical use for the regional and local training officers. In response, Darré refused to continue with his ideological training role and he was quietly dismissed. However, it is likely that Himmler manufactured this disagreement in order to oust Darré. His old friend had an independent power base as Agriculture Minister, and he was closely connected with Goering, Himmler's main rival in the political dog-fighting that determined pre-eminence within the Third Reich.

Darré continued as Agriculture Minister until 1942, when he resigned for health reasons.* He remained an honorary SS officer on Himmler's personal staff, but no longer had a significant role to play in the organisation. Ideological training eventually became the responsibility of the Main Office and it remained there until the end of the Third Reich.[10]

The standing of the Race and Settlement Office was further diminished by the activities of von Gottberg's Settlement Office. The sheer volume of cash passing through von Gottberg's settlement companies (and rumours of financial impropriety) led to them being put under the control of Pohl's administration office. But von Gottberg found a way to circumvent this by shifting the focus of his operations away from Germany and into the newly acquired 'Protectorate' of Bohemia-Moravia. In June 1939, he was named head of the Czech Land Registry. Thereafter, his seizure of land and property was so predatory that he and several of his staff were temporarily suspended. Some of his team were ultimately imprisoned in concentration camps for corruption,[11] but von Gottberg himself was eventually cleared of all charges and

---

* Darré died in 1953 from liver cancer that was probably due to chronic alcoholism.

reinstated. He eventually rose to the rank of SS-general and was awarded the Knight's Cross as Senior SS and Police Commander in Byelorussia and Central Russia. He was also Anti-Partisan Operations Commander in occupied France in 1944. Nevertheless, the settlement branch never recovered from the land-grabbing scandal, and it finally dwindled into inactivity.

Although the Race and Settlement Office eventually lost control of the Well of Life Society, and corruption finally put paid to its settlement activities, it remained active in another of its original spheres of interest right up to 1945: ideological training.

As we have seen, Himmler's ideological framework for the SS harked back to romantic ideals of chivalry and honour, and he was keen to give this aspect of his 'order' a more concrete expression. Of course, he was as ruthless as any of his colleagues in the senior leadership of the Third Reich, but he always retained a fondness for the romantic myths and legends that his father had taught him. Furthermore, while it would be misleading to overstate Himmler's belief in the occult, he was certainly prepared to accommodate some aspects of it within his world view.

In 1933, Himmler was introduced to Karl-Maria Wiligut, who claimed to be able to trace his lineage back to the Norse god Thor and the ancient German chief Arminius, whose warriors slaughtered three Roman legions in the Teutoberg Forest in AD 9. Furthermore, he said that his ancestors had been the guardians of the secret knowledge of the Irminist religion. This sect believed that the Bible was written in Germany to celebrate an Irminist God called Krist, only later to be corrupted and appropriated by Christians. Wiligut substantiated these extraordinary claims by 'channelling' the clan memories of his ancestors during clairvoyant trances in which he described the rituals and actions of the ancient German tribes.

Wiligut was born in Vienna in 1866, the son and grandson of Austrian Army officers. He followed the family tradition and entered the Imperial Officer Cadet School in Vienna at the age of fourteen, subsequently qualifying as an infantry officer. At the outbreak of the First World War, he was an infantry major and also had a moderate literary reputation, having published poems that celebrated Germanic myths, nature and regimental history.[12] He had a good war, being decorated for bravery and rising to the rank of colonel, and retired from the army in January 1919 to live with his wife and two young daughters in Salzburg. It was now that the mystical Wiligut started to emerge. He founded an extreme anti-Semitic group and edited a periodical called *The Iron Broom*, which attacked Christians, Jews and Freemasons. This generated a devoted circle of admirers who genuinely believed Wiligut's fantasies. However, according to his wife, he was a violent and unpredictable alcoholic who routinely beat her and threatened her with a loaded revolver.[13] She also took to locking their daughters' bedroom doors at night, after becoming concerned about the degree of physical affection Wiligut displayed towards them.[14]

By November 1924, his wife had finally had enough, and she had Wiligut forcibly committed to the Salzburg mental asylum and certified insane. He was diagnosed with schizophrenia and megalomaniac and paranoid delusions. The asylum's report on his mental state also noted his domestic violence, eccentric behaviour, history of grandiose projects and occultism. A court that examined his case unsurprisingly ruled that he was unable to look after his own interests. Nevertheless, Wiligut's admirers continued to believe in him, and when he was discharged from the asylum in 1927, he resumed his activities as a Germanic mystic.

In 1932, he settled in Munich, having adopted the name 'Weisthor' (Wise Thor). Nevertheless, the following year, he was sane enough to recognise that his own obsession with the Germanic past was congruent with the ideology of the new National Socialist regime. And Himmler was sufficiently impressed by Wiligut to ask him to act as an adviser on early Germanic history and traditions. He was inducted into the SS as an officer in September 1933, and appointed head of a department of pre- and early history within the Race and Settlement Office.

In January 1933, Himmler had stayed in Grevenburg Castle in Westphalia and had been most impressed by the region. Consequently, he decided to acquire a Westphalian castle for the SS, perhaps to act as an education centre. After consulting Wiligut, he visited Wewelsburg Castle, near Paderborn, and bought it for the SS in April 1934. Renovation work quickly began, but at the urging of Wiligut, Himmler soon abandoned the idea of using the castle merely as an education centre. Wiligut reported a local legend that predicted that Westphalia would be the site of an apocalyptic battle between East and West, in which the West would triumph and the Rhine would run red with blood. He then pronounced that Wewelsburg would be the bastion where this battle would take place. Himmler was sufficiently taken with this idea that in 1935 he placed the castle under the control of his personal staff so that it could become the headquarters of the SS as a chivalric order. Ever more grandiose plans were devised to accommodate this new role, and vast resources were directed towards it. Eventually, the castle boasted a 'Grail Room', in which a complex lighting system illuminated a large rock crystal that was reputedly 'a magical stone of light which had fallen from the diadem of an ancient sun god',[15] as well as a great chamber with a round table, modelled on the Arthurian legend, at which the National Leader could confer with his twelve senior officers. In the west wing, there was a museum that displayed a diverse collection of ancient artefacts (and replicas) which ranged from a diorama reconstructing an ancient peasant farm dwelling to the fossil of a large aquatic dinosaur. Most of these items were acquired by the museum's curator, an artist and archaeologist named Wilhelm Jordan.

The Wewelsburg project was never fully completed, even though a concentration camp was erected close by primarily to supply slave labour. Niederhagen was opened in May 1939 as a sub-camp of Sachsenhausen, with the prisoners initially accommodated in tents in the castle grounds. However, in 1941 they were moved to a permanent camp that operated independently. Nearly 4000 prisoners passed through its gates, of whom 1285 are known to have died. In 1943, when Himmler curtailed work on Wewelsburg because of the deteriorating war situation, the camp was scaled down and came under the administration of Buchenwald. Just fifty or so prisoners remained to act as maintenance workers for the complex.

Apart from Wewelsburg, Wiligut's principal contribution to the SS came in the form of ritual activities and heraldry. It was he who devised the rituals and symbolism that were employed in various SS ceremonies, including weddings, which Wiligut himself conducted at Wewelsburg while wielding an 'ivory-handled stick bound with blue ribbon and carved with runes',[16] as well as spring, solstice, harvest and Yule festivals. He also designed the *Julleuchter* (Yule lights), kitschy ceramic candleholders made by the Allach porcelain works and inscribed with runic symbols that were presented to favoured SS families; and the *Totenkopfring* (Death's Head ring), a silver ring inscribed with runes that Himmler personally awarded to SS officers with at least three years' unblemished service. The latter was a cherished item within the SS. If the holder left the organisation, the ring had to be returned to Himmler; if the holder died, it was ceremoniously taken to Wewelsburg, where it was stored to symbolise the owner's ongoing, posthumous membership of the SS chivalric order.

Wiligut 'retired' from the SS at the beginning of 1939, having achieved the rank of brigade leader. Officially, this was because of his age and poor health – he was seventy-two years old, a heavy smoker and still a chronic alcoholic – but in reality he may well have been pushed out because of his increasingly erratic behaviour. Furthermore, SS-General Karl Wolff – Himmler's personal staff officer – had visited Wiligut's wife in November 1938 and had learned of his three years in the asylum. Nevertheless, Himmler remained fond of the ageing mystic: the SS supplied him with a housekeeper/companion and accommodation until the Third Reich finally collapsed. Wiligut died after suffering a stroke in January 1946.[17]

Himmler's sponsorship of Karl-Maria Wiligut reveals his fascination with the bizarre and occult side of Germanic history, but he was similarly intrigued by more academic research. On 1 July 1935, he and Darré hosted a meeting in Berlin that resulted in the creation of a new department in the Race and Settlement Office. This was the *Studiengesellschaft für Geistesurgeschichte, Deutsches Ahnenerbe e. V.* (Society for the Study of Primordial History, German Ancestral Heritage), usually abbreviated simply to the *Ahnenerbe*.[18] Its public face was Herman Wirth, the Dutch-born son of a German university lecturer who was a well-known populariser of prehistoric Nordic folk culture. But its day-to-day operations were organised by Wolfram Sievers, an SS officer who had previously led a historical/archaeological research programme for Himmler in the Teutoberg Forest.[19]

The *Ahnenerbe* provided a focus and funding for research projects that explored the history of the Nordic race, both inside and outside Germany. In the pre-war years, it sponsored expeditions to Bohuslän in south-western Sweden, where Wirth studied ancient rock carvings that he believed held the key to a prehistoric Nordic language; to Karelia, where a team studied and recorded old Finnish folklore, sorcery and witchcraft; to the Mauern caves in the Jura, where an archaeological dig unearthed a number of Neanderthal artefacts; and, famously, to Tibet in 1938, where a team led by SS member Ernst Schäfer looked for evidence of the ancient Aryan race that had reputedly ruled Asia.[20] These investigations had mixed results: some were relatively scholarly; some were based on pure speculation; some were outright shams. But all operated within the framework of National Socialist racial ideas that had no basis in fact.

The outbreak of war brought the *Ahnenerbe*'s overseas missions to a halt, but then it took on a new role: plundering important historical artefacts from the occupied territories in conjunction with the *Reichsicherheitshauptamt* (RSHA – Reich Security Main Office – see Chapter 10).[21] It also organised medical research on behalf of the Waffen-SS, including Rascher's experiments, the testing of chemical weapons on human subjects at Natzweiler concentration camp, and the creation of a collection of more than one hundred skeletons of Jews – who were specifically murdered for the purpose – for the University of Strasbourg (with Natzweiler again being the source).

Pancke was succeeded as head of the Race and Settlement Office by SS-Major General Otto Hofmann in September 1939, who himself was replaced by SS-Lieutenant General Richard Hildebrandt in April 1943.[22] By the end of the war, the much-diminished office was primarily concerned with vetting SS applicants and their intended spouses, and acting as an advisory body on race issues.

The SD – The Intelligence and Security Wing of the SS

When the NSDAP came to power in January 1933, Heydrich's intelligence branch of the SS – the SD – consisted of about thirty paid agents scattered throughout Germany, as well as a few hundred unpaid collaborators within the political, governmental and state establishments. However, he moved swiftly to commission National Socialist lawyers and academics to represent the interests of the SS and SD within the state political police and to ensure that the political police operated within the framework of National Socialist ideology. Of course, this flies in the face of the popular perception of the SD as nothing more than a gang of radicals, thugs and faceless bureaucrats. Yet Michael Wildt has demonstrated[1] that many of those at the very heart of the Third Reich's security and intelligence apparatus came from the upper echelons of society: 'well-educated academics, not part of a marginal or excluded minority, but members of the mainstream elite'.[2] These were the men who were brought in to staff Heydrich's organisation as it expanded throughout the 1930s. And it was they who ultimately orchestrated some of the worst crimes in history.

Between 1933 and 1934, the SD's headquarters developed into

five major branches: I Organisation; II Administration; III Domestic Political Information (including intelligence collection within the National Socialist movement, religious movements, Marxist and socialist groups, science and education and the legal system); IV Counter-espionage and Overseas Intelligence; and V Freemasonry. Additionally, two 'independent desks' monitored press activity and provided technical support for all SD operations.

Despite this impressive structure and a growing reputation within the National Socialist movement as an inscrutable and effective espionage system, Heydrich's SD in fact remained an extraordinarily amateurish operation. Although Heydrich attracted a core of young, ambitious intellectuals into his organisation, none of them had any experience in intelligence collection or investigation. Outside the central headquarters, the SD's structure mirrored that of the regional and local General-SS, and the local units were encouraged to recruit contacts throughout German society to report on what was happening within their particular sphere. This reflected Himmler and Heydrich's conception of how the British Secret Service worked. They much admired this organisation and imagined it to be an informal network of high-minded, unpaid patriots who collected information out of a sense of duty to the state. But SD contacts were given vague and unfocused instructions on the type of information they should be collecting; and while SD headquarters accumulated impressive collections of Zionist books and Masonic artefacts, these were of little or no value for operational intelligence.

In fact, in its early days, the SD's most effective personnel were members of the SD in name only; they were employed primarily within the Gestapo. These included Heinrich Müller – a detective from Munich whom Heydrich made operational chief of the Gestapo in 1934 – and his Bavarian police colleagues Friedrich Panzinger, Franz Josef Huber and Josef Meisinger, all of whom had previously taken part in the Bavarian state's monitoring of the National Socialists.[3] Heydrich, though, was sufficiently realistic to understand that these men, with their practical backgrounds in police investigations, would be much more effective than his own poorly trained and inexperienced intellectuals in uncovering enemies of the state.

Nevertheless, a number of Heydrich's recruits went on to forge impressive careers within the SD and the Third Reich. Probably the most effective of them in the early days – and perhaps the best example of a highly intelligent and academically accomplished individual who was attracted by the SD – was Werner Best, a Hessian lawyer. He joined the SS in Hesse in 1931, and later that year he was working as a legal adviser to the Hesse National Socialist Party. In that capacity, he headed a team that drafted plans for a counter-revolution in the event of a communist seizure of power. Copies of these documents – known as the 'Boxheim Papers' after the house where the team's meetings were held – were seized by Hessian state authorities and became a source of much embarrassment to Hitler, who was attempting to persuade the German people that he would take power only by legal means.[4] However, Best survived the scandal and was eventually installed as Heydrich's Gestapo deputy in Munich.

On 30 January 1935, the SS-*Sicherheitshauptamt* (Security Main Office) was created as the third of the three original SS main offices – alongside the Main Office itself and the Race and Settlement Office. It had a central chancellery, a personnel branch, an administrative branch and a press office, as well as offices dealing with cultural information, enemies of National Socialist ideology; counter-espionage and counter-sabotage; and the dissemination of its findings. However, this organisational set-up proved to be short lived, as Himmler, Heydrich and Kurt Daluege gained ever more control over the whole German police force.

As the senior police officer within the federal Ministry of the Interior, Daluege spent much of 1934 and 1935 purging the police of 'undesirable elements': social democrats, liberals and Catholics, as well as any SA officers who had been transferred into the police prior to the Night of the Long Knives. In their place, the SS sought to secure paid police appointments for its members. This continued until 17 June 1936, when, after lengthy discussions, Wilhelm Frick appointed Himmler Chief of the German Police in the Ministry of the Interior. (Of course, he also retained his position as National Leader of the SS.) Less than two weeks later, Himmler created two new main offices within the Ministry: the *Hauptamt Ordnungspolizei* (Order Police Main Office), headed by Daluege; and the *Hauptamt Sicherheitspolizei* (Security Police Main Office), under Heydrich.[5]

Daluege now had command over all of Germany's uniformed police. Eventually, this would include: the municipal police forces; the rural gendarmerie; the traffic police; coastguards; the railway police; the postal protection service; fire brigades; the air-raid service; the emergency technical service; the broadcasting police (who protected radio stations and investigated illicit reception of foreign broadcasts); the factory protection police; building regulations enforcement; the health police; and the commercial police. As Inspector of the Order Police, Daluege had the authority to appoint SS officers at state and provincial levels, and from March 1937 he could make appointments and set budgets at all levels, which allowed in-depth SS penetration of the police. Existing police officers were inducted into the SS with few formalities, and graduates of the SS officer schools at Braunschweig and Bad Tölz were given police assignments after graduation. It was not obligatory to be a member of the SS to succeed in the police, but it was commonly perceived that it would certainly not do any harm, so many police officers and NCOs chose to join.* However, Himmler and the SS never enjoyed total control over the German police. The central lines of authority were clear enough, but at the local level the police remained subject to direction from provincial and city authorities. In practice, this meant that many policemen took their orders from local National Socialist Party leaders who had no particular loyalty to Himmler.

---

* They typically became unpaid members of a local General-SS or SD unit.

Heydrich's main office created an entirely new organisation: the *Sicherheitspolizei* (Sipo –Security Police). On paper, this was the amalgamation of the Gestapo (which had effectively been a nationwide force since 1934) and Kripo (headed by Arthur Nebe), the detective branch of the Prussian Police, to which the detective branches of the other state police forces were now added. (Previously, Kripo had been considered part of the regular police, so had been under the general authority of Daluege.[6]) Sipo, like the Order Police, was a branch of the state, so, for the time being, it came under the auspices of the Ministry of the Interior. But for members of the Gestapo and Kripo, much more so than for regular police officers, there were very clear career advantages to be gained from membership of the SS or the SD. Consequently, many hitherto apolitical career policemen signed up.

At this point, to avoid confusion with Sipo, the *Sicherheitshauptamt* once again became known officially as the *Sicherheitsdienst*. By now, this main office was consolidating its role as an intelligence clearing house and creating an organisational structure that would survive until the creation of the RSHA in 1939. Heydrich remained as chief, with SS-Brigadier Siegfried Taubert, an 'old fighter', as his chief of staff. Office I, under SS-Colonel Albert, was responsible for the administration and organisation of the SD, but it also included the 'press and museum' department, headed by SS-Major Franz Six.

Six has sometimes been presented as an archetype of the ruthless intellectuals that Heydrich recruited into the SD, even though his academic qualifications were somewhat derided by his colleagues. Born in 1909, by the mid-1930s he was a clever young man in a hurry who had spotted the advantages of hitching himself to the National Socialist bandwagon. He gained his doctorate at Heidelberg University (supervised by an NSDAP professor) with a thesis entitled 'The Political Structure as Represented in the Daily Press', which was written in National Socialist jargon. He had been a party member since 1929, and had worked as a part-time journalist for various NSDAP newspapers while writing his thesis.[7]

As head of the press department, he created a system under which every newspaper and periodical that might possibly contain something of interest was scrutinised and reviewed for information. Of course, this generated masses of press clippings. According to George Browder, 'Six would boast that he converted the haphazard exploitation of the press into the most reliable intelligence source in the entire SD, superior to any reports coming up from the field posts.'[8] In truth, 'open source' press reporting is used by all intelligence agencies to supplement their confidential sources of information, so if this really was the best source of intelligence that the SD had at its disposal, it was failing in its mission.

Office II, 'SD-*Inland*' (Home), was headed by SS-Colonel Hermann Behrends, a protégé of Heydrich who had acted as his representative in Berlin in the very early days of the Intelligence Service. This was subdivided into branches dealing with 'Ideological Analysis' and the 'Analysis of Spheres of Life'. The former focused on supposed ideological and political enemies of the National Socialist movement, and it was here that Adolf Eichmann began his work on the 'final solution to the Jewish problem' by building up a detailed knowledge of German Zionist and assimilationist matters.[9] The latter was headed by the academic SS-Major Reinhard Höhn. Its brief was to collect information on the cultural, community and material life of Germany. Thus, for example, the highly qualified economist Otto Ohlendorf began his SD career in the Spheres of Life branch as the 'Food Economy' desk officer. He subsequently went on to lead the branch, commanded a special task group in Russia, and was a member of a group who secretly planned German currency reform and the creation of the Deutschmark, before finally being executed by the US Army.

Under Höhn and Ohlendorf, the Spheres of Life branch conducted regular, confidential public opinion surveys. The results were then circulated throughout the upper echelons of the SS and the National Socialist Party as *Meldungen aus dem Reich* (*Reports from the Reich*). These took the form of anecdotal reports collected by SD operatives, and they were intended to give a flavour

of the public mood, particularly as the war dragged on, and the
impact of domestic and foreign propaganda on the population. A
typical example from 1943 discussed the impact of bombing raids:

> After the Russian attacks on Koenigsberg and Tilsit and the last
> British terror attacks on Rostock, Stettin, Mannheim,
> Ludwigshafen, Duisburg, Muehlheim, Oberhausen etc., the
> realisation has come to all parts of the Reich that from now on,
> no region of Germany is safe from air attack. Even in the moun-
> tainous districts, widely seen among the people as 'Germany's
> Air Raid Shelter', people are expecting that the enemy air capa-
> bility will be broadened to threaten these areas.[10]

The reports pulled few punches, and over time they became deeply
resented within party circles, where they were seen as proof that the
SD was gathering evidence of impropriety and inefficiency in the
NSDAP. Höhn, who had instigated them, was eventually forced to
leave the SD because of pressure from senior party officials; and
both Heydrich and Himmler were at pains to demonstrate that his
successor, Ohlendorf, was on a very short leash.

Office III, SD-*Ausland* (Overseas), was nominally commanded
by Heydrich, but his chief of staff was SS-Colonel Heinz Jost, a
protégé of Best. Its two branches dealt with 'Foreign Spheres of
Life' and 'Foreign Political Espionage and Counter-espionage'. It
seems that this office devoted considerable time and resources into
trying to gather information from overseas, but enjoyed very little
success, beyond acquiring material from open press sources and
some German minority groups. Certainly, there is nothing to indicate that the SD had a network of agents outside Germany, nor
even that its leaders had any idea of how such networks could be
recruited and maintained.[11]

On the other hand, Office III did provide Heydrich with a few
officers whom he used for 'cloak-and-dagger' operations outside
Germany. The best known of these was Alfred Naujocks,[12] a
young mechanic who had joined the SS in his native Kiel in 1931.

Three years later, he escaped domestic difficulties with his wife by signing on for a full-time SS role as a driver in SD-Regional Command East in Berlin, which at that time was commanded by Behrends. Then he became a clerk in the central registry. However, before long, for reasons that are not clear, Heydrich started to entrust Naujocks with special foreign missions. For instance, in October or November 1934, he sent him and another SD man to Prague to assassinate Otto Strasser. But after spending fourteen days in the city, they became concerned by Czech Police interest in them and returned to Berlin. Then, in February 1935, Naujocks and his colleague were again sent to Czechoslovakia, this time to kidnap a Strasser supporter who was broadcasting propaganda into southern Germany. They found their target but killed him in a gunfight, during which Naujocks was also wounded.[13]

In spite of this inauspicious start to Naujocks' covert career, for some reason Heydrich continued to select him for clandestine missions. In 1936 and 1937, he was sent on a tour of Europe to familiarise himself with all the major cities, including Istanbul, Ankara, Sofia, Bucharest, Budapest, Athens, Stockholm, Oslo, Copenhagen, Paris and London. Naujocks was accompanied on these trips by another SS man who worked for the industrial giant AEG, which afforded them some degree of cover. The two men stayed in the better hotels at the SD's expense and usually made contact with either AEG or German diplomatic staff. However, they made no attempt to gather information, and Naujocks regarded the trips as purely pleasurable.

By the autumn of 1937, Naujocks had been promoted to SS-captain and assigned to Office III. This was considered a prestigious posting, and Heydrich introduced him to several significant figures in the regime, including Himmler, Goering, Joachim von Ribbentrop and Goebbels. In early 1938, Naujocks became an SS-major and was made chief of the South-East Europe section of Office III. This new position gave him a good overview of how the SD attempted to collect foreign intelligence: 'he relied on reports submitted by German businessmen who travelled extensively in the countries concerned. They were not paid, but were enthusiastic National Socialists who prepared their reports on ideological grounds and expected no recompense for them.'[14]

In early 1939, Heydrich called Naujocks into his office to discuss a Propaganda Ministry official named Berndt who had evidently offended Heydrich in some way. According to Naujocks, Heydrich did not specifically order him to kill Berndt, but he did suggest that he should arrest the man with a drawn revolver and should use it at the first opportunity. However, Naujocks refused to carry out the mission; instead, he took to his bed, claiming illness. Heydrich was less than impressed, and Jost told Naujocks that he would be well advised to find a way out of the SD as soon as possible. He stayed in his post, though, and throughout the first half of 1939 was involved in a minor way in the haggling over the future of Slovakia, following the German dismemberment of Czechoslovakia.[15]

On 10 August, he was given the mission for which he is probably the best known: staging a fake attack on the German-Polish border. Heydrich informed Naujocks that his and other bogus attacks were needed to give Hitler a pretext to launch his planned offensive against Poland. Heydrich's plan was to gather a number of 'life-sentence' prisoners from concentration camps, kill them with a lethal injection, dress them in Polish uniforms, riddle them with bullets and then dump them at various locations along the border. The idea was that this would lead the world to believe that Polish soldiers had been making cross-border raids into Germany.

After he defected to the Allies in 1944, Naujocks claimed that his part in this, an attack on Gleiwitz's radio station in Upper Silesia, was just one of a number of such operations that took place throughout August:[*] 'Naujocks states that the bodies were

---

[*] Most accounts (e.g., Höhne, *The Order of the Death's Head*) suggest that the attack at Gleiwitz took place at the end of August and that it was a more or less unique attempt to give Hitler a *casus belli*. But in his interrogation in late 1944, Naujocks clearly indicated that his was one of several attacks, and that it took place in mid-August at the latest.

forwarded to the villages where they were required in packing cases labelled "preserves". Some of the victims arrived at their destinations only half-dead, having been given inadequate injections, and these had to be put out of their misery before they could be used.'[16] On Naujocks' arrival in Gleiwitz, with a team of

> five or six men . . . he arranged for a Polish-speaking German to take possession of the microphone 'by force' and to begin broadcasting an appeal to his 'countrymen' urging them to rise up against the Germans. The broadcast was then abruptly broken off, shots were fired in the studio, and finally a corpse, with which Naujocks had previously been provided, was left lying on the floor close to the microphone, riddled with bullets.[17]

Naujocks remained in Gleiwitz for more than a fortnight after this operation, and it was only when he travelled back to Berlin, passing vast numbers of German troops and equipment going in the opposite direction, that he realised war was imminent.

Dramatic as these operations doubtless were, they represent a schoolboy version of what constitutes 'intelligence' work and reflect the essential amateurism of Heydrich and his subordinates. While the SD could boast many young, ruthless, highly intelligent academics, it also included more than a few semi-educated bumblers like Naujocks. But all of these men shared a poor understanding of how to obtain and report useful intelligence against real enemies. Consequently, they were rarely, if ever, able to fulfil their designated role.

In November 1937, a further step was quietly undertaken towards the integration of the SS and the police. This was the creation of the role of *Höhere SS und Polizei Führer* (HSSPF – Senior SS and Police Leader), a 'shadow' appointment that became effective only upon mobilisation of Germany's armed forces. All HSSPFs were nominated personally by Himmler and answered directly to him (though, in practice, they were generally the regional SS commanders). Their task was to oversee the activities of SS and police units (from both the Order Police and Sipo) within their areas and to coordinate them with the civil and military authorities. Geographically, within Germany, the HSSPFs' areas of responsibility were congruous with the military districts of the armed forces, although their political equivalents were the regional leaders – the local National Socialist Party leaders appointed personally by Hitler. Once Germany had begun to acquire occupied territories, further HSSPFs were created to work in combination with the occupation authorities, be they military or civil.[18]

Although their role was not widely publicised before the war, the HSSPFs were theoretically immensely powerful. As Himmler's personal representatives, they were entitled to override directives from the SS main offices and, in an emergency, were permitted to take operational control of all police, SS and even military units in their areas of responsibility.

The major consolidation within the police and intelligence system of the SS occurred on 27 September 1939, when Heydrich's two main offices, the SD-Main Office and the Security Police Main Office, were amalgamated to create the *Reichsicherheitshauptamt* (RSHA – Reich Security Main Office).[19] This was the conclusion of months of discussions that had debated the future of the SD. Those attending these meetings had been concerned that the organisation had several 'faces'. First, it was an umbrella organisation through which Gestapo and Kripo detectives could acquire SS membership, rank and uniform, while demonstrating commitment to the regime. Second, it was a network of collaborators, contacts and information sources throughout German society. Third, it was a system of regional offices associated with General-SS area commands. Fourth, and most problematically, it was the central SD-Main Office.

There were two main issues regarding the SD-Main Office. First, in order to rationalise and streamline the system, the

Gestapo had been made the sole state security investigative agency back in 1937, which meant the SD could no longer conduct investigations or make arrests in Germany. Moreover, while it could and did conduct operations abroad, these were crude, poorly focused, and far less effective than the missions carried out by the Abwehr, the armed forces' intelligence service, headed by Canaris.* This meant that there was a credibility gap between the largely professional Sipo and the amateurish SD. Second, the SD was a party formation, not a state agency, so it was still funded by the NSDAP. The merger proposals, which were drafted by Walter Schellenberg, a highly intelligent young lawyer who had joined the SS in 1933 and had enjoyed a meteoric rise as a protégé of Heydrich, sought to bring the SD within the state fold and ensure that it could be adequately resourced.[20]

Ultimately, the structure of the new RSHA was a compromise. Some of the administrative elements of the SD-Main Office merged with their Sipo counterparts and became state agencies, but the two main branches of the SD that survived the merger, 'Home' and 'Overseas', remained party formations and therefore dependent on funding from the NSDAP treasury. Thus, the structure of the RSHA was a straightforward amalgamation of the earlier main offices, in which administrative and budgetary functions were combined: Office I covered legal and administrative issues, under the leadership of Best; Office II dealt with 'ideological investigation', under Six; Office III was SD-Home, now under Ohlendorf; Office IV was the Gestapo, under Müller; Office V was Kripo, under Nebe; and Office VI was SD-Overseas, under Jost. Best also became Heydrich's deputy chief for the whole RSHA.[21]

---

* However, the Abwehr itself was no more than adequate as an intelligence-collection organisation, primarily for structural reasons. The National Socialist state lacked a central intelligence coordinating body comparable to Britain's Joint Intelligence Committee, which meant that the Abwehr often lacked direction in its intelligence collection. Moreover, any material it did collect was not necessarily collated with that retrieved by other agencies, including the RSHA.

The creation of the RSHA as a central coordinating body was not widely broadcast, and for public purposes, the distinction between the state function of the Sipo and the party functions of the SD were maintained, with Heydrich continuing to be referred to as 'Chief of the *Sicherheitspolizei* and SD'.[22]

The most striking aspect of the RSHA was its personnel. Between 1925 and 1930, the typical SS member was an ex-soldier who could display a higher level of commitment and loyalty to the party and its leadership than a counterpart in the SA, for example. But as the NSDAP became more established and grew in popularity, the SS began to attract a different type of recruit: talented, well-educated individuals like Heydrich and Best who saw the party as the future government of Germany, and saw the potential of the SS's role as a security elite at the heart of the movement. Once the NSDAP did indeed come to power, this change became even more evident.

In his study of the leadership corps within the RSHA, Wildt has shown that it attracted a remarkable group of young National Socialist Germans. He studied 221 individuals holding senior positions in the organisation: 77 per cent were born after 1900; two-thirds had a university degree; and 50 per cent of these graduates also had doctorates.[23] Most of them came from lower-middle-class backgrounds, and most were the first members of their family to have attended university.

Interestingly, many of these men had been activists within the National Socialist Student Federation while at university,[24] indicating that they did not join the SS and later the RSHA merely through careerist opportunism. Rather, it seems they wanted to work within an organisation that was in the ideological vanguard of National Socialism because they were firmly committed to that ideology. So, when the time came for the RSHA to take a leading role in the attempted extermination of the Jews of Europe, they remained unflinching in their dedication to both the party leadership and the project itself.

Nevertheless, the leading intellectual within the RSHA did not last long as either chief of Office I or Heydrich's deputy. Although Best had been instrumental in framing the ideological and legal framework in which the SS operated between 1934 and 1939, Heydrich came to realise that he was a poor practical operator. He was a committed National Socialist but remained a lawyer at heart, and as such he always tried to work within the bounds of the law. By contrast, Heydrich sought practical solutions and was not concerned by legal niceties.[25] In 1940, Best left the RSHA and his office was split in two:* Office I was now concerned with personnel training and organisation; Office II was the administration and legal branch. (The old Office II – Six's 'ideological investigations' branch – became Office VII in the reshuffle.[26])

This final organisational structure remained in place throughout the remainder of the war. In practice, though, the importance and output of both Office III and Office VII diminished rapidly as the war continued. As we have seen, SD-Home's unvarnished reporting of public opinion became unpopular and controversial, and Ohlendorf had little freedom of operation. Meanwhile, the ambitious Six was intended to be the repository for all information relating to enemies of National Socialism, and it was assumed that his office would underpin much of the future work of the RSHA. Himmler, in typical grandiose style, described Office VII as: 'The "Defenders of the Grail" of the Third Reich.'[27] However, it proved to be no such thing. During the early years of the war, Office VII recruits were dispatched to the occupied territories to gather as much information as they could. But the department lacked the capacity to evaluate it; and, in any case, much of what was collected was of purely academic or historical interest. Six soon lost interest in his own department, and after service at the front with the Waffen-SS in 1940 he tried to find himself a niche within the Foreign Office. In his place, SS-*Obersturmbannführer* (Lieutenant

---

* Best joined the Foreign Office and in 1942 became German plenipotentiary in Denmark.

Colonel) Paul Dittel, an academic expert on Freemasonry, became acting head of the department. However, he also found much of its work futile and its staff far below the level he had expected: 'Office VII was, for the most part, a typical collection of semi-intellectuals . . . mostly old members of the National Socialist Party, including university failures, some minor officials and quite a number of simple tradesmen.'[28] If desk officers did ever display academic rigour, their efforts were generally not welcomed. Investigations by Office VII into the authenticity of the 'Protocols of the Learned Elders of Zion' (a hoax first published in 1903 concerning a purported Jewish plot to take over the world), the 'disastrous' and 'destructive' Catholic Church, and the 'subversive' character of witchcraft* reached conclusions that were completely at odds with the prejudices of Himmler and were duly criticised for 'over-objectivity'.[29] By the end of 1943, Office VII was little more than a haven for SD personnel seeking to avoid service at the front.

Both the Gestapo and Kripo remained effective executive agencies, but their primary role was investigative policing, albeit within a totalitarian society in which merely being of an 'undesirable' ethnicity, religious faith, political outlook or sexual orientation effectively rendered people criminals and liable to punishment. Müller remained head of the Gestapo until the very end of the war, and in this role he oversaw the activities of Eichmann and his Section IV B4 of the RSHA. This department was principally concerned with the transport and murder of the European Jews, as well as counter-espionage and counter-dissent activities.

One of the Gestapo's major successes, in conjunction with the Abwehr, came in its operations against the Soviet *Rote Kapelle* (Red Orchestra) espionage ring. Its detective work and interrogations during the late summer of 1942 eventually led to 118 trials,

---

* Desk VII C3 within Office VII, the *Hexen Referat*, was specifically tasked to monitor 'witchcraft, sorcery and popular superstition'.

after which 41 members of the ring were beheaded and 8 hanged.[30] By contrast, the Gestapo's record against 'serious' resistance in Germany was poor. Although it was aware of high-level opposition within the German political and military establishments – nicknamed the *Schwarze Kapelle* (Black Orchestra) by the Gestapo – the extent and intentions of these groups remained unknown until the assassination attempt on Hitler on 20 July 1944.

The Gestapo even failed to unearth an opposition group within the SS itself. In May 1943,[31] the British Minister in Stockholm was approached by a young Waffen-SS officer named Hans Zech-Nenntwich, who claimed to be a deserter with important military information and a desire to fight against the National Socialist regime. After negotiations with the Swedish government, Zech-Nenntwich was flown across the North Sea in a Mosquito for interrogation. He had an extraordinary story to tell.

Born in 1916 in Silesia, he served as a pilot in the Condor Legion in Spain in 1937 and then wanted to become a police officer. However, in order to do this, he was obliged to join the SS-Special Purpose Troops. In 1939, he was attached to the *Heimwehr Danzig* for the invasion of Poland (see Chapter 15). Thereafter, he attended the Officer Cadet School at Bad Tölz and was then posted to SS-Mounted Regiment 1, later the nucleus of the SS-Cavalry Division. He served with the Cavalry Brigade throughout 1941 and 1942 before being wounded and withdrawn to the brigade's convalescent battalion in Warsaw. In March 1943, he was arrested by the Gestapo when trying to pass captured Russian weapons to the Polish underground movement. However, fellow Waffen-SS officers helped him escape, and he eventually managed to reach Sweden via Denmark.

More significant than any of this, though, was that Zech-Nenntwich claimed he was a member of an opposition group – the 'League of Democratic Officers' – within the Waffen-SS. He said this group formed primarily as a result of the antagonism between the professional Waffen-SS officers produced by the officer schools

Members of the Stosstrupp Adolf Hitler preparing to parade in Bayreuth on 'German Day', 30 September 1923. *(Public Record Office)*

Heinrich Himmler carries the banner of the Imperial War Flag militia outside the Bavarian war ministry during the Munich Putsch on 8–9 November 1923.

(Public Record Office)

Julius Schreck (centre) with some of the earliest members of the SS, 1925.
(Bildarchiv Preussischer Kulturbesitz)

Heinrich Himmler (next to banner) with Rudolf Hess, Gregor Strasser, Adolf
Hitler and Franz Pfeffer von Salomon at the 1927 Nuremberg Rally. *(Bundesarchiv)*

Kurt Daluege (left) with Reinhard Heydrich (second from right) at a skiing competition in Kitzbühel, February 1939. *(Bundesarchiv)*

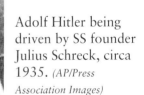

Adolf Hitler being driven by SS founder Julius Schreck, circa 1935. *(AP/Press Association Images)*

Ernst Röhm with Himmler and Daluege in August 1933, less than a year before Himmler was to orchestrate his murder. *(Bundesarchiv)*

Left: Ulrich Graf, one of Hitler's earliest bodyguards. *(Bundesarchiv)*

Right: Ernst Röhm, revolutionary, military radical and SA Chief of Staff. *(AP/Press Association Images)*

Left: Kurt Daluege, Berlin sanitation engineer turned police chief. *(Getty Images)*

Right: Prince Josias zu Waldeck-Pyrmont, one of Himmler's earliest aristocratic recruits. *(Bundesarchiv)*

Left: Oswald Pohl, business and administrative chief of the SS. *(Bundesarchiv)*

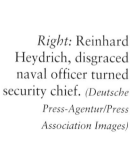

Right: Reinhard Heydrich, disgraced naval officer turned security chief. *(Deutsche Press-Agentur/Press Association Images)*

March 1933, the Nazi terror begins. A Jewish lawyer is humiliated by SS auxiliary policemen on the streets of Munich. The placard reads: 'Ich werde mich nie mehr bei der Polizei beschweren' – 'I will no longer burden the police'. *(Bundesarchiv)*

Spring 1933, a police officer swears in SS men as auxiliaries.
(Bildarchiv Preussischer Kulturbesitz)

May 1933, detainees at work at the newly established Dachau concentration camp. *(Bundesarchiv)*

May 1933, SS guards roll-call at Dachau. *(Bundesarchiv)*

Himmler standing next to his ideological mentor, Richard Walter Darré, and the police president of Berlin, Graf Helldorf, January 1939. *(Bundesarchiv)*

1939, the chiefs of the SS security apparatus: (left to right) Franz Josef Huber, Arthur Nebe, Himmler, Heydrich and Heinrich Müller. *(Getty Images)*

Left: Rudolf Diels, the Nazi fellow traveller who was first chief of the Gestapo. *(Bundesarchiv)*

Right: Theodor Eicke, creator of the SS concentration camp system, killer of Ernst Röhm and commander of the SS-Death's Head Division. *(Bundesarchiv)*

Left: Paul Hausser, former army general who founded the SS officer schools.
(Bundesarchiv)

Right: Felix Steiner, tactical guru of the early armed SS units and later commander of the 'Germanic' Panzer Corps.
(Bundesarchiv)

Left: Gottlob Berger, the Swabian PE teacher who masterminded the expansion of the Waffen-SS. *(Bundesarchiv)*

Right: Walter Schellenberg, Himmler's foreign intelligence chief and confidant in the later years of the war.
(Bundesarchiv)

and the 'old fighters' who had been promoted above their ability purely because of their political service. However, he also claimed that many of his colleagues were sickened by the atrocities being perpetrated against Jews in the East, and Zech-Nenntwich himself 'was particularly revolted by the bestial treatment of the Poles by the Gestapo'.[32] He concluded by naming forty-four members of this opposition group, and its leader – SS-Brigadier Wilhelm Bittrich.

It was never firmly established that this story of an opposition group within the SS was true. But, equally, British intelligence never found any evidence to disprove it, and Zech-Nenntwich was treated as a genuine defector. His personal anti-National Socialism certainly seemed sincere, and he spent the rest of the war making propaganda broadcasts and advising on the interrogation of SS prisoners of war. He was also never forgiven by the German establishment for his betrayal: he was harassed by the German government throughout the 1950s and was eventually put on trial and convicted in 1964 for his own role in atrocities against Jews in 1941. Imprisoned for four years' hard labour in a German prison in Braunschweig, he managed simply to walk out, after bribing his guards, and fled to Egypt, although he did later return to serve his sentence.[33]

The Gestapo had more success in dealing with less well-organised resistance groups and individuals because so many ordinary Germans were willing to denounce their fellow countrymen. The fate of the *Weisse Rose* (White Rose) group from Munich University exemplifies this. It had six core members: the brother and sister Hans and Sophie Scholl, Christoph Probst, Alex Schmorell and Willi Graf, all of whom were students, and Kurt Huber, who was a professor of philosophy. Between June 1942 and February 1943, the group printed and distributed six anonymous leaflets calling on Germans to oppose the National Socialist regime. On 18 February, while handing out their leaflets at the university, they were seen by a caretaker and promptly denounced to the police. The Scholls and Christoph Probst were tried, convicted and executed just four days later; Schmorell and Huber were executed on 13 July; Graf on 12 October.[34]

As far as foreign espionage was concerned, Office VI, SD-Overseas, achieved something of a coup in November 1939 when an operation led by Schellenberg and Naujocks kidnapped two British MI6 officers, Major Richard Stevens and Captain Sigismund Payne Best, at a café in Venlo on the German-Dutch border. Payne Best had been liaising with German anti-National Socialist refugees in the Netherlands for some time and believed that he was dealing with members of the German armed forces who were planning a coup. In fact, his contact was an agent provocateur inserted into German émigré circles by the SD. This agent persuaded Stevens and Payne Best to attend two meetings with a 'Major Schaemmel', supposedly an anti-NSDAP conspirator but actually Schellenberg. At their third meeting, on 9 November, they were ambushed by a team led by Naujocks and bundled across the border for interrogation. A Dutch intelligence officer, Major Klop, who was also at the meeting, was shot and fatally wounded during the ambush.

Payne Best and Stevens were taken to the Gestapo office in Dusseldorf. They were not allowed any contact with each other, and were interrogated at length and in detail. Stevens was the head of station for MI6 in the Hague, under the cover of being a 'passport control officer'. However, he was a relatively new recruit to MI6 and had limited knowledge of the service's agents and operations. On the other hand, Payne Best was a member of the 'Z Organisation' – a parallel and supposedly more secretive network that MI6 operated in Europe under the personal control of Claude Dansey, a senior MI6 officer who had been working with Payne Best for the best part of twenty years. Both men eventually revealed extensive information under duress, and a summary of what they said about MI6 was circulated by the RSHA in early 1940. However, this may not have been the success it seems. When Schellenberg was interrogated after the war, he maintained that Payne Best and Stevens had disclosed little useful information, particularly about the leading personalities of the British Secret Service; and Schellenberg's poor understanding of the organisation of MI6 was a source of considerable amusement to British intelligence personnel.[35]

In fact, the post-war interrogation of Schellenberg and other Office VI personnel revealed that they never gathered significant information on British, Soviet or US capabilities or intentions.[36] An attempt to insert agents into enemy territory was similarly unsuccessful. Office VI expended considerable effort in training and equipping two Irishmen and then parachuting them into the Irish Republic in December 1943. They had instructions to report on the naval, military and political situation in the UK, but they were arrested almost immediately, after details of their operation were uncovered by the 'Ultra' intelligence-gathering system. This appears to have been Office VI's only serious attempt to plant agents in Britain.[37]

Heydrich continued as chief of the RSHA until 1942, but in September 1941 he was appointed acting *Reichsprotektor* of Bohemia and Moravia, a role that took up much of his time and energy. He adopted a largely successful carrot-and-stick approach to increase war production in the region, much to the dismay of Czech resistance groups.

In the spring of 1942, a team of Czech commandos trained in Britain by the Special Operations Executive was parachuted into Czechoslovakia with the task of eliminating Heydrich. The team's reconnaissance work revealed that he drove from his residence to the Hradcany Castle in Prague every morning, and this seemed to be when he was at his most vulnerable. On 27 May, the four commandos, led by Jan Kubis and Josef Gabcik, struck. They set an ambush on a hairpin bend and waited for Heydrich to appear. When he did, Gabcik jumped into the middle of the road, raised his sub-machine gun and pulled the trigger. But the gun jammed. Heydrich's car screeched to a halt and he pulled his pistol from its holster and opened fire. At that point, Kubis lobbed a grenade under the car. It detonated, but then, to the Czechs' astonishment, Heydrich emerged from the cloud of smoke, shouting and still shooting. A running battle developed as the commandos tried to escape from their athletic and apparently unharmed enemy. Kubis managed to slip between two passing trams and escape on a bicycle he had positioned near by; but Gabcik seemed to be in real danger of being caught. However, Heydrich suddenly reached for his stomach, threw down his pistol and slumped to the ground. His driver, who had been slightly wounded in the blast, commandeered a passing bread van and took Heydrich to the nearest German military hospital. It was discovered that Heydrich had multiple shrapnel wounds, and he deteriorated over the next few days, despite being treated by Germany's leading doctors. He died on 4 June from septicaemia, aged thirty-eight.[38]

Daluege replaced Heydrich as acting *Reichsprotektor* and initiated a wave of terror against the Czech population in revenge for his predecessor's assassination. This culminated in the destruction of the village of Lidice on 9 June, when all 198 adult male inhabitants were shot, all the women were deported to Ravensbrück concentration camp, and every child was taken to Germany for adoption. Daluege stepped down from the Czech role in August 1943 after suffering a serious illness that also forced him to hand over control of the Order Police Main Office to his deputy, Alfred Wunnenberg, a professional police officer.[39]

Himmler himself had become chief of the RSHA in the wake of Heydrich's death, but he handed over day-to-day responsibility to Ernst Kaltenbrunner, hitherto Senior SS and Police Leader Danube, based in Vienna. Kaltenbrunner, an Austrian lawyer and long-time member of the SS, assumed full leadership of the RSHA in January 1943 and held the post until the end of the war. But his relationship with Himmler was never as close as Heydrich's had been, and he enjoyed far less independence than his predecessor. Where Heydrich had been an active pioneer, working closely with

Himmler to expand and develop the role of the SS in intelligence, security and policing, and later organising the murderous special task groups in occupied Europe, Kaltenbrunner was an appa-ratchik who was only really interested in securing his own position. He achieved this through the political in-fighting that characterised the upper reaches of the National Socialist state, especially towards the end of the war.[40]

11

The Path to Genocide

The SS was relatively insignificant in the early stages of the Holocaust. Historians have categorised the steps towards the Holocaust as 'identification, concentration and extermination',[1] and it was only in the latter phases that Himmler's branch of the National Socialist state assumed primacy. Although, of course, members of the SS had played their part in the brutalisation of Germany's Jews even before the NSDAP gained power.

The first steps in the National Socialist regime's persecution of the Jews were taken through legislation introduced by the Interior Ministry. On 7 April 1933, the Law for the Restoration of the Professional Civil Service decreed that government officials of 'non-Aryan descent' were to be retired. Four days later, a supplemental regulation – the so-called *Arierparagraph* (Aryan Paragraph) – defined 'non-Aryans' as 'any person who had a Jewish parent or grandparent'.[2] This law had a marked effect because 'government official' did not merely refer to civil servants: a wide range of professions (including teachers, university lecturers and so on) were employees of the state and so subject to the measure. Although this law was characterised by the NSDAP as racial, and thus in line with National Socialist policy, Jewishness was defined by a religious rather than a racial criterion: if the parent or grandparent followed the Jewish religion, their offspring was deemed 'non-Aryan'; but someone with an ethnically Jewish, non-observant parent or grandparent fell outside the law's scope. Similar laws were enacted later the same month. One was supposedly aimed at preventing overcrowding in schools. It imposed a strict quota on the number of non-Aryans who could attend state-funded schools, which had the effect of forcing Jewish children out of the state education sector and into private Jewish schooling. Another law prevented Jewish doctors from treating patients under the national health insurance scheme. And a third restricted entry of Jews into the legal profession.[3]

Enacting these early laws created a number of practical difficulties for the new regime. First, several foreign nations, including Japan, found the implication that non-Aryans were inferior to Aryans deeply offensive. In response, the German Foreign Office instructed its overseas missions to explain that the laws were designed merely to identify 'physical and spiritual qualities' within each race,[4] rather than to rank them. Unsurprisingly, this failed to satisfy the Japanese. Second, numerous experienced public officials now had to be dismissed, and this was especially destructive after 28 February 1934, when General von Blomberg, the Minister of War, extended the Aryan Paragraph to the army.[5] Some senior officers who had served in the First World War were exempted, but several hundred men – mostly of mixed backgrounds but also a few 'full' Jews – were forced to leave the service.

As a corollary to this, it was decided that the term 'non-Aryan' was unsatisfactory. Everybody knew that the legislation was primarily intended to discriminate against the Jews, rather than non-Aryans in general, so the regime needed to formulate a precise definition of what it meant to be Jewish. This came to a head at the National Socialist Party rally at Nuremberg in September 1935. Hitler ordered a decree to be drafted under the title 'Law for the Protection of German Blood and Honour'. The principal purpose of this law was to prohibit intermarriage and extra-marital sexual intercourse between Jews and citizens of German or related blood, but it also went much further than the earlier law in legally excluding Jews from participation in the German state. Further provisions banned Jews from employing Germans under the age of forty-five as domestic staff, and a separate law forbade Jews from raising the Reich flag. The next day, the Reich Citizenship Law was drafted. This excluded Jews from German citizenship – they became 'subjects of the state' – and finally legally defined the term 'Jew'. This definition was fairly straightforward. It included: anyone who had three or four Jewish grandparents; anyone who had two Jewish grandparents and was a member of the Jewish religious community on or after 15 September 1935; and anyone who was married to a Jewish person on or after 15 September. Furthermore, anyone born as a result of a marriage involving a Jew that was contracted after the Law for the Protection of German Blood and Honour had come into force, or anyone born out of wedlock from a relationship involving a Jew after 31 July 1936, would be considered a Jew.

This legislation also created a host of 'semi-Jews'. Anyone with two Jewish grandparents who did not practise the Jewish religion, and was not married to a Jew, was now considered *Mischlinge* (mixed race) of the first degree. Anyone with a single Jewish grandparent was *Mischlinge* of the second degree. In coming years, the *Mischlinge* were subjected to harassment, but they were not persecuted to the same extent as 'full Jews' (although many *Mischlinge* of the first degree were murdered in the Holocaust). They were normally barred from National Socialist party and state positions, but, for instance, they could serve in the armed forces.*

One of the key outcomes of the passing of these so-called

---

* The *Mischlinge* could be exempted from the provisions of the racial laws under various circumstances; and they could petition the state for 'liberation'. Over the years, several attempts were made to re-categorise them as Jews, but none of these succeeded.

'Nuremberg Laws' was that they introduced criminal sanctions based on race, and it was this that formally brought the machinery of the SS security apparatus into action against the Jews. Hitherto, the SS had been just one of several party formations involved in the harassment of Jews. And, of course, SS posts had collected information on Jewish activities since the early days of the organisation. But by criminalising the everyday lives of Jews, Sipo and the SD would clearly have major roles to play in their persecution in the future.

The Gestapo had been conducting surveillance on Jewish groups and individuals ever since the National Socialists had come to power, but the extent of that surveillance was largely decided by the local Gestapo commander. For instance, Robert Gellately's study of Gestapo activity in the Franconian town of Würzburg suggests that the political police's interest in Jewish activities was limited. Between 1933 and 1935, pressure against the Jewish population largely emanated from the party, rather than the state. To some extent, the Gestapo and other police elements even reined in party members' excesses. While it was certainly official (party *and* state) policy to reinforce negative images of the Jews, party-sponsored activities such as trade boycotts tended to damage foreign relationships, international trade and the tourist industry, so they were not always encouraged.

This changed with the introduction of the Nuremberg Laws. In November 1935, the Gestapo office in Münster noted: 'after the promulgation of the Jewish laws at the Party meetings in Nuremberg, a certain tranquillity set in with regard to the "Jewish question". Excesses against Jews, as well as individual actions against Jewish businesses, have not taken place again in the past month.'[6] This probably reflected a general satisfaction within the National Socialist-supporting population that, after years of propaganda against the Jews, the government had finally taken some concrete steps to back up its rhetoric.

The Gestapo's remit evolved into the defence and enforcement of National Socialist ideology, and in many respects it was free to act outside the law. But the Nuremberg Laws also gave it a legal framework within which it could persecute the Jews. For instance, between 1933 and 1945, the Würzburg Gestapo investigated 175 cases of *Rassenschande* (race defilement) – the criminal offence of sexual intercourse between a Jew and an Aryan – and 'friendship towards Jews'.* Although the latter was not a criminal offence, it was taken to indicate a refusal to accept the spirit of National Socialist racial doctrine and so was suggestive of opposition to the regime. The Würzburg office (and its sub-unit at Aschaffenburg) covered the whole of Lower Franconia, comprising a population of some 800,000, of whom only around 25,000 were Jewish. Consequently, it seems fair to conclude that the local Gestapo's investigations into 'Jewish crimes' comprised a relatively small proportion of its work.

The lack of surviving data makes it difficult to draw a nation-wide picture of the Gestapo's role in the persecution of the Jewish population in the early years of the Third Reich. But it seems that 'the police role in all this was not extraordinary, it was simply police work directed to whatever conclusion the state directed'.[7] Each local office attempted to apply National Socialist law and policy to the Jews, but in no sense did the Gestapo lead the persecution.

In fact, the first SS agency to take a serious interest in the 'Jewish question' was the SD. As we have seen, Office II dealt with all 'enemies' of National Socialism. But from mid-1935, the Jews became the specific responsibility of Office II 112. Heydrich appointed SS-*Untersturmführer* (Second Lieutenant) Leopold Edler von Mildenstein to lead it. Born in Prague in 1902, von Mildenstein trained as a civil engineer but seems to have spent most of his time before joining the SD as a traveller and writer. He

---

* Most of the 175 investigations were launched after accusations were made by members of the public. Seventy-one of them ultimately proved to have no foundation in fact, which would seem to indicate that making accusations to the Gestapo was often used to settle private scores.

came to Heydrich's attention because of an article he wrote for *The Attack*, the Berlin-based NSDAP newspaper, in which he described a visit to British-mandated Palestine and the prospects for creating a Jewish state there. Considering where this article appeared, it was quite a moderate piece, and von Mildenstein was not a conventional Jew-baiting National Socialist. Along with others in the SD, he recognised that harassment and persecution of Jews might cause more problems than it solved, and he was convinced that a better solution to the 'Jewish question' was to persuade Germany's half-million Jews to emigrate. This had been proposed before, but had always foundered on the unwillingness of other Western countries to accept large numbers of German-Jewish emigrants. As a way round this, von Mildenstein suggested that Germany's Jews should be 'exported' to Palestine. He undoubtedly came to this conclusion partly because he was in friendly contact with a number of Zionist leaders and had even attended Zionist congresses in the past.[8]

Von Mildenstein had a heavy workload, so he was given permission to take on an assistant. The man recommended for the role was an SD NCO who was currently employed in the organisation's museum of Freemasonry, where he catalogued seals and medallions. His name was Adolf Eichmann.

In her account of Eichmann's trial in Jerusalem in 1961, Hannah Arendt portrayed him as an unintelligent, simple man who was not overtly anti-Semitic. She argued that he became, in effect, the logistician of the Holocaust simply because it represented professional advancement for him. Certainly, the Eichmann who appeared in the dock did not come across as a monster: he was puny in appearance and mild and submissive in manner. But there can be no doubt that he accepted the SS's ideological framework and believed that the *Volk* had to be protected from Jewry. That was what motivated him to behave as he did. Eichmann was not conscripted into the SS: he volunteered when the SS was at its most selective; and he was accepted because he demonstrated the 'correct' outlook.

Adolf Eichmann was born on 19 March 1906 in Solingen in the Rhineland. At the time, his father was an accountant for the Solingen Light and Power Company, a subsidiary of AEG, but when Eichmann was just seven the family moved to Linz in Austria. His father became commercial director of the local power company, and Eichmann attended the Kaiser Franz High School – Hitler's alma mater – until the age of fifteen.[9] By that point, his father had gone into business for himself, opening a shale oil mine and taking an interest in a machine shop in Salzburg. Eichmann attended the local engineering vocational college, but he was pulled out by his father because of his poor results and sent to work in the mine. After a few months of this he did an apprenticeship at his father's old company. He remained there until 1928, when he became a travelling salesman for the Vacuum Oil Company. He also joined a monarchist youth group called the Young Veterans' Association, through which he came into contact with the NSDAP for the first time. At a National Socialist meeting in late 1931 or early 1932, Eichmann bumped into an acquaintance, Ernst Kaltenbrunner, who invited him to join the local branch of the SS. Eichmann later recalled: 'Ernst Kaltenbrunner put it to me straight from the shoulder: "You're going to join us!" That's how easy it was in those days, all very free and easy, no fuss. I said: "Alright." So I joined the SS.'[10]

In 1933, Eichmann was made redundant by the Vacuum Oil Company and decided to move to Germany to try his luck there. By this stage, Austrian NSDAP, SA and SS activities were being suppressed by the government, and the Upper Austrian Regional Leader had already fled over the border. Kaltenbrunner needed to get some documents to his party boss, and he entrusted Eichmann with the task. Having handed over the papers, Eichmann asked for some help finding work. Instead, the Regional Leader suggested that he should join the newly formed SS-Special Purpose Troops and 'play soldiers'[11] for a while. With nothing better to do, Eichmann joined the SS-Regiment *Deutschland*. He was one of the older members of the unit, as well as competent and organised, so he was quickly made his company's administrative NCO and given the rank of *Oberscharführer* (sergeant). After originally forming up at Kloster Lechfeld, the unit moved to the Munich suburb of Dachau, where they occupied quarters outside the concentration camp.

Eichmann stayed with the regiment until September 1934, but by then he was bored and looking for a way out. He volunteered for the SD in the hope that he would be appointed to one of the security escorts that guarded the NSDAP's leaders. He was wrong: when he arrived at the SD's headquarters at 102 Wilhelmstrasse, he was dismayed to find that he would have a desk job under the eccentric, self-styled Freemasonry expert SS-Major Schwarz-Bostunitsch. Eichmann later admitted that he 'would have gone in with the devil himself just to get away from that business with the seals',[12] but as it happened he found von Mildenstein 'an open-minded, friendly sort'.[13]

Eichmann was interested in his new work and applied himself assiduously to his specific task of monitoring Zionist groups. Having taught himself the Hebrew alphabet so that he could read Yiddish, he studied their key texts and periodicals and went as far as to visit their offices in plain clothes to make contact with their leaders. He even tried to learn Hebrew itself, but when he sought a grant from SD-Main Office to pay for lessons from a rabbi, he was rebuffed. Nevertheless, his efforts earned him a spurious reputation among the young intellectuals in the SD as a genuine expert on the 'Jewish question'.

In the spring of 1936, von Mildenstein moved on. In Eichmann's version of events, he joined the *Organisation Todt* – the National Socialist civil engineering organisation – and was sent to the United States to study the highways system.* Eichmann applied for his job but did not get it. Instead, a brash young SS-NCO, Kuno Schröder, was appointed and Eichmann continued with

* Other accounts suggest he joined the Foreign Ministry or the Propaganda Ministry.

his work on Zionism. By this time, he had been joined by Theodor Dannecker, a Bavarian lawyer who was a few years younger than Eichmann. Dannecker's job was to monitor assimilationist Jews.

When describing the SD in this period, historians often highlight its lack of any kind of executive arm and the fact that its role often overlapped with that of the Gestapo. However, this is a fairly common model for domestic intelligence collection, where political police forces are routinely separated from intelligence agencies. At this stage, Office II 112 was an intelligence staff rather than an executive unit: its role was to receive – and, to some extent, collect – information, process it, but not act upon it. However, as members of the team developed expertise in their field, their recommendations started to carry increasing weight. Therefore, it is far from remarkable that Office II 112 began to exert influence on the issue of the 'Jewish question'.

Schröder left Office II 112 in March 1937. Again, Eichmann was overlooked, and Dieter Wisliceny took over leadership of the department. The tubby East Prussian was preferred for the role because he had studied theology at university. However, he and Eichmann got on well – in conversation, they would address each other with the familiar *du*. At this point, most of the office's energy was being devoted to compiling a card index of all the Jews in Germany. This had initially proved too much for the small team, but then the organisational changes instituted by Himmler came to their aid. First, Heydrich – by now Chief of the Security Police (Gestapo and Kripo) and the SD – ordered that Office II 112 should have access to all information gathered during Gestapo raids on Jewish organisations and interrogations of Jewish community leaders. Then, in July 1937, Six (head of Office II), Wisliceny, Eichmann and Herbert Hagen (a young ex-journalist and now a member of Office II 112) attended a meeting with representatives of the Gestapo. The SD men asked for access to the Gestapo's files on Jews and Jewish organisations, and Werner Best (Heydrich's deputy) agreed that the entire Gestapo card index should be turned over to them.[14] This was a clear acknowledgement of Office II 112's growing significance – it placed the department right at the centre of SS involvement in the formulation of Jewish policy.

However, those outside Office II 112 were not always comfortable with its activities, particularly in respect to its cultivation of contacts within the Zionist movement. Eichmann was especially active in developing the links that von Mildenstein had forged with Zionists who sought German support for mass Jewish emigration to Palestine. For instance, his interest was piqued after reading an article in *Haint*, a Yiddish newspaper published in Warsaw, about the Haganah, an underground Zionist self-defence and intelligence organisation that was based in Palestine. Eichmann summoned Dr Paul Eppstein, one of the leaders of the National Socialist-controlled *Reichsvertretung der Deutschen Juden* (Reich Representatives of German Jews) and a regular source of information on Jewish matters, for questioning on Haganah. Eppstein claimed to know nothing about the organisation, but Eichmann remained interested. Then, in February 1937, Otto von Bolschwingh – a friend of von Mildenstein and a part-time SD spy – told Eichmann that a Haganah officer, a Polish Jew named Feivel Polkes, was coming to Berlin. Having sought permission from Six and Heydrich, Eichmann arranged to meet him.

The two men had lunch at a restaurant near Berlin Zoo on 26 February. Eichmann's account of the meeting and what followed, given under interrogation before his trial in Israel, was somewhat anodyne:

I took the gentleman to lunch. He knew who I was and I knew he was from Palestine. He told me all about the Kibbutzim, about construction and development projects, things I already knew because I had read about them, but now I began to take a real interest. There was no hostility. We both said what we had to say, and neither of us – I had the impression – kept anything back, because we believed that our aims converged. After a second lunch, the gentleman invited me to Palestine. He wanted me to go and see the country for myself, and said they'd show me everything. I was more than willing. I reported that, too, and I submitted a report of our discussion, which went as far as Heydrich. And something I hadn't thought possible: Heydrich authorised me to accept the invitation. This came as a surprise to my colleagues. It sparked off a race between them: Wisliceny wanted to come along, so did Hagen. Hagen won out.[15]

In effect, Polkes was offering information in return for the SD's help in promoting Jewish emigration to Palestine. He might also have been seeking weapons, although there is no evidence that any were handed over. Eichmann's report of the meeting noted that Polkes 'was prepared among other things to give powerful support to German foreign policy interests in the Middle East . . . on condition that German currency regulations were relaxed for Jews emigrating to Palestine'.[16]

Eichmann and Hagen, under cover as a journalist and a student, finally set off for Palestine at the end of September. Their trip took them by train through Poland and Romania to the port of Constanza, where they boarded a steamer. They reached the port of Haifa on 2 October. Then chance stepped in: an Arab uprising in September had forced the British authorities to close Palestine's borders. Eichmann and Hagen were given permission to disembark from their ship for twenty-four hours but were told not to journey elsewhere in Palestine. After doing a little sightseeing the next morning, they continued on to Alexandria and from there took a train to Cairo.

They stayed in the Egyptian capital for twelve days, met Polkes again, and persuaded him to become a paid SD agent (he was given a salary of £15 per month). They also applied to the British authorities for permission to enter Palestine. According to Eichmann, 'we were told: "I'm sorry, nothing doing."' I seem to remember that there had been some kind of disorders in Palestine at the time, maybe bombings. It's also possible that British Intelligence had caught on to us.'[17] This was quite likely. During this period, British embassies' and consulates' 'passport control offices' were usually staffed by MI6 operatives; and even if the British had no knowledge of Eichmann and Hagen's mission, suspicions would have been aroused by the two men's arrival.

Eichmann and Hagen returned from the Middle East with the former resigned to the fact that their mission had been a failure. But this view was not shared by his superiors, particularly Heydrich, who was now convinced that Office II 112's Zionist contacts could be used to further the SD's influence. Before long, the department was hosting a 'Jewish Day', a seminar outlining the SD's position on the 'Jewish question'. Records of this event reveal that, despite its supposed expertise on Jewish matters and its rejection of the crude extremism of many party members, Office II 112's thinking was still broadly in line with typical National Socialist attitudes. In Eichmann's closing address – on the connections between world Jewry and the Jews of Germany – he painted a ludicrous picture of Haganah and other Zionist conspiracies being perpetrated by foreign-born Jews in Germany. But, as his biographer points out: 'This fantasy was not simply driven by ideology: the SD needed to find conspiracies in order to justify its operations and its budget.'[18]

Eichmann's work gave him a thorough grounding in the 'Jewish question', and he certainly saw emigration to Palestine as the best solution to it. At this point, neither he nor any of the other experts on Jewry in the SD considered the mass extermination of the Jewish population as a feasible 'final solution', and it would be several years before they became involved in it. In the meantime, the Austrian *Anschluss* gave them an opportunity to put some of Office II 112's ideas into practice.

In early 1938, the SD was told to prepare for an upcoming action in Austria. Its offices immediately set to work drawing up lists of organisations and individuals that they intended to target. The German Army crossed the border on 12 March, and before long they were joined by the full panoply of the National Socialist security apparatus. Hagen moved to Vienna to establish a 'special unit' of Office II 112, while Eichmann – who had finally been made an officer on 30 January – followed him on 16 March, bearing lists of prominent Jews to be arrested and organisations to be raided. At his trial, more than twenty years later, he tried to give the impression that he acted as the Jews' protector in Vienna. In reality, he personally took part in many of the raids and arrests, and only when this first wave of terror had left Austrian Jews cowering and intimidated did he move on to the next phase. Having consulted with the local Sipo leadership as well as Berlin, he decided that he needed a degree of cooperation from the Jewish community in order to begin the forced emigration process. So, from his headquarters in the Hotel Metropol, he summoned Jewish community leaders to a series of meetings.

Ultimately, he chose a Viennese lawyer, Josef Löwenherz – a vice-president of the main Jewish community group – to be his chief enforced collaborator. Eichmann sent Löwenherz back to his cell and ordered that he should be held there 'until he produced a plan for the mass emigration of Austrian Jews'.[19] The plan that was eventually formulated was effectively a system of expropriation: 'The majority of Austria's 300,000 Jews were destitute and could not produce the minimum capital demanded by the receiving countries; the National Socialist regime, on the other hand, was short of foreign currency and could provide no funds. The richer Jews were accordingly compelled to subsidize the exodus from their own resources.'[20] The SD knew that these wealthy Jews would need little persuading to leave. The problem lay with getting them to take the poorer ones with them.

Eichmann's Central Office for Jewish Emigration was established in a former Rothschild family palace on Prinz Eugen Strasse in Vienna. Here he set up a 'conveyor-belt' system to handle the bureaucracy, with representatives of all the interested departments located in the building to speed up the process. Within the first eight months of the *Anschluss*, this office had organised the emigration of 45,000 Austrian Jews; within eighteen months, 150,000 had been forced from their homes.[21]

But even as the SD's pro-emigrationists were driving out the Austrian Jews, the anti-Semitic hard core of the NSDAP was gearing up to wrest Jewish policy-making away from them. In March 1938, the government of Poland, under pressure from the nationalist, anti-Semitic right, announced that all Poles who had lived abroad for more than five years were to be deprived of their citizenship. This measure was explicitly designed to rid the country of the seventy thousand Polish Jews who were residing in Germany and Austria. A further decree on 6 October announced that all Polish passports would be cancelled unless they received a validation stamp – available only in Poland – before the 31st of the month. The German government quite rightly concluded that this was simply another attempt by its eastern neighbour to dump Polish Jews on Germany. In response, Heydrich arrested some twelve thousand Polish Jews living in Germany and transported them to the border. On the night of 28–29 October, they were driven across the frontier and marched two kilometres to the Polish town of Zbaszyn. But the Polish frontier guards refused to accept them into the country, so they remained stuck in no man's land as winter drew in. They were fed only intermittently by the Polish Red Cross and Jewish aid organisations.*

Among the twelve thousand were Sendel and Rivka Grynszpan, a couple who had emigrated to Hannover in 1911. Thereafter, Sendel ran a tailoring business in the town. They took Polish nationality at the end of the First World War but remained in Hannover. Like most Jews in Germany after the National

---

* Ultimately, the Polish government relented and allowed the expellees to move into refugee camps within the Polish frontier. After Poland began expelling German citizens from its territory in retaliation, the German government relented and allowed the Polish-German Jews to return to their homes to collect property, before leaving for good.

Socialists came to power, they were frightened for themselves and their children, and in 1936 they arranged for their youngest son, fifteen-year-old Herschel, to travel to Belgium. They hoped he would be able to emigrate to Palestine from there, but instead he entered France illegally and went to live with an uncle in a small Jewish enclave in Paris.

Two years later, Rivka sent Herschel a postcard from Zbaszyn, begging him to try to organise emigration for her and Sendel to the United States. On 7 November, Herschel asked his uncle for some money to pursue this, but he refused and a furious row erupted. Still fuming, Herschel stormed out of the house, went to a gun shop and bought a pistol and some ammunition. Then he walked to the German Embassy and asked to see a diplomat. He was shown into the office of Ernst vom Rath, a young National Socialist Party member, whereupon he drew his pistol and shot vom Rath three times. The diplomat died two days later – the fifteenth anniversary of the Munich *Putsch*.

Leading National Socialists, including Hitler, always marked 9 November with a meeting in Munich. This year, the Propaganda Minister, Josef Goebbels, was intending to make an incendiary speech that he hoped would incite a pogrom against the Jews. Of course, Goebbels was a rabid anti-Semite, but he was planning to launch this particular attack for peculiarly personal reasons. The previous year, he had started an affair with a Czech actress, Lida Baarova, whom he had met through the Propaganda Ministry's UFA film studios. However, his wife Magda – a favourite of Hitler – learned of Goebbels' philandering and complained to the Führer, who duly ordered his minister to end the affair. Goebbels responded by offering his resignation (which Hitler refused) and then, on 15 October 1938, allegedly made a half-hearted attempt at suicide. An infuriated Hitler decided that the only solution was to order Himmler to remove Baarova from the country. Although this ended the affair, Goebbels' reputation had been seriously tarnished, and it seems that his speech was designed to curry favour with Hitler by raising the party's anti-Semitic hackles.

Then, just as the meeting was beginning, news of vom Rath's death reached Munich. This gave Goebbels the ammunition he needed to make his address to the meeting even more explosive. He was seen in earnest conversation with Hitler, who then left suddenly, without making his customary speech. Of course, the precise details of their conversation are not known, but Höhne believes that Goebbels 'informed the Führer that in certain areas anti-Jewish demonstrations had already taken place. The Führer had thereupon decided that such demonstrations were neither to be prepared nor organised by the Party; should they occur spontaneously; however, no action was to be taken to stop them.'[22] Goebbels then rose to relate what had just been discussed to the 'old fighters' who were gathered in the Old Town Hall. They had all been in the party long enough to understand exactly what was now expected of them. Soon they were hurrying to issue orders to SA units and party groups throughout Germany.

Goebbels' speech unleashed a wave of violence across Germany and Austria. In total, 1574 synagogues and more than 7000 Jewish-owned businesses were damaged or destroyed; around 26,000 Jewish men were taken to concentration camps and at least 91 Jews were killed, often beaten to death in front of their families. This turn of events came as a complete surprise to the leaders of the SS. Of course, both Himmler and Heydrich had been in Munich, but the first Heydrich knew of the violence was when a synagogue close to his hotel went up in flames. He hurried to issue orders to Gestapo, regular police and SS units, telling them to protect Jewish businesses and houses to the best of their ability, and to arrest looters. Nevertheless, many individual SS men, as well as local units, were certainly enthusiastic participants in the violence.

The riots became known as *Kristallnacht** (Night of the Broken Glass), reflecting the shattered windows of Jewish shops and businesses, and they marked a significant turning point in anti-Semitic policy in the Third Reich. Hitherto, most of the pressure against

---

* In Germany, it is now generally known, less euphemistically, as *Pogromnacht*.

the Jews had been applied legally, economically and socially. From now on, it was increasingly physical, applied brutally in the 'protective custody' of the concentration camps.

In the immediate aftermath of *Kristallnacht*, Hitler turned to Goering, rather than Himmler or Heydrich, to find a solution to the 'Jewish question'. He convened a meeting of interested parties and announced:

> I have received a letter written on the Führer's orders requesting that the Jewish question be now, once and for all, coordinated and solved one way or another . . . I should not want to leave any doubt, gentlemen, as to the aim of today's meeting. We have not come together merely to talk again, but to make decisions, and I implore competent agencies to take all measures for the elimination of the Jew from the German economy, and to submit them to me.[23]

It was decided to increase the pressure on Jewry, completely exclude them from the economy and, above all, step up the SD's emigration programme. Heydrich set about creating a nationwide replica of the Viennese Central Office for Jewish Emigration, commanded by Heinrich Müller of the Gestapo. Like Eichmann, he also co-opted Jewish community leaders to ensure that it ran smoothly.

The main problem for the SD, though, was where to send the Jews. In an attempt to halt inter-communal violence in Palestine, Britain had imposed a strict limit on the number of Jews it would allow to move there over the next five years: 75,000. Germany had nearly 500,000 Jews within its borders, and it wanted to expel all of them as soon as possible. Some of them could be accommodated elsewhere in Europe or in the United States, but these countries also had limits on the number of immigrants they could, or would, accept. Despite the widespread international condemnation of Germany's treatment of its Jews, no country was prepared to increase its quota to meet the demand. So, once again, the SD turned to the Zionists.

In 1937, Haganah had organised a special unit – *Mossad le Aliyah Bet* – to smuggle as many Jews as possible into Palestine, using a network of contacts throughout Europe. According to Höhne:

At about the time of Kristallnacht, two representatives of Mossad, Pino Ginzburg and Moshe Auerbach, journeyed to Adolf Hitler's Third Reich to offer the SS their assistance in the matter of Jewish emigration. They were prepared to accelerate the Zionist re-education programme for Jews willing to emigrate, and to ship the Jews to Palestine. Emigration figures had already begun to fall and so the SD leapt at the idea and guaranteed Mossad their co-operation.[24]

These 'illegal' convoys began in March 1939. Jews were usually transported from Germany or Austria to a third country, where they were loaded on to a ship and taken to Palestine. The British attempted to counter this influx with a naval patrol off the Palestinian coast, and they intercepted a number of the transports. Nevertheless, at least ten thousand Jews managed to escape from Germany before the start of the Second World War brought this form of emigration to an abrupt end.

In total, some 40,000 Jews got out of Germany in 1938, while some 78,000 escaped in 1939. The SD could therefore claim that its emigration policy was something of a success. Should Hitler not have been determined to fight a war of conquest, it even seems likely that the 'Jewish question' in Germany would have been solved in this way, without recourse to the grisly horrors that were to come. Of course, part of the tragedy was that many of the Jews who emigrated to Germany's European neighbours – and for a time must have believed they were reasonably safe – subsequently fell back into National Socialist hands as their new homes were occupied.

The rigorous pursuit of the emigration policy illustrates that, prior to the war at least, extermination of the Jews was not seriously considered as an option by the men who were dealing with the 'Jewish question' at the coal face. In fact, many of the SD's 'experts' were sharply critical of the crude anti-Semitism of their counterparts in the party. They recognised that the logical conclusion of National Socialist hate propaganda was to kill the Jews, but they simply did not believe that this was feasible, for numerous political and legal reasons. Tragically, though, they had no moral objections to it, which meant that most of them shifted effortlessly from forced emigration to mass murder and extermination as soon as the 'final solution' was devised.

Euthanasia and the Beginning of Mass Murder

In parallel with the regime's measures against the Jews, from an early stage the National Socialists targeted individuals suffering from supposedly hereditary diseases as well as the mentally and physically handicapped. It was through the implementation of these policies that many of the individuals who later participated in the Holocaust became desensitised to and trained in mass murder. It could even be said that the measures introduced against the sick and disabled in the 1930s set the Third Reich on the route to the 'final solution of the Jewish question' in the 1940s. SS personnel were involved from the start, although the euthanasia programme was officially the responsibility of Hitler's private office, the *Kanzlei des Führers* (Führer Chancellery).

There is a sense in which National Socialism was 'politics as applied biology'. The movement's theorists genuinely believed that it might be possible to resolve social and political problems by biological means. The first manifestation of this ideology – and the model for German eugenic legislation thereafter – was the Sterilisation Law of July 1933. Eugenicists had been advocating the sterilisation of 'inferior and degenerate types' for decades, and proposals for voluntary sterilisation had already reached state legislatures in Germany. But the new law introduced a new element: compulsion. Its preamble read: 'Any person suffering from a hereditary disease can be sterilised if medical knowledge indicates that his offspring will suffer from severe hereditary physical or mental damage.' The following conditions were classified as 'hereditary' under the law:

1. Congenital feeble-mindedness.
2. Schizophrenia.
3. Manic depression.
4. Epilepsy.
5. Huntington's chorea.
6. Blindness.
7. Deafness.
8. Severe physical deformity.
9. Severe alcoholism.[1]

The structure for enforcement was straightforward. If a person with one of these conditions did not voluntarily apply for sterilisation, it could be sought by health service doctors and directors of hospitals, care homes and prisons. A system of hereditary health courts was instituted, consisting of three members: a judge and two doctors. A more senior appeal court was structured in the same way.

In the first year in which sterilisation was in operation, some 388,400 people were reported to the hereditary health courts, 75 per cent of them by their own doctors. This was too much work for the courts to handle: just over 80,000 of these cases were reviewed, with 62,000 resulting in a sterilisation order. Of these people, just under half were actually sterilised (usually by vasectomy for men and Fallopian ligation for women) because of a lack of capacity in hospitals. It seems the system did not manage to clear the backlog even by 1939.[2] But this was not due to a lack of enthusiasm in the medical community: on the whole, German doctors welcomed the sterilisation scheme. It gave them enhanced prestige as implementers of government policy as well as a much greater range of paid tasks to perform – such as filling out forms and giving evidence to hereditary health courts.

However, the 'science' underpinning the Sterilisation Law was flimsy, at best:

> The sterilisation measures could never have been successful: seen from a biological point of view, they are useless, absolutely nonsense, because they do not calculate spontaneous mutations, environmental poisons and things like that. So it was a measure that would never have led to real success even if they had practised it more harshly than they did.
>
> So it was senseless from the beginning, but it was an important part and a kind of sign for the biological takeover that National Socialism was planning ... They had more than 350,000 people sterilised between 1933 and 1945, so it was also a kind of discrimination against people who didn't fit into the picture of National Socialist society. So everything else, looking bad, looking ill, looking strange, had to disappear.[3]

To some extent, the number of people who could potentially be affected by the Sterilisation Law was finite. For instance, there were only so many hereditarily blind or deaf people in Germany, and objective medical analysis was needed before they could be placed on the sterilisation lists. However, 'congenital feeble-mindedness' and 'alcoholism' were far more open to subjective interpretation. 'Intelligence tests' were introduced supposedly to determine the former, but in reality they were no such thing. Rather, they simply examined acquired learning. Moreover, many subjects passed the test but were still sterilised because they allegedly displayed 'feeble-minded appearance and behaviour'.

A popular joke in Germany in the 1930s summed up the paradox of the senior National Socialists' enthusiasm for eugenics and racial classification in its definition of an Aryan: 'He must be blond, like Hitler; thin, like Goering; handsome, like Goebbels; virile, like Röhm – and called Rosenberg.' Discriminatory laws based on eugenics continued to be enacted throughout the decade and were eventually complemented by laws that confined *Asozialen* (antisocial individuals) to state hospitals or asylums, imposed protective custody on habitual criminals, and restricted the right of gypsies to travel and trade. (The latter law effectively classified gypsies as antisocial criminals purely on the basis of their race.) These measures brought all such individuals within the purview of the SS security apparatus, and eventually led many of them to suffer the same fate as the Jews.

The next groups to be targeted were those who were considered a drain on society. Just as the National Socialists' faith in eugenics led them inexorably towards compulsory sterilisation of people with 'hereditary' diseases, so their warped social theories soon led them to attack anyone with an incurable disease or a permanent disability.

The issue of euthanasia had been raised in Germany even before the First World War. Back then, liberal progressives had argued that scarce resources should be directed towards the healthy workforce rather than unproductive cripples. At the time, this argument garnered little support in a society that still espoused Christian values and conventions. However, the brutal experience of war soon changed that. The mass slaughter of the First World War had a devastating impact on the moral climate in Germany. By the end, the German people were all too familiar with death on an industrial scale, and in a sense they abandoned their traditional views on the sanctity of human life and adopted a much harsher view of the world. Karl Bonhoeffer, the chairman of the German Psychiatric Association and father of Dietrich Bonhoeffer, a theologian and prominent opponent of Hitler, said in 1920:

It could seem as if we have witnessed a change in the concept of humanity. I simply mean that we were forced by the terrible exigencies of war to ascribe a different value to the life of the individual than was the case before, and that in the years of starvation during the war we had to get used to watching our patients die of malnutrition in vast numbers, almost approving of this, in the knowledge that perhaps the healthy could be kept alive through these sacrifices. But in emphasising the right of the healthy to stay alive, which is an inevitable result of periods of necessity, there is a danger of going too far: a danger that the self-sacrificing subordination of the strong to the needs of the helpless and ill, which lies at the heart of any true concern for the sick, will give ground to the demand of the healthy to live.[4]

In the same year as Bonhoeffer made this speech, Karl Binding, a lawyer, and Alfred Hoche, a psychiatrist with a morbid interest in the brain activity of recently guillotined criminals, wrote a pamphlet entitled 'Permission for the Destruction of Life Unworthy of Life'. Both men were right-wing German nationalists who put loyalty to the 'national community' above any notion of individual rights. Binding died before their article was published, but Hoche went on to become an aggressive apostle of euthanasia.

In the article, they stressed that the Judaeo-Christian tradition of respect for human life was a relatively recent phenomenon in human history. To back up this claim, they cited the example of the Spartans, who had routinely killed weak infants; and the Inuit, who had killed their ageing parents. Taking this argument further, they suggested that society should also kill off 'incurable idiots', the terminally ill and the critically injured. Perhaps in a feeble bid to display compassion, they said that the latter two groups should be given the right to choose to die on their own terms through a painless, medically administered procedure. (Then, as now, doctors routinely eased the final agonies of terminally ill cancer patients with overdoses of painkillers, but Binding and Hoche argued that such treatment should be enshrined as a right, and that the doctors who carried it out should never have to worry about legal consequences for their actions.) However, the crux of the pamphlet was the claim that certain individuals were 'unworthy of life'. By this, Binding and Hoche meant people who were so 'inferior' that there was no value in their continued existence. The argument they put forward was rooted in both eugenics and economics:

> If one thinks of a battlefield covered with thousands of dead youth . . . and contrasts this with our institutions for 'idiots' with their solicitude for living patients – then one would be deeply shocked by the glaring disjunction between the sacrifice of the most valuable possession of humanity on one side and on the other the greatest care of beings who are not only worthless but even manifest negative value.[5]

It is easy to find the source of this fury: Hoche's only son had been killed at the Battle of Langemarck, and he never recovered from his loss. But underlying his and Binding's argument was something much more sinister than the death of a loved one: the suggestion that the 'feeble-minded' and 'idiots' were not fully human. The claim was that their minds were so degenerate that they could not be said to have human personalities. In conclusion, Binding and Hoche argued that patients themselves, their relatives and/or physicians should be able to apply for euthanasia when the patient's life had become 'unworthy', and that the state should then be the arbiter of whether it should be carried out.

This pamphlet was widely debated in inter-war Germany, but it received no official approval or acceptance during the Weimar era. It was only when the National Socialists came to power that euthanasia started to be seriously discussed as a state policy. Paradoxically, in part this was facilitated by a revival in mainstream psychiatry.

The psychiatric profession had lost a good deal of its prestige during and shortly after the First World War – partly because of the misdiagnosis of 'shell-shock', partly because of the appalling state of Germany's wartime asylums, in which around seventy thousand patients died from starvation, and partly because certain psychiatrists had been happy to label post-war revolutionaries 'insane' with no basis in fact. However, during the 1920s, occupational therapy was introduced and proved highly successful in Germany's asylums, and community clinics were established throughout the country. Leading these reforms were Gustav Kolb and Hermann Simon, who were quick to point out the economic – as well as the medical – benefits of what they were doing. For instance, the new community clinics could treat far more patients for much less money than the old, grim asylums. At the same time, great claims were being made, initially at least, for new types of treatment, such as electro-convulsive therapy and insulin coma therapy. All of this changed the mood in the psychiatric profession from pessimism to optimism in a few short years. Moreover, asylums and institutes for the mentally ill started to be widely viewed as hospitals with a range of treatments at their disposal, rather than as warehouses for the storage of the permanently handicapped.

However, all of these improvements in the care of many mentally ill patients started to draw attention to the few who remained stubbornly unresponsive to any form of therapy. This latter group was now pushed even further to the margins of what was already a very marginalised sector of society. They started to be criticised for their inability to work, and euthanasia started to worm its way back on to the agenda of the medical profession.

Hitler followed the euthanasia debate closely, as is clear from a speech he gave in 1929 at an NSDAP rally:

If Germany was to get a million children a year and was to remove 700–800,000 of the weakest people then the final result might be an increase in strength. The most dangerous thing is for us to cut ourselves off from the natural process of selection and thereby rob ourselves of the possibility of acquiring able people. The first born are not always the most talented or able people. Sparta, the clearest case of a racial state in history, implemented these racial laws in a systematic way. As a result of our modern sentimental humanitarianism we are trying to maintain the weak at the expense of the healthy.[6]

While at first sight this appears to be an argument for eugenic infanticide, another interpretation is that Hitler was actually suggesting a trade-off between healthy infants and the sick, weak and disabled.

Hitler returned to the subject on numerous occasions. For instance, Hans Lammers – an honorary SS officer – recalled that Hitler introduced the topic of euthanasia when he was being advised on the details of the Sterilisation Law in 1933. And Dr Karl Brandt, one of Hitler's personal physicians, remembered him saying two years later, 'if war should break out, he would take up the euthanasia question and implement it',[7] because resistance from the churches and other bodies would be diminished in wartime. Notwithstanding these private conversations, euthanasia initially remained too controversial to form any part of the official National Socialist programme. But it was clearly on Hitler's mind, and he had no problem in telegraphing his feelings to those subordinates who were in a position to do something about it.

The start of the euthanasia programme can be traced to a specific event that occurred in Leipzig. In the winter of 1938–39, a baby was born to a family called Knauer. The infant was blind, missing one leg and part of an arm, and was, according to Karl Brandt, 'an idiot – at least, it seemed to be an idiot'.[8] Apparently encouraged by the baby's grandmother, the Knauers petitioned Hitler to grant permission for their child's doctor to perform a 'mercy killing'.

This petition was submitted to the Führer Chancellery, which had been established as a forum for ordinary party members to present their problems directly to Hitler. This allowed him to play the part of the conscientious leader, even though, of course, he rarely dealt with any of the letters personally. On this occasion, however, it seems that Philipp Bouhler* did actually consult with Hitler before passing the case on to Brandt, who recalled:

> [Hitler] ordered me to talk to the physicians who were look-
> ing after the child to find out whether the statements of the
> father were true. If they were correct, then I was to inform
> the physicians in his name that they could carry out euthana-
> sia . . . I was further ordered to state that if these physicians
> should become involved in some legal proceedings because of
> this measure, these proceedings would be quashed by order
> of Hitler.[9]

There were at least two other appeals for euthanasia around the same time: a middle-aged woman dying of cancer; and a labour service official who was terribly injured in an industrial accident. These cases all seem to have been widely discussed (although there are no records of any of the meetings), and the end result was a directive from Hitler to Bouhler, dated 1 September 1939, in which he states that 'authorised doctors' should be permitted to carry out 'mercy killings'.

The first victims of the euthanasia programme were children. From the autumn of 1939, doctors and healthcare workers were ordered to register all children with Down's syndrome, micro- and hydrocephaly, serious physical deformities (such as missing limbs and late development of the head and spine) and cerebral palsy. Once registered, these children – who ranged in age from new-born infants to teenagers – had their records examined by three 'referees': Werner Catel, the director of the University of Leipzig

---

* Bouhler was born in 1899. The son of an army officer and a veteran of the First World War, he was an early member of the NSDAP and became the party's 'second secretary' in the autumn of 1922. He was made Reich Secretary three years later and head of the Führer Chancellery in November 1934. He committed suicide after being arrested by the Americans in 1945.

paediatric centre; Hans Heinze, director of the asylum at Branden-burg-Görden; and Ernst Wentzler, an eminent paediatrician. Each man was paid an allowance of 240 marks a month for his con-tribution. If all three doctors agreed, the Reich Committee for Hereditary Health – a secret body that was subordinate to the Führer Chancellery – directed the relevant local public health authority to arrange for the child to be admitted to a designated regional clinic. Then the child was killed.

It is worth noting that Catel, Heinze and Wentzler assessed each case purely on paper, without conducting any physical exam-ination of the children themselves. It is also worth noting that most of the children were killed by pseudo-medical means: they had their nutrition withdrawn or were given overdoses of seda-tives in order to induce respiratory problems, bronchitis and pneumonia. The doctors and nurses who carried out these 'pro-cedures' swore an oath of secrecy and were paid extra to ensure their silence. Many of them undoubtedly found this work dis-turbing, and a number demanded transfers out of the designated clinics. Equally, however, many others simply got on with the job without complaint. It seems that they were prepared to accept that the good health of the nation required this slaughter of the innocents.

As in the case of the Knauer family, it is likely that a number of the parents welcomed, even if they did not actively seek, their chil-dren's deaths. Nevertheless, the National Socialists never felt sufficiently confident about this policy to sanction it in German law, nor did they ever make it public. That meant the whole oper-ation had to be carried out by subterfuge. Parents might be persuaded to part with their child after promises that they were being taken away to receive specialist medical treatment. Once the child was in a killing centre, spurious reports of their progress were often issued by doctors to reassure the parents. Then the tone of the reports would change, to indicate that the child had taken a turn for the worse. Shortly afterwards, inevitably, there would be a confirmation of death.

In all, some six thousand children were murdered between 1939 and 1945 in the children's euthanasia programme,[10] with some of these deaths taking place *after* Germany's unconditional surrender. Many more were killed as part of the wider 'T-4' programme that is described below.

For adult incurables, Bouhler and Brandt set up a secret-service-style operation to ensure that everything ran smoothly. The headquarters were in a villa at Tiergartenstrasse 4 in central Berlin; hence, the operation became known as T-4. Bouhler and Brandt's first task was the recruitment of personnel. Initially they turned to friends and students of the senior T-4 officials, who learned of the new operation through word of mouth. Others were recruited from the wider medical profession, because this was to be mass murder disguised as medical procedure. Finally, police officers and SS men joined the operation to perform the actual killing. One such was Franz Stangl.

Stangl was an Austrian policeman and National Socialist Party member who was summoned to Berlin by Himmler. His superior, Detective Werner, told him what he would be required to do in his new role:

> Werner told me that it had been decided to assign me to a very difficult and demanding job. He said that both Russia and America had for some considerable time had a law which permitted them to carry out euthanasia – 'mercy-killings' – on people who were hopelessly deformed. He said this law was going to be passed in Germany – as everywhere else in the civilised world – in the near future. But that, to protect the sensibilities of the population, they were going to do it very slowly, only after a great deal of psychological preparation. But that in the meantime the difficult task had begun, under the cloak of absolute secrecy. He explained that the only patients affected were those who, after the most careful examination – a series of four tests carried out by at least two physicians – were considered absolutely incurable

so that, he assured me, a totally painless death represented a
real release from what, more often than not, was an intoler-
able life.[11]

After receiving this explanation, Stangl accepted the new position
and became a 'security officer' at Hartheim Castle, one of the main
killing centres of the euthanasia programme. He was one of a
number of SS personnel who joined T-4. Around Christmas 1939,
SS-Sergeant August Becker, a professional chemist, was sent to
meet SS-Senior Leader Viktor Brack, who had been an SS and
party member since 1929 and had been working for Bouhler since
1932. Brack, who would later become the day-to-day administrator of T-4, explained that all incurable 'idiots' and mental
patients were to be eliminated from Germany. It had already been
agreed that the best means to achieve this was poison gas, so the
acting head of the chemistry department of the Criminal Technical
Institute of Kripo, Dr Albert Widmann, had been asked to find a
suitable agent.

This was a highly significant development. In effect, the SS was
preparing to implement National Socialist ideology: Himmler had
taken it upon himself and his organisation to 'improve' the
German race. He conceived of the SS as the *Staatsschutzkorps*
(state protection corps), whose role had previously been to protect
the state against external and internal ideological enemies. Now it
also included protecting Germany against biological enemies.

Widmann had decided that the best poison for his purposes
was carbon monoxide, so fifty steel canisters were dispatched to
IG Farben in Ludwigshafen and filled with the gas. These were
then transported to the former castle of the dukes of Württemberg at Grafeneck, which was being used as an asylum by the
Evangelical (Protestant) Church in Stuttgart. The building was
requisitioned from the church in October 1939, and shortly
afterwards a group of ten SS NCOs who had been seconded
from Death's Head units arrived. They were dressed in civilian
clothes and were supposedly working for the *Gemeinnutzige*

Stiftung fur Anstaltspflege (Charitable Foundation for Institutional Care) – T-4's cover designation. Using local craftsmen and labourers, the unit quickly began the process of turning the castle into an extermination centre: they converted an old coach shed into a gas chamber and installed two crematorium furnaces in a nearby hut.

In mid-January 1940, the gassing process was tested at the old prison in Brandenburg, near Berlin. Among the spectators were Widmann, Brack, Brandt, and a former Stuttgart detective, Christian Wirth – a coarse bully who had been selected as head of administration at the Hartheim killing centre, near Linz, Austria.*
A group of fifteen to twenty naked men were escorted into the gas chamber and sealed in, and then either Becker or Widmann released the carbon monoxide. Within a few minutes, all of the men were dead. Later that day, Widmann injected eight men with scopolamine and curare, two highly toxic paralysing agents, but these failed to kill the men, so all eight were placed in the gas chamber to be murdered. A further gassing was then carried out, this time with Dr Irmfried Eberl operating the controls.

In the weeks following these tests, Becker travelled to the other killing centres to demonstrate installation and operation of the equipment. Perversely, considering that this process was as far removed from medical treatment as it was possible to get, Brack decreed that only qualified doctors should be allowed to turn on the gas.

As with the children's euthanasia project, the murder of adult incurables remained entirely extra-legal, and it was carried out by deception and subterfuge. In September 1939, the Reich Doctors' Leader, Leonardo Conti, had written to all public and private asylums in Germany, requesting general statistical information and asking them to register all patients who were '(1) suffering from

---

* In addition to Hartheim and Brandenburg, the other major T-4 killing centres were at Hadamar in Hesse, Sonnenstein in Saxony, Grafeneck in Baden-Württemberg and Bernburg in Saxony-Anhalt.

schizophrenia, epilepsy, senile dementia, therapy-resistant paralysis, feeblemindedness, encephalitis and Huntington's Chorea, who were incapable of anything other than purely mechanical work; (2) patients who had been in the asylums for more than five years; (3) the criminally insane, foreign nationals and "racial aliens"'.[12] This last group is worth noting, because the simple fact of being Jewish overrode any medical considerations: virtually every Jew within the German asylum system was murdered during the course of the first year of T-4 in 1940.

The recipients of Conti's letter were told that the registration process was 'economic planning', and most hospital, asylum and clinic directors accepted this at face value. They assumed that the government was merely trying to identify additional sources of labour from among their patients. Tragically, this led some doctors to exaggerate some of their more able patients' symptoms in the misguided belief that this would save them from being used as forced labour. Of course, in reality, it served as a death sentence.

Once the completed forms had been returned to T-4, they were copied before being sent on to 'expert referees' for scrutiny. Again, each form supposedly required three referees to agree before the victim was marked for death. However, the referees were each expected to process some 3,500 cases per month, in addition to their normal duties, so it is highly unlikely that they gave any of the forms more than a cursory glance. Nevertheless, they were paid 400 marks a month for their time. Each and every form was then supposedly checked by Professor Werner Heyde, the senior referee, before the lists of victims were passed on to the Patients' Community Transport Service – T-4's transport fleet, driven by SS men in civilian clothes. They collected the patients from their 'home' asylums and took them either to a 'transit' asylum or directly to one of the killing centres. Even at this stage, the medical pretence was maintained. Typically, when the victims arrived, they were met by doctors, nurses and orderlies in medical garb and taken to changing rooms, where they were stripped, sometimes photographed, and given a further cursory examination, often to ascertain whether their corpses might be used later for scientific dissection or autopsy. Only when all this had been done were they led into gas chambers disguised as shower rooms. The doors were then sealed and the carbon monoxide was released to kill them.

This method of killing was anything but 'merciful' or 'humane'. Acute carbon monoxide poisoning typically causes headache, dizziness, nausea, confusion and convulsions, and even at relatively high concentrations death is unlikely to occur before fifteen or twenty minutes have elapsed. Usually, the victims were left in the gas chambers for an hour to ensure that they were all dead before extractor fans were turned on and the bodies were removed by teams of 'burners' (or 'disinfectors', as they termed themselves). Any gold teeth were extracted before he corpses were carted to nearby furnaces for cremation. Later, an urn of ashes was sent to each victim's family (of course, any ashes would do, as far as the killing centres were concerned), together with a letter of condolence and a death certificate that gave a plausible cause of death.

Notwithstanding all of this deception, T-4's attempts to keep the programme secret were doomed to failure almost as soon as it got under way. When the first group of patients left the asylum at Kaufbeuren-Irsee for Grafeneck, few of the asylum staff suspected that their charges were about to be executed. However, a few days later, the victims' clothing and personal effects – stained with vomit, blood and faeces – were returned to the asylum. The medical staff instantly guessed what had happened to them, and word soon spread among the rest of the staff and the patients about the true destination of the grey buses. This pattern was repeated in all of the other asylums. Scared patients often tried to hide when the transports arrived and physically resisted being loaded aboard. Some were then manacled to their seats to stop them escaping. This should come as no surprise. Although National Socialist propaganda attempted to portray incurable psychiatric patients as frightening, sub-human monsters, in reality only a small minority could not comprehend what was happening to them. And many of the groups that were targeted – such as epileptics and paralytics – were not reason-impaired at all. At least one of the eighty or so patients who were forced on to the second transport from Kaufbeuren-Irsee asked for a priest so he could make his final confession.

Word of what was happening also spread in the localities of the killing centres as the personnel talked freely in pubs and cafés. And, of course, the local residents saw the buses arriving, followed shortly afterwards by smoke and fumes from the crematoria chimneys. It was so obvious what was going on that railway workers at Grafeneck removed their hats out of respect as transport trains passed through their station.

Furthermore, some of the victims' families knew that the authorities were lying to them. Inevitably, mistakes were made by the administrators, so, for example, a sister might be told that her brother had died of acute appendicitis, even though he'd had an appendectomy fifteen years before. But even more importantly, the vast majority of the incurables were much-loved sons and daughters, brothers and sisters, mothers and fathers. Their families genuinely cared for them, were concerned about their fate and did not want them arbitrarily killed at the whim of the state. Therefore, as the death toll grew, so did resistance to the euthanasia programme. This reached surprisingly vociferous levels, given that it took place in Hitler's Germany.

At first glance, this might be interpreted as an indication of pure compassion among the citizens of the Third Reich; as evidence that they were not prepared to accept the wholesale slaughter of innocent people purely because they were different from the rest of society. However, before drawing this conclusion, it should be remembered that there were no comparable demonstrations when the extermination of the Jews got under way. And there is nothing to suggest that the general population of Germany held particularly enlightened views about how the disabled and the mentally ill should be treated. In fact, they seemed to take issue with the manner in which the killing was carried out, rather than with the killing itself: no law had been passed to authorise the programme; relatives were not informed of the victim's true fate; and the process appeared to have no rules. It may well have been the arbitrary nature of the programme that caused most concern, with many people understanding that anybody might need psychiatric treatment at some point in their life or might suffer an injury that leaves them permanently disabled. This would have been especially appreciated in Germany in 1940, because so many people had been through the horrors of the First World War and had seen friends and family members wounded or struck down by 'shell-shock'.*

Whatever it was that motivated the protesters, they made their voices heard. Some organised rallies outside the killing centres. Others took their concerns directly to the asylums and managed to extricate their relatives from the clutches of T-4. Others, ironically, petitioned Hitler through the Führer Chancellery, not realising that this organisation was orchestrating the whole project. However, the most effective protests came from members of the Catholic Church. Foremost among these was the Bishop of Münster, Clemens August Graf von Galen.

Von Galen was a member of an old aristocratic family – ultra-conservative, snobbish, racist and reactionary. A Jesuit, he had long publicly opposed the National Socialist regime, but principally because he thought it was led by social upstarts and foreigners. He first received information about T-4 as early as July 1940, but was dissuaded from denouncing the project by Cardinal Bertram, the Archbishop of Breslau. However, the following year, the Gestapo seized Jesuit property in Münster and von Galen decided to act. On 3 August, he delivered a ferocious sermon from his pulpit in the Lambertikirche, which concluded:

---

* There is little concrete evidence that German soldiers were killed in the euthanasia programme, but it does appear to have happened. At the trial of a T-4 nurse in 1948, it was alleged that she had given lethal injections to soldiers who had gone 'mad' during the winter of 1941–42.

We are not dealing with machines, horses and cows whose only function is to serve mankind, to produce goods for man. One may smash them, one may slaughter them as soon as they no longer fulfil this function. No, we are dealing with human beings, our fellow human beings, our brothers and sisters. With poor people, sick people, if you like, unproductive people. But have they forfeited the right to life? Have you, have I the right to life only so long as we are productive, so long as we are recognised by others as productive?[13]

The sermon attracted attention both outside and inside Germany. It was reported by the BBC and in British newspapers, and transcripts were dropped by the RAF as propaganda pamphlets.*

Other representatives of the Catholic Church had been in secret negotiations to stop the killings since late 1940, but von Galen's open denunciation spurred further public criticism. The disquiet reached such a pitch that even Himmler recommended that the killings should be stopped. Later in August 1941, Hitler duly ordered Brandt to call a 'temporary' halt to the killings. However, by that stage, more than seventy thousand victims had already been murdered, and T-4 had almost achieved its original goal of killing one 'incurable' patient for every thousand of the general population. So it seems likely that, rather than being swayed by public opinion, Hitler merely thought that this particular project had reached its conclusion.

Furthermore, although the centrally organised killing of psychiatric patients was now wound down, the euthanasia programme *per se* did not end. The children's programme continued, T-4 still collected data and registered 'incurables', and the killing centres at Bernburg, Sonnenstein and Hartheim remained open.† Now,

---

* Von Galen's status and popularity among the devout meant that the regime was wary of moving against him, but he was kept under virtual house arrest until the end of the war.
† Brandenburg and Grafeneck ceased operation.

though, they focused on the sick from the original concentration camps. Although the latter were models of brutality, where the murder of inmates was routine, they were not equipped for mass killing.

The killing of concentration camp prisoners was organised by 'Operation 14 f 13', a name derived from the code used by camp administrations for inmates who died in custody. (14 f 5 indicated a prisoner killed while trying to escape; 14 f 8 a prisoner who committed suicide; 14 f 14 an executed prisoner, and so on.) From mid-1941, T-4 doctors toured the camps and made selections from preliminary lists of prisoners that had been drawn up by the SS camp administrators. This meant that the T-4 extermination net started to spread wider, because, in addition to the sick, these lists of those deemed unable to work included: antisocials (defined as 'human beings with a hereditary and irreversible mental attitude who, due to this nature, incline towards alcoholism and immorality, have repeatedly come into conflict with government agencies and the courts and thus appear unrestrained and a threat to humanity'[14]); political prisoners; criminals; and Jews.

The launch of 14 f 13 caused some problems for the SS. By March 1942, the Inspectorate of Concentration Camps had seen such a decline in the number of prisoners available for work that it ordered the camps to select for extermination only those who were *genuinely* unfit.[15] Nevertheless, by the next year, the labour shortage was still so acute that Himmler ordered the end of 14 f 13. Thereafter, the killing would be confined only to inmates with mental problems who could be dealt with within the camps themselves. The gas chambers at Bernburg and Sonnenstein were duly dismantled. The Hartheim killing centre continued to operate until December 1944, primarily to murder prisoners from the nearby Mauthausen concentration camp. These victims were selected by the camp authorities, without any involvement of T-4 staff.

Adult euthanasia, however, continued on a decentralised basis, in a similar way to the children's programme, with a number of doctors authorised to kill selected patients in designated hospitals. As with the children, the adult victims were starved or overdosed until a fatal condition was induced, then cremated to destroy the evidence. Finally, a bogus death certificate was issued. According to Henry Friedlander: 'In fact, more victims of euthanasia perished after [Hitler's] stop order than before.'[16] Long-term mentally ill patients from the asylum system continued to be murdered, but now the victims also included many Germans who had more recently succumbed to mental illness under the pressure of Allied bombing raids and other aspects of the war, as well as foreign labourers who had been conscripted into the service of the Third Reich from the occupied territories of Europe. Any forced labourer who became sick – either physically or mentally – was vulnerable: they were only in Germany to provide labour at minimal cost, so their long-term medical care was deemed economically prohibitive. Consequently, if their condition suggested they would not make a speedy recovery, they were killed.

The sterilisation and euthanasia programmes are key elements in the history of the SS, even though the organisation itself played only a supporting role in them. Ever since details of the programmes first came to light, sociologists have attempted to explain how so many members of the medical profession – traditionally regarded as an essentially altruistic group – were so quickly and easily converted into enthusiastic mass murderers. Partly, it seems, they were stimulated by the idea of working in supposedly revolutionary times. The National Socialists constantly emphasised the need to 'improve' the German *Volk* and rid Germany of other races and associated 'inferior' elements. By taking part in the sterilisation and euthanasia operations, doctors and nurses placed themselves in the front line of this 'national improvement' project, which not only gave them a sense of importance and prestige, but allowed them to continue to believe in their own altruism: to their minds, they were no longer caring merely for individuals, but for the whole of German society.

More prosaically, they were materially rewarded for taking part. In addition to extra pay and allowances, they had access to, for example, a 'rest centre' at a castle near Salzburg, which provided meals that were not available to the heavily rationed ordinary people. Such VIP treatment contributed to their sense that they constituted an elite.

Even those with moral qualms about the programmes could manage to convince themselves that there was some scientific benefit from what they were doing. An unprecedented supply of corpses became available for dissection as a result of the euthanasia programme, and physicians were in the novel position of being able to combine clinical and pathological observations. In practice, this meant that doctors like Julius Hallervorden, of the Kaiser Wilhelm Institute for Brain Research in Berlin, would visit the killing centres and personally select individuals. Once they were killed, Hallervorden would remove their brains and take them back to Berlin for dissection.

The 'mercy killing' of the incurably ill still attracts adherents to this day. So, especially given the moral and ideological context of the Third Reich, it is scarcely surprising that well-educated, intelligent doctors and nurses became advocates of it. However, in reality, the overwhelming majority of the killings were far from merciful: gassing and starvation, the two principal means of death that were employed, inflicted great suffering on the victims. Moreover, as the programmes progressed, it is clear that those involved lost any moral compass they may previously have possessed.

This is well illustrated by the case of Dr Valentin Faltlhauser, director of the Kaufbeuren-Irsee asylum. In the early 1930s, Faltlhauser was a leading figure in the renaissance of German psychiatry and a vocal opponent of euthanasia. However, his position began to change after the National Socialists took power. Soon, he became one of the regional experts in sterilisation. He appeared before the hereditary health courts and initiated sterilisation proceedings, and his theories changed to accommodate National

Socialism and eugenic thought. By the late 1930s, when funding for asylums and psychiatry was being drastically reduced, he was differentiating between those patients who could be cured and those who could not – directing resources towards the former at the expense of the latter. The euthanasia programme 'solved' many of his financial difficulties as an asylum director. And after Hitler's stop order, Faltlhauser was an enthusiastic advocate of differential diets – starving the incurable to death while feeding those who responded to treatment. His ultimate moral bankruptcy is revealed by the case of Ernst Losser.

Ernst's father was an itinerant pedlar who was classified as 'asocial' and sent to Dachau (he was suspected of being a gypsy), while Ernst himself and his two siblings were put into orphanages. But Ernst was poorly behaved at the orphanage – refusing to attend school and stealing from the other children – so at the age of ten or eleven he was referred to Kaufbeuren-Irsee for psychiatric evaluation. The psychiatrist took the view that Ernst could not be changed by education, and recommended that he should be transferred to the children's unit at Kaufbeuren, even though he had neither psychiatric problems nor learning difficulties.

The transfer was duly made, and the staff at Kaufbeuren soon grew fond of Ernst: he responded much better to adult company, was friendly and liked to play. At least one member of staff even went so far as to take him home for the weekend, because they felt he should never have been in the asylum in the first place.

Before long, Ernst discovered that many of the patients at the asylum were being starved, so he started to sneak down to the kitchens at night to steal food – bread, apples and other staples – and then distributed them to the grateful inmates. When this came to the attention of Faltlhauser and the other psychiatrists, they determined that Ernst was a 'bad character' and decided to eliminate him. A T-4 nurse was instructed to carry out the killing. Ernst was too streetwise to drink coffee laced with sedatives, but he was eventually given a lethal injection after being woken up in the middle of the night. He was dead within a few hours.

Faltlhauser was also responsible for the last death in the euthanasia programme. Four-year-old Richard Jenne was killed at Kaufbeuren on 29 May 1945, twenty-one days after Germany's unconditional surrender and thirty-three days after United States troops had occupied the local area. The Americans had not occupied the hospital because they had been warned that it might contain typhus patients, so Faltlhauser and his staff had simply got on with their work.

Faltlhauser was a well-educated, intellectual, previously moralistic doctor who became a remorseless mass killer in the context of the Third Reich; and he was far from the only member of the medical establishment to follow this path. Such men and women were easily persuaded that euthanasia and sterilisation were not only acceptable but positively desirable, so it should come as little surprise that much less sophisticated, 'ordinary' people were willing to staff the concentration camps, special task groups, police battalions and extermination camps that carried out the Holocaust. The propaganda that convinced the doctors they were doing the right thing worked just as well – if not better – on the camp guards.

The euthanasia programme also provided the SS with the technical expertise that would soon be used in the extermination of the Jews. Even as the first victims of T-4 were being gassed, large numbers of Jews – and other supposed enemies of Germany – were being shot by SS special task groups in German-occupied Poland. This was time-consuming, manpower-intensive and stressful for the killers, so an alternative, more efficient means of mass murder was sought, and the euthanasia programme pointed the way. To a large extent, the procedures that had been used in the killing of the mentally ill were applied without adaptation in the killing of Jews. For instance, the gas chambers at Grafeneck and at Auschwitz were disguised as shower rooms for precisely the same reason – to try to preserve order among those who were about to be murdered. Moreover, many of the personnel from the T-4 killing centres were subsequently redeployed to the death camps: for instance, Christian Wirth, Franz Stangl and Irmfried Eberl all had roles in the extermination centres on the River Bug.

There is one final parallel between the euthanasia programme and the Holocaust. There can be little doubt that the former was a long-held dream of Adolf Hitler: he discussed eugenic measures in *Mein Kampf*, and mentioned the subject on several occasions in the late 1920s and 1930s. However, the only practical measure he took towards implementing it was to secretly authorise 'mercy killings' in October 1939. Partly this was because he feared a public backlash (in Germany as much as abroad) if he were ever to legalise euthanasia. For similar reasons, while he maintained a bitter hatred of the Jewish people and certainly welcomed their annihilation as a race, any instructions that he gave for the commencement of the extermination programme were kept entirely secret.*

---

* Some participants in the Holocaust, such as Eichmann, have claimed that Hitler did give such an order and indeed that they saw it on paper. But no documentary evidence has ever been found to prove these claims.

13

Origins of the Waffen-SS

The combat history of the Waffen-SS – the armed military units of the SS – has been recounted in numerous books since the early 1960s. These have ranged from scholarly, exhaustively researched accounts at one end of the scale to schoolboyish hagiographies at the other. However, the background story of the Waffen-SS still remains shrouded in myth and misconception. For some, this organisation was nothing more than an integral part of the apparatus that murdered millions of Jews, gypsies, Poles, Russians and others. On the other hand, there is a band of enthusiasts who argue that the Waffen-SS was a superb military elite, a fourth – superior – branch of the German armed forces that was barely related to the killers of the concentration camps, special task groups and extermination centres, with whom it merely shared administrative arrangements.

In part, this dispute stems from a continuing misapprehension about what the Waffen-SS really was and its complex relationships with the NSDAP, the state and the armed forces. Some of this misapprehension can be addressed fairly easily. The Waffen-SS was certainly not a military elite: in all, roughly 900,000 men served within its ranks during the course of the war in some 38 divisional-sized combat formations, many regimental- and brigade-sized units, and numerous smaller units and sub-units. The leadership, training, equipment and tactical effectiveness of these formations varied from excellent to abysmal. Some of its longer-established formations – primarily composed of native German volunteers and led by men who had been through officer training school – were of a very high standard indeed: the likes of the *Das Reich* and *Totenkopf* divisions were among the most effective field formations the Germans had, be it in the regular army or the SS. However, the Kossovar-Albanian *Skanderbeg* Division and the *Weissruthenisch* (Byelorussian) 'volunteers' of the Waffen-SS 30th Grenadier Division were of such dubious loyalty and utility that they barely functioned as fighting units. Most German members of the Waffen-SS and some volunteers from the occupied territories saw themselves as part of a *corps d'élite* – as was expected within the SS's ideological framework – but this was as much racial/political as it was military. Himmler was keen to establish an effective fighting force, but he was much more interested in the SS's role in the rejuvenation of the Germanic/Nordic race. Consequently, racial and political criteria were given much more weight than military considerations in recruitment to the Waffen-SS.

Another myth is that the Waffen-SS did not participate in the Holocaust. During the war, *any* member of the SS could fulfil his obligatory national military service within the Waffen-SS[1] – without joining the army, navy or air force – and thousands did just that. So a member of the Waffen-SS was just as likely to be a guard at Auschwitz as he was to be a grenadier in the *Das Reich* Division. For instance, Rudolf Höss, commandant of Auschwitz from May 1940 to November 1943, held his rank in the Waffen-SS, not in one of the other branches of the SS.[2]

Occasionally, distinctions are drawn between the combat formations of the Waffen-SS and other parts of the organisation. For instance, one former Waffen-SS regimental commander wrote: 'Formations such as the Dirlewanger unit and the Guard Battalions of the Concentration Camps were not considered to be fighting troops and their inclusion in the Waffen-SS was [merely] a matter of administrative convenience.'[3] However, this is completely spurious. Waffen-SS formations serving in the front line came under the operational command of the *Wehrmacht* (German Armed Forces), but these same units were subordinated to the SS-Leadership Main Office when they were not in the combat zone. This was as true of the elite *Leibstandarte* Adolf Hitler as it was of a humble disciplinary unit like Dirlewanger's. (See Chapter 19 for details of Dirlewanger.) The difference was simply one of duration: the major combat divisions were in demand at the front in a way that the lesser units were not, and thus spent more time under conventional military command.

On the other hand, Waffen-SS units are often accused of committing more battlefield atrocities than their conventional army counterparts. This should be treated with scepticism, but that should not disguise the fact the Waffen-SS committed numerous war crimes, most notably against prisoners of war and civilians. For instance, in May 1940, members of the *Leibstandarte* Adolf Hitler – then a motorised regiment – murdered around eighty British Army prisoners near Calais. Around the same time, members of the Death's Head Division massacred ninety-seven members of the 2nd Royal Norfolks. (See Chapter 18 for further details of both of these war crimes.) These were terrible atrocities, but so were those committed by the German Army. For instance, 140 civilians were murdered by the 225th Division at Vinkt, Belgium, and hundreds of disarmed prisoners of war were killed by army units during the Polish campaign of 1939. Later, in September 1943, at least five thousand disarmed and defenceless Italian soldiers were murdered on the Greek island of Cephalonia by members of the army's supposedly elite Mountain Infantry.*

---

* This incident features in the novel and film *Captain Corelli's Mandolin*. A further four thousand prisoners subsequently died when the ships transporting them from Cephalonia struck mines and sank.

So how did the German Army retain its reputation for battle-field decency while the Waffen-SS was deservedly castigated for all of its atrocities? The answer is fairly straightforward. In the aftermath of the Second World War, the army's war crimes were downplayed and even trivialised by *all* sides for political reasons. The newly created Federal and Democratic republics (West and East Germany, respectively) both needed to establish functioning armed forces and both needed to recruit former officers and NCOs of the *Wehrmacht* to lead them. Under these circumstances, it was convenient to imply (if not outright declare) that the vast majority of war crimes had been committed by the Waffen-SS – an organisation that was already beyond redemption because of its involvement in the Holocaust. In reality, the Waffen-SS and the German Army were both guilty of war crimes, as each was a component of the National Socialist state's machinery of war.

Notwithstanding this, in many respects, the Waffen-SS was unique. First and foremost, it was a primarily military force created out of a primarily political organisation. As we have seen, the SS was founded to protect the leadership of the NSDAP, and many aspects of its expansion after the National Socialists came to power can be viewed as logical extensions of this role. The creation of the Sipo, the concentration camps and central control of policing were all understandable adjuncts to the activities of a security-obsessed, violently inclined political organisation that had achieved absolute power.

However, the creation of a relatively small military force to operate in parallel to the conventional armed forces is less easy to explain. At the time, the government claimed that military intervention was inappropriate for many internal security tasks, so it needed a new, politically controlled force to deal with them. This is unconvincing: when the new units were set up, any physical threat from political opponents of the NSDAP was little more than a distant memory, while dissenters within the National Socialist movement itself had long since been purged. Furthermore, by then, the SS had acquired complete control over the regular, uniformed police. Equally, the armed SS units never rivalled the strength of the regular armed forces, so it seems unlikely that they were established to counter the threat of a coup. Indeed, in 1944, when elements within the army did attempt to seize power, all agencies of the SS – armed and otherwise – proved powerless to intervene. Rather, it was left to other army units to come to Hitler's aid. According to Gottlob Berger, the guiding force of the Waffen-SS towards the end of the war, the army originally treated the idea of an armed SS force with contempt. He quoted *Generalfeldmarschall* (Field Marshal) von Fritsch, Commander-in-Chief of the Army, as remarking: 'If the Reichs Transport Minister has his militarily trained Railway Police, why shouldn't Himmler also play at soldiers?'[4] This is perhaps the most accurate explanation for why the military SS units were created: they gave Himmler the opportunity to indulge in the type of military career that had eluded him as a young man. He wanted the SS to take a pioneering role in the colonisation and 'Germanisation' of the conquered lands in the East, but it seems he never seriously envisaged the Waffen-SS supplanting the army. According to Berger, the intention was to reduce the strength of the Waffen-SS after the war to seven full-strength divisions and five reserve, or 'cadre', formations. Three of the regular divisions would be formed from non-German nationals: *Das Reich* from ethnic Germans from South-East Europe; *Germania* from ethnic Germans from elsewhere in the world; and *Wiking* from other Germanic races.[5]

No matter what Himmler's future plans for the organisation may have been, the creation of a new, modern military force from scratch was a daunting task. However, he and his subordinates had the advantage of being able to use the proven and highly successful German military system as a template. Between 1934 and 1945, they created a parallel recruiting, training and logistics system, with its own officer-training schools, NCO schools and combat arms schools; hospitals; procurement, manufacture, research and development establishments; and even operational headquarters up to army level. All of this was separate from the established armed forces, and, to some extent, put the SS in competition with the regular army for funding and manpower. As the Waffen-SS continued to grow throughout the war, it demanded resources that could have been utilised by the conventional armed forces, In so doing, it became an entirely self-imposed limitation on Germany's ability to wage total war.

The Waffen-SS had its origins in the formation of full-time, armed SS units in the wake of the National Socialist assumption of power in January 1933. As we have seen, the Reichstag Fire Decree enabled Hitler's coalition government to suspend human rights, and two months later the Enabling Act gave him the power to rule by decree without reference to the Reichstag. However, despite holding this unprecedented degree of power, Hitler remained anxious about his position. On 17 March 1933, he ordered Sepp Dietrich – who had been commanding the SS-Group North in Hamburg – to set up an armed SS guard unit in Berlin, similar to the troop that already protected him when he was in Munich. Dietrich recruited some 120 volunteers, primarily loyalists who were personally known to him from SS-Regiment 1 in Munich, to form what was initially called 'SS-Staff Guard Dietrich' before being renamed 'SS-Special Unit Berlin'. They quartered themselves in the barracks of the old cadet school at Berlin-Lichterfelde* and provided armed guard details for Hitler inside his offices at the Chancellery. (For the time being, members of the regular army remained on guard outside the Chancellery building.) Although a party organisation, from September 1933 they received their pay from the Prussian Ministry of the Interior and were under the disciplinary and administrative jurisdiction of the Berlin Police President. Immediate command authority for all of their activities outside the Chancellery came from the Lichterfelde garrison commander, Police Lieutenant Colonel Wecke.

---

* This building is now the headquarters of the Berlin branch of the German Federal Archives.

During the Nuremberg National Socialist Party rally of September 1933, Hitler renamed the unit the *Leibstandarte* Adolf Hitler; and on the tenth anniversary of the Munich *Putsch* on 9 November, its members swore a personal oath of loyalty to him. By then, the unit had been granted the status of a special organisation, still separate from but with a comparable status to the army.[6] At the time, few people noticed that all of this had effectively created an armed force whose loyalty was not to the state, nor even to the head of state, but to the leader of a political party. Even Himmler, the National Leader of the SS, was cut out of this particular loop.

While the *Leibstandarte* was being formed in Berlin, local National Socialist organisations were mobilising their SA and SS contingents as auxiliaries. SS units of company strength and below – armed with privately owned weapons – acquired the status of *Sonderkommandos* (special units), while larger formations were termed *Politische Bereitschäfte* (political readiness units). These formed up in Hamburg, Dresden, Munich, Ellwangen, Arolsen and many other towns and cities,[7] where they operated as auxiliary police squads assigned to intimidate the National Socialists' political opponents – notwithstanding the fact that, by then, almost all physical opposition to the ruling regime had already been eliminated. Meanwhile, other armed, full-time squads were created to act as guards at the newly established detention centres and concentration camps. The political readiness units were not particularly large at this stage: for instance, SS-Regiment 1's political readiness unit in Munich could call on only two hundred men in 1934.[8] Nor were they particularly controversial in the context of 1930s Germany: as we have seen, squads of armed toughs had been doing the dirty work of the state ever since the end of the First World War.

However, this began to change on the Night of the Long Knives – 30 June 1934. The majority of the killings on that night and throughout the following week were undertaken by political readiness units, especially the *Leibstandarte*, which provided the firing squad in Stadelheim Prison. Their reward came on 26 July, when Hitler declared that the SS was now an independent organisation within the NSDAP. This was followed by his directive that the organisation should press ahead with the creation of 'a politically dependable SS security force, distinct from the army, upon which he could call for prompt action in times of stress or crisis for the protection of the German people and the State'.[9] After discussions in September between Himmler and the Ministry of Defence, a directive was issued on the 24th by Defence Minister General von Blomberg, setting out the organisational structure of the new armed force – the SS-Special Purpose Troops. The directive also stated that they were to be recruited from members of the political readiness units.

As originally envisaged, the force was to comprise three regiments that would be organised, equipped and manned in the same way as regular army infantry regiments, together with a separate signals battalion. (In December 1934, it was decided to add a reconnaissance battalion, based in Satzweld, and an engineering battalion, based in Dresden, to this order of battle.) Training and logistical support were to be provided by the army (which would be reimbursed by the SS); pay would be provided by the Ministry of the Interior, and would follow the appropriate military scales. An official decree issued by Hitler on 2 February 1935 gave these arrangements legal force, and further explained that the Special Purpose Troops would be organised into a division in time of war – with a divisional headquarters, artillery and 'divisional troops' supplied by the regular army. This decree also specified that the concentration camp guards of the Death's Head units were to receive military training under the supervision of the Ministry of Defence.

The command relationships within the Special Purpose Troops in peacetime were complex. Military training and organisation were the responsibilities of the army, through local military district and garrison commanders, but non-military matters were handled by the regional SS command system. In wartime, everything was to be placed under army control.

While all of this was being clarified, Himmler took the opportunity to establish the status of each branch of his organisation.[10]
Henceforth, the SS would consist of three distinct elements: the
Special Purpose Troops (including the *Leibstandarte*), which
would be the organisation's full-time military force; the guard
units (later the Death's Head units), comprising concentration
camp guards and other specialised guard and security details; and
the *Allgemeine-SS* (General-SS), consisting of 'all former active SS
units not quartered in barracks'[11] – in effect, members of the old
political SS who had largely political duties. With this established,
Himmler's primary task was to find volunteers for the new military branch. The *Leibstandarte* and the political readiness units
had originally been staffed from the General-SS, but the creation
of the Special Purpose Troops had added a new element: service
in either them or the *Leibstandarte* would now fulfil an individual's obligation to perform national military service. Clearly, this
required a different type of man from the typical SS political
bruiser, but the principle of strict selectivity in recruitment would
still apply. The key stipulations were that applicants had to be
under twenty-three years of age and prepared to enlist for five
years. They also had to be at least 1.7 metres tall and must not
need spectacles. On application, they had to show their eligibil-
ity for military service by presenting their defence registration
number, as well as a certificate of medical fitness, a police reference or a copy of their police record and a reference from a
previous employer. Finally, they had to draw up a family tree to
prove their 'Aryan' ancestry. At this stage, applicants from the
General-SS were permitted to transfer into the Special Purpose
Troops and retain their existing rank or grade. The application
criteria were made a little stricter the next year, when the minimum height was increased to 1.74 metres. Furthermore, members
of the General-SS could no longer take their rank with them if
they joined the Special Purpose Troops. On the other hand, the
enlistment period was reduced to four years.

In December 1936, the selection criteria were reviewed yet

again. The 'Leaflet for Enlistment in the SS-Special Purpose Troops and Death's Head Units' issued the following guidelines:

SS-Special Purpose Troops volunteers to report for recruiting for the spring entry by 31 Oct the previous year; and for the autumn entry by 30 April.

SS-Death's Head units volunteers can report at any time of year.

All applicants must be:
- German nationals.
- Able to prove Aryan ancestry back to 1800.
- Morally, spiritually, physically and racially problem free, of basic National Socialist outlook and must have a strong desire for SS service.
- Free of any criminal record (with the exception of crimes committed on behalf of the movement).
- Unmarried.

Minimum period of service in the SS-Special Purpose Troops: 4 years; SS-Death's Head units: 1 year.

Minimum heights:
- *Leibstandarte*: 1.78m
- Foot units: 1.74m
- Pioneer, signals and music units; SS-Death's Head units: 1.72m

Minimum ages:
- SS-Special Purpose Troops: completed 17th year.
- SS-Death's Head units: completed 16th year.

Maximum ages:
- SS-Special Purpose Troops: completed 23rd year.
- SS-Death's Head units: completed 23rd year.

Compulsory Labour Service: All SS-Special Purpose Troops recruits must have completed it; SS-Death's Head units recruits must have either completed it or been discharged from it.

The first two years of service in the SS-Special Purpose Troops constitutes compulsory military service but volunteers for the SS-Death's Head units must still fulfil their military obligations in the SS-Special Purpose Troops or the *Wehrmacht*.

Younger volunteers may join with the written permission of their parents.

Dental examination is necessary before joining.

Spectacle wearers may not join.

Applicants may follow an officer career. After a successful first year, candidates may be sent to an SS officer school for 1 year. Officer careers are open to every member of the SS.

NCO candidates have the opportunity of a 12-year career.

SS-Special Purpose Troops members have all the benefits of a *Wehrmacht* career (subsequent service in the police, etc.); Death's Head units members are paid under the SS system and will be cared for if they receive any service injury.

Anyone not fulfilling the requirements for SS membership but who is a member of an NSDAP organisation may volunteer for service in the Regiment General Goering.[*][12]

Seven years later, in a speech to naval officers, Himmler famously remarked: 'Until 1936, we did not accept a man in the *Leibstandarte* or Special Purpose Troops if he had even one filled tooth. We were able to assemble the most magnificent manhood in the early Waffen-SS.'[13] This was an exaggeration: the stringent conditions set by Himmler were unsustainable and they simply had to be relaxed. In December 1938 he issued the following instruction:

* This was a militarised unit of the Prussian Police, rather than the similarly named Luftwaffe unit created some years later.

In the coming years we cannot completely enforce the health standards for SS applicants as, in their childhood and youth during the emergency of the Weimar Republic, they will have suffered and starved. So:

- Six or fewer dental cavities or faults are not grounds for rejection.
- Poor posture, shortness and muscular faults caused by rickets or malnutrition are not decisive for rejection.
- Spectacles up to 4 dioptres are acceptable, as is astigmatism.

Minimum heights:

	General-SS	Death's Head units	Special Purpose Troops
17 years	1.65m	1.67m	1.69m
18 years	1.66m	1.68m	1.70m
19 years	1.68m	1.70m	1.72m
20 years	1.69m	1.71m	1.73m
21 years	1.70m	1.72m	1.74m[14]

As the war continued, all pretence at maintaining even these standards was abandoned outside of high-profile, specialised units such as Hitler's *Kommando* escort. In practice, the physical criterion for SS membership was essentially reduced to no more than basic medical fitness.

14

Militarising the 'Political Soldiers'

The armed SS units required officers at all levels. In the early days, these were primarily SS members with experience of low-level command in the German Army or the Free Corps – men like Sepp Dietrich, who had been a sergeant major in the Tank Regiment and a police NCO. However, to create a credible force, an injection of higher-level military talent was required, so Himmler began the process of recruiting senior officers. Of course, like their subordinates, all of these men had to display a suitable outlook.

The most important of these officer recruits was Paul Hausser, born in 1880 to an aristocratic Prussian family. He joined the German Army as a cadet in 1892 and graduated from Lichterfelde to become an infantry officer in 1899. In the 1900s, he attended the Prussian *Kriegsakademie* (War College) and was selected for the General Staff – the true elite of the German Army. He was promoted to captain shortly before the outbreak of the First World War.

Hausser's war record was steady rather than spectacular. He served on the staffs of a number of formations, as well as on Prince Rupprecht of Bavaria's personal staff, and was a major by the time of the armistice. Thereafter, he briefly commanded an infantry regiment and border-defence units along Germany's east-ern frontier before joining the newly constituted, post-Versailles 100,000-man army. His career continued in its unspectacular fashion: after a series of promotions, he reached the rank of major general in 1931. The next year, according to Hausser's SS file, political differences with the army forced his resignation. He left with the honorary rank (and pension) of a lieutenant general.

Hausser then became a regional leader for the broadly nation-alist *Stahlhelm* Old Comrades' Association. When this group was incorporated into the SA, he was happy to accept the 'reserve' rank of SA-colonel. A little later, when Himmler came looking for a suitable candidate to oversee the creation of an officer-training system for the SS, Hausser was equally happy to move across to the SS, which he did on 15 November 1934. He became member 239795, a number that reflected the startling growth of the SS since 1929.

The first SS officer-training school had already been set up by SS-Colonel Paul Lettow, a former army colonel and police tacti-cian, in the centre of the Bavarian town of Bad Tölz in October 1934. Hausser now established his school in a former castle of the dukes of Brunswick (Braunschweig). In the absence of experi-enced officers in the SS, he recruited the majority of his staff from former members of the army. A typical example was Fritz von Paris, born in Münster, Westphalia, in 1886. During the First World War, Captain von Paris had served in South-West Africa, where he was captured by the British Army in 1917. Later, he joined the Free Corps, but he showed no particular interest in pol-itics until he joined the SS as an officer in February 1934. As an SS-*Obersturmführer* (lieutenant), he was appointed *Taktiklehrer* (tactics instructor) at the Officer Cadet School Braunschweig on 1 February 1935.

The aim of the cadet schools was to produce flexible, adaptable officers who would be able to perform a role in any part of the SS, be it in a concentration camp, a combat unit, the police or the wider SS organisation. Thus, while the course concentrated on mobile small-unit tactics – raids, ambushes, patrols and so forth – the cadets gained a wider appreciation of all military planning and logistical issues. However, Richard Schulze, the last commander of the school at Bad Tölz, later claimed: 'in addition to the purely military training which occupied first place . . . great stress was laid upon training corresponding to the English educational ideals, which included character training, the most vital point being self-control, chivalry, decency, and love of truth, differing from the German ideal, which was based upon the pure acquisition of knowledge, often overlooking shortcomings in favour of this development'.[1] Hans Zech-Nenntwich, the Waffen-SS officer who defected to Britain in 1943, told his interrogators that 'both [cadet schools] are essentially professional, i.e. non-political, in atmosphere'.[2] Clearly this was not true – there was ideological instruction on the course and throughout the SS – but the intention was to create an atmosphere of professionalism that would motivate young German men to join the SS officer corps, and add to the prestige of the organisation in German society as a whole.

On average, the process of training an SS officer took about nineteen months. In a nod to National Socialist egalitarianism, candidates were supposedly identified within SS units on the basis of aptitude rather than social class or educational achievement (although, inevitably, recruits from the 'right' background were viewed as potential officers). In theory, this should have been an efficient way to select high-quality cadets; in practice, it was not. In 1940, an inspection of the officer schools suggested that as many as 40 per cent of the cadets were not fit for the role because of gaps in their education or basic military training as well as character failings.[3] Partly this was due to similar failings among the men who were selecting the cadets, the senior SS officers, who were often political appointees rather than experienced military leaders. As Bernd Wegner has pointed out, this was a typical situation within the SS: 'one the one hand, [it was] ideally suited, like no other branch of the regime, to break down social and educational barriers; on the other, [it was] debilitated by structural weaknesses anchored in their very beginnings'.[4]

The course normally consisted of approximately six months' basic training and probationary service in an SS-Special Purpose Troops or concentration camp unit, followed by ten months at Braunschweig or Bad Tölz. Exams were taken after four months and ten months, with failures returned to their units (the failure rate was usually 30 to 40 per cent). Finally, there would be two to three months' training within the individual cadet's specialist area at an SS or Army school.

A typical week of training might break down roughly as follows:

Tactics and manoeuvre (including map reading)	10 hours
Political education	5 hours
Weapons training	16 hours
Military affairs	3 hours
Practical training (target practice, tactics, instruction)	7 hours
Physical education	2 hours
Instruction in weapons	1 hour
Combat engineering	1 hour
Automotive mechanics	1 hour

Additionally, cadets were expected to use as much as one-third of their off-duty time in sport and physical recreation. They 'were required to ski, swim, sail, ride, fence, box and partake in organised track and field events',[5] and were encouraged to take part in an equally wide range of non-mandatory activities, all designed to produce the alert, fit, situationally aware officer who came to represent the SS ideal. As if to emphasise the 'English educational ideal', one of the sports offered at Bad Tölz was cricket.

Throughout their training, the cadets held NCO ranks, initially as SS-*Junker* (cadet corporal) until they had passed their first set of exams; then as SS-*Standartenjunker* (cadet sergeant) until they had passed their final exams; and finally as SS-*Standartenoberjunker* (cadet sergeant major) during their 'special-to-arm' training. If they were successful in this, in the pre-war and early war period a graduation ceremony was held in Munich on 9 November, when the cadets were commissioned with the rank of SS-*Untersturmführer* (second lieutenant) and presented with a ceremonial SS officer's dagger.

In total, with the notable exception of the ideological element, this course was entirely comparable with a modern officer-training syllabus. However, there was no attempt to combine military instruction with academic learning: in contrast to West Point in the United States or Duntroon in Australia, the SS schools were not degree-awarding institutions. Instead, they focused on practical elements. Requiring the cadets to serve a probationary period in a unit should have ensured that little, if any, time needed to be devoted in the syllabus to teaching basic military skills, such as weapons handling and foot drill; but, as we have seen, these were still taught by the schools. Inclusion of such elements in the training meant that the SS schools could never be called 'revolutionary'. In fact, in many respects, their syllabuses were strikingly similar to those already in use in Germany and elsewhere. However, they could be considered evolutionary, because they provided an effective, professional military education to a much more heterogeneous group than would be found in similar institutions at the time.

Even so, the rapid wartime expansion of the Waffen-SS meant that a minority of senior officers in the organisation had been trained at the schools: by July 1944, only about 20 per cent of all majors and 12–13 per cent of more senior officers had attended.[6] The great majority of junior officers during the war received their training through truncated courses and reserve officer courses.*

* During the course of the war, two further officer schools were opened in Klagenfurt (November 1943) and Prague (July 1944).

The most significant weakness in the SS officer selection system was the extent to which politics was allowed to intrude: although the recruiters claimed to make their selections primarily on the basis of the candidate's aptitude, in reality that was often judged in terms of political zeal. Indeed, right until the end of the war, many Waffen-SS officers had received virtually no formal military training. Instead, they owed their positions entirely to their political activities and personal connections. In 1944, a substantial majority of the senior officers – major and above – had been members of the General-SS and/or the NSDAP before joining the Waffen-SS.[7]

Training of the soldiers in the SS-Special Purpose Troops was equally rigorous in the early years of the organisation. As with the officer training, great emphasis was placed on physical fitness, and this was carried through into the field units of the Special Purpose Troops, where regular individual and team sports were used to foster comradeship between officers, NCOs and soldiers. This was a key feature of the Special Purpose Troops and later the Waffen-SS: the formal hierarchies of the German Army were rejected in favour of a system in which 'The comradeship was terrific, the relationship between Officer and man the most democratic I have known, yet the discipline was solid as a rock.'[8] That was the opinion of a Sandhurst-trained ex-British Army officer turned RAF pilot, Railton Freeman, who served in a Waffen-SS unit in 1944–5. Great efforts were made to develop trust and cooperation in these units. In barracks, doors and cupboards were routinely left unlocked; and officers and men socialised with each other. This was all a far cry from the formality of the *Wehrmacht*.

In October 1936, Himmler created the Inspectorate of Special Purpose Troops and named Hausser (who had been promoted to the rank of SS-major general that May) as the Inspector. He was responsible for overseeing the development, training and equipping of the organisation. At the same time, the various scattered elements of the Special Purpose Troops (together with the *Leibstandarte*) were brought into two infantry regiments: *Deutschland*, under SS-Colonel Felix Steiner in Munich; and *Germania*, under SS-Colonel Karl Maria Demelhuber in Hamburg. Of the two colonels, Steiner had by far the greater impact on the development of the Waffen-SS.

Born in East Prussia in 1896, he joined the Prussian Army shortly before the outbreak of the First World War. Commissioned at the beginning of 1915, he served as an infantry officer on both the Eastern and the Western fronts, commanding machine-gun units and taking part in the 'stormtroop' operations that seemed to presage a new, groundbreaking form of warfare. At the end of the war, he served briefly in an East Prussian Free Corps, taking part in the fighting for control of Königsberg, but then he found a place as an officer in the regular army.[9] This says something about the esteem in which he was held by the army leadership, because the stipulations of the Versailles Treaty meant that there were very few available officer positions.

He left the army in early 1933 to take a job as a military training specialist on the staff of Röhm at SA headquarters. This was at the height of Röhm's ambitions to convert the SA into Germany's 'people's army', and Steiner, a captain with the acting rank of major, may well have thought that his new superior was going to succeed. Of course, subsequent reversals in the fortunes of both Röhm and the SA would have forced him to revise his opinion, and he joined the SS in April 1935, initially as a battalion commander in the SS-Special Purpose Troops.

Steiner greatly enhanced the reputation of the emerging Waffen-SS. While Hausser shaped the officer corps through the two cadet schools, Steiner – as commander of the *Deutschland* Regiment – produced the soldiers. His training regime emphasised physical fitness and individual initiative to produce the 'hunter, poacher, athlete' type of soldier, rather than the traditional well-drilled, obedient infantrymen who had populated mass armies for well over a century. There was nothing particularly new about this concept: the more independent, 'light' infantryman (*Jäger* in German military nomenclature) had been around for many years.

However, these troops had operated as specialists in small units, working discretely from large formations. Steiner's innovation was to apply the idea to the regular, 'heavy' infantry. His idea caught on quickly within the Special Purpose Troops and characterised much, although not all, of the subsequent Waffen-SS.

Even so, the Special Purpose Troops' training was not revolutionary; it simply focused on producing the kind of adaptable soldiers demanded by Steiner. All of its elements would have been entirely familiar to most professional soldiers of the period. Stein, in his history of the Waffen-SS, writes: 'SS combat exercises were conducted with live ammunition and actual barrages of artillery "so that every man became accustomed to his weapons and also to being within 50 to 70 metres of the explosions of his own artillery fire".'[10] Some fantasists have taken this to mean that armed SS units regularly exercised against each other with live ammunition. But, of course, that would have been an act of abject lunacy in an organisation where manpower was precious. Stein is actually describing 'field firing' ranges – marksmanship training under simulated combat conditions – that all military forces employ from time to time. In fact, Special Purpose Troops veterans could recall only one instance of live artillery fire being used at very close quarters during their training: for an infantry demonstration in front of Hitler in 1938.[11]

While Steiner was making great strides with the *Deutschland* Regiment, Hausser was having problems coordinating the training for the Special Purpose Troops as a whole. Principally, this was due to Sepp Dietrich and his *Leibstandarte*. Although the *Leibstandarte* was of regimental strength, Dietrich was an SS-general and so outranked Hausser within the SS system; he also enjoyed a good personal relationship and easy access to Hitler as commander of the 'palace guard'. Consequently, Dietrich and his officers felt free to ignore Himmler's and Hausser's orders almost at will. Hausser finally snapped in May 1938 and wrote to Himmler to complain about Dietrich's non-compliance. He also put forward suggestions for improving the *Leibstandarte*'s military performance, including cross-posting NCOs and officers between the *Leibstandarte* and the remainder of the Special Purpose Troops. Naturally, Dietrich resisted, but Hausser's proposals were ultimately adopted in time for the *Leibstandarte* to achieve a reasonable level of combat readiness before the Second World War began.[12]

In addition to operating in a slightly different manner to the German Army, the Special Purpose Troops looked different. In 1935, when the army assumed responsibility for the initial military training of the armed SS, the latter swapped their black service uniforms for the traditional field grey of the German Army for reasons of convenience and security (Germany was still notionally bound by the restrictions of the Versailles Treaty). But this was anathema to Himmler, who took a peculiarly close interest in uniforms, military heraldry and insignia. He wanted to differentiate *his* soldiers from those of the army, so, for a while, the Special Purpose Troops wore 'earth grey' (a kind of muddy khaki) uniforms. However, these had to be abandoned in 1938, when the SS armed units started to take part in live operations with the army. Clearly, in those circumstances, all the soldiers had to wear the same basic uniform for identification purposes, and it was the traditional army one that was adopted.

Nevertheless, the Special Purpose Troops were able to differentiate themselves in another way: through their innovations in the use of camouflage clothing. After the war, credit for this was claimed by Gottlob Berger, the chief of SS recruiting. His story was that he wore a camouflage jacket when hunting bustards in Pomerania, and mentioned the item to Dietrich. The latter then recognised the jacket's potential application in warfare and ordered a large number for the *Leibstandarte*.[13] This was probably a tall tale, but, none the less, from 1938 onwards, the Special Purpose Troops sported mottled camouflage smocks – with reversible green (spring and summer) and brown (autumn) patterns – and camouflage helmet covers. These, more than anything else, set them apart from the regular army.

Under Hausser and Steiner's leadership, a number of other ex-German Army officers flourished in the SS. Herbert Otto Gille served as an artillery officer in the First World War and joined the SS in 1932. He was made platoon leader of the Political Readiness Unit Ellwangen in 1934, and subsequently commanded the defence company and the machine-gun company under Steiner when these units were incorporated into the *Deutschland* Regiment. Later, he transferred into the *Germania* Regiment, where he was promoted to captain and placed in command of the 2nd Battalion. During the war, he commanded the *Wiking* Division and the IV SS-Armoured-Corps. In the process, he became the most decorated member of the SS, and one of the most highly decorated members of the German armed forces.[14]

Hans Jüttner also began his SS career under Steiner and Hausser. An infantry officer in the First World War, seeing service in Syria and Iraq, he joined the NSDAP in 1931 but did not enter the SS until 1935, when he became a battalion commander in *Deutschland*. The next year he moved to the Inspectorate, where he worked under Hausser. He went on to become chief of the SS-Command Staff (in effect the general staff) of the Waffen-SS in 1943.[15]

These men were forward thinking and progressive, and they presided over an organisation with a novel military ethos. However, the whole set-up remained entirely untested until the Third Reich embarked on the path of military and physical expansion that would ultimately lead to its annihilation.

15

Expansion of the Militarised SS

As we have seen, the German Army initially held the armed units of the SS in thinly disguised contempt. Its leaders were grateful to the SS for helping to eliminate the seemingly much greater threat of the SA; but other than that, they felt the police-type squads and concentration camp guard units were scarcely worthy of their consideration. That attitude changed on 2 February 1935, when Hitler decreed that the SS-Special Purpose Troops would be organised into a division in time of war. The decree caused some perturbation among the German Army's High Command because Hitler's accommodation with the army had included the promise that they would remain the sole bearer of arms within the state. This had also underpinned his calculation that the army was a more important ally than the SA. There is no compelling evidence that Hitler, Himmler or anyone else within the National Socialist hierarchy saw the SS as a future replacement for the army, but it was typical of Hitler to keep his options open by creating a force that was entirely at his disposal and need not worry about constitutional niceties.

Some of the military leadership's concern was assuaged in March 1936, when Hitler decided to reintroduce universal conscription in order to create a standing army of thirty-six divisions.

In comparison, the Special Purpose Troops were tiny. Even so, hostility and suspicion remained. Both Minister of Defence von Blomberg and General von Fritsch, Commander-in-Chief of the Army, objected to the formation of an SS division* or any further expansion of the armed formations.

At this point, the situation changed again. In January 1938, the sixty-year-old von Blomberg married Erna Gruhn, who was twenty-six. It was a quiet ceremony, even though Hitler acted as a witness and Goering was the general's best man. A few days later, while the happy couple was on honeymoon, a Berlin Vice Squad detective who was analysing a batch of seized pornographic photographs realised that one of the women in the pictures was the new Frau von Blomberg. Further background checks revealed convictions for prostitution. Seemingly shocked and embarrassed by this revelation, Hitler summoned the Defence Minister when he returned to Berlin and demanded an annulment of the marriage. Much to Hitler's incredulity, von Blomberg refused, apparently believing that his comrades in the army would rally to his support. When they did not, he resigned all of his posts.[1]

The obvious replacement as Defence Minister was von Fritsch. But there were question marks about his propriety, too. In 1935, a criminal named Otto Schmidt admitted to blackmailing a number of closet homosexual establishment figures, including a 'General Fritsch'. Recognising the name, the police passed details of the case on to the Gestapo, who investigated further and concluded that Schmidt's story may well have been true. Himmler showed Hitler the von Fritsch file in August 1936. At that moment, Hitler was entirely uninterested. Von Fritsch was a key figure in the expansion of the Army, and Hitler needed him. Consequently, just as he had done previously with Röhm, Hitler put aside any qualms about von Fritsch's homosexuality and

---

* They resisted this official designation even though they were well aware that the Special Purpose Troops were now of divisional strength.

ordered Himmler to destroy the file. By the end of 1937, though, von Fritsch was exhibiting a distinct lack of support for Hitler's proposed war of conquest in Europe. In November, the investigation into the Schmidt/von Fritsch affair was quietly reopened; and, if anything, Hitler was looking to get rid of him, rather than hand him the Defence Ministry.

The only other serious candidate was Goering, Commander-in-Chief of the Luftwaffe, and he was prepared to put a lot of effort into securing the job. It seems that it was Goering who informed Hitler of Frau von Blomberg's past, and then, twenty-four hours later, presented him with an updated version of the von Fritsch file.[2] Von Fritsch was summoned to Hitler's office, where he found the blackmailer Schmidt waiting for him. Von Fritsch gave his word of honour that he had not met Schmidt before, but Hitler refused to accept his assurances.

Clearly, von Fritsch would not now be succeeding von Blomberg, but at this point Goering's plan unexpectedly unravelled, too. Von Blomberg, embittered by the lack of support he had been given by his colleagues within the armed forces, suggested during his farewell interview with Hitler that the Führer should take control of the Defence Ministry himself. Hitler agreed, although with one small adaptation: he gave it a new name. On 4 February, he dissolved the Ministry and created the *Oberkommando der Wehrmacht* (OKW – High Command of the Armed Forces), with himself as Supreme Commander and *Generaloberst* ('colonel general' – a rank roughly equivalent to a four-star general in the UK or US Army) Wilhelm Keitel as his chief of staff. This did not remove all of the obstacles to further SS expansion, but it certainly undermined them. Obviously, Hitler hoped to maintain a balance between the *Wehrmacht* and the SS, to keep his senior military commanders on side, but he now had much more freedom to do as he wished in respect to Germany's armed forces.

The von Fritsch affair had an appropriately squalid end. Although von Fritsch retired and was replaced as Commander-in-Chief of the Army by the more malleable Walther von Brauchitsch, he demanded an opportunity to clear his name. A court martial was duly convened, presided over by none other than Hermann Goering. Before it started, Heydrich and Himmler already knew the truth. The Gestapo's enquiries had revealed that Schmidt had actually blackmailed a retired *captain* called von *Frisch*. However, they had kept quiet about what was clearly a case of mistaken identity in order to oust von Fritsch. Heydrich, in particular, had allowed the accusations to continue long after he had known they were groundless. This could have caused a great deal of trouble between the army and the SS security apparatus, but ultimately nobody seemed to care too much. While the court martial fully exonerated von Fritsch, no senior army officer emerged from the woodwork to demand his reinstatement. A number of middle-ranking Gestapo officials were disciplined and demoted, while most of the blame fell on Schmidt, who was shot on Himmler's orders.[3] Von Fritsch remained a broken man, but he was made honorary commander of the 12th Artillery Regiment. He fell in action in Poland on 22 September 1939, with many believing that he had actively sought an honourable battle-field death.

The von Fritsch court martial coincided with – and was briefly interrupted by – the German annexation of Austria. This saw the first major combat use of the SS-Special Purpose Troops under army command. The *Leibstandarte*, the SS-Engineer Battalion and the SS-Signals Battalion were mobilised under General Guderian's XVI Army Corps; the *Germania* Regiment was attached to VII Army Corps, with two battalions of the Death's Head *Oberbayern* Regiment providing security on lines of communication; while the *Deutschland* Regiment and a further battalion of the *Oberbayern* Regiment were attached to Infantry Regiment 61 and Mountain Infantry Regiment 98, respectively, for the occupation of the Austrian Tyrol.[4] There seems to have been no friction between the SS and army soldiers on the ground, although there were some logistical difficulties. SS units reportedly caused traffic congestion because of their lack of training and experience in large-scale road moves, and some of their commanders were disgruntled because they were assigned purely supporting roles. This prompted an immediate order from Hitler to Keitel to motorise the hitherto horse-drawn Special Purpose Troops. But a little later, on 17 August, he issued a much more significant decree. This clarified the position of the armed SS and, in effect, created what soon became known as the Waffen-SS.

The decree began by stating that the General-SS was a political formation of the NSDAP and therefore did not require military training or arms. However, 'for special internal political tasks . . . or for use within the wartime army in the event of mobilisation', the Special Purpose Troops, the officer cadet schools, the Death's Head units and the police reserves of the SS were to be organised, armed and trained as military formations. In peacetime, these forces would be commanded by Himmler as National Leader of the SS and Chief of the German Police, and they would carry out internal political tasks. The SS would pay for their weapons and equipment, which would be supplied by the *Wehrmacht* as and when required.

The order went on to state:

The Special Purpose Troops are neither a part of the *Wehrmacht* nor a part of the police. They are a standing armed unit exclusively at my disposal. As such, and as a unit of the NSDAP, their members are to be selected by the National Leader of the SS according to the philosophical and political standards that I have ordered for the NSDAP and for the SS. Their members are to be trained and their ranks filled with volunteers from those who are subject to serve in the army who have finished their duties in the Obligatory Labour Service. The service period for volunteers is 4 years. It may be prolonged for SS [NCOs]. Such regulations are in force for SS leaders. The regular compulsory military service (par. 8 of the law relating to military service) is fulfilled by service of the same amount of time in the Special Purpose Troops.[5]

Similarly, the Death's Head units were neither part of the *Wehrmacht* nor part of the police, but were an armed SS force at Hitler's disposal for the resolution of internal political problems. At this stage, service in the Death's Head units did not count as compulsory military service, but the decree made a clear link between them and the Special Purpose Troops, and envisaged that members of the former would be transferred into the latter in time of war to act as their reserve.

In the aftermath of the *Anschluss*, a third Special Purpose Troops regiment, *Der Führer*, was established in Vienna and Klagenfurt, as was an Austrian Death's Head regiment. So the peacetime strength of the SS armed formations was now set as:

- Headquarters
- *Leibstandarte* Adolf Hitler (motorised)
- three foot regiments (*Deutschland, Germania* and *Der Führer*)
- two motorcycle reconnaissance battalions
- one combat engineer battalion
- one signals battalion
- one medical unit.[6]

Elements of the Special Purpose Troops were again mobilised under army control for the march into the Sudetenland in October 1938; and for the occupation of the remainder of Bohemia and Moravia the following March. Once more, the army had some minor quibbles about their performance, but generally there seemed to be few problems.

Two months later, Hitler attended a demonstration by *Deutschland* at the Münsterlager training area. He was so impressed that he finally gave orders to the army's High Command to assist the

Special Purpose Troops in creation of a full divisional organisation with integrated artillery support. This should have been fairly straightforward as the SS-Artillery Regiment had already been established and placed under the command of Herbert Gille. However, the reorganisation was postponed in the summer of 1939 to avoid disruption in the run-up to the invasion of Poland.

When that offensive was launched in September 1939, it was the first time that the armed SS had faced serious opposition. In many respects, it was a baptism of fire. Their marches into Austria and Czechoslovakia had been practically unopposed, but the invasion of Poland was a real shooting war against a determined, if massively outgunned, enemy. Once again, the Special Purpose Troops were committed piecemeal, attached to army formations. *Deutschland* was grouped with the SS-Artillery Regiment, the SS-Reconnaissance Battalion and an army tank regiment in the 4th Panzer Brigade under command of an army general. *Germania* was allocated to the 14th Army in East Prussia. The *Leibstandarte*, together with the SS-Engineer Battalion, were assigned to von Reichenau's 10th Army, which attacked into western Poland from Silesia. In Danzig, a new unit had been created in July and August from local General-SS members, the 3rd Battalion of the Death's Head *Ostmark* Regiment (which was based in Berlin-Adlershof), and members of other Death's Head units smuggled in by ship from Oranienburg. This motley group of between 1500 and 2000 men was named the *Heimwehr Danzig* (Danzig Home Guard) and took part in covert actions in and around the city as soon as the invasion began.

Again, the SS armed formations received mixed reviews from army commanders. They were criticised for taking heavy casualties (the *Leibstandarte*, for example, suffered around a hundred men killed in action and three hundred wounded during the campaign[7]); for poor performance within a division; and for their inability to conduct complicated 'combined arms' operations.[8] The SS's response was to say that the army kept them starved of support, supplies and even their own heavy weapons, and denied them the opportunity to train in a divisional context. All of this was largely true.

More friction was caused by the actions of the special task groups and police units operating in the rear. Then, as now, it was difficult to draw a clear distinction between the strictly combat formations of the SS and their comrades in the 'special' units, if indeed there was any difference: the Special Purpose Troops may have been militarised members of the SS with a specific wartime role, but the basis of their existence was exactly the same as that of the men who were engaged in killing politicians, priests, intellectuals and Jews in the wake of the advancing forces.

As a consequence of the problems thrown up by the Polish campaign, it was decided to press ahead immediately with the formation of the Special Purpose Division. Furthermore, members of the SS and the police would no longer be tried through the military court martial system. Instead, the military penal system would be applied in their own special courts.

Hausser, still the Inspector of the Special Purpose Troops, had secured a position as liaison officer to the army in the field. Having returned to Berlin, on 10 October 1939 he was appointed chief of the newly formed *SS-Verfügungsdivision* (Special Purpose Division). At this point, he was an SS-major general, but the fact that he was now in command of an armed division meant that he had to be given formal rank equivalence with his army counterparts. This was the first time that a rank in the SS – which, it should be remembered, was still primarily a voluntary political organisation – was officially equated with a military rank.

The new division was created by the simple expedient of officially combining the three Special Purpose Troops foot regiments – *Deutschland*, *Germania* and *Der Führer* – with the artillery, reconnaissance, engineering and medical elements. Meanwhile, the *Leibstandarte* was reinforced, but kept separate from the division: it received a fourth battalion of infantry, a motorised 'infantry gun' battalion, and ultimately (in April 1940) a full artillery battalion.

Detachments from the unit still provided personal security for Hitler, and in January 1940 he ordered the creation of a 'light' *Leibstandarte* battalion to do the job on a permanent basis.* It was to be based in Berlin.

In spite of the army's criticism, the armed units of the SS therefore survived and even profited from their baptism of fire in Poland. But it was left to other SS groups to start to forge the organisation's notorious wartime reputation during that campaign. Their mission went far beyond the occupation of a neighbouring territory: it began the process of putting the merciless SS ideology into practice.

* This came about after he spent Christmas Eve with the *Leibstandarte* at their barracks in Koblenz.

16

The Invasion of Poland and the Special Task Groups

The invasion and occupation of western Poland in September 1939 signalled a major change in German policy towards the Jews. Hitherto, National Socialist racial policies had targeted *German* Jews: people who were assimilated into mainstream German society, spoke German, and, to a large extent, 'looked' German. However, despite their loathing for all things Jewish, Hitler and other senior National Socialists had been forced by institutional constraints and public opinion to make limited concessions towards Germany's Jews. For instance, they appreciated that there would be an outcry if they unleashed unrestricted attacks on Jewish veterans of the First World War, or on those who had served Germany in the civil service or public life. So the persecution of Germany's Jews had been pursued carefully, gradually and usually within the framework of German law, debased as it had become. Measures against the Jews had to be given considerable thought in order to stop them rebounding on ethnic Germans, who, for example, might have close business relationships with Jewish partners.

In Poland, the situation was entirely different. The National Socialists regarded the Poles themselves as an inferior race who were deserving of no particular consideration. So the country's Jews – who made up some 10 per cent of the population of 33 million – were regarded as the lowest of the low: *Untermensch* (sub-humans), in National Socialist terms. Their persecution began suddenly, violently and with very little restraint. First, though, the rest of Germany's eastern neighbour had to be subdued.

As the plans for the invasion of Poland had been finalised in August, Hitler had summoned Himmler to entrust him with a special task. Hitler was not really invading Poland to resolve the issue of the 'Free City' of Danzig and the so-called 'Polish Corridor', his pretext for action. In fact, his intention was to destroy Poland and reduce its people to German slaves. This was to be phase one of his drive to acquire *Lebensraum* (living space) in the East. The main role for the SS and the police would be to cut off the head of the Polish nation by eliminating its ruling class: politicians, clerics, aristocrats and the intelligentsia were all to be liquidated. Hitler knew that the generals of the army would baulk at this task – codenamed 'Operation Tannenberg' – which was why he handed it over to Himmler and the SS.

Heydrich set up five special task groups of personnel drawn from or seconded to the SD, and commanded by SD officers: Bruno Streckenbach (who had commanded the Hamburg Gestapo), Dr Emanuel Schäfer, Dr Herbert Fischer, Lothar Beuthel and Ernst Damzog. These groups were assigned to the five armies of the invasion force, with each being of roughly battalion strength, subdivided into four *Einsatzkommandos* (special task units) of between 100 and 150 men (equivalent to company strength). Each of these task units was then allocated to an army corps. Two more special task groups were created shortly after the beginning of the invasion, including one commanded by SS-Major General Udo von Woyrsch, which was ordered to follow the German 14th Army into Galicia. Additionally, a battalion of Daluege's uniformed Order Police joined each army corps, with orders to secure the army's rear by sweeping up any remnants of the Polish forces bypassed by the rapid army assault.

Although their mission had come directly from Hitler, Himmler and Heydrich felt it necessary to conceal the true nature of their role from the *Wehrmacht*. As a result, they operated under the cover that they were securing the army's rear through counter-espionage, the arrest of political opponents, the confiscation of weapons and so forth. In fact, both their men and the police battalions unleashed a wave of terror against Poland's ruling classes. Working from prepared lists, they rounded up their targets, took them to hastily prepared 'reception camps' at Stutthof (near Danzig), Muhltal (near Bydgoszcz), Soldau, Torun and Fort VII in Poznan, and then, largely out of sight of the army, executed them. On 27 September, Heydrich reported: 'Of the Polish upper classes in the occupied territories, only a maximum of 3% is still present.'[1] In other words, tens of thousands of civilians had been murdered in less than a month.

A secondary role for the special task groups was to secure the active military cooperation of the local German population through the formation of local self-defence units. At the onset of the invasion, Poles, particularly in western Prussia, had fallen upon the ethnic German population, driving them from their homes and killing several thousand.[2] As soon as the *Wehrmacht* started to gain the ascendancy, the remaining ethnic Germans demanded revenge. The special task groups gave them the organisation to achieve it.

As we have seen, there was already a German military formation within Danzig: the Home Guard. For the most part, it operated and fought as a military unit 'behind enemy lines', but one of its sub-units, a guard battalion commanded by thirty-nine-year-old SS-Major Kurt Eimann, supported the special task group operating in the Danzig area. Some of Eimann's men became guards at local POW and concentration camps, including Stutthof, while others formed a mobile killing squad. In early October, they executed thirty or so Polish postal officials who had been captured at the Polish Post Office in Danzig on 1 September (the Polish postal workers had been attempting to resist the German takeover.

They surrendered after the – German – Danzig Fire Brigade had pumped petrol into the cellars and ignited it). They were also ordered to 'clear' the inmates of a number of Pomeranian asylums that Himmler had designated for other purposes (one of them, at Lauenburg, became a Waffen-SS NCO training school). This involved none of the pseudo-medical procedures that were being employed by T-4. Eimann's men simply took the patients into some woods and shot them. They were then thrown into ditches dug by prisoners from Stutthof. Once the three thousand patients had been executed, the gravediggers were killed, too, and thrown into their own ditches.[3]

Asylums in East Prussia were also 'cleared', this time by an SS unit commanded by Herbert Lange and drawn from the guards at the Soldau concentration camp. Between 21 May and 8 June 1940, Lange's unit murdered some 1558 mental patients in a gassing van that was disguised as a coffee delivery truck. This caused some strife within the SS. The killings had been ordered by SS-Major General Wilhelm Rediess, the Senior SS and Police Leader in Königsberg, who had promised Lange a 'bounty' of ten marks per death. But he reneged on the deal and refused to pay once the murders had been committed. Lange complained to SS-Major General Karl Wolff, Himmler's adjutant, who eventually secured payment for the unit out of T-4's coffers.[4]

The special task groups' final task was to identify and 'concentrate' Poland's Jewish population. Heydrich held a meeting on 19 September with the army's Quartermaster General, Eduard Wagner, to thrash out the details of the final 'clear-up' of Poland's Jews, intelligentsia, clergy and nobility. Wagner wanted to keep the army's hands relatively clean – although he did not object in principle to what was about to happen – so insisted that these measures should begin only once the military had handed over authority to the civilian authorities who were already being lined up to take control of occupied Poland.[5] Two days later, Heydrich convened a meeting with senior officers of the RSHA and recalled the heads of the special task groups to give them their instructions. The 'concentration' was to be drastic and brutal. Jews were to be cleared from all rural areas, and from the German-speaking parts of Poland – Danzig, West Prussia, Poznan and Polish Upper Silesia – which would be incorporated into the Third Reich as soon as the fighting was over. The uprooted Jewish population was then to be forced into ghettoes in major cities with good railway communications. This latter point was important because the plan, even at this stage, was eventually to push the Jews out of Poland. However, where they would be going had not yet been decided.

At this meeting, Heydrich issued written guidelines to the special task group commanders with regard to the 'Jewish question':

1. Jews to be moved to the towns as soon as possible;
2. Jews to be moved out of the Reich and into Poland;
3. The remaining 30,000 gypsies also to be moved into Poland;
4. Jews in the German territories (that is to say those previously held by Poland) to be systematically deported by goods train.[6]

Shortly afterwards, these instructions were modified. On 1 October, Himmler personally ordered that the special task groups were to 'initiate only preparatory measures' regarding the deportation of Jews. Further action would have to wait for another time.[7] There was a second element to this order, too. In an echo of the measures that Eichmann had implemented in Germany and Austria, each Polish Jewish community would be obliged to form a council of 'Jewish elders' who would undertake the registration, transportation, maintenance and housing of all Jews under the direct command of the SS.

With fighting between the *Wehrmacht* and the last remnants of the Polish forces continuing, the thinly stretched special task groups were in no position to do much more than the 'preparatory work' specified by Himmler. However, during a raid on a Jewish community centre in Warsaw on 4 October, members of the local special task group identified the chemical engineer Adam Czerniakow as chairman of the community group. He was taken to the newly established Security Police headquarters and told to organise a Jewish council.

By then, special task groups and other units of the SS and Order Police had carried out a number of largely uncoordinated attacks against individual Jews and small communities. For example, on 8 September, von Woyrsch's task group burned down the synagogue and its neighbouring Jewish residential quarter in the Upper Silesian town of Bedzin. Then, over the next forty-eight hours, they shot as many as five hundred local Jews, including women and children.[8] The next day, the same unit torched the synagogue in Katowice. However, systematic persecution of Poland's Jews did not begin in earnest until after combat operations had ceased at the beginning of October.*

The new civil administration was inaugurated on 26 October. Poland was now divided into five parts, four of which were to be incorporated into the 'Greater German Reich', with a rump state that would officially remain under German occupation for the time being. Two entirely new regions (*Gaue*) were created: Danzig–West Prussia, the northern part of the 'Polish Corridor', was placed under the former Danzig Regional Leader, Albert Forster;[†] while the Warthegau, the southern part of the Corridor, centred on the city of Poznan (renamed Posen by the Germans), came under the control of Arthur Greiser.[‡] Meanwhile, large parts

---

* Warsaw surrendered on 27 September, while isolated resistance continued until at least 5 October. However, the final Polish collapse had been inevitable once the Soviet Union had invaded from the East on 17 September.

† Born in 1902, Forster joined the SA in 1923 and he was one of the earliest members of the SS in 1925. In the power struggles that characterised the upper echelons of the Third Reich, he was an implacable but largely untouchable opponent of Himmler. He was hanged for crimes against humanity in 1952.

‡ Born in 1897, Greiser was a pilot in the First World War. He joined the NSDAP and the SA in 1929, and the SS in 1931. He was tried and executed by the Polish government in 1946.

of formerly Polish territory were incorporated into Regional Leader Erich Koch's East Prussia and Regional Leader Josef Wagner's Silesia.[*]

The Polish rump state was named the *Generalgouvernement* (General Government) and organised into four districts, centred on Warsaw, Cracow, Radom and Lublin.[†] One of Hitler's closest collaborators, Hans Frank, was appointed General Governor. Born in Karlsruhe in 1900, Frank joined the army in 1917 and served in the Free Corps after the war, when he also joined the DAP (forerunner to the NSDAP). He qualified as a lawyer in 1926 and immediately became Hitler's personal legal adviser. He was elected to the Reichstag in 1930, became Minister of Justice in Bavaria once the National Socialists came to power, and joined the government as Minister without Portfolio in 1934.

Unlike the regional leaders in the newly created regions of Germany, Frank had virtually unlimited power within his domain. While the regional leaders and their administrations were in place to coordinate the activities of central and local government, Frank was answerable only to Hitler. A vain man, he insisted that his officials should obey no orders but his own. However, there were three exceptions to his absolute power: the army, which continued to operate under its own command and had responsibility for dealing with external threats, internal unrest, transport, communications and military procurement; the railway system, which as a strategic asset was directly controlled from Berlin; and the SS and police security apparatus.

As we have seen, in November 1937, the German Ministry of

---

[*] Born in 1899, Wagner was dismissed as Regional Leader and from the NSDAP in 1941, when the Silesia region was split into two parts. Lower Silesia was put under the command of Karl Hanke (1903–45), and Upper Silesia under Fritz Bracht (1899–45). Wagner was arrested by the Gestapo in 1944 after the failed bomb plot against Hitler. He died the following year, although whether he was killed by the SS or by the advancing Red Army is not clear.
[†] A fifth district, centred on Lvov/Lemberg, was added when the Germans overran Galicia after the invasion of the Soviet Union in 1941.

the Interior had created the position of 'senior SS and police leader' to coordinate the activities of the SS and the police at military district level during wartime. Himmler had not waited for the war to begin, though, and had appointed the first of these officials in September 1938, 'in order to finally ensure the union of the SS and the police in the highest positions of command authority'.[9] However, his new appointees had soon caused problems: 'the civil administration refused to countenance the intrusion of SS functionaries who had no official place in the police hierarchy and the Reichsführer was compelled to confine his Senior SS and Police Leaders to purely formal representative duties'.[10]

The situation was very different in Germany's new eastern colony. Both the newly incorporated territories and the General Government had been entirely deprived of their administrative structures by the German takeover, so there was a vacuum to fill. Himmler appointed SS-Major General Richard Hildebrandt as Senior SS and Police Leader in Danzig–West Prussia; in the Warthegau, he installed SS-Major General Wilhelm Koppe; and for the General Government, his representative in Cracow was SS-Lieutenant General Friedrich-Wilhelm Krüger. These appointments, and others which followed as the SS and police network spread across Europe, were of considerable significance. There were relatively few constraints on the freedom of action of the senior SS and police leaders outside pre-war German territory. They exercised direct operational control over SS and police units garrisoned within their area and therefore became key agents in the implementation of occupation policy.

Krüger was a controversial choice: he was hated by many of the 'old fighters' for playing a role in the Night of the Long Knives and was also known as 'a scandalmonger and a pedant'.[11] But that made him just the kind of man Himmler wanted: an SS loyalist who owed his entire career to the National Leader. Frank was alive to the problems created by having an outsider – Himmler – in control of his security apparatus, so he sought to circumvent these by appointing Krüger State Secretary for Security while allowing him to continue in his original role as Senior SS and Police Leader. But this backfired and resulted in several years of antagonism between Himmler and Frank over who was in charge of security within occupied Poland.

As Senior SS and Police Leader for the General Government, Krüger had command authority over the Commander-in-Chief of the Security Police, who controlled roughly two thousand Gestapo, Kripo and SD men, and the Commander-in-Chief of the Regular Police, who exercised authority over the police battalions, gendarmerie detachments and individual policemen. At the district level, four SS and police leaders (*SS- und Polizeiführer* – SSPF) – a level of command unique to the General Government – exercised authority over the *Kommandeure der Sicherheitspolizei* (KdS – commanders of the Security Police) and the *Kosmmandeure der Order Police* (KdO – commanders of the Order Police). The SSPFs were based in Warsaw, Radom, Cracow and Lublin; while, in theory, they were subordinated to the district governors, in practice their primary loyalty was to Krüger and ultimately to Himmler.

The separation of the military, security and administrative components of the General Government led to considerable friction. As we have seen, SS and police formations had a different mission – in effect, the destruction of the whole Polish nation – to that of the *Wehrmacht*, which was solely concerned with the destruction of Polish combat power. Many of the *Wehrmacht*'s generals seem not to have grasped that their military victory against the Polish Army was simply a precursor to Hitler's main objective: a race war against all Polish people and particularly the Jews. Even before the fighting had finished, some *Wehrmacht* commanders were complaining about the activities of the special task groups. On 20 September, 14th Army reported that their soldiers had witnessed mass shootings of Jews and civilians by Woyrsch's unit. These reports led General Gerd von Rundstedt to order the special task group's withdrawal. However, it is doubtful that this order was based on humanitarianism. After all, the 14th Army itself used very harsh measures to drive the Jewish populations in its zone to the east, into the hands of the Soviets.[12] More likely, *Wehrmacht* officers were simply concerned that the actions of the SS and police personnel would have a detrimental effect on their own forces' discipline. Nevertheless, General Blaskowitz, Commander-in-Chief of the Army in Poland, instructed *Wehrmacht* commanders to collect evidence of any unauthorised activities by members of the SS and police.

One particularly horrific example took place in Ostrow Mazowieck. Following a fire on 9 November that was blamed on Jewish arsonists, members of Reserve Police Battalion 11 gathered together the Jewish population of the town and requested reinforcements from the Warsaw Police Regiment. Two days later, members of Police Battalion 91 arrived and, with little further ado, shot 366 Jewish men, women and children on the edges of pre-dug mass graves.[13]

A letter from General Wilhelm Ulex to Blaskowitz gives an indication of the day-to-day harassment and intimidation suffered by other Polish Jews in the first few months of the occupation:

On 28.10.39 a Pole, despite having a driving permit issued by the Warsaw *Kommandantur*, was stopped by SS members and had his truck confiscated at pistol point.

In Tschenstochau, during the night of 31.12.39, around 250 Jews were held in an icy-cold street, then taken for some hours to a school, where they were searched for gold. The women were made to strip naked and the policemen even searched their private parts.

In Radom on 8.1.40, two SS men searched the home of the Polish female official Bugacka and stole personal possessions and 2 bank books.

On 18.2.40 two sergeants of 3/Police Battalion 182 in Petrikau took, at pistol point, the 18-year-old Jewess Machmanowic and the 17-year-old Jewess Santowska from their parents' homes, drove them to the Polish cemetery and raped one of them there. The other had her period, but they said they would come back in a few days and promised her 5 zlotys.[14]

The army's leaders pointed out that these measures would be counter-productive by engendering sympathy and support for the Jewish victims from the majority Catholic population, and would lead to ill-discipline and declining morale in the army. Once again, this merely indicated that they did not understand the true purpose of the occupation: to destroy the Polish nation and wage a war of annihilation against the Jewish people. Himmler feigned concern and referred the complaints to the SS legal service, which investigated and then did nothing.

By then, the generals had more pressing concerns, as they and their troops had been ordered westwards, to begin the assault on France.

17

The SS and the Polish Jews

Once the civil administration and the security apparatus had been established, the 'concentration' and elimination of the Jews could begin in earnest. As we have seen, before the war, the SS and the SD expropriated Jewish citizens and eventually coerced them to leave Germany and German-occupied territories. Furthermore, some Zionists actively cooperated with the Third Reich in this process to further their aim of establishing a Jewish state in Palestine. The onset of war drastically reduced the number of potential destinations for Jewish 'voluntary' emigration, so the programme was swiftly abandoned. However, the acquisition of new territory in the East offered an opportunity for *involuntary* deportation.

Eichmann, the SD's Jewish affairs expert, had spent much of 1938 and 1939 in Vienna, managing the Central Office for Jewish Emigration, but he was summoned back to Berlin by his superior, SS-Senior Leader Heinrich Müller, in October 1939. Müller, who had recently become chief of the Gestapo and was now running the Central Office for Jewish Emigration for the entire Third Reich, had just received a personal order from Hitler: to remove all of the Jews from Katowice, which was about to be incorporated into the Reich as part of the reconstituted region of Silesia.

Müller, in turn, had chosen Eichmann for the task. This was to be the first step in the deportation of all remaining 300,000 Jews of German nationality.[1] Now Eichmann had to decide where to send them. The conquest of Poland provided an obvious answer: the unincorporated but occupied territory of the General Government.

Eichmann returned to Vienna and, over the next few days, set the wheels in motion for the deportations to begin. On 9 October, he briefed his staff on his plans. First, a labour force would be deported and forced to build crude, wooden, barracks-type accommodation. The Jewish community itself would be extorted to pay for the builders' transportation, supplies and materials, and would then be deported *en masse* to join the advance party.

The following day, Eichmann summoned the leader of the Viennese Jews and ordered him to supply between a thousand and twelve hundred able-bodied Jewish labourers.[2] Similar orders were given to Jewish leaders in Mährisch-Ostrau and Katowice. However, at this stage, Eichmann still did not know precisely where he was going to send the labour parties. So, on 12 October, he flew with Franz Stahlecker, his deputy in Prague, to Warsaw and then drove south-east towards Lublin. Eventually, they came upon the small village of Nisko on the banks of the River San, which had good rail and road communications. It would do.

On 17 October, a train loaded with 916 Jewish men, prefabricated huts, building equipment and food supplies set off from Mährisch-Ostrau, followed three days later by a train from Vienna with 875 men and one from Katowice with 1029 labourers and their supplies.[3] Eichmann was at Nisko to meet them. He gave them a pep talk to the effect that they were the brave pioneers of a new 'home' for the European Jews, and told them that if they worked hard, they could make a go of it.

In theory, the deportation of the Jews was meant to run in parallel with another vital component in Hitler's Third Reich. There were scattered German-speaking communities of ethnic Germans as far east as the River Volga. Now, Hitler planned to 'bring them home to the Reich' and settle them on the 'living space' that was being created by the expulsion of the Poles and Jews. They would simply be installed in the previous occupants' homes and on their farms, and would go a long way to solving Germany's acute labour shortage. From his large cast of racial zealots, Hitler selected Himmler as *Reichskommissar für die Festigung Deutsche Volkstums* (RKF – Reich Commissar for the Strengthening of 'Germandom'), and he and Heydrich set to work on the logistics.

The scale of this scheme was enormous.[4] The intention was to bring roughly 500,000 ethnic Germans into the Reich, which meant that existing Polish populations would have to be shunted around to accommodate the new arrivals. It was simply too ambitious at a time when the transport system was severely stretched by the demands of war. By late October, the decision had already been taken in Berlin to suspend both the deportations of the Jews and the German resettlement scheme for the time being.

Eichmann allowed the second wave of transports from Vienna, Mährisch-Ostrau and Katowice to go ahead as planned on 26 October, but after this they were halted. The Jewish labourers who were struggling to build their accommodation were more or less left to fend for themselves. The Nisko 'settlement' struggled on for several months in the face of increasingly poor weather, malnutrition, disease and harassment from local SS and police units. Many of the workers were forced into the Soviet-occupied zone of Poland, while others voluntarily entered the labour camp at Sosnowiece. In April 1940, the settlement was officially abandoned and the remaining Jews were told to go home; only three hundred of the six thousand who had been deported eventually did so.

In a sense, Himmler brought the administrative problems on himself. The *Volksdeutsche Mittelstelle* (Central Office for Ethnic Germans), had been set up in 1936 by Rudolf Hess to coordinate the interaction of state and party offices with overseas German communities. But the original head of the office, Otto von Kursell, a party official, had lacked the influence to compete with the various other bodies that had an interest in the subject, so Hess had turned to the SS to make it work. The chief of SS-Regional Headquarters North-West, SS-Major General Werner Lorenz, was duly appointed in von Kursell's place.[5] When Himmler became Reich Commissar and gained total authority over the office, he planned to use it to implement what he regarded as his great project: the resettlement of Eastern Europe by Germans.* As he saw it, the Central Office for Ethnic Germans would organise the repatriation of the German communities; the Race and Settlement Head Office (RuSHA) would ensure their racial suitability; and the Reich Security Head Office (RSHA) would weed out any undesirables and anti-state elements.

All of this was fine in theory, but Himmler needed to convince his rivals within the National Socialist hierarchy that they should go along with the idea. Of course, the project had the full backing of Hitler, and Goering was on board, too. (As head of the Four-Year Plan – the National Socialists' strategic economic programme – Goering was fully aware of the Third Reich's labour shortage and he saw the resettlement scheme as a potential solution.) But others were much more resistant. For example, both Erich Koch, Regional Leader of East Prussia, and Albert Forster, Regional Leader of West Prussia, refused point blank to allow any ethnic Germans to resettle within their territories. This immediately scuppered Himmler's plan to move the Baltic Germans to Prussia. Meanwhile, Alfred Rosenberg – who held the ministerial portfolio for the occupied territories in the East – added to the pressure on Himmler by criticising the treatment of the Baltic Germans. (He was one himself so took a keen interest in their welfare.) Rosenberg claimed that they had been forced to live in unpleasant transit camps because of the failure of the Central Office for Ethnic Germans to find them somewhere to settle when they reached the 'homeland'.

---

* This was a goal that harked all the way back to Himmler's time as a member of the Artamanen Society.

But it was General Governor Hans Frank who complained loudest and longest about the scheme. While Himmler and Heydrich saw the General Government as little more than a dumping ground for unwanted Jews, Frank firmly believed that it could be economically viable, and he intended to make it so. Depositing large numbers of Jews inside his borders and giving them nowhere to live and nothing to eat would put a huge strain on a system that was already fragile, at best.[6]

In November 1939, Heydrich ordered the deportation of 80,000 Jews and Poles from the newly annexed territories into the General Government; and Eichmann, as the officer charged with coordinating the process, was planning to move 600,000 more in the New Year. It was at this point that the plan truly hit the buffers, because Frank categorically refused to accept them. As a temporary solution, many of the Jews who had already been uprooted were moved to Lodz, now in the Warthegau (and renamed 'Litzmannstadt' by the National Socialists), where a ghetto would be established while the problem was sorted out. By February 1940, the conflict between Himmler and Heydrich, on the one hand, and Frank, on the other, had become so heated that Goering was forced to intervene. He took Frank's side, and the whole resettlement programme was effectively stymied. There was no transport available because the military had priority claims on it; there were disputes about who took control of property left behind by the deportees and who should pay for the expulsions; and now the man running the area designated as the destination for those deportees was not prepared to accept them. Furthermore, the civil governments in the newly annexed areas were becoming increasingly concerned by the condition of the Jews who were waiting to be expelled. Their homes, property and money had been plundered, they had been stripped of all political rights, and they were beginning to suffer from disease and malnutrition. On 30 April, supposedly as a health measure, the ghetto area of Lodz was sealed off to prevent the spread of typhus outside the Jewish population.[7]

However, these practical difficulties did not deter Himmler from planning a future for a re-engineered Europe. In May 1940, he wrote a secret memorandum entitled 'Thoughts on the Treatment of Foreign Populations in the East'. In it, he argued that the 'Polish' populations of the General Government and the incorporated territories needed to be subdivided into ethnic groups and assessed, so that 'valuable' racial elements could be brought into Germany for assimilation into the *Volk*. The remainder would then provide a pool of labour for Germany, and their individual racial identities, such as Ukrainian, Lemke, Goral and so on, would slowly disappear. A different fate awaited the Jews: they were to be evacuated 'to a colony in Africa or elsewhere', which Himmler argued was the 'mildest and best' solution 'if one rejects the Bolshevik method of physical extermination of a people out of inner conviction as being un-German and impossible'.[8]

Himmler presented this memorandum to Hitler on 25 May, by which point German tanks were on the Channel coast and the French and British armies were in disarray. Hitler liked what he saw and suggested that Himmler should show the memo to Frank. Himmler then asked permission to distribute the memorandum to the regional leaders in the East, and this was granted. Consequently, Himmler's odd, racist, musings had become official state policy.

Germany's unexpectedly rapid, crushing victory in the western campaign gave new momentum to the National Socialists' Jewish policy. In early June, Franz Rademacher – a lawyer and diplomat who had recently returned to Germany from the German Embassy in Chile to take over the Jewish Affairs Desk at the Foreign Ministry – submitted a paper. In it, he suggested deportation of the Jews of Western Europe to either the French-controlled island of Madagascar or South America. Meanwhile, the Jews of Eastern Europe could be held as hostages to prevent American Jews agitating for the USA to join the war against Germany. Foreign

Minister von Ribbentrop seized on these proposals as a way to involve himself in Jewish policy and the paper was circulated for comment.

Himmler and Heydrich's curt response was to point out that Goering had given *them* the authority to resolve the 'Jewish question', but they were still clearly interested in Rademacher's ideas. Eichmann, whose Section II 112 of the SD had now become Section IV B4 within the RSHA,* was set to work to flesh out the proposals. In mid-August, Eichmann presented his detailed plan, which expanded Rademacher's concept to include the eastern Jews as well. Using the methods that had already been employed in Germany, Austria, Czechoslovakia and Poland, the Jews of Bohemia-Moravia, Poland, France, Belgium, the Netherlands, Norway, Denmark, Luxembourg and Slovakia would be registered, assembled, plundered and shipped out of Europe to Madagascar at the rate of three thousand per day. First to go would be workers with the skills to build the settlements, then the remainder. Each deportee would be allowed to take only twenty kilos of baggage; the rest of their possessions would be expropriated to fund the operation. On Madagascar, the German Navy would establish naval bases to suit its requirements. The rest of the island – with its estimated population of four million Jews, plus indigenous inhabitants – would be governed by the SS.

It seems that this Madagascar plan was seriously considered at the highest levels of the National Socialist establishment as a potential solution to the 'Jewish question'. And Hitler was still discussing it as late as February 1941 in conversation with Dr Robert Ley, the chief of the National Socialist Labour Front.[9] However, it was only ever viable for a very brief period during the war. In June and July 1940, the assumption throughout Europe was that

---

* The rebranding was partly a result of a simple reorganisation of the RSHA, but it also reflected the fact that the section was now an operational unit, rather than an information clearing house. It was officially an office of the Gestapo, so Eichmann reported directly to Heinrich Müller.

Great Britain would soon be forced to negotiate a peace settlement with Germany. After all, the German Army was massed on the Channel coast and the Luftwaffe seemed certain to win air superiority before too much longer. Once a peace agreement was agreed, Britain's naval blockade against Germany would be lifted, and the evacuation fleet could set sail for East Africa. However, as we now know, Winston Churchill did not sue for peace; and it was the RAF rather than the Luftwaffe that gained command of the skies in the Battle of Britain. Consequently, the naval blockade remained in place and the Madagascar plan evaporated as a practical proposition.

The plan is significant because it strongly suggests that a resettlement solution to the 'Jewish question' was still being considered just a year before the extermination of the Jews began in earnest. Some historians have taken this to indicate that Hitler never really planned the extermination of the Jewish people; rather, that it came about because he was left with no other option. However, Daniel Goldhagen is dismissive of this argument, suggesting that the plan was 'a phantom of a solution',[10] and would merely have been an interim step towards extermination. Madagascar would simply have been an island prison, housing Jews until they died or were killed. In effect, it would have been a replica of the Polish ghettoes off the coast of East Africa.

There can be no doubt that the welfare of the Jews was not a factor in Eichmann's planning for Madagascar, but at this stage it seems clear that the aim was to get the Jews as far away from Germany as possible, rather than to eliminate them. What we cannot now be sure about is whether the plan represented a preferred non-lethal 'final solution' or simply that those responsible for the Holocaust had yet to persuade themselves that extermination was a practical possibility.

The uncertainty created by the plan stalled the programme of mass deportations, which precipitated a return to the ghettoisation inaugurated by Heydrich's instructions to the special task groups in September 1939. The authorities walled off the Warsaw ghetto in October 1940 and the Jewish district of Cracow in March 1941. Ghettoes were also created in Radom, Lublin, Csestochowa and Kielce the following month.[11] All of these were established to isolate the Jewish population both physically and economically. Inside them, authority was held by Jewish councils set up by the Sipo (but subsequently placed under the control of the civil administration), in a bid to restrict the ghettoes' contact with the outside world.* These councils organised the distribution of the meagre food supplies, allocated accommodation and provided whatever medical care and other public services could be arranged, as well as maintaining security through their own police forces. The external cordons around the ghettoes were secured by units of the Order Police and the Polish Police Force, often supplemented with a physical barrier: Warsaw's ghetto, for example, was encircled by a large brick wall, with twenty-eight manned gates where permitted individuals could enter and exit; Lodz's was surrounded by barbed wire. The Lublin ghetto could not be physically sealed off, but Jews still had to show permits to pass through its outer limits.[12]

At first, the German civil authorities viewed the ghettoes with anything from indifference to outright hostility, fuelled by the erroneous belief that they had adequate reserves of wealth and food to survive but were choosing not to use them. When it became clear that this assumption was wrong, two camps emerged with contrasting opinions of what to do with the ghettoes. Some believed that they had to become productive contributors to the Reich so that they did not become a drain on scarce resources. Others had a more drastic 'solution': the Jews should be left to starve to death. Eventually, after much discussion, the first group won the argument.[13] This was not a humanitarian decision: it was taken simply because the civil administrations of late 1940 could

---

* In reality, this was a somewhat futile hope. Hilberg, in *The Destruction of the European Jews*, notes that some 53,000 people held passes to enter or leave the Warsaw ghetto at one stage.

not countenance letting hundreds of thousands of prisoners die through hunger and disease.

The result was that the ghettoes were steadily industrialised. Machinery that had been expropriated from Jewish businesses was returned to them, and before long the ghettoes were producing a wide range of goods, from footwear to furniture, under contract to German businesses. Of course, the desperate workers were paid rock-bottom wages. Oskar Schindler's German Enamel Works was established near the Cracow ghetto in order to utilise its vast pool of skilled, cheap labour. Meanwhile, in Lodz, five thousand workers were manufacturing textiles and clothing in the ghetto in October 1940; by the spring of 1943, the number was eighty thousand.[14]

Nevertheless, the ghettoes still could not pay their way. The Jewish councils had no comeback when suppliers failed to fulfil orders or delivered insufficient or substandard goods; and many of the National Socialist authorities robbed and expropriated anything they wanted. Regional Leader Greiser of the Warthegau imposed a 65 per cent tax on Jewish workers' wages, which was paid directly into the coffers of the NSDAP. By contrast, in Warsaw, confiscations were stopped to encourage free enterprise and this appeared to bear fruit. By the summer of 1942 – the point at which the population of the ghetto started to be liquidated – they were producing significant quantities of revenue-earning 'exports'.[15]

Irrespective of the contribution they were making to the German war economy, conditions within the ghettoes remained dire. Starvation was rife and with that came increased susceptibility to infectious diseases, exacerbated by the absence of medical supplies, decent sanitation and fuel for heating and cooking. The original plan had been for the Jews to purchase foodstuffs collectively through the councils, but their resources were quickly used up, so then there was much debate over whether to supply the ghettoes with food. It was finally decided that the inhabitants of the Lodz ghetto, for example, would receive 'prison fare',[16] as long as this did not adversely affect the food supply outside. Such rations were never enough: the death rate in the Warsaw ghetto in the summer of 1941 reached over 5500 per month, and conditions were similar in the others. Hilberg estimates that more than 600,000 people – most of them Jews[*] – died in the ghettoes from privation and disease.[17]

None of this was centrally planned. The ghettoes were established as brutal but temporary transit camps for the Jews. They became death traps only when the National Socialists proved incapable of working out where to send their inhabitants.

[*] Some gypsies were also confined in the ghettoes.

Gottlob Berger and the Creation of the Waffen-SS

Until the conclusion of the Polish campaign, the armed SS was a curiosity. Much attention had been lavished on it by Hitler, Himmler and others, but it remained an odd mixture of the political and the military, and it had achieved only moderate results. Its main problem was its size: it was too small to have a decisive impact on any of the operations in which it was involved; yet it was sufficiently large to prove burdensome to the regular armed forces. The experience of the Polish campaign should have convinced the National Socialist leaders to scale down the armed SS units. Then they could have continued to perform their core function – preserving the security of the regime – without causing any more trouble for the army. Instead, the opposite happened. Partly this was due to the efforts of one man: Gottlob Berger – in many respects, the 'father' of the Waffen-SS.

Berger proposed a clever scheme that would more than double the strength of the armed SS without infringing the recruiting rules laid down by the OKW. Hitler's decree of 17 August 1938 had allowed the SS to use members of the Death's Head units and police reinforcements to bring the Special Purpose Troops up to

strength; and a further decree of 18 May 1939 had authorised
Himmler to increase the strength of the Death's Head units to
between forty and fifty thousand as 'police reinforcements' in
wartime. Berger's suggestion was to transfer sufficient members of
the existing Death's Head units and police formations into the
Special Purpose Troops to create two new infantry divisions, and
then to replenish the 'reinforcement' formations with army-trained
members of the General-SS (then some 240,000 strong) and the
Order Police. Hitler approved the plan, and by the end of
November 1939, more or less at the stroke of a pen, the armed SS
formations had grown from four infantry regiments, a few support
battalions and a motley collection of concentration camp guard
units into a force of three infantry divisions (two of which were
motorised), a heavy motorised infantry brigade and a pool of some
fifty thousand trained reinforcements/replacements. These three
new divisions were the SS-Special Purpose Division, the SS-Death's
Head Division and the SS-Police Division. The Death's Head
Division was a motorised infantry formation with a nucleus of
6500 former concentration camp guards. They were largely
equipped with Czech heavy weapons and were commanded by
Theodor Eicke, the brutal and irascible Inspector of Concentration
Camps. The Police Division was a horse-drawn infantry division
manned by 15,800 members of the Order Police, commanded by
Karl von Pfeffer-Wildenbruch.

It was at this time that Berger first coined the phrase 'Waffen-SS'
(literally 'Weapons-SS') to describe the armed military formations
of the SS.[1] He did so in a bid to end the friction between the Special
Purpose Troops and the Death's Head units. The former viewed
themselves primarily as soldiers – indeed, as a military elite –
whereas Eicke's men regarded themselves as members of the (political) General-SS. The Death's Head's units had always been obliged
to undertake military training, but under Eicke – whose own army
career had been spent behind a desk – this fell well short of the
required standard. Therefore, they were now on a steep learning
curve. The designation 'Waffen-SS' was designed to smooth over

this distinction between the two organisations to create a single armed branch of the SS. After the war, several former Special Purpose Troops commanders claimed that the new set-up had been 'an insult to any soldier',[2] but there is no evidence of them raising any objections to it at the time.

The Waffen-SS established its reputation – both bad and good – during the invasion of the Low Countries and France in the spring of 1940. The Police Division spent most of the early part of this campaign in reserve before being deployed across the River Aisne and the Ardennes Canal on 9–10 June, and then moving into the Argonne Forest, fighting a series of engagements against French rearguard troops along the way. By contrast, the *Leibstandarte* and the Special Purpose Division were engaged from the early stages of the campaign.

The *Leibstandarte* formed part of Mobile Group North for the attack on the Netherlands. Its initial role was to thrust forwards from Gronau towards the River Yssel when the attack was launched on 10 May. Dutch resistance was so light that elements of the *Leibstandarte* had penetrated more than forty-five kilometres beyond the river by that evening. Following this, they were attached to the 9th Panzer Division and moved west to link up with German parachute units that had seized key bridges on the southern approaches to Rotterdam. On the afternoon of 14 May, a Luftwaffe airstrike on Rotterdam levelled much of the city centre, killing nearly a thousand civilians, and the town's garrison commander surrendered. The *Leibstandarte* was ordered to move through the city and head on towards the Hague, but en route they encountered a group of armed Dutch soldiers (who were probably heading towards a POW collection point) and engaged them with machine-gun fire. This would have been reckless and irresponsible even if they had not hit and severely wounded General Kurt Student, commander of the German 7 Luftdivision parachute unit as he stood at the window of his command post. Almost simultaneously with this, the Dutch High Command ordered a ceasefire.

Meanwhile, the Special Purpose Division had crossed into the Netherlands on 11 May via the Gennep Bridge, which had been seized in the early hours of the previous morning by army special forces. In company with the 9th Panzer Division, they headed first towards Moerdijk, but were then diverted to intercept a French column that was attempting to block the German advance into North Brabant. Having dealt with this threat, they moved into Zeeland to engage the last remnants of French and Dutch resistance. By 17 May, this part of the assault was over and the division was ordered south to join the French campaign.

As the *Leibstandarte* and the Special Purpose Division were moving from the Netherlands and into France, the Death's Head Division was brought out of reserve in Germany to join in the fighting. All three formations participated in the attacks on the British and French forces that were cut off and squeezed against the north-east Channel coast of France; and all three suffered casualties and reverses. On 21 May, the Death's Head Division (together with Rommel's 7th Panzer Division) was on the receiving end of a British counter-attack near Arras that briefly caused near panic in the German ranks. On 25 May, the Special Purpose Division was forced to withdraw from the town of St Venant by another British counter-attack. And the next day, Sepp Dietrich himself was forced to hide in a ditch when his car was hit by British machine-gun fire. He smeared himself in wet mud to avoid being burned by petrol from the blazing vehicle.

It was during this period that the *Leibstandarte* and the Death's Head Division carried out two separate atrocities that have helped to seal the Waffen-SS's reputation as an essentially criminal force.

On 26 May, the Death's Head Division was pressing hard against the British rearguard holding the canal line between Bethune and Robecq. By mid-afternoon, members of the battalion headquarters and the Headquarters Company of the 2nd Battalion, the Royal Norfolk Regiment, were trapped in and around the Cornet Farm on the outskirts of Le Paradis. They were short of ammunition and cut off from any other British forces. The commanding officer, Major Ryder, sought guidance from HQ 4 Brigade, who asked him to try to hang on until darkness before attempting to withdraw. He knew that would be impossible, so he ordered his men to stop fighting and try to escape. A few slipped out of the farmhouse's side door and hid near by, but the major- ity exited through the main door to the cowshed, with the intention of surrendering. One of the hiding soldiers describes what happened next:

> At first they were met by a hail of bullets then at the second attempt the Germans came rushing out shouting. They were knocked about by rifle butts and kicks, then taken across to some more buildings and searched. After a while they were marched across a road to a farm and as they marched along- side a building two machine guns opened fire and mowed them down. The Germans then went along and shot anybody that moved. By a stroke of luck Bert Pooley and Bill O'Callaghan, although wounded, survived underneath and eventually crawled away.[3]

The Death's Head soldiers were members of the 4th Company of the 1st Battalion, Death's Head Infantry Regiment 2, commanded by Lieutenant Fritz Knöchlein, who gave the orders for the mas- sacre. He was not a popular officer, even within the Death's Head Division. Born in 1911, he was one of the earliest cadets at the Officer Cadet School Braunschweig, and he served in several post- ings without particular distinction before being transferred from the *Deutschland* Regiment to the Death's Head Division at the end of 1939. His fitness reports labelled him 'cocky' and suggested that he 'requires a strong hand'.[4] At his post-war trial, his defence was that the British had used 'dum-dum' ammunition against his men.[*]

---

[*] Dum-dum bullets were developed at the British Military Arsenal in Dum-Dum, India, in the nineteenth century. They were designed to inflict particularly griev- ous wounds by expanding on impact.

This was a ludicrous claim: 'dum-dum' ammunition had been out-lawed by the Hague Convention of 1899 and had not been issued to British soldiers since before the First World War. In reality, Knöchlein's company had simply faced infantry soldiers trained to a high standard of marksmanship. The bullets used by the British Army could certainly produce devastating wounds – one Death's Head soldier described exit wounds of 'hand size'[5] – but they were not dissimilar to those used by the German infantry. And it is highly unlikely that any of the British soldiers in Le Paradis would have had the time or the inclination to alter their ammunition.

As the British witness noted, Privates Pooley and O'Callaghan survived the massacre, even though Knöchlein ordered members of his unit to shoot and bayonet any survivors of the initial shoot-ing – a process that appears to have taken more than an hour.[6] They were both severely wounded, but were cared for by a local Frenchwoman and surrendered to soldiers of the German Army two days later.

News of the massacre spread quickly on the German side, and the commander of the Death's Head Division's higher formation, General Hoeppner of XVI Army Corps, initiated an investigation. However, nothing came of it, and the historian of the division spec-ulates that both Eicke and Himmler intervened to protect Knöchlein.[7] The incident certainly never harmed his wartime career. He was awarded the Iron Cross, (second class) just four days later and finished the war as a lieutenant-colonel, having commanded the partly Norwegian *Norge* Regiment within the *Nordland* Division. However, the Allies were not so forgiving: Knöchlein was hanged as a war criminal in January 1949.[8]

Only a day after the Le Paradis killings, members of the *Leibstandarte* murdered about eighty British prisoners from the 2nd Battalion of the Royal Warwickshire Regiment and attached units on a farm near Wormhoudt-Esquelbecq. The details of this massacre are more obscure than those of the Le Paradis murders, but it certainly took place. It appears that members of the 2nd Battalion of the *Leibstandarte*, under the command of Captain

Wilhelm Möhnke, assembled the prisoners in a cowshed. The British assumed that they were being provided with shelter from the rain, but then a group of SS men surrounded the building and started to throw in hand-grenades. When a British officer ran outside to protest, he was gunned down. Then the Germans shouted for five prisoners to come out. When five did, they were shot one by one on the command of a *Leibstandarte* officer or NCO. Then the call went up for another five to come out. Gunner Brian Fahey, one of the young British soldiers who was in the cowshed, takes up the story:

> I struggled to my feet and a lad about nineteen with a Birmingham accent helped me. We shook hands and took our places. He was at number four, I was at number five.
>
> The officer gave the command. 'Eins!' A shot. After what seemed an eternity (in reality, about two seconds), 'Zwei!' and another shot. It was surprisingly easy to show no panic. I could only stand on my good leg so movement was impossible. The situation was so hopeless that it was almost a relief to think that it would soon be over.
>
> 'Drei!' The third rifle fired and despatched its victim. I tried to concentrate my thoughts on my past life and on my family.
>
> 'Vier!' The fourth rifle fired and I saw from the corner of my eye the boy with the Birmingham accent fall. My mind was buzzing with half-remembered sights and sounds. My father practising the cello; the cricket nets on the middle playground at Colfe's; the smell of the fats and rags and bones in my uncle's Marine Store at Margate.
>
> 'Funf!' It was just like a sharp blow from a fist in my chest that knocked me over. As I hit the ground everything left my mind except the sensation of raging thirst and the certainty that I was dead.
>
> When I opened my eyes I saw the grass and the khaki of my battle-dress. The thought gradually came to me that I was not dead. I lay perfectly still and strained my ears. There was

no sound, I raised my head from my arm and felt the pains in my chest and leg. My spectacles were close by and unbroken and that seemed more important. I put them on and looked at my watch. It was four o'clock. The massacre had taken place at noon.[9]

After shooting the first few groups of five, the SS men had abandoned the procedure as too slow and simply fired their weapons into the cowshed until there was no more movement. But several of the British prisoners escaped injury by feigning death, while others, like Fahey, were unconscious and presumed dead or at least mortally wounded. After several days lying untreated in the shed, the wounded men were found by a German Army patrol and taken to hospital.

No one is certain what motivated this massacre. Some have suggested that Möhnke's battalion believed that their commander, Dietrich, had been killed in the course of the attack that left him cowering in a ditch, and the atrocity was their revenge. More likely, it resulted from pure frustration. The British rearguard units were conducting a layered defence, which meant that a new obstacle appeared after every previous one had been breached, bypassed or captured by the Germans. *Leibstandarte* casualties were particularly heavy that day – veterans remembered it as the hardest single day of the whole western campaign[10] – so their comrades may simply have lashed out at defenceless targets. Either way, no charges were ever brought. Möhnke was captured by the Soviets rather than the British at the end of the war, and they had no inclination either to hand him over or to prosecute him themselves. Much later, in 1988, a German investigation concluded that there was insufficient evidence to bring charges against him.

It seems likely that the Le Paradis and Wormhoudt massacres were carried out as local initiatives by relatively junior officers, rather than on the orders of the respective formation commanders. These were isolated events at this stage, and it would be wrong to draw general conclusions about the behaviour of all Waffen-SS units from them. Even so, it may be more than a coincidence that the two SS units that committed the atrocities were predominantly composed of the more 'political' element within the Waffen-SS. The *Leibstandarte*, as Hitler's bodyguard, tended to attract politically conscious SS recruits, while the Death's Head Division was fashioned around a core of men who had practised the casual brutality of National Socialist totalitarianism over several years in the concentration camp system.

While the field units of the Waffen-SS were fighting in the West, Himmler and Berger were dealing with the consequences of the organisation's rapid expansion. At the beginning of the Polish campaign, the Special Purpose Troops had a strength of some 18,000 men;[11] on 1 May 1940, following the creation of the Death's Head and Police divisions, the total strength of the Waffen-SS was 124,199.[12] In the short term, this represented considerable combat power; but Berger's difficulty now was to sustain it. In December 1939, he had persuaded Himmler to create a full-scale SS recruiting service (SS-*Ergänzungsamt*) within the SS-Main Office, with himself as its head. He then opened an SS recruiting office (*Ergänzungstelle*) within each regional headquarters, and thus within each of the coterminous *Wehrmacht* military districts. However, while Berger was now free to attempt to recruit young men, the *Wehrmacht*, which controlled the draft, was under no obligation to let them join the Waffen-SS rather than the regular armed forces. Each year, the army, air force and navy were allocated medically fit young men according to strict quotas, while the Waffen-SS* recruited its

---

* In March 1940, it was agreed that the Waffen-SS comprised the *Leibstandarte*, the Special Purpose Division, the Death's Head Division, the Police Division, the officer cadet schools, the Death's Head regiments and their *Ersatz* (replacement) units. The German military system divided military formations into field and replacement units. Each formation had a replacement unit that was responsible for training and holding soldiers in reserve until they were needed by the field unit.

members from individuals who volunteered for the organisation from within these quotas. The *Wehrmacht* was willing to allow the Waffen-SS sufficient recruits to maintain its existing formations, but it was not prepared to let the SS create more reserve units that might subsequently be used as the basis for expansion. After all, both the army and the OKW viewed the Waffen-SS as a small and relatively insignificant part of the German armed forces; and, to a large extent, they wanted to keep it that way. Consequently, Berger had to look elsewhere for recruits.

Making Up the Numbers: Foreign Volunteers and Criminals in the Waffen-SS

One of the most striking aspects of the SS was the extent to which non-German nationals were welcomed, and indeed co-opted, into its ranks. Robert Gelwick claims that 'nearly half or more than half of the 910,000 men believed to have served in the Waffen-SS were not Germans or German nationals'.[1] Initially, the recruitment of non-Germans was handled carefully, to tie in with Himmler's vision of the SS as the wellspring for all 'good blood' within Europe. However, as the war continued, the supposedly crucial racial element was put to one side, and non-Germans – particularly those from Eastern Europe and Asia – were recruited *en masse* to enhance the combat power of the Waffen-SS.

The first non-German nationals to join the SS were Austrians, who were recruited even before Hitler came to power. The Austrian NSDAP was, in effect, a subsidiary of the German movement, but, predictably, it placed special emphasis on *Anschluss* – the legal and political union of Germany and Austria. From January 1933 onwards, the Austrian National Socialists stepped up their challenge to the government of Austria through demonstrations and acts of terrorism and sabotage. The government, led by the author-itarian Engelbert Dollfuss, responded in June with a ban on the Austrian NSDAP and its subsidiary organisations (it had its own SA and SS). Consequently, many Austrian SA and SS members crossed the border into Germany as refugees, with around six thousand of them setting up an SA camp at Lechfeld, near Augsburg.[2] As we have seen, Adolf Eichmann was among their number:

> So then they sent me to Kloster Lechfeld . . . It was a big training station from First World War days, set up by the old army. There were barracks, lots of them, and nearby there was a monastery and a brewery. Those barracks weren't new, and there had also been a big canteen there. Bavarian state police were in charge of our training. We were all known as the Austrian Legion [*Österreichische Legion*] . . . There was a complete Battalion of SS, three *Stürme*, but probably more than five hundred men. And probably quite a lot more SA men. Training was given. To all intents and purposes there were only two branches of service, infantry and engineers. The engineers were given shock troop training . . . I went to the shock troop because I was stronger then than I am now. We were trained mostly in street fighting.[3]

Subsequently, in December 1933, the SS battalion was moved from Lechfeld to Prittlbach, and from there to Schleissheim. Meanwhile, in response to diplomatic protests, the Austrian Legion itself was formally dissolved. In 1934 the Austrian battal-ion was absorbed into the nascent Special Purpose Troops as 2nd Battalion, SS-Regiment 1 (which would eventually become the *Deutschland* Regiment).

In addition to the Austrians, a number of other non-Germans joined the SS in the 1930s. Probably the most important of these was the Swiss physician Dr Franz Riedweg. Born in Lucerne in

1907, Riedweg was politically well connected in both Switzerland and Germany, in the latter through his marriage to one of Field Marshal von Blomberg's daughters.[4] He joined the SS in July 1935 and served initially as a doctor with the Special Purpose Troops, but by mid-1943 he had risen to become chief of staff of the *Germanische Leitstelle* (Germanic Administration) – the branch of the SS-Main Office responsible for recruitment throughout occupied Europe and beyond. Riedweg was thus a key figure in the formulation of the SS's unique policy towards foreign volunteers.

Howard Marggraff never rose anywhere near as high as Riedweg in the SS hierarchy, but his case is intriguing in another way – because Marggraff was an American, from Milwaukee. Born on 16 October 1916, he apparently came from a relatively well-off family. He visited Europe in the summer of 1936, during which time he watched some of the Berlin Olympics and spent three weeks in the Soviet Union. He evidently decided that he preferred fascism to communism, because he returned to Germany in February 1938 and joined the *Reichs Arbeits Dienst* (Reich Labour Service) for seven months.[*] In September, he began a course at Berlin University.

Marggraff later claimed that he was invited to join what he termed either the 'Free Legion of Volunteers' or the '*Freischar*' in early 1939.[5] He characterised this as a branch of the SS for foreign volunteers. However, aside from his account, there is no evidence that this organisation ever existed. It is possible that he invented it simply for exculpatory reasons, because by July 1939 at the latest, Marggraff was a full-time member of a Death's Head unit – the Danzig Home Guard. By his own account, he served with the Home Guard during the German invasion of Poland in September, when the unit was subordinated to the 207th Infantry

---

[*] It is likely that he took one of the service's academic courses – which were designed specifically for foreign volunteers – in addition to providing physical labour.

Division. Which means he would have been with it on 8 September, when it executed thirty-three Polish civilians in the Pomeranian village of Ksiazki (Hohenkirch).[6] On 29 September, with the Polish campaign won, the Home Guard paraded through its 'home' city before being transferred to Dachau, headquarters of the Death's Head units.[7] From there, Marggraff and the rest of his unit participated in the invasion of France in May and June 1940.

The following February, Marggraff was released by the Waffen-SS to work as an English-language propaganda broadcaster for the German Radio Service. However, two years later, he skied through the Alps to neutral Switzerland and presented himself to the US Embassy.[*] He received a distinctly uncordial reception,[8] and never revealed what had prompted him to join the SS four years earlier.

It is easier to establish what motivated some other pre-war foreign volunteers. In July 1939, an Englishman wrote to Rudolf Hess, Deputy Leader of the NSDAP:

39 Tomson Avenue
Radford
Coventry
England

Dear Sir,

I hope you don't mind me writing to you like this. But as you are deputy of the Fuhrer, I thought you would be the best one to write to. Could it be possible for me to become a member of the SA or SS? I hope you don't think this funny of me but I am very much interested in it, and I think very much of Deutschland, and its people who I like very much. I would like very much to serve the Fuhrer, and his movement. I am coming over for a holiday in September for the National

---

[*] He was accompanied on this journey by his two brothers, Eugene and Norman, who had joined him in Germany before the outbreak of war. However, it is unclear whether they had also enlisted in the SS.

Socialist Congress as I have many friends in Deutschland. My very best friends. Could it be possible for me, as I would do anything to be able. I could become a German subject even. Please help me won't you dear sir.

Heil Hitler

Your Friend

M. C. Murphy[9]

Himmler's personal staff made enquiries about Murphy through the NSDAP's *Auslandsorganisation* (Overseas Organisation), but these yielded no information about him. Then, with the outbreak of war, his application was not pursued.

One Englishman who did succeed in joining the SS was Thomas Cooper, a young Londoner. His father, Ashley Cooper, was a veteran of the Boer War who established a photography business in Berlin and married a young German woman, Anna Maria Simon. When the First World War broke out, Ashley was interned as an enemy alien in Berlin, while Anna remained free. Thomas was born exactly nine months after the armistice, back in England, where the couple had moved to try to rebuild their lives.

The Coopers eventually settled in Hammersmith, west London, and in due course sent Thomas to Latymer Upper School. He did well enough academically to be remembered by his headmaster as 'a clever boy who was interested in foreign languages'. His 'character appeared sound',[10] too, but in December 1936 he was unable to follow the majority of his classmates into higher education because of lack of money. Instead, he went to work as a clerk for an importer of essential oils in Hackney. Cooper was soon disenchanted with this job, so he made a series of applications to more prestigious organisations. However, he was turned down by the Foreign Office, the Royal Navy, the Royal Air Force and the Metropolitan Police. (Both he and his parents blamed these repeated rejections on his mother's nationality.) Finally, an embittered Cooper joined his local branch of the British Union of Fascists (BUF).

In July 1939, Cooper and his mother travelled to Chemnitz in Germany. They stayed with relatives and Cooper entered a student exchange scheme run by the Reich Labour Service. However, he soon left to find work teaching at a language school in the Taunus Mountains. He was still there when war was declared between Britain and Germany in September. This would normally have led to internment for the duration of the war because Cooper was an enemy alien of military age, but he had a trump card to present to the authorities: his mother had obtained a certificate that classified him as an ethnic German.[11] This left Cooper in a kind of limbo: as a British national, he was treated with suspicion; but as an ethnic German, he was entitled to most of the privileges enjoyed by a German citizen. After taking a variety of odd jobs, he followed up a suggestion from the *Volksdeutsche Mittelstelle* (VOMI – Ethnic German Central Administration) to join the 'German Army'.[12] However, on 1 February 1940, he reported for duty at 163 Finckensteinallee in Berlin-Lichterfelde, the training depot of the *Leibstandarte* Adolf Hitler.

By that stage, he was far from being the only non-German in the armed branch of the SS. Three months later, the Waffen-SS conducted an audit of its manpower.[13] Out of its 124,199 officers, NCOs and men, more than 40,000 had their origins outside the pre-1933 borders of Germany. The membership broke down as follows:

German citizens from:
- Germany (pre-1933 borders)   83,442
- Austria   14,694
- Sudetenland   7693
- Bohemia and Moravia   799
- Memelland   143
- Baltic States   516
- South Tyrol   781
- Upper Silesia   2803
- Warthe and Vistula   10,809

- Volhynia   359
- General Government   1123
- Saarland   103
- Danzig   237

Ethnic Germans from:
- Romania   110
- Hungary   24
- Denmark   40
- New Guinea   1
- France   84
- Switzerland   21
- Slovakia   83
- Italy   15
- USA   8
- Holland   7
- Latvia   2
- Japan   2
- Sumatra   2
- Danzig   2
- Russia   81
- Belgium   7
- German South-West Africa   3
- German East Africa   2
- Saarland   5
- Yugoslavia   48
- China   3
- Brazil   4
- Luxembourg   4
- Spain   2
- Great Britain   10
- South America   2
- Ukraine   5
- Bosnia   1
- Bulgaria   1

- Palestine   2
- Australia   1
- Hultschiner Ländschen*   1
- Mexico   1

Foreign volunteers of 'Germanic' blood from:
- Hungary   1
- Switzerland   44
- Dutch East Indies   1
- Denmark   1
- Great Britain   8
- Greece   3
- Poland   3
- Italy   3
- Holland   4
- Finland   1
- France   8
- Yugoslavia   1
- Belgium   4
- Romania   2
- German South-West Africa   2
- Sweden   3
- Ukraine   1
- German East Africa   4
- Palestine   1
- USA   5
- Russia   1
- General Government   10

Howard Marggraff was probably classified as a Germanic volunteer, making him one of the five in that category from the USA, all of whom served in the Death's Head Division. Thomas Cooper was probably included among the ten British ethnic Germans,

* An ethnic German area of Czechoslovakia.

three of whom were in Death's Head regiments. (By May 1940, Cooper was serving in a Death's Head training unit in Radolfzell, near the Swiss border.) The seven others were in the Police Division.

At this point, foreigners were not specifically targeted by the Waffen-SS for recruitment, and if any did find their way into the organisation, they were not segregated from the German members. However, both of these policies were about to change.

With opportunities for recruiting young German nationals restricted by the *Wehrmacht*, Berger hit on the idea of bringing in ethnic Germans from the rest of Europe. He calculated that there were up to 1.5 million ethnic Germans of military age in Central and South-East Europe, none of whom would be included in the *Wehrmacht* draft. Crucially, though, they did still meet the racial criterion demanded by the SS. Berger's own son-in-law, Andreas Schmidt, was a leader of the German community within Romania. In the spring of 1940, he had smuggled more than a thousand young ethnic Germans out of the country and into the waiting arms of the Waffen-SS. Delighted by this, in August 1940 Berger proposed launching a recruitment campaign among the ethnic Germans of Romania, Hungary and Yugoslavia, 'with or without the agreement of their Governments'.[14] Himmler gave Berger the green light to proceed, which he duly did, but with only limited success.

Nevertheless, the recruitment of foreign nationals into the Waffen-SS was about to shift into a higher gear. This came about because of the conquest of Western Europe, which began with the invasion and occupation of Denmark and Norway. The two Scandinavian countries were attacked simultaneously on 9 April 1940. In addition to straightforward empire-building, this was a strategic move to pre-empt British disruption of the transport of iron ore from Sweden to Germany. Denmark, which possessed an army of just fourteen thousand men (eight thousand of whom had been serving for under two months), fell within a few hours. The campaign in Norway was more protracted, lasting two months and costing the lives of around twelve thousand men (German, British and Norwegian), but eventually it fell, too. The occupation of these two countries gave the SS direct access to potential recruits who, while not ethnically German, fell within the organisation's definition of 'Nordic' or 'Germanic'. As such, they were eligible to join as part of the wider Germanic family. As early as 20 April, Hitler ordered that the SS-*Nordland* Regiment 'was to be established from Danish and Norwegian volunteers'[15] and would undertake 'police duties'.[16] In fact, the unit was an infantry regiment. Hitler probably represented it as a police formation in a bid to avoid antagonism between the SS and the *Wehrmacht*.

In the 1930s, neither Norway nor Denmark had a particularly large fascist movement. The Danish National Socialist Workers' Party (DNSAP), founded in 1930, managed to attract just over 31,000 votes in the Danish parliamentary elections of 1939, winning three seats. In Norway, the *Nasjonal Samling* (NS – National Union Party), founded by Vidkun Quisling in 1933, was even less effective – it had not managed to gain even a single seat on a local council prior to the German occupation. Unsurprisingly, then, the SS's hopes of persuading thousands of Scandinavian racial idealists to join the organisation soon proved unfounded. When recruiting started in the autumn of 1940, no more than a few hundred signed up in either country.

Back in the spring, as the western campaign progressed, the *Westland* Regiment – designed to accommodate Dutch and Belgian-Flemish volunteers – was founded on 25 May 1940.[17] This was fast work: while the Netherlands had fallen within four days of the German invasion on 10 May, Belgium was still resisting (and would continue to do so until 28 May). The rush probably reflected Himmler's expectation that the SS would be inundated with volunteers from both Holland and Flanders. In the Netherlands, Anton Adriaan Mussert's *Nationaale-Socialistiche Beweging* (National Socialist Movement) had imitated Germany's NSDAP while also stressing its Dutch character. This tactic had helped it to secure 294,284 votes in the municipal elections of

1935, and 4 per cent of the vote in the 1937 national elections.* In Flanders, Flemish nationalists seeking independence from Belgium had traditionally accepted patronage from Germany, and in the 1930s they had been strongly influenced by fascism. Therefore, the Germans had genuine grounds for optimism as far as recruitment was concerned; and, indeed, the Dutch subsequently provided the largest single contingent of Western European volunteers in the German armed forces.

Some post-war apologists and revisionists have argued that these volunteers and the few to sign up in Scandinavia were motivated by anti-communism or perhaps even a sense of pan-Europeanism. But that seems highly unlikely in the spring and summer of 1940, when relations between the Third Reich and the Soviet Union were officially cordial. It is much more credible to suggest that the new recruits to the *Nordland* and *Westland* regiments were either pro-National Socialist cranks or simple opportunists.

In order to process their applications, recruiting offices were established in Oslo, the Hague, Antwerp and Copenhagen. Furthermore, a former French Army barracks at Sennheim, Alsace, was commandeered by the SS-Main Office to be used as a premilitary training depot for the assessment and indoctrination of volunteers before suitable applicants were formally inducted into the Waffen-SS. This new infrastructure was hardly overworked. In July 1940, the organisation inducted 908 recruits from Denmark and the Netherlands; then 310 in August; and 330 in September.[18]

Nevertheless, Himmler remained an enthusiastic supporter of the recruitment campaign. He wanted the SS to gather the best 'Germanic' blood from all over the world, not just from Germany, and he viewed the work in Scandinavia and the Low Countries as the start of that project. More prosaically, it was now abundantly clear that the SS had to look outside of Germany for its manpower.

---

* This gave the party four seats in the hundred-member lower house and four in the fifty-member upper chamber.

In July 1940, Berger estimated that the *Wehrmacht* would permit the Waffen-SS to recruit no more than 2 per cent of all eligible German youths from each year group. At most, that would amount to twelve thousand men per year,[19] which was simply not enough to maintain existing Waffen-SS units, let alone raise new ones.

The mood in Germany in the late summer of 1940 was understandably triumphant. By then, plans were well under way for the future conquest of the Soviet Union; and some thought was also being given to the post-war administration of Europe after what seemed the inevitable German victory. Hitler decreed that the future strength of the German Army should amount to some sixty-four divisions.* Meanwhile, the Waffen-SS should comprise the *Leibstandarte* (at brigade strength), the Special Purpose Division, the Death's Head Division, the Police Division, and a future division that would be 'recruited, for the most part, from foreign nationals'.[20]

The *Nordland* and *Westland* regiments would provide the basis of this 'foreign' division, and preparations for its formation continued throughout the autumn. Finally, on 3 December 1940, the SS-Command Staff decreed that *Nordland* and *Westland*, together with the *Germania* Regiment from the Special Purpose Division, the newly formed SS-5th Artillery Regiment and other minor units would form the fully motorised *Germania* Division: the fourth combat division of the Waffen-SS. Eighteen days later, though, amid concerns that this name would cause confusion, it was changed to *Wiking*.

In reality, the claim that this division was formed 'largely from foreign nationals' was a fraud that was designed to pull the wool over the eyes of the *Wehrmacht*. The *Germania* Regiment had been recruited primarily in north-west Germany; and while the

---

* To put this into perspective, the modern British Army consists of just two operational divisions, only one of which can be deployed at any one time.

Nordland and *Westland* regiments contained several hundred foreign volunteers from Scandinavia and the Low Countries, the great majority of their personnel comprised either native German citizens or ethnic German recruits from Romania and Slovakia. Himmler and Berger were not remotely concerned about exceeding their recruitment quotas of eligible German manpower, as long as they could get away it. All that really mattered to them was to build up the Waffen-SS to such a size that the organisation could demand a place alongside the *Wehrmacht* in the councils of war. Moreover, the command cadre of the 'foreign' division at this stage was almost entirely German. The divisional commander was Felix Steiner, the former chief of the *Deutschland* Regiment, who now held the rank of SS-brigadier.

However, Steiner proved to be a powerful champion of the Germanic volunteers within the *Wiking* Division. Of course, this was an uphill struggle, given the profoundly racist philosophy of the SS. No matter how much Himmler preached that the Nordic and Germanic peoples were from the same racial family as the Germans themselves, the average Waffen-SS officer or NCO was almost certain to view them as second-class soldiers from conquered nations. Yet, ultimately, Steiner managed to persuade the German elements to accept the Germanic volunteers as full members of the SS order purely through the force of his stubborn, mulish personality. By the end of the war, they were fully integrated into the *Wiking* Division – and the *Nordland* Division, which was formed from it – and were treated in much the same way as their German national and ethnic German counterparts.

Berger continued to be on the lookout for recruits who were not eligible for the *Wehrmacht* draft, and he found some to form one of the most notorious units within the Waffen-SS: the *Sonderkommando* (Special Unit) Dirlewanger. This formation could be viewed as a link between the regular combat units of the Waffen-SS and the special task groups that began the extermination of the Jews. Initially, though, it was not even under the formal control of the SS-Command Main Office, although its commanders were members of the Waffen-SS or the police. In its early stages, most of its German personnel were convicted criminals (often poachers), assigned to the formation to redeem themselves through combat. Once there, they were subjected to a brutal disciplinary regime that involved beatings, formal floggings and, frequently, summary execution. They were treated like kicked dogs and reacted in much the same way – lashing out whenever they were let off the leash.

The idea of using convicted criminals in such units might have originated with Hitler himself. Certainly, SS-Major General Karl Wolff portrayed it in that way. On 23 March 1940, Himmler's personal adjutant phoned the Ministry of Justice to say: 'The Führer proposes to postpone punishment of the so-called "decent" poachers and, provided they acquit themselves well at the front, to guarantee them amnesty.'[21] He then went on to ask for details of any poachers currently being held within the criminal justice system. Later, at the post-war Nuremberg trials, Berger said that Hitler held all hunters in 'scorn and ridicule'* and seized any opportunity to rile them.[22] However, he also mentioned a petition sent to the Führer Chancellery by the wife of an 'old fighter' who was serving a two-year jail term for poaching deer, which suggested that he might be able to redeem himself at the front.[23] This letter could well have led Hitler to the idea of the poachers' unit. Equally, though, the concept might have come from Berger. As we have seen, he was a keen hunter himself, so perhaps he saw the potential of utilising poachers' expert fieldcraft on the front line.

A week after Wolff's phone call, Himmler himself wrote to the Justice Ministry: 'The Führer has directed that all poachers – particularly of Bavarian and Austrian origin – who have broken the law by hunting with guns rather than snares may, through service in the SS, particularly in sharpshooter companies, for the duration

---

* Hitler's indifference towards human suffering formed a bizarre contrast to his sentimental affection towards most animals.

of the war, be freed of the consequences of their punishment, and through good service may be considered for amnesty.'[24]

In May and June 1940, eighty-eight convicted poachers were assembled in Block 36 of Sachsenhausen concentration camp; and on 1 July, fifty-five of them were deemed usable and transferred to the 5th Death's Head Regiment in nearby Oranienburg to begin military training. It seems that Berger himself made the final selection,[25] and he had a large role to play in choosing the unit's leader, too. Appropriately, he picked a man with a criminal record to lead this band of convicts.

Oskar Dirlewanger was born into a middle-class family in Würzburg on 26 September 1895. He seems to have had a relatively conventional, if nationalistically inclined, upbringing.[26] In October 1913, he joined the Machine-Gun Company of the 123rd Regiment of Grenadiers as a 'one-year volunteer'.[27] This should have allowed Dirlewanger to train as a reserve officer before he embarked on a business or professional career; but, of course, Europe descended into war before his year was up, and in August 1914 he found himself leading a platoon into Belgium and France. Thereafter, he had a distinguished First World War.[*] He received his commission as a *Leutnant der Reserve* on 14 April 1915 and continued to command his platoon. However, he was injured in action five months later and was excused further front-line service.[†] In November 1916, he was assigned to run machine-gun training courses, but the following year he volunteered to return to the front and was placed in command of the Assault Company of the 7th Infantry Division. Later, he was given command of his

---

[*] He was awarded the Iron Cross, second and first class, and the Gold Württemberg Bravery Medal.

[†] Dirlewanger was injured on three separate occasions during the war. In one of his very first actions in France in August 1914, he was shot in the foot, sabred in the chest and received shrapnel wounds to the head. Then, in September 1915, he received a gunshot wound to his hand and a bayonet wound to his leg. Finally, in April 1918, he was shot in the left shoulder. At the end of the war, he was classified as 40 per cent disabled.

old Machine-Gun Company in the 123rd Grenadiers. His final –
temporary – appointment was command of the 2nd Battalion of
the 121st Regiment of Grenadiers in the German occupation force
in the Ukraine. When hostilities ended in November 1918, he led
his battalion home across Romania, Hungary and Austria in order
to prevent their internment.

Unsurprisingly, Dirlewanger joined various Free Corps units
after his demobilisation from the regular army. Between 1919 and
1921, he took part in actions in a number of towns and cities as
a member of the *Epp*, *Haas*, *Sprösser* and *Holz* groups, and he
commanded an armoured train that was instrumental in liberat-
ing the town of Sangerhausen from the control of socialist
revolutionaries. He was also jailed on two occasions in 1920–21,
apparently for firearms offences. However, it would be incorrect
to infer that he was a full-time counter-revolutionary at this time.
He enrolled at a business college in Mannheim in 1919 and graduated two years later. Then he entered the University of Frankfurt
to read for a doctorate in political science.*

Alongside his studies and his paramilitary activities, Dirlewanger was active in right-wing politics. He joined the NSDAP in
October 1922, receiving the membership number 12517, and it
seems that he tried and failed to hijack some police armoured cars
for use in the Munich *Putsch*. Thereafter, he let his party membership lapse, rejoined in 1926, then left again two years later,
when he became an executive for the Jewish-owned Kornicker textiles company in Erfurt. Nevertheless, he continued to make
financial contributions to the SA.[28]

Dirlewanger rejoined the NSDAP yet again in March 1932, and
later that year he signed up with his local SA unit, where he was
appointed a platoon commander. The following year, he secured
a job as deputy director of the Employment Office in Heilbronn.[29]
At this point, Dirlewanger should have been well set on the path

---

* On 12 April 1921, he was injured yet again – another head wound – but this
does not seem to have impeded either his studies or his soldiering.

to success: he enjoyed prestige as a distinguished 'old fighter' and war hero, and he was in tune with the opinions of the new regime. However, he was soon branded a disruptive influence by the SA, his local NSDAP and the Employment Office. The root cause of this was his alcoholism, a condition that he never managed to overcome. In July 1934, in the wake of the Night of the Long Knives, he went for a drunken drive around Heilbronn in his official car. He caused two road accidents and left the scene of both. Even more disturbingly, during the course of this binge, he had sex with a thirteen-year-old member of the *Jungmädel* (Young Maidens),[*] and it was later alleged that he sexually abused girls from this organisation on a routine basis.

Dirlewanger lost his job, was expelled from the party and the SA, and received a two-year prison sentence. He admitted that he 'did wrong',[30] but vehemently denied that he was a serial child abuser, claiming that he thought the girl in question was sixteen. A subsequent investigation by the SD suggested that the local NSDAP leadership might have put pressure on the court to find him guilty. Furthermore, when Dirlewanger tried to have his case reopened after his release from prison in 1936, the local party leaders almost immediately placed him in 'protective custody' in a local concentration camp, presumably to shut him up.

Dirlewanger's rehabilitation began in April 1937, when Gottlob Berger, who seems to have been a friend, helped to find him a post as a company commander in the Condor Legion – the quasi-official German military presence in Spain during the civil war. At one point he was summoned back to Germany to be investigated for 'political unreliability', but Viktor Brack of the Führer Chancellery intervened to ensure Dirlewanger's release and return to the fighting. The next time he returned to Germany, in May 1939, he was awarded the Spanish Cross in Silver by the OKW (to go with two Spanish Nationalist decorations).

---

[*] The Young Maidens was the junior branch of the NSDAP's *Bund Deutscher Mädel* (League of German Maidens), the female equivalent of the Hitler Youth.

With a much larger war now in the offing, Dirlewanger wrote to Himmler in July 1939 to apply for one of the SS military units. However, he was initially turned down, pending the outcome of a fresh appeal he had made against his conviction five years earlier. Finally, in May 1940, following the presentation of a new testimony, Dirlewanger's conviction on the underage sex charge was overturned and he was exonerated of guilt. Ultimately, he was also allowed back into the NSDAP.

It is impossible to know whether Dirlewanger's friends in high places pulled some strings on his behalf, just as it is impossible to know whether his original conviction was secured by political enemies. Whatever the truth, Berger now felt free to champion Dirlewanger. He reminded Himmler of this potentially promising commander, and suggested that he should be placed in charge of training the new poachers' unit. Himmler agreed, and on 17 June 1940 orders were issued to transfer Dirlewanger from the army reserve into the Waffen-SS with the rank of SS-reserve lieutenant.

However, just as Dirlewanger arrived at Oranienburg to take up his new post, the whole project hit a snag. One of the poachers wrote a letter home, and this found its way into the hands of an NSDAP leader in Hettstedt. The party man subsequently complained that there was 'general indignation, both in party circles and in the SS',[31] at the very idea of convicted poachers serving in Himmler's supposedly elite service. As convicts, these men were deemed to be *Wehrunwürdig* – unworthy to carry arms in the service of the state – and thus could not be drafted by the *Wehrmacht*, and yet here was the SS seeking to recruit them. A cunning way was found to dampen this criticism: it was decided that the unit would not be *part of* the Waffen-SS but a special formation *under the control of* the SS. Likewise, while the unit's commanders were to be drawn from the Waffen-SS, the poachers, in effect, were to be employed by the SS but could not be members of it until they had redeemed themselves in combat.

With this established, Dirlewanger supervised the basic training of the eighty[32] poachers at Oranienburg. Then, in the autumn of 1940, he was ordered to take the unit to Poland. Although it had been renamed *SS-Sonderbataillon Dirlewanger* (SS-Special Battalion Dirlewanger), it was organised at this stage as an infantry company. In Poland, its members undertook a variety of tasks: for instance, they were involved, probably as slave-labour guards, in the digging of anti-tank ditches on the defensive 'Otto Line' that was prepared against possible Soviet attack; they supervised Jewish slave labourers from a concentration camp at Dszikow; and they swept up remnants of the Polish Army hiding in the forests near the demarcation line between the German and Soviet zones.[33] There is no concrete evidence for how they behaved at this time; however, given their conduct later in the war, it is safe to assume that they were casually brutal towards both their enemies and their prisoners.

More is known about what life was like for the poachers themselves at this time. One of the original members of the unit recalled: 'We learned from the beginning that Dirlewanger was "Lord of Life and Death"; he treated us as he wanted. He could pronounce sentence of death and carry it out. He didn't need to carry out a trial. These powers were given to him by the National Leader of the SS.'[34] This was certainly true, but it appears that Dirlewanger also had a certain degree of affection for his men, and he could treat them decently, provided that they observed absolute obedience to him and maintained an iron discipline.

As we have seen, the Waffen-SS was hardly deluged with volunteers when it tried to recruit ethnic Germans and the 'Nordic' races from occupied Europe. However, that recruitment campaign was a roaring success in comparison with its various attempts to persuade significant numbers of Allied nationals to join its ranks.

A British volunteer unit fighting in the Third Reich's 'crusade against Bolshevism' was first seriously mooted in the winter of 1942. Its proponent was John Amery, the elder son of a member of Churchill's government, who had thrown in his lot with the

Third Reich and moved to Berlin several months earlier. Eventually, despite considerable effort over the next two years, this would turn out to be the smallest independent foreign volunteer unit of the Waffen-SS.

Amery's father Leo, a contemporary of Churchill at Harrow, was elected to Parliament in 1911 and was soon being touted as a rising star of the political right. Over the next thirty years, he established a reputation as 'One of the best informed and most intellectually sophisticated men in British public life.'[35] Indeed, his speech to the House of Commons on 7 May 1940 helped precipitate the fall of Chamberlain's government and Churchill's assumption of power.

John Amery, who was born the same year his father entered Parliament, was an entirely different character. A strange and difficult boy from a very early age, he suffered from a personality disorder that seems to have left him more or less indifferent to the consequences of his actions. He ran away from school on several occasions, drank heavily, contracted syphilis at the age of fourteen, stole, lied, ran up huge debts, wrecked cars and married bigamously on two occasions (his three 'wives' were all prostitutes). He was living in southern France in the spring of 1940 – supported by an allowance from his family – and spurned a number of opportunities to return to Britain. By then, he had a fairly unique political philosophy, combining his father's British Conservative imperialism with French-tinted fascism and virulent anti-Semitism; which was particularly peculiar, as his grandmother had been a Hungarian-Jewish refugee. These political views – and his connection to Churchill's government – earned him considerable suspicion from the Vichy government, and he was incarcerated in a concentration camp at Vals les Bains in November 1941.

Released after a few weeks, Amery began to look for ways to improve his situation. Enthused by the German invasion of the Soviet Union, he approached the Finnish and Italian governments and asked to join their forces, but then he was contacted by the German Foreign Ministry in August 1942 and invited to visit

Berlin under safe conduct. Fired up with vanity and self-importance, he accepted. The Germans, of course, merely wanted to see if this anti-Semitic fascist sympathiser with a direct link to the British establishment might be of use to them. Amery met with Dr Fritz Hesse, chairman of the German inter-departmental 'England Committee', around Christmas 1942. Hitler was kept informed of these meetings and seemed to think that Amery might provide Germany with a major propaganda coup. It was agreed that Amery should make a series of 'pro-peace' (anti-British) broadcasts on German radio, but Hitler was also interested in the Englishman's suggestion that he should recruit sympathetic British prisoners of war to fight for the German cause on the Eastern Front. On 28 December, Ambassador Walter Hewel, the Foreign Ministry's representative at Hitler's headquarters, telegrammed Hesse: 'The Führer is in agreement with the establishment of an English Legion . . . [recruited from] former members of the English Fascist Party or those with similar ideology – thus quality not quantity.' Immediately, the England Committee decided to exclude Amery entirely from the recruitment process.

The SS did not become formally involved in the formation of the 'English Legion' until September 1943. By then, an effort had been made to identify fascists among the sixty thousand or so British POWs being held by the Germans, and to concentrate them at two special camps in the suburbs of Berlin: Zehlendorf for officers; and Genshagen for other ranks. A rumour was started that these two camps were 'holiday centres' for long-term prisoners, where they would have access to better food, sports facilities, entertainment and even sight-seeing trips around Berlin. In reality, they were run by a member of the England Committee, Arnold Hillen-Ziegfeld. Under his direction, supposed British fascist sympathisers were installed as the permanent trusties of the camp and ordered to identify and recruit other potential volunteers.

It seems that the Zehlendorf camp was a complete failure, but the same cannot be said of the Genshagen camp. Among the

'German' staff there were Oskar Lange, an army NCO who had lived in New York for many years, and Thomas Cooper, who was now an SS-corporal. Cooper had spent most of 1941 and 1942 officially as a member of the guard unit at Sachsenhausen concentration camp, but actually detached to the Heidelager training area at Debica, where he had supervised slave labourers working on construction projects. At the beginning of 1943 he and other NCOs from his unit had been drafted into the Waffen-SS Police Division and sent to the Eastern Front. Cooper received severe leg wounds during the fighting around Leningrad and was seconded to Genshagen to recuperate.

The British 'camp leader' was Battery Quartermaster Sergeant J. H. O. Brown, a pre-war member of the BUF and a notorious figure among British POWs because of his black-marketeering and collaboration. However, Brown was playing a double game. He had been a genuine fascist before the war, but his loyalty to his country far outweighed any political allegiance. By late 1942, he was sending coded intelligence back to Britain via the POW mail system. His permanent staff at Genshagen included: Francis MacLardy, a sergeant pharmacist from the Royal Army Medical Corps who had been a district secretary of the BUF; two former commandos and ex-BUF members – Corporal Paul Maton and Lance Corporal William Charles Britten; Frederick Lewis, a merchant seaman and also an ex-BUF member; and Roy Courlander, a British-born New Zealander with no previous history of fascist sympathies. Brown did not realise that MacLardy, Maton and Courlander had already individually volunteered to serve in the Waffen-SS, and the other fascist sympathisers in the camp had agreed to recruit others. Consequently, while Lange, Cooper and the other fascists busily canvassed the 'holidaying' POWs, Brown and several confidants in the camp did all they could to undermine the project.

In August 1943, the senior British POW in Germany, Major General Victor Fortune, sent Brigadier Leonard Parrington to inspect Genshagen. Parrington took the camp at face value and gave permission for the prisoners to participate in recreational activities under parole.* This was misinterpreted by the fascists within the camp, who assumed that Parrington was endorsing their recruitment campaign.† Not long after, they left Genshagen to form the nucleus of the new unit.

In September 1943, Hesse wrote to Gottlob Berger to suggest that the SS-Main Office should assume control of the administration of the British unit. Berger was unconvinced, but as the British were regarded as a 'Germanic', it made sense for the new formation to come under the auspices of the SS. Berger grudgingly appointed a young, English-speaking artillery officer, SS-Captain Hans Werner Roepke, to act as 'liaison officer' and acting commander until a suitable British officer could be found to lead the unit. Roepke then convened several meetings with the volunteers (there were only six of them) to thrash out some administrative details. It was decided that the unit would be called the British Free Corps; that it would be active only on the Eastern Front against the Soviets; that its members would wear German uniforms with distinctive insignia; that it would be led by British officers, if any could be recruited; that members would not be subject to the full range of German military law;‡ and that they would receive normal German military rates of pay. Roepke also explained that the unit would have to be fully trained and number at least thirty personnel before it could be committed to the front.

Recruitment continued at Genshagen and was also launched at Stalag IIIa, Luckenwalde. Here, a different approach was taken. Luckenwalde was a large POW camp near Berlin, but it also served as a tactical interrogation centre, where a small team of

---

* They had to sign a statement agreeing not to attempt to escape if they were allowed outside the confines of the camp.

† Subsequently, they even proposed that Parrington should be the nominal commander of the British unit. However, this suggestion never reached him, and he never had anything to do with it.

‡ This was standard practice for foreign volunteers, who generally served on a contract basis in the German armed forces and did not have the same legal obligation as German citizens to undergo military service.

renegade British and Canadian soldiers were used as 'stool pigeons' to wheedle intelligence out of newly captured military POWs. In October and November 1943, this interrogation team succeeded in browbeating fifteen or twenty British, Canadian and South African soldiers into 'volunteering' for the British Free Corps. However, when these men arrived at the fledgling unit's accommodation block in Pankow, Berlin, they protested so strongly that most were allowed to return to Luckenwalde. Thereafter, the Luckenwalde operation was abandoned; instead, it was decided that existing members of the British Free Corps would concentrate their recruitment efforts on the general POW population.

On 1 January 1944, the British Free Corps was formally established as a unit of the Waffen-SS. The following month, the ten or so members moved to Hildesheim to begin their training. Meanwhile, desultory recruitment efforts continued until April 1944, primarily focusing on known fascist sympathisers. However, only a couple signed up. The recruiters also had no success with James Conen and William Celliers. They had been prisoners of war in Italy, had escaped after the armistice in 1943, but had been recaptured by a German unit to find themselves prisoners of the *Leibstandarte* Adolf Hitler. Thereupon, they had been sworn in as auxiliary volunteers and taken to Russia, where they were employed as drivers. On the *Leibstandarte*'s return from the Eastern Front, Conen and Celliers were sent to the British Free Corps, but both declined the offer to join.

Towards the end of April 1944, the dozen members of the unit were issued with special insignia: three heraldic leopards on the right collar patch, a Union Flag shield on the left sleeve, and a cuff-title reading 'British Free Corps' in English. On the 20th, they paraded in front of Roepke in their new uniforms and were issued with SS identity documents and side-arms. Roepke announced a series of promotions and then the members of the unit were dispatched on a full-scale recruitment drive. Over the next few months, usually working in pairs, they visited the majority of

POW and civilian internment camps. They left fliers and wherever possible spoke to potential volunteers. Anyone who came forward was immediately transported to a house in Berlin, supervised by Cooper, while a cursory background check was conducted. If they passed, they then joined the unit in Hildesheim. By June, all of this effort had yielded about eleven new recruits.

On 13 June, a meeting was convened to discuss these recruitment difficulties. One of the attendees was SS-Major Vivian Stranders, an Englishman who had served in the British Army in the First World War before becoming a naturalised German in 1933.[*] He had done some propaganda broadcasting to England at the beginning of the war and was now the 'England Desk Officer' at the Germanic Administration in the SS-Main Office. Astonishingly enough, this long-standing British member of the NSDAP and SS was also Jewish – a fact known to at least some of his colleagues[36] – and was widely suspected of being a British spy. At the meeting, he suggested that the 'German' leaders of the British Free Corps – Roepke and Cooper – were incompetent, and proposed using carefully selected English-speaking Germans as recruiters. After all, they could do no worse than the British had over the spring.

Meanwhile, the unit itself was already rupturing. One of its first recruits had been a captured British commando called Thomas Freeman. He had volunteered from Stalag XVIIIa in Austria along with two friends: an Australian called Lionel Wood and a Belgian civilian named Theo Menz. However, these three had joined with the intention of either escaping or sabotaging the unit from within. Freeman especially worked hard to split the unit into those who had joined for ideological reasons and those who had more materialistic motives. The idealists, led by MacLardy, were characterised as the 'Nazi Party', while Freeman himself formed a

---

[*] He had been convicted by a French court of espionage on behalf of Germany in 1927 and sentenced to two years in prison, and he may have been working as a German agent even before the First World War.

faction that called itself the '*Kohlenklau*' (Coal Snaffler), after a German propaganda character. By June, Freeman had managed to persuade fifteen out of the twenty-three members of the unit to sign a petition requesting that they be allowed to return to their POW camps. He and Menz were identified as the ringleaders and dispatched to Stutthof concentration camp.* Roepke then decided that the only way to keep the unit intact was to get rid of the genuine fascists, too: MacLardy was transferred to a Waffen-SS medical supplies depot in Berlin, while Courlander and Maton went to the Kurt Eggers Regiment, the Waffen-SS's war correspondent and psychological operations unit. Nevertheless, disciplinary problems continued in the British Free Corps throughout the summer, and only a handful of new members were recruited. No more than twenty-nine British and Commonwealth soldiers served in the unit at any one time, while the total number associated with it in any way – including those who 'volunteered' from Luckenwalde – never reached sixty.

The tiny unit remained in Hildesheim until October 1944, when it was transferred to the Waffen-SS combat engineering school in Dresden. Shortly after this move, both Roepke and Cooper were removed from their posts. Roepke was replaced by SS-Lieutenant Kühlich, a former member of the *Das Reich* Division who was no longer fit for active service after being wounded on the Eastern Front. Unlike his predecessor, he did not command his new charges personally, opting instead to remain at the British Free Corps liaison office in Berlin. Roepke went on to serve in a Waffen-SS special forces unit, while Cooper was sent to the depot of the *Leibstandarte* Adolf Hitler, where he remained until April 1945. Recruitment under the new commander was as poor as ever, but a few new volunteers turned up during the autumn and winter of 1944. Among their number were three South Africans and five New Zealand Maoris. The latter were rejected on the basis that it was a 'whites only' unit.

* Menz was murdered there, while Freeman eventually managed to escape.

In January 1945, six of its members attempted to escape. They headed east in the hope that they would be able to hide out and then surrender to the Russians. However, they were detained by military policemen in German-controlled Czechoslovakia and eventually returned, under armed escort, to Dresden. Three of them were immediately sent to an isolation camp that had been established for British Free Corps 'rejects' at Drönnewitz, while the other three rejoined the unit. They were still there when Dresden was bombed by a massive Allied air strike on 12–13 February. Only one member of the unit was slightly injured during the raid, and thereafter took part in the rescue and clear-up operation alongside other soldiers from the barracks. However, a few days later, an ex-girlfriend of one of the members denounced the unit to the Gestapo for having signalled to the RAF bombers. These ludicrous accusations were taken seriously, and the whole corps was arrested and briefly detained. On 24 February, they left Dresden for Berlin and all attempts to recruit any new members ceased. Kühlich remarked to his British senior NCO: 'The British Free Corps has had a damned good run, now they must prove they are sincere.'[37]

They hung around in Berlin for two weeks until a decision could be made about where they should go next. In the end, each member of the unit was given a choice: the isolation camp at Drönnewitz or the front line against the rapidly advancing Soviets. Amazingly, twelve of them – not one of whom was an ideological fascist or a National Socialist – opted to fight. Another member of the unit recalled: 'They didn't want the Jerries to think they were frightened, so they just went.'[38] Over the next few days, they were fitted out with new combat equipment and sent on a hurried close-combat course. Then, on 15 March, they were transported to Germanic Panzer Corps, in reserve at Stettin on the Baltic Coast. They waited there for a further week before being assigned to the 3rd Company of the Armoured Reconnaissance Battalion of the 11th SS-Panzer-Grenadier *Nordland* Division, in reserve on the western bank of the River Oder, awaiting the next Soviet offensive.[39] This battalion was probably the most cosmopolitan in the German armed forces, including volunteers from all over Scandinavia, the Baltic States, the Low Countries, as well as native Germans and ethnic Germans from throughout Europe, but even they had not expected to see a British unit joining their number.

Their commanding general, Felix Steiner, was equally surprised by the British Free Corps' appearance at the front:

> In view of the general situation the appearance of these volunteers seemed to me to be more than superfluous and senseless, an opinion which I expressed . . . I drove to this unit in order to inspect it while training and to see the English volunteers. I found them at their bivouac in the wood. They were about 12 or 14 men, tall, well built, with decent open faces. I welcomed them, and told them to get used to things and to keep good comradeship . . . The whole company was then drawn up in a semi-circle and I spoke to them about the great seriousness of the situation, saying that we had to use our last strength to stop the Russians who were threatening not only Germany but the whole of Western culture. The men who had done extremely well in the past years, especially in west Latvia, and who knew me well, appreciated the full meaning of these words. As for the English volunteers, I had the impression that they were suffering from an inner conflict. Their conduct was faultless; they had no special personal wishes and seemed to get on well with the troops, but I nevertheless had the impression that they were depressed. At my arrival at Corps battle HQ I mentioned the matter to the Corps adjutant and the ADC. We all agreed that we could not take the responsibility of letting the English volunteers fight as they would be driven into a humanly unbearable inner conflict. I thought about the matter and on about 10 April I discussed it with Lieutenant Colonel Riedweg, who shared my opinion that it would be unfair on our part to

throw these young men into this battle sector which would probably turn out to be their last. I therefore decided to withdraw the English volunteers from their unit and to employ them in some way as auxiliaries at a rear medical unit of the command. At the same time I issued instructions that in the case of British troops approaching from the West, they were to be given an opportunity somehow to get in touch with their compatriots. This solution I believed to be best in the circumstances . . .

One day between the 10th and the 14th I met some English volunteers during one of my journeys to the front. They were marching west along the *Autobahn*.[40]

It was while the British Free Corps were suffering their 'inner conflict' at the front that the last British volunteer joined the Waffen-SS. Douglas Berneville Webster Claye was a bizarre character. Born in south London in 1917, his father was a regular soldier in the Royal Army Service Corps. Claye himself spent three years at the Army Apprentices' College in Chepstow, but he left the army in 1935 and spent the next five years in a variety of jobs, including riding instructor and journalist. Soon after the outbreak of war, he volunteered for the RAF as an aircrew trainee, but he was discharged after going absent without leave to marry his pregnant girlfriend bigamously. At this point, his behaviour became more erratic. He joined a Home Guard unit in Leeds, and took to wearing an officer's uniform adorned with RAF pilot's wings (neither of which he was entitled to wear, of course). Before long, he was involved in a traffic accident while wearing his bogus uniform and was sent to an officers' hospital to recover, whereupon he stole some money from a fellow patient. An investigation revealed his true identity and he was fined for impersonating an officer. At that point, he joined the army as a private soldier. Once in the ranks, he claimed he had been educated at Charterhouse and had attended both Oxford and Cambridge universities. He also subtly changed his name to the more aristocratic Douglas Webster St

Aubyn Berneville-Claye. This social-climbing ruse worked, and he was soon selected for officer training and commissioned as a second lieutenant. Sent to Egypt in 1942, and now calling himself 'Lord Charlesworth', he served in the Special Air Service commando unit. He was captured during an operation behind enemy lines in December 1942, and was eventually sent to Oflag 79 in Braunschweig.

By the end of 1944, Claye's fellow prisoners suspected that he was acting as an informer. He was removed from the camp early the next year and then volunteered for the Waffen-SS. Given the rank of SS-captain, he was sent to the headquarters of the 3rd Germanic Panzer Corps, much to the bemusement of Steiner:

About 8 or 9 April the Corps adjutant came to see me and told me with an amused smile that an English officer, who wished to fight against Bolshevism, had now also arrived . . . His papers had been examined carefully and found in order. The . . . adjutant told me that he was a pleasant young officer with most agreeable manners . . . A few minutes later a smart man of about 27 years of age, fair haired and of medium build was introduced to me. He spoke broken German and wore a grey German uniform with a Captain's badges of rank and the colour of the armoured troops . . . He had a lively and determined look, was sure of himself, although unassuming, and had very good and pleasant manners. He answered my questions most freely. I told him I was naturally surprised to find an English officer who was apparently willing to fight against Bolshevism of his own free will and decision, at a time when Germany was in a most serious and even hopeless position, and asked him to tell me where he came from and what had prompted him to this decision. He . . . had heard about the deep penetration of the Russians into German territory, had asked for permission to volunteer for employment in the front line, and after receiving permission had been sent to the SS Depot Berlin where he . . .

received permission and took possession of the necessary papers. He had heard that armoured units of the Waffen-SS were lying north-east of Berlin and on his request had now been sent here.

I thereupon asked him if he knew what the situation was, and briefly pointed out its seriousness. He answered that it was the very seriousness of the situation which had moved him to take this step, as he was an anti-Bolshevist and felt not only English but also European.[41]

The next day, Steiner sent Claye to visit the British Free Corps, who were still with the *Nordland* Division at this stage. They had been through a series of surprises. The first of these was the return of Thomas Cooper, who had been summoned by the SS-Main Office from his job with the *Leibstandarte* to take control of the BFC. Cooper had by then persuaded senior officers of the Germanic Panzer Corps that the BFC could only be a hindrance in battle and had organised a non-combatant role for them. The next shock was the appearance of Claye and they were even more surprised when he announced that he was the son of an earl and a captain in the Coldstream Guards and was going to lead them against the Russians. He also told them that they would be in no trouble with the British authorities, because Britain would be at war with Russia within a few days. None of this went down well with his audience: 'You've come to drop them back in the shit after I just got them out of it!'[42] Cooper shouted. Apparently taken aback, Claye commandeered a vehicle and made his way westwards, eventually meeting a British unit in the vicinity of Schwerin.

A few days later, the other British volunteers were withdrawn to the corps headquarters, where they were employed as drivers and on traffic control duty. As Germany collapsed around them, they were ordered further west. They surrendered to a US Army unit at the beginning of May.

After the war, John Amery pleaded guilty to high treason and was sentenced to death. He was executed in December 1945. Thomas Cooper was given the same sentence at his trial, but this was commuted to life imprisonment on account of his youth and his German ancestry. He eventually served just seven years. The majority of the British volunteers were given sentences ranging from life imprisonment to a few months. A few got away scot-free, including Claye, who flatly denied ever having served in the Waffen-SS.

Of the handful of Britons who served elsewhere in the Waffen-SS, only one, an RAF officer and former member of the British Union of Fascists, faced a court-martial. Railton Freeman had served for six months in the Kurt Eggers Regiment at the end of the war, having previously broadcast propaganda on German radio. During his interrogation in May 1945, he claimed to have seen a file containing more than eleven hundred applications from British POWs who wanted to fight the Russians but were not prepared to join the British Free Corps. He also suggested that the Waffen-SS hierarchy had seriously considered forming a British SS 'regiment' – separate from the corps – possibly to be called the Oliver Cromwell Regiment.[43] He was ultimately sentenced to ten years in prison.

The Indian Legion was perhaps the most bizarre foreign contingent within the Waffen-SS. Its existence was due largely to the efforts of one man: Subhas Chandra Bose.

Bose was born in India in 1897, the son of an affluent lawyer and Indian nationalist. After education in India and at Cambridge University, he joined the Indian civil service but soon resigned to become a full-time activist in the independence movement. In contrast to the non-violence espoused by Mohandas Gandhi and his followers, Bose advocated a confrontational approach to the British rulers. As a result, he spent most of the inter-war years in prison or in exile. Nevertheless, he established himself as one of the leading radicals within the Indian National Congress, and he was a prominent politician in Calcutta.

However, the outbreak of war in 1939 caused deep divisions in the Indian independence movement. Most Indian politicians were hostile to the Axis and wished to help the Allied cause while still moving towards independence. A minority led by Gandhi opposed any Indian involvement in the war because of their adherence to non-violence. While an even smaller group, centred on Bose, argued that the Axis should be supported because the British were the real enemies of India. Bose was never a fascist, but he had travelled extensively in Europe in the 1930s, was married to an Austrian woman,* and admired the European dictatorships: for instance, he believed that an authoritarian political model would be required in the early stages of Indian independence.

Bose organised several anti-British demonstrations in Calcutta in October 1939, and as a result he was placed under house arrest. However, on 19 January 1941, he slipped away from his house, drove to Peshawar on the North-West Frontier, and was then spirited across the border into independent Afghanistan. From Kabul, he travelled to Moscow, then Rome and finally Berlin, where he arrived at the beginning of April. He was reunited with his wife and started work on his 'Free India' movement, under the sponsorship of the German Foreign Office.

Just as Bose was doing this, General Erwin Rommel's forces in North Africa managed to capture the 3rd (Indian) Motorised Brigade – which was attempting to defend Allied gains in Libya – almost intact. When news of this reached Berlin, Bose sensed an opportunity to canvass support for a Free India force within the German armed forces. A Luftwaffe intelligence officer was dispatched to speak to all of the English-speaking Indians in the brigade in mid-May, and twenty-seven were transported to Berlin a few days later. Meanwhile, plans were made to move the rest of the brigade, together with other Indian prisoners, to a special camp at Annaburg.

---

* Emilie Schenkl Bose (1910–96), who had been Bose's secretary and whom he married in 1937.

Bose and other members of the Free India Committee spent the next six months trying to persuade the prisoners to join their cause. Finally, in January 1942, the committee, the German Foreign Office and the OKW jointly announced the formation of the Indian National Army at a ceremony in Berlin. Some six thousand potential recruits were moved to a new camp, *Arbeitskommando* (Labour Unit) Frankenburg, where military training commenced under the cover that the soldiers were still a prisoner-of-war labour unit. Then, in July, approximately three hundred of these Indians were moved again, this time to Königsbrück, where they were issued with German Army uniforms. These had a flash on the right sleeve depicting the green, white and orange tricolour of India with a leaping tiger superimposed on it, as well as the motto '*Freies Indien*' – 'Free India'. Several Hindi-speaking German NCOs were drafted in to act as interpreters, but primarily English was used as the working language of the formation.

Over the following months, recruitment continued – using a combination of persuasion and compulsion – and by the spring of 1943 the Indian National Army (which was now also known as the Free India Legion) consisted of some two thousand men organised into three battalions and formally designated as Infantry Regiment 950.

Bose's original hope had been that this new force would spearhead a German invasion of India, but this fantasy had been dispelled as soon as Germany had launched its attack on the Soviet Union. Instead, the Indian soldiers' first assignments, in May and August 1943, were to construct defences on the Dutch North Sea coast and the west coast of France. Thereafter, they kicked their heels until August 1944, when they joined the general evacuation of German forces from France, heading east until they reached the comparative safety of Hagenau, in Alsace. It was during this retreat that the legion saw its only action of the war – a series of skirmishes with resistance elements that left three Indian soldiers dead and a number of others wounded.

In September, control of the legion was handed over to the Waffen-SS, but this had minimal practical impact. SS-Senior Colonel Heinz Bertling was appointed commanding officer, but he took little interest in his new role and *de facto* command remained in the hands of the army's Lieutenant Colonel Kurt Krappe, who had commanded the legion since its first deployment in the Netherlands. However, personnel records show that several Indians formally became officers of the Waffen-SS on 1 September,[44] and new insignia – comprising an embroidered tiger's head collar patch[45] – were worn by both Indian and German members of the legion. The unit travelled on to Heuberg and remained there until the very last stages of the war, when it retreated towards Lake Constance before disintegrating.

Bose himself had left Germany in March 1943, before the legion had even been deployed for the first time. He managed to reach Japan, from where he sponsored the vastly more credible Far East version of the Indian National Army and set up the provisional government of 'Free India' in Singapore. It is believed he died in an airplane crash in the last days of the war, although his body was never found.

Hitler gave his opinion of the German version of the Indian National Army in March 1945, when the Red Army was poised to cross the Elbe:

> The Indian Legion is a joke. There are Indians that can't kill a louse and would prefer to allow themselves to be devoured. They certainly aren't going to kill any Englishmen . . . I imagine that if one was to use the Indians to turn prayer wheels or something like that, they would be the most indefatigable soldiers in the world. But it would be ridiculous to commit them to a real blood struggle . . . the whole business is nonsense. If one has a surplus of weapons, one can permit oneself such amusements for propaganda purposes. But if one has no such surplus it is simply not justifiable.[46]

He was right. Once the German campaign had stalled in the Soviet Union, there was really no justification in maintaining the Indian National Army. With no prospect of it ever entering India, it was simply an insignificant work detail of dubious loyalty in possession of weapons and equipment that could have been better employed elsewhere. Furthermore, there was considerable internal strife between the true volunteers and those who had been press-ganged into the unit, and even more between Muslim, Sikh and Hindu recruits. At least one NCO – Corporal Mohammed Ibrahim, who had been an enthusiastic volunteer – was murdered by his own men.

Aside from Howard Marggraff, only a handful of US volunteers joined the Waffen-SS. Bizarrely, two of them were from Missouri.

Martin James Monti came from a prosperous, middle-class St Louis family, descended from Swiss and Italian immigrants on his father's side, and German immigrants on his mother's. They were staunchly Catholic and isolationist, rather than pro-Axis or anti-American. Monti joined the US Air Force in January 1943 and was posted to Karachi in August 1944, aged just twenty-two. However, he became unpopular in his unit because of his views on the war in Europe, and on 2 October he went AWOL before hitching a lift on a military aircraft flying to Cairo.[47] From there, he travelled to Naples and managed to steal a P-38 fighter, which he piloted behind German lines near Milan. He convinced his captors that he was a genuine defector, and at the end of November was transferred to Berlin. After more interrogation, this time by the Abwehr, he was released from captivity to work as a propaganda broadcaster. He recorded a few programmes – using his mother's maiden name, Wiethaupt – but these were deemed unsuccessful by the authorities.

With his broadcasting career seemingly over as soon as it had begun, Monti fell in with another Missourian Waffen-SS officer. The self-styled 'Comte Pierre Louis de la Ney du Vair' had been born Perry Regester De Laney in Holcomb in 1907. De Laney's father died when he was just seven years old but his uncle paid for his education at a military high school in Bell-Buckle, Tennessee. During this time, he came under the influence of an aunt, a Frenchwoman who emphasised his own French origins (the De Laney family had emigrated to North America in the early eighteenth century), taught him French and called him 'Pierre'. After high school, while working on the St Louis *Post-Dispatch*, De Laney converted to Catholicism, having been raised a Lutheran, and was eventually offered a scholarship to study in Rome, which he duly accepted. He returned to St Louis in 1932 and became Professor of Theology at Fontbonne College. However, while in Rome, he had applied for and been granted French citizenship via the French Embassy. Consequently, in 1935, he was called up for military service in the French Army. By now, he was going by the grandiose name of Pierre de la Ney du Vair and claiming lineal descent from the counts of Vair. He undertook his military service with great enthusiasm, gaining a reserve commission and serving with the 152nd Infantry Regiment at Colmar, Alsace. In May 1940, he and his family were living in Lausanne, Switzerland, where du Vair was supposedly operating as a French military intelligence agent. However, after the German invasion, they moved to occupied France.

Du Vair could best be described as a monarchist, French nationalist reactionary, but he was also a supporter of the anti-Semitic Charles Maurras, leader of *Action Française*, and was strongly Anglophobic. As such, his political views were quite in tune with those of the Vichy regime. He resigned his French Army commission in 1941, joined Pétain's *Légion Française des Combattants* (a paramilitary ex-services organisation) and then transferred to the *Légion des Volontaires Français* – the French legion within the German Army – with whom he saw action in the Soviet Union. After returning from the Eastern Front, he served with the collaborationist Vichy militia, the *Milice Française*, before transferring to the Kurt Eggers Regiment and working as a radio propagandist.

In Berlin, it seems that the sophisticated, highly educated du Vair took the immature Monti under his wing. He arranged for Monti to visit the scenes of Soviet atrocities in Hungary and compile reports to broadcast to American audiences. Monti formally joined the Waffen-SS at the beginning of April 1945, just as the Kurt Eggers Regiment was starting to disintegrate in the face of the Soviet advance. Du Vair was killed in an American air raid a few days later,[48] while Monti left the German capital at the end of the month. Accompanying him were the Kurt Eggers Regiment's commander, Gunter D'Alquen, SS-Major Anton Kriegbaum, Railton Freeman and several others. Commandeering an aircraft in Potsdam, they flew south-west before going their separate ways: Freeman remained in Bavaria, where he was arrested by the British; the Germans headed towards the mythical 'Alpine Redoubt';* while Monti travelled through Austria and into Italy, where he surrendered to an American unit. Tried and convicted initially for 'desertion and misappropriation of government property',[49] and later for treason, he was eventually sentenced to twenty-five years' imprisonment. He was paroled in 1960.[50]

There is some evidence that a number of US prisoners of war had volunteered for German service in the final months of the war. In early March 1945, Berger reported to Himmler:

[T]wo complete [prisoner] work commandos have volunteered to work in the *Wehrmacht* rear logistic services ... This concerns one work commando of 120 American POWs and a further one of 100. After previous experience, this breakthrough was to be expected with American prisoners first. Further incomplete messages, as yet unconfirmed by commanders, have been received from Military District VII.[51]

* Supposedly where the last stand of the Third Reich would take place. It never materialised.

Himmler seems to have been distinctly underwhelmed by this 'breakthrough'. His adjutant, Rudi Brandt, noted:

> I spoke with SS-General Berger on 5.3.45 about his suggestion regarding the employment of the American prisoners of war and conveyed to him the opinion of [Himmler]:
>
> 1. The question of the employment of the American and British prisoners of war is very problematic.
> 2. It would have to be guaranteed that really only genuine volunteer enlistments are considered.
> 3. Who questioned the prisoners and what were the circumstances?
>
> The final decision can be made only if these three questions are answered and if a list of the prisoners with each man's signature is provided.[52]

What became of these volunteers was not recorded.

Overall, then, the Waffen-SS's attempts to recruit foreigners from the Allied nations proved almost entirely fruitless. Some Americans may have volunteered to fight the Bolsheviks; but even if they did, their offer came far too late in the war to help the Germans. The Indian Legion was large enough to function as a military unit, but it ended up as a work party on the French coast. Meanwhile, the British Free Corps was conceived as little more than a propaganda operation, but it was ineffective even in that limited role: there seem to have been only two public mentions of it during the war, both in Norwegian collaborationist newspapers. Such paltry returns were hardly commensurate with the effort that went into its recruitment.

In a way, the failure of these projects mirrored that of the Waffen-SS as a whole. The domestic threat to the National Socialist regime had been rendered negligible by the time the armed SS units came into being: opposition political parties and their associated paramilitary groups had already been banned, disarmed and suppressed. Realistically, only one force – the army – had the power to remove Hitler; and the armed SS would never be sufficiently strong to challenge that. Consequently, the Waffen-SS was never more than a modest adjunct to the German military machine. In fact – as a result of the complications which it caused in logistics, procurement, recruitment and so on – it probably diminished rather than enhanced the German state's ability to wage war effectively.

20

The Waffen-SS Heads East

By October 1940, Benito Mussolini had grown envious of his German ally's military conquests in the West. Consequently, he launched an invasion of Greece through Albania. However, to the Italians' surprise, the Greeks proved to be extremely tough opponents. The invasion force was grossly under-strength and was forced back into Albania before the harsh winter led to a cessation of hostilities. Hitler chastised Mussolini for his 'regrettable blunder', but felt compelled to intervene to prevent a collapse of the Axis position in the Balkans.

Germany now pressured the government of Yugoslavia to join the Axis in order to facilitate a German assault on Greece. This was anathema to the Yugoslavs; but with the only alternative seeming to be a German invasion, the government eventually signed the Tripartite Pact on 25 March 1941. However, two days later, elements within the Yugoslavian armed forces allied with Serbian nationalists to launch a *coup d'état*. They deposed the Regent, Prince Paul, and proclaimed the eighteen-year-old King Peter II as the new ruler. Enraged by this affront, Hitler immediately ordered an invasion of Yugoslavia to run in tandem with the attack on Greece. This meant that the planned invasion of the Soviet Union would have to be postponed.

Once again, Waffen-SS units were to be at the forefront of the German assault. The Special Purpose Division had spent the winter of 1940–41 in eastern France, training for the proposed invasion of Great Britain. In December, it had been renamed the *Deutschland* Division – which of course caused confusion with the regiment of the same name – so shortly thereafter it had been re-designated the *Reich* Division. On 28 March, it was ordered to move into south-western Romania. There it joined the XLI Panzer Corps to take part in the main thrust towards Belgrade. Meanwhile, the *Leibstandarte*, which was now of brigade strength and subordinated to the 12th Army, was to attack from Bulgaria, across southern Yugoslavia and into Greece.

The assault was launched on 6 April. In Yugoslavia, resistance was virtually non-existent. A combat group of the *Reich* Division, led by SS-Captain Fritz Klingenburg, raced across the country and reached Belgrade on 13 April, whereupon Klingenburg accepted the surrender of the city. The Yugoslavian Army surrendered four days later. The Germans lost just 151 dead in the entire campaign.

Resistance in Greece was somewhat stiffer, but the outcome was the same. A British expeditionary force had been rushed into the country during March, but it was ill equipped and its air support was no match for the large numbers of combat aircraft available to the Germans. In danger of being stranded, the British began an evacuation on 21 April. With no prospect of holding back the Germans, the Greek Army capitulated two days later. For the whole of the next week, the British fought some desperate rearguard actions as they sought to protect their evacuation sites. By 30 April, German troops controlled the whole country.

Now, a little behind schedule, Hitler was finally able to turn his attention to what had always been his primary target.

At 3 a.m. on 22 June 1941, the largest military force ever assembled in Europe began to cross into Soviet territory: one hundred and fifty-three divisions, organised into three army groups[*] (North, Centre and South, commanded by Field Marshals von Leeb, von Bock and von Rundstedt, respectively), comprising more than 3.5 million soldiers and 3600 tanks, and supported by three tactical air forces with around 2700 aircraft. The front stretched from the Baltic in the north to the Black Sea in the south. Astonishingly, the invasion came as a surprise to the Soviets. Although their intelligence had watched the build-up of forces with increasing anxiety, Stalin had convinced himself that Hitler would not move east until Britain had been decisively defeated. After a decade of terror in the Soviet Union, no one was prepared to contradict him.

Of course, the destruction of the Soviet Union and its 'Jewish Bolshevism' was at the core of Hitler's personal belief system. He had floated the idea in Mein Kampf in 1924, but 1941 was probably the first realistic opportunity that he had to carry it out. It was a colossal gamble but he took it, perhaps feeling that the forces under his command were invincible after their lightning successes in the West, perhaps genuinely believing that the 'inferior' Russians would be unable to put up any significant resistance. In spite of Germany's shortage of men and matériel (at least when compared to the almost limitless resources of the Soviet Union), Hitler seems to have convinced himself that victory was inevitable. Then, once the Third Reich had conquered the USSR, it would have access to vast amounts of land, untold natural resources and millions of 'primitive' people who could be forced into the largest slave labour force the world had ever seen. Hitler viewed it as the twentieth-century equivalent of Britain's subjugation of India in the nineteenth, and envisaged similarly rich rewards.

As with the invasions in the West and the Balkans, the Waffen-SS played a full role in the opening stages of the campaign in the East. The Leibstandarte was re-designated as a division in June

---

[*] An army group usually comprised two or more conventional armies, commanded by a general of at least four-star rank.

1941 – becoming the *Leibstandarte* Adolf Hitler Division – even though it boasted only eleven thousand men, significantly below conventional divisional strength. It was then attached to Army Group South, along with the newly formed *Wiking* Division. The *Reich* Division was placed in von Bock's Army Group Centre, while the Death's Head and Police divisions were subordinated to Army Group North for the push towards Leningrad.[1]

On paper, another new Waffen-SS division should also have been heavily involved in Operation Barbarossa (the codename of the invasion). In late 1940, the 6th and 7th Death's Head regiments – comprising concentration camp guards and reservists – had been transferred to southern Norway to act as a garrison and security force. A few months later, these regiments were combined with a signals unit to form the *Nord* Battle Group, which was under the tactical command of the army. Then, on 17 June 1941, the unit was re-designated the *Nord* Division after the addition of a reconnaissance unit, an anti-aircraft battery, logistics units and so on. Five days later, it was on the Finnish-Soviet border, eager to join the offensive. However, it was far from ready for action: it had fired its artillery only once, its men were barely competent with their small arms, and its officers had had virtually no military training. Its performance in the opening few days of the invasion was so appalling that General von Falkenhorst, commanding the XXXVI Army Corps, had no option but to withdraw it from combat to reconstitute.[2]

Elsewhere, though, the opening months of Barbarossa seemed to be a massive success for the German armed forces: their tanks swept through the western Soviet Union, bypassing vast numbers of helplessly disorganised Soviet troops as they did so. By the beginning of December, Germany and its allies had virtually cut off Leningrad in the north; and they were within eighteen miles of Moscow's Kremlin in the centre. However, they had also reached the limit of their manpower and *matériel* strength.

Then, on the night of 5–6 December, a Soviet counter-offensive took von Bock by surprise, causing a near collapse of the German front to the west of Moscow. By the time that the front stabilised in January, the Germans had been pushed back 150 kilometres. Although they still held vast swaths of Soviet territory, in six months of fighting they had already lost 918,000 men killed, captured, wounded and missing. The Soviets had lost many more – 3.35 million had been captured alone – but they had a far larger population in reserve. By contrast, the German losses represented a whole generation of the nation's manpower, and the blow had fallen just as heavily on the Waffen-SS as it had on the *Wehrmacht*.[3]

Despite these colossal casualties, it did not become apparent that the tide was turning against Germany for more than a year. Although the forces of Army Group Centre had been stymied in their push towards Moscow, in the north the German forces laid siege to Leningrad from September 1941 until January 1943. Meanwhile, Axis forces* pushed ever further to the south-east, towards the River Volga and the Caucasus oilfields, throughout the first half of 1942. They reached Stalingrad in July. The setbacks of the previous winter were glossed over as the German commanders demonstrated their operational flair against their lumbering Soviet opponents.[4]

This invasion created a number of recruiting opportunities. Right-wing 'patriots' in countries occupied by the Germans, and anti-communists in neutral countries, convinced themselves that Hitler's action was the first step in a crusade against Bolshevism, and offers of help began to trickle into German diplomatic offices from individuals and organisations anxious to play their part. As early as 29 June 1941, Hitler gave his assent to the formation of 'legions' of foreign volunteers, which would soon be hurled into the fighting.[5]

Of course, foreign legions have played significant roles in warfare for centuries: George III deployed Hessian mercenaries during the American War of Independence; Napoleon maintained his Polish

---

* Romania and Italy also contributed troops to this theatre of Operation Barbarossa.

Lancers; and even today the Pope has Swiss Guards and the British Army has Nepalese Gurkhas. Most, if not all, of these foreign fighters have been motivated primarily by material advantage, joining prestigious regiments in the hope of achieving a better quality of life. Those who fought for the Axis against Soviet Russia were different: in the main, they were driven by fervent anti-communism.

The day after Hitler gâve the go-ahead for the formation of the foreign units, the German Foreign Office called a conference that was attended by representatives of the OKW, the Waffen-SS Command Main Office and the Overseas Organisation of the NSDAP. This meeting decided that 'national' contingents would be recruited by the Waffen-SS and the army to fight in German uniform (with distinguishing badges), under the same pay and conditions as the German soldiers and as part of the German armed forces. However, wherever possible, they would be directly commanded by officers of their own nationality. The Waffen-SS was given responsibility for Germanic recruits, while the army would deal with all the others, including Frenchmen, Walloons (French-speaking Belgians) and Spaniards (the famous Spanish Blue Division was already in the process of being formed).[6]

After the meeting, the Waffen-SS set to work organising four separate national contingents for its volunteers: the Netherlands Legion, the Flanders Legion, the Norway Legion and the Denmark Free Corps. Once again, the organisation was hardly swamped with applications, but the Netherlands Legion eventually fielded a force of just over two thousand men, while the others each mustered over a thousand.[7]

Ultimately, the national legions proved to be a relatively short-lived experiment. They served on the Eastern Front throughout 1942 and into 1943, but as they started to lose men in the fighting they found it impossible to recruit more to take their place. This was partly because they were in competition for recruits with the SS's own *Wiking* Division, which had suffered severe casualties as part of Army Group South. Before long, the decision was taken to pull the surviving Western European volunteers out of the line in the summer of 1943. This would allow them to be reformed into new national formations that would be integral parts of the Waffen-SS, rather than attached to it. If these formations were short of men, they would be supplemented by German nationals and ethnic Germans (with the latter coming mainly from Romania). The original intention was to create a division called *Nordland* comprising Danish and Dutch motorised infantry regiments and a Norwegian light reconnaissance regiment. Meanwhile, the Flemish Legion would be expanded into an infantry brigade named *Langemarck*. These would then be combined with the *Wiking* Division to form a new Germanic Panzer Corps.[8]

However, the Dutch National Socialist leader, Mussert, strongly objected to these plans on the grounds that he did not want his countrymen fighting in a mixed-nationality division. Moreover, many of the foreign volunteers themselves were unhappy: a significant number of them had signed on with the legions for only two years, so they were due for release in mid-1943. As it turned out, the OKW was unable to release the *Wiking* Division from combat to form the new corps. In order to compensate for this, it was decided to expand the Netherlands Legion into a Panzer-Grenadier brigade called *Nederland* while grouping the Norwegian volunteers in the *Norge* Regiment of the *Nordland* Division. Formation of the Germanic Panzer Corps began in April 1943 under the command of Felix Steiner. It was deployed for the first time on anti-partisan operations in Croatia in September that year.

It is worth noting that, despite the nomenclature, there were never many Scandinavian volunteers in the *Nordland* Division. On average, at any one time, it could boast about 1200 Danes and about 600 Norwegians. Around 25 per cent of the division were German nationals, and roughly 35 per cent ethnic Germans from Romania.

Germanic Western Europeans and Central European ethnic Germans obviously fitted in well with the creed of the Nordic SS order; but in order to maintain their intended expansion of the

Waffen-SS, Himmler and Berger had to cast their net wider. As a result, the organisation's next foreign formation seemed to fly in the face of all previous SS racial ideology.

In Yugoslavia, bands of communist and nationalist partisans were vying with the German occupiers and each other for control of the country. The German response, in 1942, was to form a Waffen-SS mountain division known as the Prinz Eugen Division, which comprised ethnic Germans from Romania, Croatia and Hungary.[9] However, it soon became clear that this unit was not up to the task, so Himmler and Berger looked for more potential recruits to supplement it. They hit upon the idea of enlisting the Muslim population of Bosnia-Herzegovina. It is easy to see why they thought this might work. The Bosnian Muslims had been persecuted by both Serbs and Croats for centuries, so Himmler rightly predicted that they would possess a natural hostility to these nationalities, which made up the majority of the partisan forces. He hoped to turn them into an infantry formation that could be used to secure territory while better-equipped German and ethnic German units acted as mobile, highly manoeuvrable strike forces.[10]

Hitler granted permission to begin recruitment of the Bosnians on 10 February 1943, but finding volunteers was not easy, partly because the Croatian puppet regime* was loath to lose potential manpower from its own forces. Nevertheless, by July 1943, some twenty thousand Bosnians and a few hundred Kossovar Albanians had been enlisted, either voluntarily or through conscription and press-ganging. They were then transferred from Croatia to Le Puy in southern France to begin training.[11]

The division was organised around an officer cadre of German citizens and ethnic Germans, many of whom had previously been in the Prinz Eugen Division. But these officers found it very difficult to come to terms with the new recruits. They could not

---

* The fascist Ustaša movement, headed by Ante Pavelić, ruled Croatia from 1941 until the end of the war.

understand and did not respect the rules and customs of Islam, even though a group of Bosnian imams had been recruited for the soldiers' benefit and to liaise with the German command cadre. This, together with infiltration by a number of partisans, led to considerable unrest. In mid-September 1943, a group of 'Mujos' (as the Germans called the Muslims) mutinied at Villefranche-sur-Roche, killing several SS officers and NCOs before loyalists in the division managed to quell the uprising. A number of Muslims from each side died, too; and, later, some of the ringleaders were court-martialled and shot. (Several others escaped and took refuge with French resistance units in the area.)[12] Shortly thereafter, the division – now named the *Handschar* Mountain Division – began a short period of training in Silesia. It was finally deployed in northern Bosnia in February 1944 as part of the 5th SS-Mountain Corps.

This ramshackle infantry unit of doubtful competence and reliability could hardly have done much to buttress the elite image of the Waffen-SS, but it did finally remove Berger and Himmler's recruiting inhibitions. Over the next eighteen months, SS divisions were formed from Ukrainians, Latvians, Estonians, Kossovar Albanians, Byelorussians and Hungarians; French and Walloon formations were transferred from the army to the Waffen-SS; and the Dutch and Flemish SS brigades were expanded into divisions. Similar expansion occurred in more dubious formations, including the Dirlewanger unit: its recruiting charter was extended to include former Soviet POWs, political prisoners from concentration camps as well as convicted military criminals from the *Wehrmacht* and the Waffen-SS.[13]

Inevitably, this massive expansion caused the Waffen-SS to lose some of its original character. In 1940, it had legitimately been able to claim that it was an elite: a small, well-equipped, well-trained and well-led showpiece force of the 'best' German and Nordic human material. In May of that year, it had a strength of 90,368, excluding the Police Division. By 1 September 1942, this had risen to 236,099. By 1 December 1943, it was 501,049. And by 30 June 1944, it stood at 594,443 (368,654 of them combat troops).[14] Around half of that final figure were non-German nationals. Whatever ideology they espoused, it was hardly likely to be entirely congruent with German National Socialism. The Waffen-SS's German national divisions remained among the Third Reich's best military formations. But the bulk of the organisation's combat units were manned by soldiers who could often barely speak German and were, at best, dubiously motivated. In no military sense could they ever be described as a *corps d'élite*.

21

Operation Barbarossa and the First and Second Sweeps

Hitler blamed the Jews for Russian Bolshevism throughout his political life. Communism, as far as he was concerned, was an artificial ideology created by the Jews to weaken and subdue the Aryan race. It is likely that he concocted this notion just after the First World War, when he became convinced that socialist attempts to seize power in Bavaria were being orchestrated by Jewish revolutionaries. Two decades later, he viewed the showdown with the Soviet Union as a racial war. In his mind, the only way to destroy Soviet Bolshevism was to destroy its Jewish progenitors.

However, it seems that it was only in the spring of 1941 that the rest of Germany's military and political leaders truly comprehended the full and terrible implications of this philosophy. General Alfred Jodl, chief of operations for the *Wehrmacht* High Command, noted on 3 March that Hitler had said that the 'Jewish–Bolshevik intelligentsia' would need to be eliminated during Operation Barbarossa, and that this must be discussed between the High Command and the SS. Heydrich duly met with General Eduard Wagner, the army's Quartermaster General, ten days later. During their discussions, Heydrich outlined the role he envisaged the RSHA's special task groups playing in Russia.[1] Then, over the next couple of months, Wagner and Walter Schellenberg worked out the details. (Heinrich Müller had originally represented the RSHA but Wagner, who found Müller arrogant and uncouth, asked for him to be replaced.) On 4 April, Wagner sent Heydrich a draft agreement on the role of the special task groups, which stated: 'within the framework of their instructions and upon their own responsibility, the Special Units are entitled to carry out executive measures against the civilian population'.[2] It went on to say that the groups would operate in the army's rear areas; that they would be administratively subordinated to whichever military headquarters they were 'supporting'; that the army would provide their logistical support, quartering, rations, fuel and ammunition; but, crucially, that their operational tasks would be set by the RSHA in Berlin. This draft document was eventually amended to allow the special task groups to operate right up to the front line, thus ensuring that they would be able to catch their intended victims by surprise. It was this amended version of the agreement that was signed by Heydrich and Wagner at the end of May.

The intention was to form four special task groups for the Russian campaign: one allocated to each of the three army groups; and the fourth, smaller group attached to the 11th Army, which was to strike into the Caucasus on the southern flank of Army Group South. As in the Polish campaign, the groups were originally of approximately battalion strength, just under a thousand men, subdivided into company-sized special task units. Special Task Group A, commanded by SS-Brigadier Franz Walther Stahlecker, was placed in Field Marshal von Leeb's Army Group North. Stahlecker had joined the NSDAP in 1932 and served as Gestapo chief in Württemberg and SD chief in Vienna before clashing with Heydrich and transferring to the Foreign Office, becoming its representative in Bohemia-Moravia and Norway. Special Task Group B, attached to von Bock's Army Group Centre, was commanded by SS-Brigadier Arthur Nebe, head of the Kripo. Nebe had volunteered for the post in April 1941, when Heydrich had told his RSHA heads of division of the 'heavy task' of securing and pacifying Russia. It seems that Nebe was keen to add some combat decorations to those he had amassed during the First World War. Special Task Group C, commanded by Dr Otto Rasch, was assigned to von Rundstedt's Army Group South. Rasch had already participated in special task group operations in Poland, where he had set up the Soldau concentration camp that had murdered many members of the intelligentsia. Special Task Group D was commanded by SS-Colonel Otto Ohlendorf, the unpopular head of SD-Home. He had twice refused to serve in occupied Poland, and it seems he agreed to lead Special Task Group D only to avoid a reputation for cowardice.[3]

Manpower for the special task groups was drawn from a variety of sources. In Special Task Group A, with an initial strength of 990, 9 per cent came from the Gestapo, 3.5 per cent from the SD, 4.1 per cent from Kripo, 13.4 per cent from the Order Police, 8.8 per cent from 'foreign auxiliary police' and 34 per cent from the Waffen-SS.[4] The remainder were administrative and technical support staff: clerks, cooks, drivers, mechanics and so on. At a time when the bulk of the German armed forces remained horse-drawn, the special task groups were fully motorised in jeeps, on motorcycles and in trucks, to give them a quick response time and enable them to keep up with the vanguard of the German forces.

The leadership cadre of the groups was varied, too. However, most were highly intelligent and well-educated men: Rasch had earned a doctorate in law; Franz Six – who commanded the *Moskow Vorkommando* (Advance Unit) within Special Task Group B – had been a senior academic at Berlin University while still in his late twenties; Ernst Biberstein, commander of Special Task Unit 6 in Special Task Group C, was, of all things, a Protestant pastor; and Paul Blobel, the alcoholic commander of Special Task Unit 4a, had qualified as an architect.* They also generally showed a strong commitment to the NSDAP and National Socialist ideology:

---

* According to his somewhat sketchy SS personal file, at any rate.

Ohlendorf had been a party member since 1925; Nebe was an early SA member; and while Blobel joined the party only in 1931, he seems to have been a wholehearted convert, espousing the SS's perversely named 'Belief in God' doctrine,[5] which renounced religious belief.[*] None of these men seems to have taken great pleasure in their 'heavy task',[†] but nor did they seek to avoid it: this was the mission of the SS.

In late May 1941, the special task groups assembled at the Border Police Academy in the small town of Pretzsch, near Wittenberg, on the Elbe. They were met there by SS-Brigadier Bruno Streckenbach, chief of personnel in the RSHA and himself a former special task group commander in Poland. Among other grim crimes, he had arrested and executed many of the academic staff of Cracow University. The briefing Streckenbach gave was sketchy. One witness recalls him telling the assembled troops that they would be engaged on 'a war assignment which would be concluded by December at the latest'.[6] Over the course of the next three weeks, they were given ideological lectures – designed to bolster their belief in the justice of the race war they were about to fight – and did basic weapons training, rangework and one or two field exercises. Their weapons were primarily light small arms: rifles, submachine guns, pistols, grenades and light machine guns. The men were not trained to take part in serious combat; rather, they learned how to protect themselves, and how to flush out and kill individual victims. Their officers and NCOs were given a rough idea of the kind of task they would have to fulfil; but it seems that only the commanders and their deputies received a full briefing at this stage. At his post-war trial, Ohlendorf stated:

---

[*] Adherents to this doctrine proclaimed themselves to be *'Gottgläubig'* rather than adhering to any particular religion.

[†] Nebe, especially, seems to have found his task in Russia distasteful, to say the least. It may well have been his experiences there that led him to flirt with the bomb plot against Hitler in July 1944, for which he was executed the following year.

On the basis of orders which were given by Brigadier Streckenbach, Chief of office I of the RSHA, by order of the head
of the RSHA, to the chiefs of the Special Task Groups and the
Kommandoführer at the time of the formation of the Special
Task Groups in Pretzsch (in Saxony); and which were given
by the *Reichsführer*-SS to the leaders and men of the Special
Task Groups and Special Task Units who were assembled in
Nikolaev in September 1941. A number of undesirable elements composed of Russians, gypsies, and Jews and others
were executed in the area detailed to me. All Jews who were
arrested, as such, were to be executed within my area. It was
my wish that these executions be carried out in a manner and
fashion which was military and suitably humane under the
circumstances.[7]

Hilberg has characterised the actions of the special task groups in
the opening months of Operation Barbarossa as the 'First Sweep'.[8]
Broken down first into special task units, then into platoon-sized
sub-units, the killing squads followed closely behind the front-line
formations of the army. Their initial progress was remarkable:
'We'll only have to kick in the door and the whole rotten structure
will collapse,' Hitler had claimed at a conference with *Wehrmacht*
commanders in April 1941, and his prophecy appeared to be
coming true. Within days of the launch of the invasion, the killing
operations began.

At stake were the lives of some four million Jews who lived in
areas that would soon be occupied by the Germans: 260,000 in
the Baltic States, 1.35 million in eastern Poland (which had been
occupied by the Soviets in autumn 1939), 300,000 in Bessarabia
and Bukovina, and over 2 million in Byelorussia, the Ukraine and
the Russian Soviet Republic.

The number of Jews who were killed by each special task group
was determined to a large extent by the density of the Jewish population and the speed of the German advance in that area. Special
Task Group A, operating on the relatively short northern axis of

advance along the Baltic, had conducted some 112 separate killing operations in 71 localities by 1 December 1941.[9] This reflected the fact that the group had been able to move backwards and forwards within its area of operational responsibility to ensure thorough execution of its tasks. SS-Colonel Karl Jäger, a police officer commanding Special Task Unit 3, reported his group's elimination of some 137,000 Jewish men, women and children. He concluded:

> Today I can confirm that our objective, to solve the Jewish problem for Lithuania, has been achieved by EK 3. In Lithuania there are no more Jews, apart from Jewish workers and their families . . .
>
> I consider the Jewish action more or less terminated as far as Special Task Unit 3 is concerned. Those working Jews and Jewesses still available are needed urgently and I can envisage that after the winter this workforce will be required even more urgently. I am of the view that the sterilization program of the male worker Jews should be started immediately so that reproduction is prevented. If despite sterilization a Jewess becomes pregnant she will be liquidated.[10]

By contrast, the smaller Jewish population of Estonia, being further east, had some time to escape. Consequently, Special Unit 1a of Special Task Group A was unable to claim that it had liquidated the entire Estonian Jewish population. On 12 October 1941, the unit reported:

> At the beginning of 1940 about 4,500 Jews were living in Estonia. About 1,900 to 2,000 of them were living in Tallinn, larger Jewish communities were at Tartu, Narva, and Parnu, while only few Jews were living out in the flat country.
>
> The deportations carried out by the Russians, as far as they concerned Jews, cannot be established in numbers. According to inquiries made so far, Jewry had hardly been

affected by them. With the advance of the German troops on Estonian territory, about half of the Jews made preparations for flight and, as these Jews had collaborated with the Soviet authorities, they left the country with them going east. Only few of them were seized in Tallinn because their escape route had been cut off. After the occupation of the country, there were probably still about 2,000 Jews left in the country.

The Estonian self-defense units, which had been formed when the *Wehrmacht* marched in, started immediately to arrest Jews. Spontaneous demonstrations against Jewry did not take place because there was no substantial enlightenment of the population.

The following orders were therefore issued by us:

1. The arrest of all male Jews over 16.
2. The arrest of all Jewesses fit for work between the ages of 16 and 60, who were utilized to work in the peat bogs.
3. Collective billeting of female Jewish residents of Tartu and vicinity in the synagogue and a tenement house in Tartu.
4. Arrest of all male and female Jews fit for work in Parnu and vicinity.
5. Registration of all Jews according to age, sex, and fitness for work for the purpose of billeting them in a camp which is in the stage of preparation.

All male Jews over 16, with the exception of physicians and the appointed Jewish elders, were executed by the Estonian self-defense units under supervision of the Special Unit. As for the town and country district of Tallinn, the action is still under way as the search for the Jewish hideouts has not yet been completed. The total number of Jews shot in Estonia is so far 440.

When these measures are completed, about 500 to 600 Jewesses and children will still be alive.

The village communities are already now free from Jews. For the Jews residing at Tallinn and vicinity a camp is at present being prepared at Harku (District Tallinn), which after receiving the Jews from Tallinn is to be expanded to contain all Jews from Estonia. All Jewesses fit for work are employed with farm work and cutting of peat on the property of the nearby prison so that the questions of feeding and financing are solved.[11]

This report and others from Special Task Group A allude to attempts to foment pogroms against the Jews by local populations. The indigenous Baltic populations' resentment of Bolshevik rule was never in doubt, but the special task groups assumed that they also conflated Bolshevism with Judaism. This turned out to be far from true, especially outside Lithuania:

In Lithuania this [a pogrom] was achieved for the first time by partisan activities in Kovno. To our surprise it was not easy at first to set in motion an extensive pogrom against Jews. Klimatis, the leader of the partisan unit mentioned above, who was used for this purpose primarily, succeeded in starting a pogrom on the basis of advice given to him by an Advance Unit operating in Kovno, and in such a way that no German order or German instigation was noticed from the outside. During the first pogrom in the night from 25 to 26 June, the Lithuanian partisans did away with more than 1,500 Jews, set fire to several synagogues or destroyed them by other means and burned down a Jewish dwelling district consisting of about 60 houses. During the following nights about 2,300 Jews were made harmless in a similar way. In other parts of Lithuania similar actions followed the example of Kovno, though smaller and extending to the Communists who had been left behind.

These self-clearing operations went smoothly because the army authorities, who had been informed, showed understanding for this procedure. From the beginning it was obvious that only the first days after the occupation would offer the opportunity for carrying out pogroms. After the disarmament of the partisans the self-clearing operations automatically ceased.

It proved much more difficult to set in motion similar clearing operations in Latvia. The essential reason was that the entire stratum of national leaders had been assassinated or deported by the Soviets, especially in Riga. It was possible though, through similar influences, for the Latvian auxiliary police to set in motion a pogrom against Jews also in Riga. During this pogrom all synagogues were destroyed and about 400 Jews were killed. As the population of Riga quieted down quickly, further pogroms were not feasible.

So far as possible, both in Kovno and in Riga evidence by film and photography was established that the first spontaneous executions of Jews and Communists were carried out by Lithuanians and Latvians.

In Estonia, by reason of the relatively small number of Jews, no opportunity presented itself for the instigation of pogroms. The Estonian home guard rendered harmless only some individual Communists whom they especially hated, but generally they limited themselves to carrying out arrests.[12]

One of the most infamous actions of the special task groups took place in Kiev between 29 September and 11 October 1941. Special Unit 4a of Special Task Group C had arrived in the city on 25 September in the wake of Field Marshal von Reichenau's 6th Army, which had captured the Ukrainian capital six days earlier. Meanwhile, a number of explosions had rocked the city as mines and booby traps left behind by the retreating Soviets had detonated. One of these explosions killed the 6th Army's artillery commander, General von Seydlitz, but others started fierce fires that burned out of control, destroying many buildings and leaving some 25,000 Ukrainians homeless. A meeting was convened between Rasch, Blobel, SS-General Friedrich Jeckeln (who had recently been appointed Senior SS and Police Leader South) and Major General Eberhardt (the military commander in Kiev). Between them, they decided to take radical action. On 28 September, a notice was posted around the city, addressed to the Jewish population:

> All Jews living in the city of Kiev and its vicinity are to report by 8 o'clock on the morning of Monday, September 29, 1941, to the corner of Melnikovsky and Dokhturov Streets (near the cemetery). They are to take with them documents, money, valuables, as well as warm clothes, underwear, etc. All who do not carry out this instruction will be shot. Anyone entering flats evacuated by Jews and stealing property will be shot.[13]

Some thirty thousand Jews arrived at the designated location in the belief that they were about to be evacuated to labour camps. Instead, they were met by a group consisting of Sipo and SD men from Special Unit 4a; a company of Waffen-SS soldiers who were attached to Special Task Group C; members of the Order Police from Special Unit 4a and from Police Regiment South; and some Ukrainian auxiliary policemen recruited as reinforcements by the Order Police. The Jews were then marched in groups of a hundred or so through the Jewish cemetery to the ravine of Babi Yar. Once there, they were ordered to strip naked and pile their belongings neatly. Kurt Werner, a member of Special Unit 4a, described what happened next:

> Soon after my arrival at the execution site I was ordered to the bottom of the ravine, together with other comrades. After a short time the first Jews were brought to us via the slopes

of the ravine. The Jews had to lay face down at the edge of the ravine. Three groups of marksmen were in the pit, around 12 marksmen. Jews were constantly brought from above to these groups of marksmen. The Jews following had to lie down on the corpses of the Jews who had already been shot. The marksmen stood behind the Jews and killed them by shots in the neck. Today I still remember the horror of the Jews who saw the corpses in the pit. Many Jews were shocked, and screamed. One cannot imagine the nervous strain involved in carrying out this dirty job in the pit. It was horrible . . .

The whole morning I had to stay in the ravine. There I was ordered to shoot again and again for a while, and then I was busy filling MP (machine pistol) magazines with ammunition. During this time other comrades were detailed for shooting. At noon we were allowed to leave the ravine, and in the afternoon together with others comrades I had to bring the Jews towards the pit. During this time other comrades carried out the shooting in the pit. We brought the Jews to the border of the pit; from there they ran down the slopes themselves. On this day the shooting went on until approximately 5 or 6 p.m. Then we were ordered back to our quarters. That evening alcohol was handed out again.[14]

The official report was more prosaic, but the writer's satisfaction at what Special Unit 4a had accomplished was clear:

Partly because of the better economic situation of the Jews under the Bolshevist regime and their activities as informers and agents of the NKVD, partly because of the explosions and the resulting fires, the public feeling against the Jews was very strong. As an added factor it was proved that the Jews participated in the arson. The population expected adequate retaliatory measures by the German authorities. Consequently all Jews of Kiev were requested, in agreement with the city commander, to appear on Monday, 29 September by 8 o'clock at a designated place. These announcements were posted by members of the Ukrainian militia in the entire city. Simultaneously it was announced orally that all Jews were to be moved. In collaboration with the Special Task Group staff and 2 Kommandos of the Police Regiment South, the Special Unit 4a executed on 29 and 30 September, 33,771 Jews. Money, valuables, underwear and clothing were secured and placed partly at the disposal of the NSV [National Socialist Party Public Welfare Organisation] for use of the racial Germans, partly given to the city administration authorities for use of the needy population. The transaction was carried out without friction. No incidents occurred. The 'resettlement measure' against the Jews was approved throughout by the population. The fact that in reality the Jews were liquidated was hardly known until now, according to up-to-date experiences it would, however, hardly have been objected to. The measures were also approved by the *Wehrmacht*. The Jews who were not yet apprehended as well as those who gradually returned from their flight to the city were in each case treated accordingly.

Simultaneously a number of NKVD officials, political commissars, and partisan leaders was arrested and liquidated.[15]

Unsurprisingly, given the speed with which the atrocity had been carried out, some of the victims had been wounded rather than killed. Three days after the main massacre, Anton Heidborn, another member of Special Unit 4a, returned to the site:

On arrival we saw a woman sitting by a bush, having obviously survived the execution. This woman was shot by an SD man who joined us, name unknown. Furthermore, we saw a person waving to us with their hand out of a pile of corpses. I don't know if it was a man or a woman. I assume that this person was shot by the SD man but I did not see it. That day we started to cover the heaps of corpses. For this purpose civilians were used. In addition some walls of the ravine were partially blown up. After that day I did not return to the execution site. For the next several days we were busy smoothing banknotes from the property of the shot Jews. I estimate that it must have amounted to millions. I don't know what the money was used for. It was packed in bags, and sent away.[16]

The method of execution employed at Babi Yar was typical of that used throughout the Soviet Union. Hermann Graebe was a German engineer employed on building projects in the Ukraine who witnessed another massacre, this time by members of Special Unit C:

I walked around the mound, and found myself confronted by a tremendous grave. People were closely wedged together and lying on top of each other so that their heads were visible. Nearly all had blood running over their shoulders from their heads. Some of the people shot were still moving. Some were lifting their arms and turning their heads to show that they were still alive. The pit was already two thirds full. I estimated that it contained about 1,000 people. I looked for the man who did the shooting. He was an SS man, who sat at the edge of the narrow end of the pit, his feet dangling into the pit. He had a tommy gun on his knees and was smoking a cigarette. The people, completely naked, went down some steps which were cut in the clay wall of the pit and clambered over the heads of the people lying there, to the place to which the SS man directed them. They lay down in front of the dead or injured people; some caressed those who were still alive and spoke to them in a low voice. Then I heard a series of shots. I looked into the pit and saw that the bodies were twitching or the heads lying already motionless on top of the bodies that lay before them. Blood was running from their necks. I was surprised that I was not ordered away, but I saw that there were two or three postmen in uniform nearby. The next batch was approaching already. They went down into the pit, lined themselves up against the previous victims and were shot. When I walked back around the mound, I noticed another truckload of people which had just arrived. This time it included sick and infirm persons. An old, very thin woman with terribly thin legs was undressed by others who were already naked, while two people held her up. The woman appeared to be paralyzed. The naked people carried the woman around the mound . . .

On the morning of the next day, when I again visited the site, I saw about 30 naked people lying near the pit – about 30 to 50 meters away from it. Some of them were still alive; they looked straight in front of them with a fixed stare and seemed to notice neither the chilliness of the morning nor the workers of my firm who stood around. A girl of about 20 spoke to me and asked me to give her clothes, and help her escape. At that moment we heard a fast car approach and I noticed that it was an SS detail. I moved away to my site. Ten minutes later we heard shots from the vicinity of the pit. The Jews still alive had been ordered to throw the corpses into the pit; then they had themselves to lie down in this to be shot in the neck.[17]

The majority of the Order Police and Waffen-SS members of the special task groups had simply been labelled unsuitable for combat operations at the front – in general, because they were too old. In other words, they had not been selected for the special task groups because they had exhibited particular fanaticism, or because they were sadists or psychopaths. Indeed, many of the commanders recognised that the executions, particularly of women and children, placed their men under great psychological strain. Several methods were employed by various commanders to minimise this. In Special Task Group D, Ohlendorf insisted that the murders had to be carried out in what he imagined was a 'military' way. Thus, the firing squads had no contact with their victims until the last moment, and three riflemen were allocated to each person to be shot. This was designed to alleviate individual guilt among the execution squads. Rasch took a different tack. He insisted that every member of his unit participated in the killings, ensuring a sense of collective, and shared, guilt.

In August 1941, Himmler – accompanied by his adjutant, Karl Wolff, and SS-Lieutenant General von dem Bach-Zelewski – observed a mass execution near Minsk, organised by Arthur Nebe's Special Task Group B. As the victims awaited their fate, Himmler is said to have spotted a tall, blond, blue-eyed man of about twenty whom he engaged in conversation:

'Are you a Jew?'
'Yes.'
'Are both of your parents Jews?'
'Yes.'
'Do you have any ancestors who were not Jews?'
'No.'
'Then I can't help you.'[18]

Standing close to the pit, Himmler became increasingly distressed as the shooting commenced. According to Wolff: 'After many volleys, I could see that Himmler was trembling. He ran his hand across his face and swayed. "You could have spared yourself and me this," I said to him. His face was almost green. And then he said, "A piece of brain just splattered in my face." He immediately threw up.'[19] Once the killing was over, Himmler made a speech to the men in which he exhorted them to 'see it through'. However, he asked Nebe to devise a less gruesome means of mass execution than simply shooting people.

Nebe summoned the gassing expert Albert Widmann from the Criminal Technical Institute in Berlin to carry out some experiments.[20] The first method to be tested was explosives. Two wooden

Odilo Globocnik (second from the right), commander of Operation Reinhard, with unidentified Nazi officials in 1943. *(Yad Vashem)*

SS personnel at Belzec death camp, 1942. The camps employed relatively few SS men. Much of the dirty work fell to Ukrainian auxiliaries. *(Instytut Pamieci Narodowej Muzeum Regionalne w Tomaszow Lubelski, courtesy of Zygmunt Klukowski)*

Above left: A Waffen-SS NCO of a Special Task Group prepares to murder a Ukrainian Jew as other Waffen-SS and Reich Labour Service members look on. *(Library of Congress Dokumentationsarchiv des Oesterreichischen Widerstandes, United States Holocaust Memorial Museum (USHMM), YIVO Institute for Jewish Research, courtesy of Sharon Paquette)*

Above right: Lithuanian militiamen – under SS direction – force Jewish women to undress before murdering them, Panevezys, 1941. *(USHMM, Institut Pamieci Narodowej Lietuvos Nacionalinis Muziejus, courtesy of Saulius Berzinis Mrs Bukowska)*

Special Task Force members murder a Jewish family, Ivangorod, 1942.

SS soldiers conduct a selection on the *rampe* at Birkenau, circa 1944. It is likely that the column of prisoners on the far side of the tracks is being led to the gas chambers. *(Yad Vashem)*

The SS leadership at Auschwitz, 1944: (left to right) Richard Baer, Josef Mengele, Josef Kramer, Rudolf Höss and Anton Thumann. *(USHMM, courtesy of anonymous donor)*

Left: Erich von dem Bach-Zelewski, SS anti-partisan chief in central Russia. *(Bundesarchiv)*

Right: Otto Ohlendorf, the economist who led the SD-*Inland*, but also commanded a Special Task Group during the invasion of the Soviet Union. *(Bundesarchiv)*

Left: Adolf Eichmann, the 'Jewish Expert' who masterminded the persecution and later extermination of Jews throughout Europe. *(AP/Press Association Images)*

Right: Christian Wirth, pioneer of the use of gas for mass murders of Jews. *(Holocaust Research Project)*

Left: Franz Stangl, the Austrian police officer who commanded the Sobibor and Treblinka death camps. *(Topham Picturepoint/PressAssociation Images)*

Right: SS-Lieutenant Heinz Macher, a highly decorated Waffen-SS officer who accompanied Himmler during his attempted escape in May 1945. *(Bundesarchiv)*

Otto Skorzeny (left), commander of Waffen-SS special forces on the Eastern Front, spring 1945. *(Public Record Office)*

Recruiting poster for the British Free Corps.
(Bundesarchiv)

YOUR PLACE IS HERE!

A Sikh member of the Free Indian Legion, stationed on the Atlantic coast of France, spring 1944. *(Bundesarchiv)*

Two members of the British Free Corps of the Waffen-SS – Kenneth Berry (left) and Alfred Minchin (right) – with German Army soldiers on a visit to a naval internment camp, April 1944. *(Public Record Office)*

Sepp Dietrich (left), who led the first armed SS unit in 1933, also commanded the largest, the 6th SS Panzer Army, during the Ardennes offensive in winter 1944–5. *(Bundesarchiv)*

Members of the Dirlewanger battalion of convicted criminals and political prisoners taking part in street fighting during the Warsaw Rising of August 1944.

(Bundesarchiv)

Members of the Waffen-SS and German Army who had escaped across the River Elbe to surrender to the US Army rather than the Soviets, May 1945. The prisoner (centre) with a bandaged head is also a member of the Dirlewanger battalion.

(Time & Life Pictures/Getty Images)

An SS-sergeant major, under British supervision, carrying the body of a dead prisoner to a mass grave at Belsen concentration camp, May 1945. *(Time & Life Pictures/Getty Images)*

SS personnel captured by the British Army at Belsen. *(Public Record Office)*

bunkers were packed with explosives before twenty mental patients were herded inside. Then the dynamite was detonated. This first explosion did not kill all of the patients, so the wounded were placed back in the bunkers with even more dynamite. A work detail spent much of the next day retrieving body parts from nearby trees and undergrowth.[21]

The next method to be tried was gassing. A number of gassing vehicles had already been built for Operation T-4, which utilised them as mobile gas chambers. The passenger cab was hermetically sealed, and the driver operated a switch that pumped carbon monoxide into the back of the truck. Nebe's version was more rough and ready. He and his assistants travelled to an asylum at Mogilew and ran a hose from their car exhaust into a sealed room containing mental patients. This didn't seem to be working quickly enough, so they swapped the car for a truck. The victims were dead within eight minutes.

The eastwards expansion of the Third Reich created the need for both civil administration and a security apparatus in the conquered territories. Himmler therefore appointed three new senior SS and police leaders to assume control of the security forces in these areas: SS-Major General Prutzmann in the North, based in Riga; SS-Lieutenant General von dem Bach-Zelewski in the Centre, based in Minsk; and SS-Lieutenant General Jeckeln in the South, based in Kiev. Each of these men controlled a regiment of Order Police as well as various Waffen-SS units and locally recruited militias. All of these forces were used to attack the surviving Jewish populations that had been missed or bypassed by the initial wave of special task groups. Hilberg characterises these operations as the 'Second Sweep';[22] they were often deliberately misrepresented as 'anti-partisan' actions.

A typical example was the massacre of Jews at Józéfow in eastern Poland that was carried out by the 101st Reserve Police Battalion in July 1942. This came about because a shortage of transport had led to a temporary hiatus in traffic from Poland's ghettoes to the Operation Reinhard death camps (see Chapter 22). Frustrated by the lack of killing, the SSPF for Lublin, Odilo Globocnik, ordered the police battalion to travel to Józéfow, pick out any young male Jews who could be employed by the work camps, and murder the rest of the Jewish population. This they duly did. Unusually for such an operation, the commander, a Major Trapp, excused some members of his battalion – which comprised mostly middle-aged reservists from Hamburg – from taking part in the actual shooting. Nevertheless, over the next six months, this same battalion killed Jews in Lomazy, Miedzyrzec, Serokomla, Kock, Parczew, Konskowola, Miedzyrzec again and Lukow.[23] In total, they are estimated to have murdered some 38,000 Jews and to have deported some 45,000 more. Although they operated within the framework of the Lublin SSPF, not one of the battalion's policemen was a formal member of the SS.

Waffen-SS units deployed on security operations in the East came under the auspices of the Command Staff of the National Leader of the SS. This operational headquarters was formed by the SS-Command Main Office to provide combat formations under Himmler's direct military control that were used to round up Soviet stragglers, fight partisans and execute Jews. The two major formations were: the 1st SS-Brigade (motorised), which comprised the 8th and 10th Death's Head regiments; and the SS-Cavalry Brigade, consisting of a hodge-podge of General-SS equestrian units under the command of Hermann Fegelein.

Fegelein was born in 1906 in Bavaria, the son of an army officer. He briefly attended university, spent six months in the army, then enlisted in the Bavarian Police for two years. He left the police to work at his father's riding school in Munich, while also gaining a reputation as a competitive horseman. He joined the SS in 1933, served within various mounted units, and was appointed commander of the main SS riding school in Munich in 1936.[24] A good-looking man with a glamorous reputation, Fegelein used his position at the riding school to butter up senior SS officers, a tactic that clearly worked as he became an SS-colonel within a year of taking up the post. When the first Waffen-SS cavalry unit was formed in 1940 (the Death's Head Mounted Regiment), he was made a lieutenant colonel* and placed in command, despite his lack of formal officer training.

On 28 July 1941, after a meeting with von dem Bach-Zelewski and Fegelein, Himmler issued orders to comb the Pripyat Marshes – in Byelorussia and north-western Ukraine – which were a centre of partisan resistance. However, his oral instructions to his two subordinates were less equivocal: 'all Jews must be shot. Drive the females into the swamps.'[25] The sweep operation lasted for just ten days, from 2 to 12 August. When it was over, SS-Major Franz Magill, the detachment commander who led the forces on the ground, reported that some 6526 men – the overwhelming majority of them Jews – had been shot. By 16 August, the overall operation (including the contributions made by police and army units) had murdered 15,878 men and captured 830 prisoners.[26] A tiny proportion of the victims were undeniably partisans, but the vast majority were not, as is attested by the fact that no more than 500 rifles, 30 machine guns and 20 artillery pieces were recovered during the operation.[27]

Meanwhile, Himmler's other main unit, the 1st SS-Brigade, had been equally busy. On 7 August, it had killed a total of 7819 Jews around Minsk. Both it and the Cavalry Brigade subsequently became fully fledged combat divisions of the Waffen-SS: the 18th *Horst Wessel* SS-Volunteer Panzer-Grenadier Division and the 8th *Florian Geyer* SS-Cavalry Division.

Another special unit that was rampaging around Byelorussia at this time was Oskar Dirlewanger's band of ex-convicts. The unit had been placed under the Command Staff of the National Leader of the SS by an order dated 29 January 1942, and transferred to Byelorussia the following month. Part of the reason for this seems to have been an ongoing investigation by an SS judge, Dr Konrad

---

* He was a full colonel in the General-SS, but this did not equate with a military rank.

Morgen, into allegations of 'race defilement' against Dirlewanger.
He was accused of having had sexual relations with a number of
Jewesses while in Lublin, and his friend and protector Gottlob
Berger had deemed it prudent to get him away from the area.*
That was a terrible decision for the people of Byelorussia, because
Dirlewanger's troops then looted, raped and murdered their way
through the republic's villages and settlements over the next two
years. Even Fegelein, who was no stranger to atrocities, described
them to Hitler as 'real scoundrels'. Their behaviour was so
appalling that prosecutors presented it at Nuremberg as evidence
of the general criminality of the Waffen-SS.

While the likes of the Dirlewanger unit roamed the countryside,
the original special task groups that had accompanied the army
into the Soviet Union and the Baltic States transformed themselves
into static Sipo posts under the command of the senior SS and
police leaders. They collected intelligence on partisans, Jews and
other threats (real and imaginary), and coordinated action against
them after consultation with their senior SS and police leader. The
subsequent campaign against the partisans of Byelorussia, western
Russia and the Ukraine was as dirty a war as has ever been fought.
It was primarily conducted by the German Army's security divisions, but – as the activities of the Dirlewanger unit prove –
Waffen-SS and police formations were heavily involved in it, too.

---

* There were further allegations that Dirlewanger had subsequently had these
lovers murdered to keep them quiet.

22

The Wannsee Conference

As we have seen, almost as soon as Himmler witnessed for himself the grim reality of 'open air' executions in Minsk, it was decided that a more efficient method was needed to kill the large numbers of Jews now being targeted for extermination. This ultimately led to the Operation Reinhard death camps and Auschwitz, but Jews were being gassed in static locations – largely on the initiative of local commanders – before that process even began.

On 16 July 1941, SS-Major Rolf-Heinz Höppner wrote to Adolf Eichmann to inform him that, over the forthcoming winter, 'there is a danger that not all of the Jews can be fed anymore. One should weigh earnestly if the most humane solution might not be to finish off those of the Jews who are not employable, by some quick working device. At any rate it would be more pleasant than to let them starve to death.'[1] Four months later, an extermination camp was built in the village of Chelmno nad Nerem ('Kulmhof-an-der-Nehr' under the German administration), some seventy kilometres north-west of Lodz. It came into operation on 7 December, the day after Zhukov had launched his counter-attack to the west of Moscow.

The camp was built around an empty manor house, known as the 'Castle', and was commanded by SS-Lieutenant Herbert

Lange – the man who had earlier organised the gassing of over fifteen hundred mental patients in Poland and East Prussia. Since then, he had been employed as a Kripo investigator in Poznan. His guard force at Kulmhof comprised a fifteen-man Sipo special unit and between sixty and a hundred members of the 1st Company of the Litzmannstadt Police Battalion.

The first victims were local Jews from surrounding villages, but from mid-January 1942 the camp also started to exterminate deportees from the Lodz ghetto. Typically, the victims were transported by train to Kolo station, approximately fifteen kilometres away, where they were locked in the local synagogue until they could be transferred to the camp. Once sufficient trucks had been found, the prisoners were taken in batches to the Castle, where they were addressed by Lange (and later by his successor, SS-Captain Bothmann), who said that they were to become labourers either on the estate or further east, and that they would be treated fairly and fed well. However, first, for reasons of hygiene, they and their clothes had to be washed and disinfected.

The victims were then escorted into an undressing room on the first floor of the Castle, where they were made to strip and hand over any valuables. Next, they were taken downstairs to a corridor that led to the back of a truck. They were told that this would drive them to the baths. Many of the prisoners were even given pieces of soap in order to maintain this fiction. Walter Burmeister, one of the van drivers, described what happened next:

> The gas vans were large vans, about 4–5 meters long, 2.2 meters wide and 2 meters high. The interior walls were lined with sheet metal. On the floor there was a wooden grille. The floor of the van had an opening which could be connected to the exhaust by means of a removable metal pipe. When the lorries were full of people the double doors at the back were closed and the exhaust connected to the interior of the van . . .
> The Kommando member detailed as driver would start the

engine right away so that the people inside the lorry were suffocated by the exhaust gases. Once this had taken place, the union between the exhaust and the inside of the lorry was disconnected and the van was driven to the camp in the woods were the bodies were unloaded. In the early days they were initially buried in mass graves, later incinerated . . . I then drove the van back to the castle and parked it there. Here it would be cleaned of the excretions of the people that had died in it.[2]

Kulmhof eventually claimed the lives of at least 152,000 people – the vast majority of them Jews, but also at least 5000 gypsies, a number of Soviet POWs and at least 88 Czech children. A small number of Polish and Jewish prisoners worked in the 'forest camp', where the mass graves (and later improvised incinerators) were located, but every other prisoner who was taken there was killed there. That made it the first camp to be set up solely for extermination, and it served as a model for the Operation Reinhard camps that were established later in 1942.

On 29 November 1941, Reinhard Heydrich wrote to a number of officials from various ministries and National Socialist Party offices, inviting them to a meeting to discuss the 'final solution of the Jewish question'. To underline both the importance of this meeting and Heydrich's authority to call it, he enclosed a copy of a written order from Hermann Goering, dated 31 July 1941, which commissioned Heydrich to make preparations for a 'total solution to the Jewish question', to prepare a plan, and to coordinate the activities of the relevant government departments. The meeting was originally scheduled for 9 December, but the Japanese attack on Pearl Harbor and Germany's subsequent declaration of war on the United States necessitated a postponement. It finally took place at an SS conference centre at 56–58 Am Grossen Wannsee on 20 January 1942. The invited officials were told to arrive at 12 p.m. for a conference, which would be followed by 'breakfast'.

Those who attended were: SS-General Reinhard Heydrich (chief of the RSHA and *Reichsprotektor* of Bohemia-Moravia), chairman; Dr Josef Bühler (representative of the General Government); Dr Roland Freisler (Ministry of Justice); SS-Major General Otto Hofmann (Race and Resettlement Main Office, RuSHA); SA-Senior Colonel Gerhard Klopfer (NSDAP Chancellery); Friedrich Wilhelm Kritzinger (Reich Chancellery); SS-Major Dr Rudolf Lange (Commander-in-Chief of the Security Police, Latvia); Dr Georg Leibbrandt (Ministry for the Occupied Eastern Territories); Dr Martin Luther (Foreign Office); Regional Leader Dr Alfred Meyer (Ministry for the Occupied Eastern Territories); SS-Major General Heinrich Müller (chief of Gestapo); Dr Erich Neumann (director, Office of the Four-Year Plan); SS-Senior Colonel Dr Karl Eberhard Schöngarth (SD, assigned to the General Government); Dr Wilhelm Stuckart (Ministry of the Interior); and SS-Lieutenant Colonel Adolf Eichmann (head of Section IV B4, Gestapo), secretary.[3]

According to Eichmann's minutes, Heydrich opened the conference by reasserting his authority to coordinate policy relating to the 'Jewish question':

> At the beginning of the discussion Chief of the Security Police and of the SD, SS-General Heydrich, reported that the Reich Marshal had appointed him delegate for the preparations for the final solution of the Jewish question in Europe and pointed out that this discussion had been called for the purpose of clarifying fundamental questions. The wish of the Reich Marshal to have a draft sent to him concerning organizational, factual and material interests in relation to the final solution of the Jewish question in Europe makes necessary an initial common action of all central offices immediately concerned with these questions in order to bring their general activities into line. The National Leader of the SS and the Chief of the German Police (Chief of the Security Police and the SD) was entrusted with the official central handling of the final solution of the Jewish question without regard to geographic borders.[4]

He then went on to outline the steps that had been taken both before and during the war:

> The Chief of the Security Police and the SD then gave a short report of the struggle which has been carried on thus far against this enemy, the essential points being the following:
>
> a) the expulsion of the Jews from every sphere of life of the German people,
> b) the expulsion of the Jews from the living space of the German people.
>
> In carrying out these efforts, an increased and planned acceleration of the emigration of the Jews from Reich territory was started, as the only possible present solution.
>
> By order of the Reich Marshal, a Reich Central Office for Jewish Emigration was set up in January 1939 and the Chief of the Security Police and SD was entrusted with the management. Its most important tasks were:
>
> a) to make all necessary arrangements for the preparation for an increased emigration of the Jews,
> b) to direct the flow of emigration,
> c) to speed the procedure of emigration in each individual case.
>
> The aim of all this was to cleanse German living space of Jews in a legal manner.[5]

Heydrich next mentioned the difficulties that the emigration policy had faced, such as the increasing sums of money demanded of the emigrants at their destinations, the lack of available shipping, restrictions on entry visas and so forth. However, he then told the delegates:

In spite of these difficulties, 537,000 Jews were sent out of the country between the takeover of power and the deadline of 31 October 1941. Of these:

- approximately 360,000 were in Germany proper on 30 January 1933
- approximately 147,000 were in Austria (Ostmark) on 15 March 1939
- approximately 30,000 were in the Protectorate of Bohemia and Moravia on 15 March 1939.[6]

These figures included Jews who had emigrated to 'safe' countries outside the German sphere of influence and those who had gone to, for example, Poland, the Netherlands and Hungary, and so were now back under German control. They also included those who had been forcibly deported from German territory to the General Government. Heydrich then explained that the Jews had financed their enforced emigration themselves, having raised some US$9.5 million among Jewish organisations inside and outside Germany. However, the war situation had now forced the German government to abandon the emigration project for security reasons.

With the preamble over, Heydrich moved on to the main topic of the meeting: what was to be done with the Jews. While Eichmann's minutes are bureaucratic and neutral,* nobody present could have been in any doubt about what they were discussing. After all, mass executions had been taking place in the incorporated territories of Poland and the General Government since 1939, and a similar policy was now being pursued in the Baltic States and the western Soviet Union. The various delegates were therefore fully aware that they were there to discuss

* In the aftermath of the meeting, Heydrich instructed Eichmann that his minutes must not be a verbatim record of what had been said: Eichmann was told to 'clean them up', to eliminate such words as 'extermination' and 'liquidation'.

genocide, even though Heydrich never used the word during the meeting:

> Another possible solution of the problem has now taken the place of emigration, i.e. the evacuation of the Jews to the East, provided that the Führer gives the appropriate approval in advance.
>
> These actions are, however, only to be considered provisional, but practical experience is already being collected which is of the greatest importance in relation to the future final solution of the Jewish question.[7]

Of course, 'evacuation of the Jews to the East' was a euphemism. At the time of the conference, the military situation in the Soviet Union was far from secure, and no plans had been drafted to resettle the Jews anywhere permanently. Any 'practical experience' therefore related not to evacuation but to mass extermination. Lange, the Sipo commander in Riga, was able to give the assembled delegates precise details of the relevant 'experience' he had accumulated in the city's ghetto.

Heydrich next went on to explain the scale of the task that they faced. The Jews of Europe could be divided into two groups: those under the direct control of Germany; and those in countries that still possessed their own sovereign governments. Heydrich's figures for the first group were:

- Germany proper   131,800
- Austria   43,700
- Eastern territories   420,000
- General Government   2,284,000
- Bialystok   400,000
- Protectorate of Bohemia and Moravia   74,200
- Estonia   0
- Latvia   3500
- Lithuania   34,000

- Belgium   43,000
- Denmark   5600
- France: occupied territory   165,000
              unoccupied territory   700,000
- Greece   69,600
- Netherlands   160,800
- Norway   1300[8]

His estimates for those in the second group – who were expected to be swept up in the final solution at some point – were:

- Bulgaria   48,000
- England   330,000
- Finland   2300
- Ireland   4000
- Italy, including Sardinia   58,000
- Albania   200
- Croatia   40,000
- Portugal   3000
- Romania, including Bessarabia   342,000
- Sweden   8000
- Switzerland   18,000
- Serbia   10,000
- Slovakia   88,000
- Spain   6000
- (European) Turkey   55,500
- Hungary   742,800
- USSR   5,000,000
- Ukraine   2,994,684
- White Russia, excluding Bialystok   446,484[9]

Heydrich made it very clear what was planned for all of these people:

Under proper guidance, in the course of the final solution the Jews are to be allocated for appropriate labor in the East.

Able-bodied Jews, separated according to sex, will be taken in large work columns to these areas for work on roads, in the course of which action doubtless a large portion will be eliminated by natural causes.

The possible final remnant will, since it will undoubtedly consist of the most resistant portion, have to be treated accordingly, because it is the product of natural selection and would, if released, act as the seed of a new Jewish revival (see the experience of history).

In the course of the practical execution of the final solution, Europe will be combed through from West to East. Germany proper, including the Protectorate of Bohemia and Moravia, will have to be handled first due to the housing problem and additional social and political necessities.[10]

Although the conference concerned all the Jews of Europe, specific attention was paid to the murder of German Jews; principally, it seems, because of concerns about political protests. The T-4 programme had been wound down just five months earlier, partly in the face of vocal opposition from the churches, and the conference delegates may well have feared similar protests against the extermination of the Jews. In a bid to forestall this, Heydrich explained that Jews over the age of sixty-five and those who had been seriously wounded or had won the Iron Cross, first class, during the First World War would be exempted from 'evacuation'. Instead, they would be deported to the 'old age' ghetto that had recently been established at Theresienstadt* (now Terezín in the Czech Republic). Heydrich believed that, 'With this

---

* Theresienstadt had been established as a Jewish ghetto towards the end of 1941. It was used by the SS to reassure the outside world about the fate of the Jews, but conditions there were still harsh. Between 1941 and 1945, some 144,000 Jews were sent there, and approximately 33,000 of them died within the ghetto, mainly of hunger or disease. Around 88,000 were ultimately deported to Auschwitz and other death camps. There were just 17,272 survivors when the ghetto was liberated by the Soviet Army.

expedient solution, in one fell swoop, many interventions will be prevented.'

Another issue that the delegates had to address was the question of the *Mischlinge*. Heydrich proposed that *Mischlinge* of the first degree (those with two Jewish grandparents) should be treated as Jews unless they had married a person of German blood and that union had produced children; or if they had been granted exemption by the 'highest offices of the State' through personal merit. However, these *Mischlinge* would need to accept sterilisation as a prerequisite for being allowed to remain in Germany.

Mischlinge of the second degree (those with one Jewish grandparent) would be treated as Germans unless:

a) The person of mixed blood of the second degree was born of a marriage in which both parents are persons of mixed blood.

b) The person of mixed blood of the second degree has a racially especially undesirable appearance that marks him outwardly as a Jew.

c) The person of mixed blood of the second degree has a particularly bad police and political record that shows that he feels and behaves like a Jew.[11]

In other words, looking Jewish or having a criminal record was enough to ensure a death sentence.

Heydrich then enumerated the plans for various other permutations of *Mischlinge* and Jews who were married to each other, and to persons of German blood. Basically, all of this attention to detail was designed to prevent disquiet among the German population at the evacuation of Jewish or *Mischlinge* spouses or relatives, while also ensuring that as many people as possible fell within the scope of the 'final solution'.

There was also some discussion among the delegates about how the planned genocide would be implemented throughout Europe:

The beginning of the individual larger evacuation actions will largely depend on military developments. Regarding the handling of the final solution in those European countries occupied and influenced by us, it was proposed that the appropriate expert of the Foreign Office discuss the matter with the responsible official of the Security Police and SD.

In Slovakia and Croatia the matter is no longer so difficult, since the most substantial problems in this respect have already been brought near a solution. In Rumania the government has in the meantime also appointed a commissioner for Jewish affairs. In order to settle the question in Hungary, it will soon be necessary to force an adviser for Jewish questions onto the Hungarian government.

With regard to taking up preparations for dealing with the problem in Italy, SS-General Heydrich considers it opportune to contact the chief of police with a view to these problems.

In occupied and unoccupied France, the registration of Jews for evacuation will in all probability proceed without great difficulty.

Under Secretary of State Luther calls attention in this matter to the fact that in some countries, such as the Scandinavian states, difficulties will arise if this problem is dealt with thoroughly and that it will therefore be advisable to defer actions in these countries. Besides, in view of the small numbers of Jews affected, this deferral will not cause any substantial limitation.

The Foreign Office sees no great difficulties for southeast and western Europe.

SS-Major General Hofmann plans to send an expert to Hungary from the Race and Settlement Main Office for general orientation at the time when the Chief of the Security Police and SD takes up the matter there. It was decided to assign this expert from the Race and Settlement Main Office, who will not work actively, as an assistant to the police attaché.[12]

With the main business of the meeting now done, there were still a few issues to resolve. Neumann, Goering's representative from the Office for the Four-Year Plan, sought assurances that key Jewish war workers would not be 'evacuated'; Heydrich was happy to provide them. Then Bühler, from the General Government, made a special plea:

> State Secretary Dr Bühler stated that the General Government would welcome it if the final solution of this problem could be begun in the General Government, since on the one hand transportation does not play such a large role here nor would problems of labor supply hamper this action. Jews must be removed from the territory of the General Government as quickly as possible, since it is especially here that the Jew as an epidemic carrier represents an extreme danger and on the other hand he is causing permanent chaos in the economic structure of the country through continued black market dealings. Moreover, of the approximately 2 1/2 million Jews concerned, the majority is unfit for work.
>
> State Secretary Dr Bühler stated further that the solution to the Jewish question in the General Government is the responsibility of the Chief of the Security Police and the SD and that his efforts would be supported by the officials of the General Government. He had only one request, to solve the Jewish question in this area as quickly as possible.[13]

This was the most explicit reference to the real purpose of the 'final solution' during the meeting. If the intention was genuinely to evacuate Jews to the East, why would transportation not be an issue for the Jews of the General Government? Clearly, Bühler was under no illusions about what was about to happen to the Jews of Europe: they would be going no further east than the General Government.

Eichmann recorded: 'In conclusion the different types of possible solutions were discussed, during which discussion both

Regional Leader Dr Meyer and State Secretary Dr Bühler took the position that certain preparatory activities for the final solution should be carried out immediately in the territories in question, in which process alarming the populace must be avoided.'[14] This meant that the delegates finished the meeting – after cognac had been served – casually discussing the pros and cons of different methods of killing.

The Wannsee Conference was probably not as significant as it is often portrayed. It did not initiate any new measures, and it did not include substantive discussions about the practicalities or logistics of the mass execution of the Jewish people. Rather, by and large, it was simply a briefing by Heydrich that was designed to demonstrate his (and the RSHA's) authority and pre-eminence in policy relating to the 'Jewish question' over all other agencies and departments that might have some objections to it. It was felt that this needed to be established particularly with respect to the Foreign Ministry – which had concerns on diplomatic grounds – and the Office of the Four-Year Plan – which was worried on economic grounds. Once this had been achieved, the meeting could conclude.

23

The Extermination Camps

Bühler's plea at the Wannsee Conference for the General Government to be the first area to be cleared of Jews was already well in hand. On the evening of Monday, 13 October 1941, Himmler had held a meeting with SS-General Krüger, his representative in the General Government, and SS-Brigadier Odilo Globocnik, the Lublin SSPF. He had ordered Globocnik to build a camp at Belzec in order to begin the extermination of the General Government's Jews under the official codename '*Aktion Reinhard*' (Operation Reinhard).

Globocnik was an ideal choice for the job. He was born in 1904 in Trieste, where his father, a reserve officer in the Austro-Hungarian Army, was a postal official. Globocnik was of half-Slovene, half-German ancestry, but he seems to have considered himself German and to have felt a strong contempt for the Slavs. He was originally enrolled to study at a military school, but the First World War intervened. His father was called up for military service, so Globocnik went to live with the rest of the family in Klagenfurt, where he completed his education at the local civilian high school in 1923.[1]

For the next few years, he worked in the building trade while developing contacts and friendships in right-wing circles. In March

1931, he joined the Austrian National Socialist Party and rose steadily through its ranks; he also served several brief prison sentences for his political activities. He joined the SS on 1 September 1934, achieving officer rank as an *Untersturmführer* (second lieutenant) in 1937. In the wake of the *Anschluss*, he was appointed Regional Leader of Vienna in May 1938, an indication that he was considered one of the rising stars of Austrian National Socialism. Unfortunately for Globocnik, though, this high reputation was short lived. His new role gave him control over large amounts of money, including party funds, public funds and cash expropriated from the Jews or raised by the sale of their seized assets. Questions were raised about Globocnik's handling of this money and, amid allegations of corruption and embezzlement, he was dismissed as Regional Leader on 30 January 1939. It seems that Himmler – who was a close personal friend – protected Globocnik from prosecution, but was unable to halt the investigation entirely.* For most of the next eight months, Globocnik – who by now held the General-SS rank of SS-senior leader – participated in military training with the Special Purpose Troops, with the lowly rank of SS-*Rottenführer* (lance corporal). He then took part in the invasion of Poland as a member of the 1st Battalion of the *Germania* Regiment.

On 3 November 1939, Globocnik made the considerable jump from Waffen-SS-lance corporal back to SS-senior colonel as the SSPF for Lublin. Six days later he became an SS-brigadier (with an equivalent rank in the police). Of course, this meant he now owed a huge debt to Himmler for resurrecting his career. Thereafter, just as Himmler must have hoped, Globocnik demonstrated enormous zeal in executing – and even anticipating – the National Leader's orders.

---

* A few months later, in August 1939, Himmler awarded Globocnik the *Totenkopfring* – his personal honour that was supposedly not available to any SS member with a tarnished disciplinary record. Whether this indicates that Himmler did not believe the allegations or simply did not care is unclear.

During his tenure as Lublin's SSPF, he presided over a network of imprisonment and death that eventually comprised 57 Jewish ghettoes, including the massive Lublin ghetto itself; 143 work camps; 27 prison camps; 3 POW camps; 2 extermination camps (with a third near by); the enormous Majdanek concentration camp, which had its own gassing and cremation facilities (it was also known as the Lublin concentration camp); 6 'sub-camps' of Majdanek; 17 transit camps; 9 prisons; and 29 detention centres.[2] Additionally, his district was a centre for SS economic enterprises that utilised Polish and Jewish slave labour. It was also earmarked by Globocnik as a base for future German colonisation of the East. Himmler was so impressed by Globocnik's efforts in this area that he appointed him 'Plenipotentiary for the Construction of SS and Police Bases in the Former Russian Areas'.

According to Yitzhak Arad, Globocnik had responsibility for:

- The overall planning of the deportations and extermination activities of the entire operation.
- Building the death camps.
- Coordinating the deportations of the Jews to the death camps.
- Killing the Jews in the death camps.
- Seizing the assets and valuables of the victims and handing them over to the appropriate authorities.[3]

Globocnik assembled a team of specialists to carry out these tasks. His chief of staff was SS-Captain Hermann Höfle, who had spent the previous year overseeing the digging of a network of vast anti-tank ditches by Jewish slave labour in the Lublin district. Höfle's office was in the Julius Schreck Kaserne at Pieradzkiego 11, Lublin, separate from Globocnik's headquarters for security reasons. From there, he personally led a team of some 350 SS and police personnel, who were involved in various aspects of the extermination programme.

Another group, eventually numbering ninety-two, was attached to Globocnik's staff from the Führer Chancellery. These were members of the operational staff of the T-4 killing centres and thus, at the time, were among the most experienced mass murderers in the world. The first to arrive in Lublin, in September 1941, was Christian Wirth, who was apparently sent there to set up a euthanasia facility. When this plan was abandoned, he turned his attention towards the Jews.

By all accounts, Wirth was a brutal and sadistic man, fitting the stereotype of the SS mass killer better than most of his colleagues. A Swabian, born in 1885, he had worked as a carpenter and a policeman before the First World War. He served as a soldier on the Western Front, then worked in the building trade before becoming a member of Stuttgart Police's murder squad in the 1930s. As we have seen, he was present at the first gassing experiments in Brandenburg in 1939, and his participation in the euthanasia programme gave him indisputable expertise in mass killing.

In October 1941, he returned to Lublin with a small group of former T-4 employees, all of whom had been inducted into the Waffen-SS,* with orders to establish and operate a camp to kill Jews. The extermination facility was to be constructed on a railway spur near the small town of Belzec, in the south-east of Lublin district, out of sight of prying eyes but close to the railway and other transport links. Construction began on 1 November, supervised by SS-Sergeant Josef Oberhauser but carried out by local Polish tradesmen:

> We built barracks close to the side-track of the railway. One barrack, which was close to the railway, was 50 m long and 12.5 m wide. The second barrack, 25 m long and 12.5 m wide, was for the Jews destined for 'the baths'. Not far from

---

* This highlights the legal status of the Waffen-SS. The T-4 personnel of Operation Reinhard were supposedly performing military service in the camps, so they were given the same status as combat-unit members of the SS.

this barrack we built a third barrack, 12 m long and 8 m wide. This barrack was divided into three chambers by a wooden wall, so that each chamber was 4 m wide and 8 m long. It was 2 m high. The inside walls of this barrack were of double boards with a vacant space between them filled with sand. The walls were covered with pasteboard. In addition, the floor and walls (to a height of 1.10 m) were covered with sheets of zinc. From the second to the third barrack led a closed passageway, 2 m wide, 2 m high, and 10 m long. This passageway led to a corridor in the third barrack where the doors to the three chambers were located. Each chamber of this barrack had on its northern side a double door 1.80 m high and 1.10 m wide. These doors, like those in the corridor, were sealed with rubber gaskets round the edges. All the doors in this barrack could only be opened from the outside. These doors were built with strong planks 7.5 centimetres thick, and were secured from the outside with a wooden locking bar held by two iron hooks on either side. In each of the three chambers of this barrack a water pipe was installed 0.10 m above the floor. In addition, in the corner of the western wall of each chamber, was a water pipe 1 m above the ground with an open joint, turned toward the centre of the room. These pipes with the joint were connected through the wall to a pipe that ran under the floor. In each of the three chambers of this barrack a stove weighing 250 kg was installed. It was expected that the pipe joint would later be connected to the stove. The stove was 1.10 m high, 0.55 m wide and 0.55 m long.[4]

The camp was divided into two sectors. Camp 1, the western half, was the reception area, with the railway platform, a few garages, storerooms, accommodation for the guard force and so on. It also included the 'undressing barracks', where the victims' clothes were taken from them, and a hut in which the female victims' hair was cut off. There was a 'chute' or 'sluice' into Camp 2, separated from Camp 1 by a high fence, where the extermination facilities were located. These were the wooden 'barracks' built by the Polish labour force – in reality the gas chambers – the burial pits (and, later in the camp's existence, the incinerators) and accommodation for the few 'work Jews' who were kept alive to remove bodies from the gas chambers, sort through the victims' clothing and possessions and perform menial tasks for the guards and the SS men. The camp offices and accommodation for the SS NCOs were in the town of Belzec itself.

The guards were not members of the SS but mainly Ukrainians, trained as military auxiliary *Hilfswillige* (or 'Hiwis') at the Trawniki training camp, which was also located in Lublin district. Many accounts of the Holocaust focus on the brutality of these men, as if they were somehow a lower, less cultured order of humanity than the Germans, and that this explained their behaviour. In addition to being racist, this ignores the fact that the majority of these men were prisoners of war, captured during the first months of Operation Barbarossa. They behaved brutally and participated in unforgivable crimes but equally they had been, for the most part, treated appallingly while in captivity, and many assumed that they were left with little option but to 'volunteer' for German service in order to survive. Once they took up their new roles, they were all too aware that they would suffer if they did not perform them to the Germans' satisfaction. Undoubtedly, there were anti-Semites and sadists among their number, but the majority were simply doing whatever was necessary to give themselves a chance of surviving the war. They were given some basic training and issued with black uniforms – often requisitioned from former General-SS stocks – and a rifle. The guard force at Belzec consisted of about eighty men, formed into two platoons, commanded by Ukrainian German-speakers. They were under the overall supervision of an SS NCO, SS-Sergeant Feiks.

Belzec's task was simple: to kill as many Jews as quickly as possible. Once the camp's basic facilities had been constructed in February 1942, Wirth began experiments in how to achieve this.

Eventually, he settled on gassing with carbon monoxide, just as had been used during the T-4 programme. However, it would have been logistically difficult to transport the relatively 'clean' bottled form of the gas, and this might also have raised security questions. So, instead, SS-Sergeant Lorenz Hackenholt, a former driver and 'disinfector' for T-4, connected what might have been either a Soviet tank or an armoured-car engine to the gas chambers. Whichever type of engine it was, it proved amply efficient.

The procedure for the murders at Belzec was ultimately adopted throughout Operation Reinhard. It started with the arrival of twenty freight cars at the camp's railway 'ramp'.* The Jewish prisoners disembarked with the guards in attendance and under the supervision of two or three SS men. Next, the 'work Jews' would remove any corpses from the wagons, leaving them on the ramp to be cleared away later. Wirth or one of his subordinates would then give a speech, informing the prisoners that they had arrived at a transit camp, where they would be fed and re-clothed before being moved on to work camps. They were told that they needed to undress and tie their shoes together with the laces. The women were informed that they would have their hair cut before they were all taken to the showers for delousing. At this stage, the men and the women were separated.

The men were always killed first, to reduce the risk of any resistance. They were driven by the Ukrainian guards – with clubs and bayonets, if necessary – into the 'sluice' that connected the reception area to the gas chambers. This two-metre-wide passageway was topped with barbed wire and covered with camouflage netting. But the fiction of where the prisoners were going was maintained even here: 'To the Baths' signs adorned the walls in a bid to allay suspicions. As soon as they reached the gas chambers, the men were crammed in, shoulder to shoulder, and

---

* The trains usually set off with between sixty and eighty wagons, but this exceeded the capacity of the reception facilities in the camp, so they were split into groups of twenty for the final part of their journey.

the doors were shut. Then the engine was started by Hackenholt or one of his Ukrainian assistants. As the Jews in the gas chambers realised what was happening, there would be screams and shouts, but within a few minutes most were unconscious. In twenty to thirty minutes, they were all dead.

On 17 August 1942, an SS technical officer, Kurt Gerstein, witnessed the process from beginning to end. His path into the Waffen-SS had been anything but typical: he had joined with the sole purpose of gleaning information about the euthanasia programme, in which his sister-in-law had been murdered. Born in 1905, the son of a judge, he originally trained as a mining engineer and worked as a civil servant for the Saarland mining administration. However, he was independently wealthy, and he helped to finance Christian anti-National Socialist propaganda even though he had joined the NSDAP in May 1933. He was arrested twice before the war by the Gestapo, and was incarcerated in concentration camps. As a result, he was expelled from both the civil service and the party. Having lost his job, he went to Tübingen University to study medicine.

He volunteered for the Waffen-SS in 1941 and was accepted, astonishingly, on the basis of references that were provided by two of the Gestapo officers who had investigated him. 'The gentlemen took the view that my idealism, which they probably admired, must be of advantage to the National Socialist cause,' Gerstein reported. He did his basic training with the *Germania* Regiment in Hamburg, but was soon transferred into the Waffen-SS's technical medical service, commissioned as an SS-lieutenant (F)* and assigned to the 'hygiene' department, which specialised in the delousing of military uniforms and water purification.

In June 1942, Gerstein was ordered by SS-Major Günther of the RSHA to obtain a hundred kilos of the delousing agent Zyklon B for an undisclosed purpose. Two months later, Günther, Gerstein and SS-Major Wilhelm Pfannenstiehl, the Professor of Medical

---

* The '(F)' denotes that Gerstein was a *Fachführer* (specialist officer).

Hygiene at Marburg University, drove via Prague to Lublin, where they met Globocnik. The SSPF swore them to secrecy and briefed them on Operation Reinhard, which by then was in full swing at Belzec and two other camps: Treblinka and Sobibor. Gerstein now learned why he had been brought along. He was given two tasks: to look into the disinfection of the vast amount of clothing that had been stolen from the murdered Jews and was being sent back to Germany for use by forced labourers;* and to determine the viability of using Zyklon B in the gas chambers. To this end, it had been decided that Gerstein should witness the current gassing procedure. Gerstein recorded what happened that day:†

The next day we drove to Belzec. A small special station had been created for this purpose at a hill, hard north of the road Lublin–Lemberg, in the left angle of the demarcation line. South of the road some houses with the inscription 'Waffen-SS Special Unit Belzec'. Because the actual chief of the whole killing facilities, Police Captain Wirth, was not yet there, Globocnik introduced me to SS-Captain Obermeyer. That afternoon he let me see only that which he simply had to show me. That day I didn't see any corpses, just the smell of the whole region was stinking to high heaven in a hot August, and millions of flies were everywhere.

Near to the small double-track station was a large barrack, the so-called 'cloakroom', with a large counter for valuables. Then followed the barber's room with approximately 100

---

* By this time, Globocnik had accumulated some forty million kilos of textiles – far too much to be disinfected in existing commercial facilities. Gerstein negotiated with some commercial disinfectors, but they baulked at the scale of the task. Eventually, Globocnik and Gerstein decided simply to sprinkle disinfectant on the clothes, so that at least they smelled as if they had been disinfected.

† Gerstein's account has been criticised because it undeniably contains exaggerations as well as descriptions of events that he did not witness. Nevertheless, his presence at the gassing at Belzec on 17 August is corroborated by other witnesses and there is no doubt that his account of this specific event is largely accurate.

chairs . . . Then an alley in the open air, below birches, fenced in to the right and left by double barbed wire with inscriptions: 'To the inhalation- and bath rooms!' In front of us a sort of bath house with geraniums, then a small staircase, and then to the right and left 3 rooms each, 5 × 5 metres, 1.90 metres high, with wooden doors like garages. At the back wall, not quite visible in the dark, larger wooden ramp doors. On the roof as a clever little joke the Star of David. In front of the building an inscription: '*Hackenholt Stiftung*'.* More I couldn't see that afternoon.

The next morning, shortly before 7 a.m. someone announced to me: 'In ten minutes the first transport will come!' In fact the first train arrived after some minutes, from the direction of Lemberg (Lvov). 45 wagons with 6,700 people of whom 1,450 were already dead on arrival. Behind the barred hatches children as well as men and women looked out, terribly pale and nervous, their eyes full of the fear of death. The train comes in: 200 Ukrainians fling open the doors and whip the people out of the wagons with their leather whips. A large loudspeaker gives the further orders: 'Undress completely, also remove artificial limbs, spectacles etc.' Handing over valuables at the counter, without receiving a voucher or a receipt. The shoes carefully bound together . . . because on the almost 25 metre high heap nobody would have been able to find the matching shoes again. Then the women and girls to the barber who, with two, three scissor strokes is cutting off all hair and collecting it in potato sacks. 'That is for special purposes in the submarines, for seals or the like,' the SS-Corporal who is on duty there says to me.

Then the procession starts moving. In front a very lovely young girl. So all of them go along the alley, all naked: men, women, children, without artificial limbs. I myself stand

* 'Hackenholt Foundation' – the SS men's nickname for the gas chamber at Belzec – named after Lorenz Hackenholt.

together with Captain Wirth on top of the ramp between the gas chambers. Mothers with babies at their breast, they come onward, hesitate, enter the death chambers! At the corner a strong SS man stands who, with a voice like a pastor, says to the poor people: 'There is not the least chance that something will happen to you! You must only take a deep breath in the chamber, that widens the lungs; this inhalation is necessary because of the illnesses and epidemics.' On the question of what would happen to them he answered: 'Yes, of course, the men have to work, building houses and roads but the women don't need to work. Only if they wish they can help in house-keeping or in the kitchen.'

For some of these poor people this gave a little glimmer of hope, enough to go the few steps to the chambers without resistance. The majority are aware, the smell tells them of their fate! So they climb the small staircase, and then they see everything. Mothers with little children at the breast, little naked children, adults, men, women, all naked – they hesitate but they enter the death chambers, pushed forward by those behind them or driven by the leather whips of the SS. The majority without saying a word. A Jewess of about 40 years of age, with flaming eyes, calls down vengeance on the head of the murderers for the blood which is shed here. She gets 5 or 6 slashes with the riding crop into her face from Captain Wirth personally, then she also disappears into the chamber. Many people pray. I pray with them, I press myself in a corner and shout loudly to my and their God. How gladly I would have entered the chamber together with them, how gladly I would have died the same death as them. Then they would have found a uniformed SS man in their chambers – the case would have been understood and treated as an accident, one man quietly missing. Still I am not allowed to do this. First I must tell what I am experiencing here!

The chambers fill. 'Pack well!' – Captain Wirth has ordered. The people stand on each other's feet. 700–800 on

25 square metres, in 45 cubic metres! The SS physically squeezes them together, as far as is possible.

The doors close. At the same time the others are waiting outside in the open air, naked. Someone tells me: 'The same in winter!' 'Yes, but they could catch their death of cold,' I say. 'Yes, exactly what they are here for!' says an SS man to me in his Low German. Now I finally understand why the whole installation is called the Hackenholt Foundation. Hackenholt is the driver of the diesel engine, a little technician, also the builder of the facility. The people are brought to death with the diesel exhaust fumes. But the diesel doesn't work! Captain Wirth comes. One can see that he feels embarrassed that that happens just today, when I am here. That's right, I see everything! And I wait. My stop watch has honestly registered everything. 50 minutes, 70 minutes – the diesel doesn't start! The people are waiting in their gas chambers. In vain! One can hear them crying, sobbing . . . Captain Wirth hits the Ukrainian who is helping Sergeant Hackenholt 12, 13 times in the face. After two hours and 49 minutes – the stop watch has registered everything well – the diesel starts. Until this moment the people live in these 4 chambers, four times 750 people in 4 times 45 cubic metres. Again 25 minutes pass. Right, many are dead now. One can see that through the small window in which the electric light illuminates the chambers for a moment. After 28 minutes only a few are still alive. Finally, after 32 minutes, everyone is dead.

From the other side men from the work command open the wooden doors. They have been promised – even Jews – freedom, and some one-thousandth of all valuables found, for their terrible service. Like basalt pillars the dead stand inside, pressed together in the chambers. In any event there was no space to fall down or even bend forward. Even in death one can still tell the families. They still hold hands, tensed in death, so that one can barely tear them apart in order to empty the chamber for the next batch. The corpses are thrown out, wet from sweat and urine, soiled by excrement, menstrual blood on their legs. Children's corpses fly through the air. There is no time. The riding crops of the Ukrainians lash down on the work groups. Two dozen dentists open mouths with hooks and look for gold. Gold to the left, without gold to the right. Other dentists break gold teeth and crowns out of jaws with pliers and hammers.

Among all this Captain Wirth is running around. He is in his element. Some workers search the genitals and anus of the corpses for gold, diamonds, and valuables. Wirth calls me to him: 'Lift this can full of gold teeth, that is only from yesterday and the day before yesterday!' In an incredibly vulgar and incorrect diction he said to me: 'You won't believe what we find in gold and diamonds every day' . . . 'and in dollars. But see for yourself!' And now he led me to a jeweller who managed all these treasures, and let me see all this. Then someone showed me a former head of the *Kaufhaus des Westens** in Berlin, and a violinist: 'That was a Captain of the Austrian Army, knight of the Iron Cross 1st class who is now camp elder of the Jewish work command!'

The naked corpses were carried on wooden stretchers to pits only a few metres away, measuring 100 × 20 × 12 metres. After a few days the corpses welled up and a short time later they collapsed, so that one could throw a new layer of bodies upon them. Then ten centimetres of sand were spread over the pit, so that a few heads and arms still rose from it here and there. At such a place I saw Jews climbing over the corpses and working. One told me that by mistake those who arrived dead had not been stripped.[5]

Wirth was clearly embarrassed by the problems that had been encountered that day, and asked Gerstein not to bother conducting

---

* A large department store, equivalent to Harrods in London or Macy's in New York.

the Zyklon B experiments. Consequently, Gerstein buried the canisters in some nearby woods.

The second Operation Reinhard camp was built close to the village of Sobibor, in a densely wooded part of the eastern Lublin district. It was situated close to the River Bug, which formed the border between the General Government and the *Reichskommisariat* Ukraine, and not far from the Chelm–Wlodawa railway. Construction began in March 1942, and the layout of the camp reflected lessons that had been learned from the early murders at Belzec. For instance, a rail spur, leading from the station at Sobibor, ran straight into the camp, through a gateway in a wall constructed from concrete and 'camouflaged' with tree branches.

In April 1942, Franz Stangl was placed in command of the camp.* His story is fairly simple. He was born in 1908 in Altmünster, Austria, the son of an ex-soldier who bullied and terrorised him for the first eight years of his life. However, in 1916, Stangl's father died, and his childhood became more bearable. At the age of fifteen he was apprenticed in a local textile mill, and three years later he qualified as a master weaver, supposedly the youngest in Austria. He continued in that profession until 1931, when he joined the police in Linz. He seems to have been a reasonably competent policeman, and in July 1934, shortly after the assassination of Dr Dollfuss, the Austrian Chancellor, he discovered a National Socialist arms cache in a forest. His reward was a decoration and a posting to detectives' school. After he qualified, he joined the political police in the town of Wels, where he investigated anti-government activity.

---

* What follows is derived largely from Stangl himself. His testimony is unique among those of extermination camp commanders in that it was given – in a series of interviews with Gitta Sereny in 1970 – without a hint of compulsion. Sereny's book, *Into That Darkness*, therefore gives an unsurpassed insight into the mindset of a major perpetrator of the Holocaust. Stangl's attitude to what he did can best be described as a kind of morose, fatalistic detachment.

Stangl claimed that he was not a National Socialist supporter prior to the *Anschluss*; and thereafter, he feared that his police record might well lead to him being branded an enemy of the new regime. He therefore persuaded a contact to enter his name retrospectively on a list of secret National Socialists, which he hoped would afford him some protection. His police unit was absorbed into the Gestapo in early 1939,[6] and he was promoted to the status of an established, pensionable civil servant. He also left the Church, in line with SS policy (even though he was not yet an SS member). He continued with his police work – which by now included some tasks relating to forced Jewish emigration – until November 1940, when he was informed by his superior that he had been selected for a special role.

This was an assignment to the T-4 programme euthanasia killing centre at Hartheim. It is not clear why Stangl was chosen, but perhaps it was because he was fundamentally obedient, the sort of man who would not disobey an order from a superior, even if it conflicted with his own moral beliefs. Stangl also seemed to believe that accepting the position would help his career. He was promoted to the rank of lieutenant in the uniformed police and duly became the administration and security officer at Hartheim. He was responsible for the general smooth running of the operation, the issuing of death certificates and the return of the victims' personal effects to their families. Although he was intimately involved in all aspects of the operation, the killing at Hartheim (as in all of the euthanasia centres) was carried out by doctors and nurses, and Stangl appears to have been able to distance himself from it emotionally.

He remained at Hartheim until the centre's T-4 killings were wound down in the autumn of 1941, whereupon he moved to Bernburg to supervise the end of the T-4 programme there. As we have seen, both centres continued to kill 'incurables' from the concentration camps as part of Operation 14 f 13, but Stangl still had to resolve administrative issues associated with the end of the formal euthanasia programme. He completed this in February

1942,[7] and was then offered the choice of a return to Linz or an unspecified 'anti-partisan' task in Lublin. He had not enjoyed a good working relationship with the senior officers in Linz, so he chose the second option and travelled east in a group of about twenty T-4 personnel.

Stangl later claimed that he had no idea what was awaiting him. When he reached Lublin, in March 1942, he had a long conversation with Globocnik, who sounded him out for the role of commandant of Sobibor. However, according to Stangl, the SSPF was vague about the camp's true function. Globocnik did tell Stangl that Christian Wirth was in charge of the operation, and soon afterwards Stangl travelled to Sobibor to take up his new post. When he arrived at the camp, a small group of Polish labourers was building the camp under the supervision of a number of former T-4 personnel. They were soon supplemented by a Jewish labour detail and a company of Ukrainian guards from Trawniki. As construction continued, Stangl was summoned by Wirth to Belzec, and it was here that he finally realised the true purpose and scale of Operation Reinhard. On the day he arrived, there was a problem in the burial pits: the corpses had putrefied, expanded and spilled on to the open ground surrounding the pits. Wirth was furiously trying to deal with this situation, but he found the time to tell Stangl that he would soon be having similar problems at Sobibor.*

On his return to Sobibor, Stangl discussed what he had witnessed with Sergeant Hermann Michel, a friend and former co-worker at Hartheim, who had been appointed his deputy. According to Stangl, both he and Michel were deeply distressed, but they decided to keep their heads down and seek transfers out of Operation Reinhard, rather than protest or refuse to serve. Some days later, Wirth made an extended visit to the new camp to ensure that preparations were continuing smoothly. Wirth

---

* By his own account Stangl neither liked nor had a good working relationship with Wirth.

demanded that the gas chamber should be fully tested, so he gave the order for twenty-five of the 'work Jews' to be murdered in it.

This test revealed some deficiencies that had to be rectified, but Sobibor was ready to receive its first transport of prisoners in the first week of May 1942. The procedure was almost identical to that employed at Belzec, as SS-Sergeant Kurt Bolender recalled:

> Before the Jews undressed, SS-Sergeant Michel made a speech to them. On these occasions, he used to wear a white coat to give the impression that he was a physician. Michel announced to the Jews that they would be sent to work, but before this they would have to take baths and undergo dis-infection so as to prevent the spread of diseases ... After undressing, the Jews were taken through the so-called 'Schlauch' [sluice]. They were led to the gas chambers not by the Germans but by the Ukrainians ... After the Jews entered the gas chambers, the Ukrainians closed the doors. The motor which supplied the gas was switched on by a Ukrainian named Emil Kostenko and by a German driver called Erich Bauer from Berlin. After the gassing, the doors were opened and the corpses removed.[8]

As at Belzec, a few hundred Jews were kept alive in the camp to perform menial duties: burying corpses, cleaning trains and sort-ing through the vast amounts of goods, money, jewellery, food and clothing that were stolen from the victims before they died.

Between May and July, 90,000–100,000 Jews – primarily from the General Government but also from Austria and Czecho-slovakia – were murdered at Sobibor.[9] By most accounts, it was a more efficient camp than Belzec, having learned from its pre-cursor's mistakes, and because Stangl was a better, more sober organiser than Wirth. The pace of the murders was less frantic than at Belzec. Sobibor rarely received more than one transport per day, which usually consisted of no more than 2500 victims.

That made the process more manageable, although the maximum capacity of the gas chambers at this stage was not more than six hundred people at a time.

Engineering work on the Lublin–Chelm railway line caused a lull in the gassings between July and October 1942, but this gave the camp staff the opportunity to increase the gas chambers' capacity to some 1300 people. Between October 1942 and June 1943, between 150,000 and 170,000 Jews from the General Government and Slovakia were murdered, as well as 4000 from France and 34,000 from the Netherlands. Killing operations were wound down at Sobibor after July 1943, when the camp was transformed into a depot for captured ammunition.

Construction began on the third and largest of the three Operation Reinhard extermination camps soon after Sobibor had accepted its first transport in May 1942. Treblinka was placed under the command of SS-Lieutenant Dr Irmfried Eberl, who had been present at the first gassing experiment at Brandenburg and had then worked for T-4 both there and at Bernburg. Initially, there were three gas chambers in Treblinka, each capable of murdering between 200 and 250 prisoners at a time. In the first five weeks of its operation, in excess of 300,000 Jews were murdered there: some 245,000 from the Warsaw ghetto and surrounding areas; over 50,000 from Radom; and more than 16,000 from Lublin.[10] But while the camp had managed this industrial scale of killing, the rest of the operation was in a state of chaos. By July, the reception area was littered with the decomposing corpses of people who had died on the transports or had been too weak or too sick to make the short journey to the gas chambers and had thus been killed on the spot. Vast piles of prisoners' belongings were also piling up, because Eberl had not thought to set up work details to sort through them. This meant that valuables ended up in the pockets of the camp staff, were forwarded by Eberl to his former employers at T-4 (presumably at the instigation of T-4), or were simply left lying around. In the last week of August, Globocnik and Wirth visited the camp and saw a complete breakdown of the system: a transport train full of dead and dying Jews was waiting to be unloaded, because there was no space within the camp itself. Eberl was dismissed on the spot,* and Globocnik stated that he would have had him court-martialled, had he not been a fellow Austrian.

The dependable Stangl was brought in to re-establish order at Treblinka. He and Wirth asked Operation Reinhard headquarters to call a temporary halt to deportations to allow them to sort out Eberl's mess. This was agreed, and five hundred Jews from previous transports were set to work cleaning up the camp and burning or burying the piles of corpses. The transports resumed on 3 September, by which time Stangl had organised a prisoner work detail to deal with the arriving prisoners and their luggage. One group of prisoners removed dead bodies from the trains and buried them in the mass graves; others cleaned the freight cars; others sifted through the piles of clothing, valuables and food.

Generally speaking, each of the Operation Reinhard camps had a prisoner labour force of between five hundred and a thousand people. Unsurprisingly, their existence was brutal and extremely precarious. Roll-calls were held up to three times each day, and any prisoner who seemed ill or weak, or had irritated the SS NCOs, would be sent to the gas chamber or shot, to be replaced by a new arrival from the next transport. Those who remained alive were entirely at the mercy of the SS and the Ukrainians. There were no effective rules to regulate the behaviour of their overseers, who could – and did – beat and murder the workers at will. Survivors of the camps reported that very few of the guards behaved with any decency or humanity. The great majority of them were either indifferent to the prisoners' suffering or were

---

* Eberl subsequently served as a doctor with the army. He returned to civilian medical practice after the war, but committed suicide in custody after his arrest in 1948.

actively cruel and violent. One tiny shred of relief for the working prisoners was that food was usually plentiful: the victims tended to bring supplies with them on the transports, and this was used to supplement the basic rations provided by the SS. The working prisoners also managed to obtain cash and valuables, which they bartered with local civilians and some of the Ukrainian guards for more provisions. However, if the transports slackened off for any reason, the supply of extra food dried up and hunger added to the prisoners' misery.

Male prisoners were mostly assigned to heavy physical work, but a few women were also employed in the death camps – as laundrywomen, cooks and cleaners. They lived in separate barracks to the men and could be subjected to sexual abuse and rape by the guards, despite National Socialist strictures against 'race defilement'. In Sobibor, a love affair is said to have developed between a young Jewish woman from Vienna and SS-Sergeant Paul Groth, who had a reputation as a sadist. Groth's behaviour towards the other prisoners apparently improved as a result of the affair, but when it became known to his fellow SS men the girl was murdered.[11]

In spite of being fully aware of the consequences, the prisoners staged several acts of resistance in the Operation Reinhard camps. The first of these was the killing of SS-Sergeant Max Bialas at Treblinka in September 1942, when the camp had been in operation for only a few weeks. Bialas was in charge of the evening roll-call and was in the process of deciding which prisoners were to be murdered that night when one of the prisoners ran from the ranks and stabbed him with a knife he had been concealing. Bialas fell to the ground while his assailant – Meir Berliner, an Argentinian who had been in the camp only a few days[*] – stood over

---

[*] Berliner had been visiting relations in Warsaw with his wife and daughter when the war broke out. His Argentinian citizenship did not protect him and he and his family were deported to Treblinka a few days before his attack on Bialas. Both his wife and daughter had been murdered on arrival at the camp.

him. Berliner was beaten to the ground with a shovel by a Ukrainian guard and then shot. Meanwhile, other Ukrainians started shooting randomly into the prisoners, killing and wounding dozens. Once order had been restored, Wirth, who was in the camp at the time, demanded the immediate execution of ten prisoners. Another 150 were shot the next morning.

On several occasions, groups of prisoners fought with the guards as they were being hustled towards the gas chambers, but these acts of defiance were always doomed to fail in the tightly organised and confined conditions of the 'chute'. So it was perhaps inevitable that the major act of resistance to the Holocaust should take place where the murderers had less control over their victims. From July 1942, the SS began to clear the Warsaw ghetto of its inhabitants, with the vast majority being sent to Treblinka. By the end of September, some 300,000 had already been deported and murdered, leaving only 60,000 in the ghetto. But at that point, the Jewish Fighting Organisation came into being to offer some resistance. Led by Mordechai Anielewicz, the organisation smuggled a few weapons into the ghetto, and started to manufacture more with whatever materials they could find.

Three thousand SS, army and police troops from the Warsaw garrison, commanded by SS-Brigadier Jürgen Stroop, eventually entered the ghetto on 19 April 1943 to begin the final clearance. Using armoured vehicles, artillery and heavy machine guns, they attacked, blew up and set fire to buildings where the Jewish resisters were thought to be hiding. The defenders responded by fighting a running battle from ruined buildings, bunkers and trenches. Their ferocity shocked the German units, and Stroop could not claim victory until 16 May.* (Notoriously, he subsequently produced a bound volume of photographs and reports, as if the operation had been a considerable military victory.)

---

* Anielewicz and his command group committed suicide in their bunker on 8 May.

Even then, some Jewish resisters continued to fight until July. Overall, the fighting claimed the lives of some 14,000 Jewish inhabitants of the ghetto, but 7000 more were removed to Treblinka and exterminated, with the remainder being sent to Majdanek concentration camp. The Germans lost around 400 killed and 1000 wounded.[12]

The camps were never able to launch anything to rival the Warsaw ghetto rebellion, but prisoner committees in Treblinka and Sobibor did at least try. The Treblinka revolt occurred on 2 August 1943. There had been a lull in new arrivals at the camp since late May, when the Warsaw ghetto had finally been cleared. The prisoners' workload now comprised routine maintenance in and around the camp, and the cremation of corpses exhumed from the mass graves, which had been ordered by Himmler following a visit in the early spring. This relative lack of activity convinced many of the prisoners that the camp was about to be wound down and that they, inevitably, would not survive its closure. Consequently, they began to plan a revolt. Among the leaders were the camp elder, Bernard Galewski, a former Czech Army officer named Zelomir Bloch and several others with some military experience. Their plan was straightforward: teams of prisoners armed with whatever weapons they had managed to steal from the camp store would attempt to kill as many on-duty SS and Ukrainian personnel as possible; then they would attempt to seize as many weapons as possible; and finally they would burn down the camp and flee into the surrounding countryside.

In the event, circumstances forced the rebels to abandon even this basic plan. SS-Sergeant Kuttner, commander of the 'lower camp', where most of the working prisoners were housed, unexpectedly appeared in their barracks and began a conversation with a known informer during the early afternoon of 2 August. One of the committee leaders decided something had to be done, so he sent for an armed prisoner. In the meantime, Kuttner had discovered a young prisoner with bundles of cash, in readiness for his escape. As he led this prisoner to the gate of the barracks, Kuttner was shot by one of the rebels. Obviously, the general uprising now had to begin, but many of the stolen weapons had not yet been distributed among the prisoners. As a result, the revolt was chaotic. A group of prisoners armed with grenades attacked the camp headquarters, but they failed to kill or even injure any of the SS men inside. Others attacked the Ukrainian guards and fired on the watchtowers. Still others ignited the camp's petrol depot. However, in the confusion, nobody thought to cut the telephone line, and Stangl, who was in his office, called for reinforcements from the local police. In the extermination area of the camp, prisoners managed to kill or disarm their Ukrainian guards and set light to the wooden buildings, but they were unable to destroy the gas chambers or knock out the guards in the watchtowers. As a result, as the prisoners began to break through the fences and gates, many were cut down by rifle and machine-gun fire from the towers.

There were approximately 850 prisoners in Treblinka at the start of the revolt. Some 350 to 400 (including many of the leaders) were killed within the camp; about 100 did not make it outside the wire (some of these were too weak to try, while others clung to the hope that they would not be killed if they displayed 'loyalty'); and about 350 managed to escape. Of these, about half were captured and killed during the next twenty-four hours. Thereafter, the German security forces combed the forests and countryside for several more days. They picked up several more escapees, while a number were reputedly caught and either murdered immediately or handed over to the National Socialists by local peasants. However, an estimated hundred or so of the prisoners were never recaptured.[13]

The Treblinka uprising was an act of heroic defiance; and, in spite of the heavy cost, it was certainly a risk worth taking for the otherwise doomed prisoners. By the time it was launched, Operation Reinhard was nearly complete, because the overwhelming majority of the target group had already been eliminated. Two transports arrived from the Bialystock ghetto in the third week of

August 1943, and their occupants were exterminated, but the greatly reduced prisoner population meant that the process took much longer than had previously been the case. Thereafter, most of the Bialystock Jews were sent to Auschwitz, Majdanek and Theresienstadt.

In many respects, the revolt at Sobibor was better organised and more successful than the Treblinka uprising. The catalyst for the revolt was the arrival of a transport of Jews from Minsk on 23 September 1943. Among the two thousand prisoners was a group of about a hundred Jewish Soviet Army prisoners of war, including Lieutenant Alexander Pechersky. About eighty men from the transport, most of them from this group, were spared the gas chambers and began to work in the camp. By the end of the month, they were formulating plans for a mass escape. Pechersky's military bearing and obvious leadership ability attracted the attention of longer-term prisoners and their unofficial leaders, and a dialogue quickly opened up between the existing camp underground and the new arrivals.

Pechersky's first escape scheme involved digging a thirty-five-metre tunnel. Work began on this in early October, but after a few days of smooth excavation, heavy rain caused the tunnel to flood and it was abandoned. Pechersky decided that a more direct method was required, so he started to devise a means of eliminating the SS men within the camp, followed by a mass breakout through the gates. By this stage, the rebels had already made two discoveries that gave them hope: first, the camp commandant, Captain Franz Reichleitner, and his second-in-command, Sergeant Gustav Wagner, as well as several other members of the SS staff, would soon be going to Germany on leave; second, only those Ukrainian guards who were on duty carried ammunition for their rifles.*

---

* This rule had been introduced after several members of the guard company had fled from the camp (with their weapons and ammunition) to join the partisans.

In essence, Pechersky's plan was to kill the SS men in the camp, then assemble as if nothing had happened for evening roll-call, march towards and then rush the gates, and suppress any resistance from the guards with weapons captured from the Germans or stolen from the camp armoury. This plan was put into action on 14 October. During the afternoon, the SS staff were invited into various workshops and storerooms by prisoners, where they were killed with axe blows to the head. Among the dead were the acting commandant, Second Lieutenant Niemann, ten other SS NCOs and one Ukrainian guard. As the afternoon drew to a close, the prisoners moved on to the second phase and began to form up, as if for roll-call. It was at this stage that the plan began to unravel. A group of prisoners attacked the armoury, where they severely wounded Sergeant Werner Dubois. However, this assault, together with the discovery of a body elsewhere in the camp, caused shooting to break out, and the leaders of the revolt started to lose control as panicking prisoners began to climb the fences. Many were shot by the Ukrainian guards and two surviving SS NCOs; others died in the minefields that had been sown around the perimeter. Nevertheless, of the six hundred or so prisoners who had been in the main part of the camp, around three hundred managed to escape.

Unlike at Treblinka, the prisoners had cut the telephone lines, so it was some time before the remaining SS men were able to call for back-up. A mounted squadron of SS and police finally arrived in Sobibor by train at around midnight, followed by a company from Army Security's 689th Battalion in the early hours of 15 October. These forces immediately began to sweep the local forests. Later, they were joined by more SS and Sipo units. Many of the escapees were eventually found, while others were turned in or murdered by the local population, but around fifty managed to find refuge. A small group of the Soviet POWs joined a partisan group whom they met in the forest, and several of them, including Pechersky, survived the war. All of the Jewish prisoners still in Sobibor – numbering at least 150 – were executed on the afternoon of 15 October

on the orders of SS-Major General Sporrenberg, who had succeeded Globocnik as Lublin's SSPF.*

In principle, the decision to bring Operation Reinhard to an end
was taken in the spring of 1943, after Himmler had visited the
camps. By this stage, the great majority of the Jews in the General
Government had been murdered, and it was thought that any left
alive could be dealt with by the extermination facilities at Majdanek and, especially, Auschwitz–Birkenau.

The first of the Reinhard camps to cease operations was Belzec,
where mass murder ended in March–April 1943. From that point
onwards, all effort went into demolishing the camp and hiding the
evidence of the terrible crimes that had been committed there. A
small detail of surviving prisoners did the work: tearing down the
buildings, levelling the mass graves and planting trees across the
site. The work had been finished by July, at which point the work
detail was transported to Sobibor and murdered. Belzec's guards
were redistributed around Sobibor, Treblinka and the labour camp
at Poniatowa, where Belzec's last commandant, SS-Captain Gott-
lieb Hering, took over as camp commander.

The SS's attempt to conceal evidence was a complete failure. As
soon as the Germans had left the area, local Poles began to dig up
the mass graves in search of gold and valuables. Consequently, the
ground was soon strewn with identifiable human remains.†

The final death toll for Operation Reinhard is difficult to

---

* Globocnik was rewarded for his efforts in Lublin with promotion to the role
of Senior SS and Police Leader for the Adriatic Coastal Zone. There he had
responsibility for combating partisan activity and liquidating the local Jewish
population. Many of his staff from Operation Reinhard, including Wirth and
Stangl, accompanied him. Globocnik killed himself after being captured by
British soldiers in May 1945. Wirth was killed in action against partisans. Stangl
was extradited to West Germany from Brazil in the late 1960s. He died of heart
failure in prison in 1971, just eight months after being found guilty of war crimes
by a West German court.
† At Auschwitz, the ashes of cremated victims were ground up before disposal so
that no identifiable bones, teeth or other fragments would ever be found.

determine, not least because the SS's own records did not survive. Murdered Jews were not registered on arrival at the camps. They were simply sent there as a transport of 'x' number of Jews from the ghettoes and killed. Consequently, estimates can be based only on numbers who are known to have resided in the 'evacuated' areas prior to the war; numbers who lived in the ghettoes; and numbers who arrived in the camps on each transport. Hilberg suggests that some 1.5 million Jews died in Belzec, Treblinka and Sobibor between March 1942 and November 1943; in addition, approximately 150,000 Jews and others were murdered at Kulmhof, which, although not officially part of Operation Reinhard, killed its victims in a similar manner.[14] Arad estimates that 1.7 million died in the Reinhard camps alone.[15]

The SS conducted its own statistical estimate in early 1943. Dr Richard Korherr, chief inspector of the organisation's statistical department, was commissioned by Himmler to present a report on Europe's Jewish population. Korherr looked at the entire programme of emigration, deportation and extermination, with Eichmann's Section IV B4 his main source of information. However, his detailed figures for Operation Reinhard came from SS-Major Hermann Höfle, Globocnik's staff officer, presumably based on numbers from each transport.

Höfle sent a telegram to the commander of the Sipo in Cracow on 11 January 1943 in which he reported the number of Jews killed in all of the Reinhard camps:

- Lublin-Majdanek 24,733
- Belzec 434,508
- Sobibor 101,370
- Treblinka 713,555*
- Total 1,274,166[16]

---

* The actual figure given in the telegram was 71,355, but this was clearly a typing error.

Based on these figures (compiled more than six months before Sobibor ceased operations), a final estimate of at least 1.5 million seems entirely plausible, if not conservative.

In addition to extracting an obscene human toll, Operation Reinhard amassed an enormous amount of loot. The SS had always sought to profit from their persecution of the Jews: those who had been forced to emigrate from pre-war Germany and Austria had been obliged to pay extortionate fees for the privilege of leaving their homes, which had left many of them virtually destitute. Those who were murdered in Operation Reinhard were stripped of everything they possessed: food, clothing, cash, jewellery, art, even their hair and their gold teeth. Administration of this booty was loose, at best: some of it was taken by corrupt SS men, acting on their own initiative; some was pilfered by the Ukrainian guards; and some found its way into the hands of local Poles through black-market trading with the SS, the guards and even the prisoners. But the great majority – amounting to hundreds of millions of marks – was sorted by the prisoner labour force and sent to the WVHA. In a note dated September 1943, Globocnik recorded that he had sent some eighteen hundred rail cars of textiles to Germany;[17] and in a subsequent note to Himmler he boasted that the '"decency and honesty" of his men had guaranteed a complete delivery of assets'.[18]

Operation Reinhard comprised the largest – and most efficiently run – element of the Holocaust. Almost all of the material required for the construction of the camps, including the gas chambers, was sourced locally, and the logistical support they required was minimal. In total, the three camps required only 120 SS men and no more than 400 Ukrainian auxiliaries. All of the physical labour was performed by the continually changing roster of 500 to 1000 prisoners that each camp temporarily saved from death. The operation came to an end only because Globocnik had largely achieved his aim of annihilating the entire Jewish population of the General Government. And the industrial extermination machinery of Auschwitz could easily take care of the few who were left.

24

Auschwitz

The town of Oświęcim first appears in the historical record in the twelfth century. Originally, it was a Polish settlement, established at the confluence of the Vistula and Soła rivers, some forty-five kilometres to the west of Cracow. The following century, German settlers moved to the area, bringing with them their language and their law system. Then, in the 1300s, the Duchy of Oświęcim, centred on the little town, was incorporated into the Holy Roman Empire. However, by the end of the century, the duchy was under Bohemian rule, with Czech as its official language. In 1457, it was sold to the Polish monarchy, and it remained part of Poland until the state was carved up by Russia, Prussia and Austria in 1772. At that point, it came under the auspices of the Habsburg Empire, was renamed Auschwitz, and once again adopted the German language.[1] Thereafter, it remained under Habsburg control until the fall of the monarchy in 1918. Three years later, it was included in the region of eastern Upper Silesia that the League of Nations allocated to the recreated independent Polish state. Auschwitz once again became Oświęcim, but this time for just eighteen years, until the fall of Poland in September 1939.

Despite all of these changes of ownership and name, the population of Oświęcim remained largely Slavic until the mid-fifteenth century, when the first Jews arrived. Unlike many towns in Silesia, no anti-Semitic laws were enacted against Oświęcim's Jewish population, so they enjoyed a relatively stable, peaceful coexistence with their Catholic neighbours. Their numbers flourished up to 1939, by which time 50 per cent or more of the town's population of 14,000 were Jewish. Every mayor of Oświęcim was a Catholic, but his deputy was always a Jew.

The camp at Oświęcim began life at the end of the nineteenth century as a barracks for seasonal workers who passed through the frontier region on their way to find work in Prussia. At the end of the First World War, it became a refugee centre for people fleeing the border conflicts precipitated by the collapse of the German, Austro-Hungarian and Russian empires; but by the 1930s, it was being used primarily by the Polish Army.

Oświęcim fell to the German Army on 4 September 1939, and it was renamed Auschwitz a few days later. On 26 October, it became part of the new region of Upper Silesia. Thus, the town was now officially within Germany proper, rather than, as many assume, in the occupied territories of the East.

The SS first began to take an interest in the area around this time after Himmler had been appointed Reich Commissar for the Strengthening of 'Germandom'. As we have seen, much of the eastern region of the newly incorporated areas of Upper Silesia were originally designated to be used for the resettlement of ethnic Germans, but these plans were put on hold as soon as the logistical difficulties of ousting the existing population became apparent. As a short-term alternative, SS-General von dem Bach-Zelewski, who was in command of SS-Region South-East, suggested that the area could accommodate a new concentration camp.

During the winter and spring of 1939–40, the old camp in Auschwitz was visited by several teams of inspectors, who itemised the site's pros and cons. On the one hand, the buildings were dilapidated, the whole camp was in a low-lying, swampy area with poor drainage and there was a malaria problem. On the other, it had excellent communications and the main camp – once refurbished – could easily be converted into a prison compound. In the end, supporters of the site won out, and responsibility for the conversion of the barracks and establishment of the new camp was given to a long-standing National Socialist 'old fighter', SS-Captain Rudolf Höss.[2]

Höss was born in a farming district near Baden-Baden in the Rhineland-Palatinate in November 1900. His family was middle class and strongly Catholic. Höss was a solitary child, preferring the company of animals, and particularly his pony, rather than humans. This extended even to his family: by his own account, while he respected his parents and his sisters, he was unable to love them as other children seemed to love their families. He also began to lose his religious faith at the age of thirteen, after his confessor reported one of Höss's indiscretions to his father, who punished him for it. (He had accidentally hurt another child at school.) The following year, before the outbreak of the First World War, his father died.

Höss was fascinated by the conflict. He persuaded his mother to let him become a Red Cross volunteer, and he spent much of his free time helping wounded soldiers at hospitals, railway stations and barracks. In 1916, after several failed attempts, he was accepted into the cavalry regiment in which both his father and his grandfather had served. After basic training, he was sent to Turkey and from there to the Iraqi front. At the age of just seventeen he became the youngest NCO in the German Army, and the following year he was a senior sergeant commanding an independent cavalry reconnaissance troop composed entirely of men in their thirties.

He was in Damascus with his troop when the armistice came. Rather than surrender and face internment, he chose to fight his way home; his soldiers volunteered to join him. They rode across Turkey, took a tramp steamer across the Black Sea, then rode through the mountains of South-East Europe in the middle of winter before arriving in Germany after three months of travelling.

Höss's mother had died while he had been away at war, leaving his two young sisters in the care of relations. On arriving home, he discovered that these relations had divided his parents' belongings among themselves, put his sisters in a convent, and were now demanding that he should enter the priesthood (this had been his father's wish, too). Höss had no intention of becoming a priest, having found his vocation in the army. However, there was no place for him in the much-reduced regular armed forces, so he joined the *Rossbach* Free Corps.

He fought as a Free Corps soldier for the next few years in various trouble-spots within Germany and on its borders. In November 1922, he joined the NSDAP during a visit to Munich, but by then he had already committed the crime that would ensure he was not around to participate in its rebuilding process in the late 1920s. On the night of 31 May–1 June 1922, he had been one of a group of drunken Free Corps members who had abducted, brutally beaten, stabbed, shot and killed a schoolteacher whom they had wrongly believed to be an informer for the French occupation forces.[*] Höss was finally arrested on 28 June 1923, and on 15 March 1924 he was sentenced to ten years' hard labour in Brandenburg Prison.

He was a model prisoner, which amply demonstrated his compulsive obedience to authority – a trait he had already displayed in the army and the Free Corps. He achieved the highest level of trusty status and gave the prison authorities no problems whatsoever prior to his sudden release after six years as part of a political prisoner amnesty.

Höss spent much of the next five years as a member of the Artamanen Society, the Nordic-racist agricultural 'pioneer' group that Himmler had joined in the early 1920s. He met his wife in the society, and they quickly started a family. But in 1934, Himmler – whom Höss had known slightly since the early 1920s – asked him to join the SS. After some thought, he accepted and joined Eicke's

---

[*] Martin Bormann was also implicated in this crime, and served a year in prison for his part in it.

Oberbayern Guard Battalion. His reasons for doing so are easy to understand: he would be joining an organisation in which his favourite traits of obedience and duty were paramount; and he saw this as an opportunity to advance himself under a new regime whose goals he shared. After a brief period of training, he was promoted to corporal and posted to the concentration camp at Dachau as a block leader.

In his autobiography – with nauseating self-pity – Höss describes his 'reluctance' to act as a concentration camp gaoler. But he was evidently very good at his job, fitted in well with Eicke's severe and brutal regime, and rose steadily through the ranks. By July 1935, he was a sergeant and the following year he had become a sergeant major and the *Rapportführer* (in effect, executive officer) for Dachau's protective custody camp. In September 1936, he became an officer and was put in charge of administering the prisoners' property. In August 1938, he was transferred to Sachsenhausen concentration camp as its adjutant.

This was a key appointment. Sachsenhausen adjoined the Concentration Camp Inspectorate, which meant that Höss 'got more closely acquainted with Eicke and with the effects of his influence upon the camp and the troops . . . [and also] learned to understand the relationships within the higher reaches of the SS. In short acquired a broader view.'[3] Höss's familiarity with the system, as well as his zeal, efficiency and absolute obedience, made him the ideal choice as commandant of Auschwitz when the decision was made to establish it. He received his posting order to the new camp on 2 May 1940.

Work had begun on the renovation of the camp and construction of new facilities the previous month. Among the first workers were some three hundred Jews, provided by the local Jewish Council, but in all more than five hundred companies from throughout Germany were eventually involved in building work and the supply of equipment to Auschwitz. On 20 May, a group of specially selected German prisoners from Sachsenhausen was brought to Auschwitz and installed in the barracks to act as the nucleus of the trusties who would liaise between the SS and the rest of the prisoner population. Nine days later, forty more prisoners arrived with a truckload of barbed wire and started to enclose the compound by winding the wire around wooden poles.

The first political prisoners arrived at the camp on 14 June 1940. This was a group of 728 Poles – mostly soldiers, students and schoolchildren, including a few Jews – who had been transferred from the prison at Tarnów, near Cracow. At this time, it was intended that Auschwitz would be a similar institution to the concentration camps in Germany: a place where potential opponents of the National Socialists could be isolated, brutalised and 're-educated'. The only difference was its capacity: the new camp was designed to hold some 11,000 prisoners whereas, at the start of the war, the six German concentration camps held around 25,000 in total.[4] More prisoners soon followed those from Tarnów, travelling from other prisons throughout Germany and the incorporated territories. They were all set to work as forced labour, building the camp.

Organisationally, Auschwitz followed the model for concentration camps established by Eicke at Dachau. Department 1 was the commandant's staff, run by the adjutant,[*] with the role of managing the camp's SS personnel; Department 2 was the 'political department', staffed by members of the Gestapo, Kripo and SD, subordinated to the RSHA, and responsible for surveillance and interrogation of prisoners; Department 3 was responsible for the protective custody camp and was, in effect, the camp operations staff; Department 4 dealt with operations and logistics; Department 5 was the medical staff; Department 6 was responsible for the training and welfare of the Waffen-SS guards. The latter were originally supplied by a Waffen-SS mounted unit based in Cracow, but these were soon replaced by specialists seconded from

---

[*] The first adjutant at Auschwitz was Josef Kramer, who subsequently commanded the Natzweiler concentration camp in Alsace, the Birkenau camp at Auschwitz and finally Bergen–Belsen, where he was captured by the British Army.

other concentration camps, supplemented by reservists called up for duty within the SS-Death's Head Auschwitz Battalion.[5] As in the other concentration camps, much responsibility was also given to the prisoner trusties who were employed as supervisors and clerks on labour details and within the camp. They were distinguished by being allowed to wear civilian clothes, grow their hair and carry whips and clubs to beat their fellow prisoners. At first, as we have seen, these were exclusively German, but as time went by and the camp expanded, the net was spread more widely, with prisoners from elsewhere being employed in these roles. By late 1943, even Jews served as block seniors and Kapos.

Conditions for the prisoners during the early period at Auschwitz were probably worse than in the rest of the concentration camp system. On arrival, they were registered, stripped of their clothing, shorn of their hair and issued with a number that was also tattooed on their forearm. Thereafter, their names were meaningless within the camp system. They were given prison clothing, consisting of a shirt, a jacket, trousers and a cap, all made from a distinctive striped, coarse canvas, together with a pair of wooden clogs. Then they were issued with triangular patches to indicate their status: green for criminals; red for political prisoners; black for 'asocials', including gypsies; purple for Jehovah's Witnesses; blue for emigrants. At this stage, Jews were not being sent to Auschwitz simply for being Jewish, so any Jewish prisoner wore an additional yellow triangle underneath their primary patch, to form a crude 'Star of David'. This arrival and registration process was deliberately designed to terrorise and subdue the prisoners: it was accompanied throughout by shouting and blows from the Kapos and the SS guards, as well as the barking of aggressive guard dogs. Any prisoner showing signs of resistance or poor attitude could expect to be beaten to a pulp or even shot.

There was little improvement once the prisoners had been received into the camp. After a few days of quarantine and physical assessment by SS personnel and trusties, they were allocated to work details either within the camp or, as the Auschwitz 'complex' grew in size and scope, in one of the many industrial concerns that were established to exploit this pool of slave labour. The working day for the prisoners began around 4.30 a.m. in the summer and 5.30 in the winter. After being ordered from their bunks, they were hustled to a communal washroom and lavatory where they were given a few minutes to evacuate their bowels and wash themselves in water that could be icy cold or scalding hot. Thereafter, they were given breakfast, which normally consisted of a mug of unsweetened artificial coffee, a slice of bread, a thin slice of salami and a small knob of margarine.[6] They were not fed again until their return to the camp in the evening. Following breakfast, roll-call was taken: the prisoners would be forced to stand outside in all weathers as they were counted and re-counted. Any prisoners who had died during the night were laid out next to the living to make the figures tally. With the roll-call complete – and it could take several hours – the prisoners were marched to their work details.

The best jobs were skilled tasks in the factories and on building sites, which could be performed with relatively little harassment from the guards and overseers. Also highly prized were those tasks that allowed access to newly arrived prisoners' belongings and therefore extra food, valuables and money that could be used to bribe Kapos and corrupt SS guards, of whom there were many. The worst jobs involved hard physical work: labouring on construction sites, in stone quarries and the timber yard. The prisoner diet was inadequate for all, but those who were forced into hard labour without any means to acquire extra food were effectively given an extended death sentence. As they became increasingly malnourished, these prisoners were labelled *Musselmänner* (Muslims) in the camp vernacular. They effectively lost the battle for survival: unable to get anywhere near the front of the queue for food, they sank into lassitude. Ultimately, if they didn't die from illness or starvation, they were killed for being unable to work. The SS and the long-term inmates were skilled at spotting potential *Musselmänner* – for instance, their buttocks became soft and flabby. When Auschwitz became a death camp, this was enough to have a prisoner sent to the gas chambers.[7]

The end of the prisoners' day came in the early evening. They returned from their work details to face another extended roll-call; once again, any prisoners who had died during the day were counted alongside the living. Then the surviving prisoners received their evening meal, which usually consisted of a bowl of watery vegetable soup, thickened with potato peel and sometimes barley. Sometimes lumps of animal skin and fat would be included to give the soup slightly more nutritional value, but this happened so rarely that it had almost no impact on the prisoners' health. Food distribution was handled by the trusties, which gave them enormous scope for corruption. Routinely, when a trusty was given a loaf of bread intended for four prisoners, he would cut it into five pieces, give the four prisoners short rations, and exchange the remainder for more food, alcohol, tobacco, jewellery or some other prized commodity. These items were then used in barter with the SS guards. Moreover, a favoured prisoner would receive a ladle of soup taken from the bottom of the cauldron, where the more nourishing material could be found, while another would be given watery, nutritionally worthless slop from the top.

Homosexual relationships were commonplace, with many trusties using their control of food distribution to obtain sexual favours from younger male prisoners. If these bribes were refused, the prisoner might simply be raped.

Punishments for infractions of the numerous rules were invariably harsh and brutal. Block 11 in the main camp was designated as the punishment area. Once there, prisoners might be flogged or beaten; placed overnight in 'standing cells', where they could not lie down or rest, and then forced to do their designated work the next day; placed in 'starvation cells', where they were given neither food nor water; or hung up by their hands so that their shoulders dislocated. Those who were executed for violating the rules were either shot or hanged in a yard next to Block 11.

In February 1941, Himmler ordered that all Jews were to be expelled from the town of Auschwitz and its immediate environs, and that all indigenous Poles and all available camp inmates were to begin work on a new project. This was the construction, under the auspices of the giant IG Farben chemical company, of a huge plant to manufacture Buna – synthetic rubber and oil made out of coal – for the German war effort. The project had been presented to Himmler as a way of bringing German settlers to Auschwitz. It would also fully exploit the economic potential of the prisoners by employing them in a viable commercial operation, as opposed to one of the SS's own embarrassingly incompetent business enterprises. Himmler made his first visit to Auschwitz the following month and issued orders for how the project should proceed. First, the capacity of the Auschwitz main camp was to be expanded to thirty thousand prisoners; then, in April, these prisoners would begin construction of the IG Farben site, which was approximately six kilometres from the main camp, at the village of Dwory. Höss claimed that it was also during this visit that Himmler ordered the construction of a second camp, with a capacity of a hundred thousand prisoners, at nearby Birkenau (Auschwitz II).*

According to Höss's autobiography, during the summer of 1941, he was summoned to Berlin by Himmler, who gave the camp commandant 'the order to prepare installations at Auschwitz where mass exterminations could take place, and personally to carry out these exterminations'.[8] Höss then says that he discussed the details of the extermination programme with Eichmann, who told him that the operation should start with the Jews of Upper Silesia, then those who remained in Germany and the Protectorate, and finally those of Western Europe. The two men did not agree on the method of extermination, but Eichmann told Höss

---

* However, the latest evidence (cited in Steinbacher, *Auschwitz*, p. 90) is that Höss misremembered this at his post-war trial: it seems the order was actually given on 26 September 1941.

that he was investigating various poison gases that might prove suitable.[*]

SS-Captain Karl Bischoff, an engineer who had been put in charge of the Auschwitz Central Building Administration, arrived to oversee the start of work on Birkenau in October 1941. By then, the first experiments in mass killing with gas had already taken place. It had been policy since the beginning of Operation Barbarossa that Soviet political commissars captured by the *Wehrmacht* and Waffen-SS combat units were to be isolated from other prisoners of war, taken to the nearest concentration camp and killed. Generally, they had been shot. But in September 1941, SS-Captain Karl Fritzsch, who commanded the protective custody camp at Auschwitz, decided to try to kill a group of Russian POWs by a different method – gassing them with the Zyklon B delousing agent. The experiment was successful, and Fritzsch arranged another so that Höss could see the results for himself. However, the two men now decided that their location – the cellar of Building 11 – was unsuitable for this operation; so, for the next experiment, they moved to the mortuary of the old camp crematorium. This was easily adapted for its new role: holes simply had to be pierced in the ceiling so that the gas could be introduced. The next experiment was conducted on a transport of nine hundred Russian POWS. According to Höss:

> The Russians were ordered to undress in an ante-room; they then quietly entered the mortuary, for they had been told they were going to be deloused. The whole transport exactly filled the mortuary to capacity. The doors were then sealed and the gas shaken down through the holes in the roof. I do not know how long this killing took. For a little while a humming sound could be heard. When the powder was thrown

---

[*] Höss might have got this wrong, too. Eichmann denied this version of events at his trial in Israel, and Höss seems to have conflated a series of meetings or conversations that actually took place over several years.

in, there were cries of 'Gas!', then a great bellowing, and the trapped prisoners hurled themselves against both the doors. But the doors held. They were opened several hours later, so that the place might be aired. It was then that I saw, for the first time, gassed bodies in the mass.[9]

Soon, a second gas chamber was constructed by converting a peasant cottage within the Birkenau perimeter. This was modified by having its interior walls removed, its windows filled in and special airtight doors fitted. With the conversion done, it had five gassing rooms and a capacity of approximately eight hundred victims. It became known as the 'Bunker' and later as 'Bunker I' or the 'Red House' because of its unpainted brickwork. It was here that the first transports of Jews from Upper Silesia were brought when mass extermination began in earnest at Auschwitz–Birkenau in the early spring of 1942.

The process of killing at Birkenau was similar in some ways to the genocide at the Operation Reinhard camps. Transports of Jewish prisoners would arrive and disembark at the railhead and were then marched past the medical staff, who made cursory, superficial visual inspections. Those who appeared to be fit to work – on average 20–35 per cent of each transport – were registered in the main camp, with their prisoner numbers being crudely tattooed on their forearms. Those deemed unfit to work might be genuinely sick or disabled, but equally they might simply be elderly, small children, pregnant women, or mothers with their children. These prisoners were not registered. Instead, they were taken to the Bunker, where they were stripped of their clothing and led into the gas chambers on the pretext of delousing. When they were dead, the chambers were ventilated for a while and the bodies were removed by 'special units' of prisoners for burial.

Within a few months of the first extermination transports arriving, it became clear that more capacity was required, so a second cottage – known as 'Bunker II' or the 'White House' – was converted for gassing. Undressing huts were also erected near the two gas chambers. At this stage, all of the gassed victims, as well as prisoners who died for other reasons in Auschwitz and Birkenau, were buried in mass graves within the camps. But in the late summer of 1942, the corpses began to pollute the water table, and the decision was made to disinter and incinerate them.

Around this time, Höss was visited by SS-Colonel Paul Blobel, the former special task group officer who had commanded Special Unit 4a. Heinrich Müller had ordered Blobel to locate and eliminate all evidence of genocide in the East, primarily by digging up the mass graves that had been created by the special task groups and then burning the bodies.* The same process had already begun at the static killing centres, although this was against the wishes of Globocnik: in August 1942, he commented that, rather than concealing the killings, the SS should bury bronze plaques in the mass graves so that the world would know who to thank!

By this stage, plans were already in place to step up Birkenau's killing capacity through purpose-built gas chambers and crematoria. A conference at the end of February 1942 had settled on a basic design for underground gas chambers, from which the murdered victims could be hauled up in electric hoists to a crematorium equipped with five furnaces, each with three retorts and theoretically capable of handling up to two thousand corpses every twenty-four hours. However, it took more than a year to construct these substantial installations and bring them into operation, so, as a short-term measure, a pair of smaller extermination units were built on the surface, each with only two furnaces.

In the early days of the mass killings at Auschwitz–Birkenau, transports stopped at a railway platform between the two compounds and the prisoners were then led either to the old crematorium in Auschwitz or across a meadow to the bunkers in Birkenau. Once the purpose-built gas chambers had been constructed, a rail spur was laid to transport the victims much closer to them. On Birkenau's rail platform, members of the medical

* Blobel was possibly given this onerous task as punishment for his alcoholism.

staff, including Josef Mengele and Fritz Klein, would make their casual inspections of the prisoners, directing them right, to the camp, or left, to the gas chambers.[10] Then, as in the Operation Reinhard camps, efforts were made to conceal what was about to happen, primarily in order to maintain control over the victims and forestall any resistance. SS officers and NCOs told the prisoners that they were to be showered and deloused, and urged them to hurry so that the soup that was waiting for them did not become cold. Next, they were told to undress and hang their clothes on numbered pegs; they were even instructed to remember the numbers so that they could quickly retrieve their clothes after their shower. In most cases, this subterfuge was effective. Describing a transport from Salonika, Hilberg notes: 'The unsuspecting Greek Jews, clutching soap and towels, rushed into the gas chambers.'[11] However, when Jews from nearby Katowice, Sosnowiece and Bedzin were taken to Birkenau in the late summer of 1943, they were under no illusions about their fate. Local rumours had told them all they needed to know, and they had to be forced into the gas chambers at gunpoint by reinforced squads of tense Waffen-SS guards.[12]

The victims were usually led into the chambers by members of a special squad, Jewish inmates who were temporarily spared death to carry out the physical work within the killing areas. By and large, these prisoners cooperated in the fiction that the victims were not about to die, probably in the hope of prolonging their own lives. Of course, this was a forlorn hope: they were kept alive for a few months at most. During this time, their existence was probably marginally better than that endured within the main camp because they could obtain extra food from the possessions of the dead. However, sooner or later, they were killed too and a new group was selected to take their place. Very few members of the special units survived until the end of the war.

The gas chambers were lit by electric lights and were fitted out with fake shower heads. Once all the prisoners were inside, the members of the special unit withdrew and the gas-tight doors were sealed. At this point, the lights were switched off, which always induced panic, and SS NCOs from the sanitation department, wearing gas masks, would start to dispense the Zyklon B. It was delivered in tins, about the size of paint cans, and consisted of pea-sized blue ceramic pellets impregnated with hydrocyanic acid. The SS men would remove the lids with a hammer and chisel and then immediately throw the contents into the gas chambers. In the sub-terranean chambers, this was done through openings in the roof; the surface chambers were equipped with hatches in the side walls. The pellets began to sublimate as soon as they were exposed to the air, at which point the prisoners would start screaming. This did not last long: depending on the weather conditions and the tem-perature, everyone within the chamber was normally dead within five to fifteen minutes.

After half an hour or so, ventilators were switched on to extract the gas and the doors were opened. The prisoners were generally found close to the door, having attempted to force their way out, or heaped in piles where the stronger prisoners had scrambled on top of the dead to try to reach clean air. There were usually empty areas near the hatches where the Zyklon B was introduced. According to Höss: 'There was no noticeable change in the bodies and no sign of convulsions or discoloration. Only after the bodies had been left lying for some time . . . did the usual death stains appear in the places were they had lain. Soiling through the open-ing of the bowels was also rare. There were no signs of wounding of any kind. The faces showed no distortion.'[13] The special squads, now wearing gas masks, would drag out the bodies and hose down the chamber, which also helped to neutralise any lingering gas. The corpses were then given a cavity search for valu-able items and any gold teeth were removed. These were cleaned with hydrochloric acid before being melted down and formed into ingots in the main camp. Unlike in the Reinhard camps, it was only now that the women's hair was shorn. This was used to make felt, which provided winter insulation for the German armed forces.

The four Birkenau crematoria were equipped with coke-fired furnaces, but these also used the victims' own body fat to speed the combustion process, which meant, in theory, they could consume in excess of 4500 bodies every day. However, this figure was never reached due to persistent malfunction. The victims tended to be so malnourished that as many as five bodies could be crammed into each retort, rather than the two or three they were designed to take. This overuse, combined with poor maintenance (which, for example, left the chimneys caked with human fat), led to numerous breakdowns. Thus, during the summer of 1944, when Birkenau murdered 400,000 Hungarian Jews, open-air pits had to be dug and the victims' bodies were cremated on grids formed out of railway tracks and logs.

The minority who were spared death on arrival were registered in the camp in the normal way: stripped, shorn, showered and tattooed. Then the male prisoners were taken to Birkenau's quarantine compound. For much of its existence, this was presided over by SS-Corporal Karl Kurpanik, a brutal ethnic German from Silesia who used the ten to fourteen days during which new prisoners were under his supervision to terrorise them, partly by selecting several for the gas chambers each day.[14] Any who survived the quarantine period were allocated to work groups within Birkenau itself or were transferred to one of the sub-camps.

As in the main camp, the best places to work within Birkenau were on details that sorted through prisoners' possessions. Members of the 'ramp commando' went through the baggage of newly arrived prisoners, which was dumped on the railway siding while the selection procedure took place. They also had the task of cleaning out the freight wagons, so were probably best placed to find any food, drink and valuables that the prisoners had brought with them. The SS guards and trusties generally turned a blind eye to them eating any food they found, as long as they maintained their work-rate and handed over all the cash and valuables that turned up. The worst assignments, as ever, were on the heavy labour details, particularly the punishment company, which dug drainage ditches and laid sewerage pipes within the compound.[15]

The small minority of women who survived the selection process were accommodated in a separate camp and were kept almost entirely segregated from the men. Like the male prisoners, they were sent on various work details in the surrounding industrial complexes in addition to doing manual labour in and around the camp itself.

If anything, accommodation in Birkenau was even worse than in Auschwitz. The first buildings to be constructed were single-storey brick huts with no heating or sanitation, built on bare earth, crammed with wooden triple bunks. However, the majority of prisoners in Birkenau were housed in prefabricated wooden stable blocks built to a standard military pattern. Each was designed to shelter fifty-two horses, but in Birkenau they accommodated over four hundred prisoners, crammed together on wooden bunks.

As a result of the overcrowding, poor sanitation and lack of clean water, Birkenau was infested with lice and other vermin, while typhus and similar diseases were rampant. Furthermore, the camp's medical staff inspired fear rather than hope among the prisoners, because they were free to conduct research in any way they saw fit. This involved infecting, mutilating, murdering and dissecting any prisoners who were unfortunate enough to be selected for their experiments.

The most notorious of these scientists was SS-Captain Josef Mengele. He came from a wealthy Bavarian family who had made their money manufacturing agricultural machinery. But instead of joining the family business, Mengele studied anthropology, earning a Ph.D. in 1935 from Munich University and a doctorate in medicine three years later from Frankfurt University. He served as a medical officer with the Waffen-SS on the Eastern Front in 1941–2 before being wounded and deemed unfit for front-line service. In 1943, he was transferred to the staff of Auschwitz, initially as medical officer for the 'gypsy camp' within Birkenau and subsequently as chief medical officer within the Birkenau infirmary.[16]

Medical provision within Auschwitz was basic, and Mengele's role was hardly taxing from a professional point of view. He simply had to make snap diagnoses to determine which patients merited hospitalisation and which did not. The former would be given rudimentary treatment (no drugs were ever provided) and a few days to recover; the latter would be liquidated, either in the gas chambers or through an injection of phenol into the heart. However, Mengele had other interests outside his official tasks.

His Ph.D. dissertation had been on racial differences in the structure of the human lower jaw. Now he had the opportunity to continue his research on living human subjects. While making selections for the gas chambers on the rail platform, he would also pick out any prisoners he found interesting from a 'scientific' point of view – particularly twins and dwarfs. Once selected, they were installed in a special barracks, where conditions were marginally better than in the rest of the camp. However, thereafter, they suffered a terrible fate. Mengele injected chemicals into their eyes to try to change their colour, conducted chemical sterilisation experiments on the women, and eventually had all of his human guinea pigs killed for dissection.[17]

The selections were terrifying aspects of daily life for all prisoners in Auschwitz, Birkenau and the sub-camps. They could take place at any time and none of the prisoners could be certain what their outcome would be. Some were for the gas chambers and death; others were to find new prisoners for work details. Anyone displaying weakness or illness was liable to be killed on the spot or removed from his fellow prisoners for gassing. Sometimes, selections were ordered simply to create space for new arrivals within the barracks.

The industrial complex around Auschwitz grew at a rapid rate. Oswald Pohl's WVHA leased out prisoners to German industry at the rate of four marks a day for unskilled and six marks a day for skilled labourers. By mid-1942, 6000 Auschwitz prisoners were working for industrial concerns; by mid-1944, the number was around 42,000.[18] In addition to IG Farben's Buna plant, prisoners worked in coal mines, steel works, oil refineries, military equipment factories, textile mills, shoe factories and on the railways. The SS employed other prisoners in their own commercial enterprises as agricultural labourers and quarrymen, and to assemble weapons and make uniforms for the Waffen-SS.

Conditions in the sub-camps were generally no better than in Auschwitz or Birkenau. The guards were provided by the SS-Death's Head Auschwitz Battalion, and many of the commandants became particularly notorious. For example, the commandant of the sub-camp attached to the Fürstengrübe mine at Myslowitz-Wesoła was SS-Sergeant Major Otto Moll, who had been in charge of the original extermination bunkers at Birkenau.

The only prisoners to benefit from being in the sub-camps were skilled labourers, who were generally better treated than their unskilled colleagues. For instance, those who worked hard might occasionally be granted a *Premiumschein*, a coupon that allowed them to purchase extra rations from the canteen.[19] Even so, discipline remained brutal and ruthless, and conditions were appalling.

While the Operation Reinhard camps, Chelmno and Majdanek primarily killed Jews from the General Government, the incorporated territories and parts of the Soviet Union, the geographical reach of Auschwitz–Birkenau was much greater. As the principal extermination centre from 1943 onwards, Jews from all over Europe were brought there to be killed. This meant that Eichmann's Jewish section within the RSHA had to be reorganised and expanded, and Eichmann himself once again moved towards centre stage in the Holocaust.

As we have seen, Eichmann's section started within the SD as a clearing house for information and intelligence on the 'Jewish question'. It then metamorphosed into the central administration for forced Jewish emigration from Germany, Austria and the Protectorate. When this project came to a halt in 1940, Eichmann's principal task became organisation of the transports for the deportation of Jews, first to the ghettoes and then to the extermination centres in Poland. However, the extension of the extermination policy across Europe saw his role widen significantly, to include high-level negotiation – at the direction of Himmler via Müller – with other government agencies, including the Foreign Office and the armed forces. Thus, Eichmann had a hand in implementing all aspects of Jewish policy. The modalities of National Socialist genocide were complex and required a great deal of detailed staff work, which is where Eichmann came in. His role was not to create Jewish policy but to see that it was carried out at the operational level. He and his team used their institutional background knowledge and experience to translate the directions he received – primarily from Müller – into an efficient system for the deportation and murder of millions of Jews.

To this end, he placed representatives of Section IV B4 in many Sipo headquarters throughout occupied Europe: for example, Theo Dannecker went to Paris, while Dieter Wisliceny acted as an adviser on Jewish affairs to the Slovak regime before being dispatched to Salonika, where he organised the deportation and murder of the entire Jewish population. These men ensured that the directives emerging from Eichmann's office were implemented on the ground, which might mean negotiating with the local Sipo commander, with the military occupation authorities, or, as in occupied France, with the local civil regime. With the victims secured by these local representatives, Eichmann's office could then arrange transport to Auschwitz via the railway system.[*]

The French Vichy regime implemented anti-Jewish measures, in line with the Nuremberg Laws, soon after the armistice in 1940.[20] However, it was only in the summer of 1942 that substantial deportations of Jews from Western Europe to Auschwitz–Birkenau began. In June, the German occupation authorities started to demand the surrender of French Jews for 'evacuation' to Auschwitz.

---

[*] It has often been suggested that transporting Jews to the death camps seriously undermined the German war effort. In reality, even at the height of the transports, no more than a handful of trains were assigned to this task each day.

The Vichy regime refused to allow the deportation of any Jews with French citizenship, but it did offer up the stateless Jews and refugees who were resident in France.[21] Himmler reluctantly accepted this compromise for diplomatic reasons. Nevertheless, the French government and police soon proved to be willing and effective collaborators with Dannecker: by September, some 27,000 Jews had already been deported and, usually, killed.

Round-ups and deportations of non-French Jews continued right up to the liberation of France in 1944, but the Vichy government never relaxed its position that French Jews should not be deported, and relatively few were. One additional group of French-ruled Jews who were briefly threatened were the eighty thousand or so in Tunisia, which was occupied by the German Army following the Allied Operation Torch landings in Morocco and Algeria on 8 November 1942. The German occupation force was quickly followed by the Special Task Unit Tunis,* commanded by SS-Lieutenant Colonel Walter Rauff, a pioneer in the use of gassing vans. However, the precarious supply situation of the *Afrika* Panzer Army ruled out any deportations. Consequently, many Tunisian Jews were expropriated and forced to work as slave labourers, but there were few killings.

By the end of the war, approximately 75,000 Jews had been evacuated from metropolitan France, of whom 69,000 were sent to Auschwitz. Only a few thousand survived.[22]

In contrast to France, the Netherlands was under direct German rule, so there was no need for diplomatic niceties. The first sweep – from June to September 1942 – netted about twenty thousand Dutch Jews, and at least another eighty thousand were deported over the next two and a half years. They travelled east via transit camps set up in Westerbork and Vucht that were guarded, for a time, by members of the Dutch–Flemish *Nordwest* Waffen-SS Regiment. About seventy thousand of them ended up in

---

* This seems to have been the only SS detachment which operated outside continental Europe.

Auschwitz–Birkenau; but, as we have seen, a substantial number were also dispatched to Sobibor between March and July 1943.[23]

Deportations from Belgium began around the same time and totalled at least 25,000 by the end of the war. The majority of them died in Auschwitz.[24]

Attempts to round up and deport the Jews of Norway began in October 1942. The Norwegian Jewish population was relatively small – about two thousand – and rumours of the impending operation caused many of them to flee to neutral Sweden or go into hiding. Nevertheless, some 532 men, women and children were caught by the Norwegian Police and members of the *Germanske SS Norge* (the Norwegian imitation of the General-SS) in Oslo. They were deported by sea across the Baltic to Stettin, from where they were taken to Auschwitz. A further group of 158 from Trondheim and northern Norway were deported in February 1943; but fewer than a thousand Norwegian Jews were rounded up during the course of the war.

Denmark had about 6500 native Jews and some refugees, but here the situation was initially similar to that in France, because the Danish government had retained control after the occupation, subject to German supervision. The German representatives in the country did not usually interfere in internal Danish political affairs, and even when they did suggest that the Danes might wish to address the 'Jewish problem', their overtures were always firmly rebuffed. However, this changed in the summer of 1943 as a consequence of a rise in Danish resistance activities. By that point, the senior German representative in Denmark was SS-General Werner Best, Heydrich's former deputy in the RSHA,* who had continued the reasonably conciliatory approach to the Danish government but had no compunction about deporting Jews. In August 1943, with the situation in Denmark deteriorating, Best was summoned to meet Hitler at his headquarters, where he was given orders to

---

* The two men had fallen out in the first half of 1939 over the roles of the Sipo and SD within the state.

declare a state of emergency and intern the remnant of the army that the Danes had been permitted to keep. In response, the Danish government resigned *en masse* and Denmark came under the control of the German military commander.

Best saw this as an opportunity and sent a message to his superiors in the German Foreign Office, suggesting that this was the ideal moment to start deporting Jews. This suggestion led to Best being reinstated as the German plenipotentiary in Denmark; and, as planning continued, the pre-deportation arrests were scheduled for the night of 1–2 October. However, the operation was compromised by leaks from within the German administration, and particularly from Best's own transport attaché, so when the raids began most of Denmark's Jewish population were in hiding or had fled to Sweden. In total, 477 Jews were eventually deported to the so-called 'old people's' concentration camp at Theresienstadt, where 52 of them died. In the weeks following the attempted round-up, almost all of the Danish Jews still left in the country were able to reach Sweden by boat.[25]

Although subject to some anti-Semitic measures enacted by the Mussolini's government, the Jewish population of Italy was protected from deportation while the country remained an ally and co-belligerent of Germany up to the summer of 1943. However, after the fall of Mussolini and the German occupation of northern Italy in September 1943, this protection largely evaporated as SS-General Karl Wolff, as military governor and Senior SS and Police Leader, took control. First, a large quantity of gold was expropriated from Rome's Jewish community. Then, in mid-October, the first round-up took place, with the list of names compiled from Jewish community groups' own subscription lists. More than a thousand Jews were arrested and transported to their deaths in Auschwitz.[26] Many other Italian Jews now went into hiding, helped by the Catholic Church or even, on occasion, by Italian Fascist officials.[27] However, many were caught in the dragnet laid by Theo Dannecker. The Jews of Trieste faced a particularly notorious enemy with the arrival of Odilo Globocnik as Senior SS and

Police Leader for the Adriatic Coastal Zone. Moreover, he was accompanied by a team of hardened Operation Reinhard veterans. Globocnik and his men established a transit camp at San Sabba, from where several hundred Jews were dispatched to Auschwitz. In total, around 7500 Jews were deported from Italy between 1943 and 1945; fewer than 800 returned home.[28]

The other parts of Europe that deported large numbers of Jews to Auschwitz were the South-East and the Balkans. In Serbia between 1941 and 1942, much of the task of liquidating Jews and gypsies was undertaken in the field by the German Army, which acted in much the same manner as the special task groups further east. Around eight thousand Jewish and gypsy men were detained in the autumn and winter of 1941, after the German occupation of Yugoslavia, and shot by the army in reprisal for partisan attacks (even though the attacks had been conducted by ethnic Serbs and Croats, rather than Jews).[29] Their fifteen thousand wives and children, who were interned in the Semlin camp, near Belgrade, were then liquidated in a gassing van supplied by the RSHA.[30]

Between March and August 1943, 46,000 Greek Jews were deported from Salonika to their deaths in Auschwitz.[31] Just a few hundred were saved through the efforts of the Fascist Italian Consul General and the Spanish Chargé d'Affaires in Athens, who were able to classify them as either Italian or Spanish citizens. In 1944, several thousand Athenian Jews, as well as the Jewish populations of many of the larger Greek islands, were also sent to Auschwitz. In total, approximately sixty thousand Greek Jews were murdered.[32]

The first large group of Jews to be murdered in Auschwitz – in the spring and summer of 1942 – were Slovakian. They numbered more than fifty thousand. This was followed by a lull of more than two years, but then the deportations resumed in October 1944, when twelve thousand to fifteen thousand Jews were rounded up, with the majority going to Auschwitz.

In marked contrast to what happened in the rest of Europe, the great majority of the estimated 270,000 Romanian Jews killed during the Holocaust fell victim to their own countrymen, with encouragement but little assistance from Germany and the SS.

The last major European Jewish community to be murdered at Auschwitz came from Hungary. In 1941, there were just under 800,000 Jews in the country – about 5 per cent of the total population – but they were disproportionately well represented in the professional and commercial middle classes. Nevertheless, from 1938 onwards, the government of Admiral Miklós Horthy had been passing anti-Semitic legislation to limit Jewish economic activity,[33] largely in the hope of gaining Germany's support for territorial claims against Czechoslovakia and other neighbouring states. Hungary had also entered the war on the German side on 26 June 1941, but by the end of 1943 Horthy's government had realised its error and was seeking a way out. Sensing they were about to be abandoned by their ally, the Germans bloodlessly occupied Hungary on 19 March 1944, seizing control of key facilities and installing a more compliant government (although Horthy remained as leader). A wave of German agencies arrived in the country that same day, including Senior SS and Police Leader Otto Winkelmann and a special task group that had formed in Mauthausen concentration camp and was commanded by Adolf Eichmann.

Eichmann installed his unit in the Hotel Majestic in Budapest and immediately summoned Jewish community leaders to meet him the following morning. At the meeting, he adopted a brisk but reassuring tone: the community would need to form a Jewish council and provide a list of all Jewish property. Similar meetings between the SS and the Jewish community over the next few days clarified and extended these orders, but did so without creating any alarm.[34] Meanwhile, Germany's political representatives were pushing their Hungarian puppets into adopting new legal measures to isolate the Jewish community, including wearing the yellow Star of David, restricting travel and imposing curfews.

Eichmann's unit next began to direct the concentration of the Jews. Working through the Hungarian Police, from mid-April,

Jews in outlying towns were moved into ghettoes and makeshift concentration camps. Later, they were loaded on to trains and deported to Auschwitz at an average rate of twelve thousand people per day.

The Jewish community leaders were under no illusions about the fate of the deportees, and they started to make frantic efforts to save what was left of their people. Appeals to neutral governments and the Church were accompanied by attempts to ransom at least some of Hungary's Jews. Back in January 1943, a group of Hungarian Zionists had formed a 'rescue committee' that provided assistance to Jews who had managed to flee to the relative safety (at that time) of Hungary from elsewhere in Europe. Now, two members of the committee, Rudolf Kastner and Joel Brand, approached Eichmann's team in a bid to broker some kind of deal. Kastner subsequently claimed that Dieter Wisliceny offered to release six hundred Jews in exchange for approximately $1.6 million. The money was raised and handed over, whereupon the SS agreed to raise the number of released Jews to sixteen hundred. These were selected by the committee and then transported to the concentration camp at Bergen–Belsen, near the north German town of Celle, which at the time was being used as a holding camp for prominent Jews.[35]

This deal came to the attention of Himmler, and Eichmann was now instructed to make a new offer to the rescue committee: more Jews would be spared in return for goods that were needed by Germany – 200 tons each of tea and coffee; 10,000 trucks; 2 million cases of soap. The Hungarian Jews would continue to be sent to their deaths until these items were presented to the Germans. Brand was sent to Istanbul to negotiate this deal with the supposed leaders of 'World Jewry', but he was unable to convince the people he met of its viability. After the meeting, travelling overland to Palestine, he was arrested by the British in Syria, taken to Cairo and held in solitary confinement. Meanwhile, the deportations and murders continued.[36]

Of course, it is impossible to say whether Himmler would have kept his side of the bargain if the goods had been procured, but now the remaining Hungarian Jews' survival rested solely on how the battle between the Red Army and the *Wehrmacht* played out. On 23 June, the Soviets launched a major offensive against the German Army Group Centre. They overran Majdanek the following month and started to head towards Auschwitz. By then, Horthy had already ordered a halt to the deportations, largely because he feared that the rest of the world knew the extent of his government's collaboration. However, with the exception of those living in Budapest, who had not yet been rounded up, this came too late to save Hungary's Jews.

On 20 August, the Soviets began a series of operations designed to liberate South-East Europe. Three days later, the Romanian government requested an armistice and gave the German forces stationed in their country three days to leave. Horthy, now certain which way the wind was blowing, replaced the pro-German administration that had been forced on him in March with a government that was clearly designed to reach an armistice with the Allies. Then he requested the removal of Eichmann's task force. The Germans had no option but to agree.[37]

Nevertheless, the Jews of Budapest remained extremely vulnerable throughout the autumn. On 15 October, SS-Lieutenant Colonel Otto Skorzeny and members of the SS-*Jagdverband Mitte* (a Waffen-SS special forces unit assigned to the RSHA) kidnapped Horthy's son while tanks of the 24th Panzer Division occupied the capital. Horthy was deposed and replaced with the leader of the local National Socialist 'Arrow Cross' Party, Ferenc Szalasi. Deportations to Auschwitz were no longer possible – Himmler had already ordered a halt to the gassing operations – but the SS attempted one last throw of the dice: the evacuation on foot of able-bodied forced labourers. In the first weeks of November, some thirty thousand Jews were rounded up and sent marching west, with little or no food and no provision of shelter along the way. Many died from hunger, exhaustion or sickness; many others were shot. A few survivors were found starving in the

Mauthausen and Wels concentration camps by the Allies in May 1945.

Estimates for the total number of Hungarian Jews murdered range from 180,000 to 550,000. The true figure is probably around 400,000. And it should be remembered that all of these murders were committed at a time when the perpetrators knew that the war was as good as lost. This, perhaps more than any other SS atrocity, illustrates the murderous ferocity of the ideology that Himmler instilled in his 'order', because his men stuck to their task even as Germany spiralled towards inevitable military collapse. Meanwhile, Himmler himself was prepared to barter the lives of National Socialism's supposed mortal enemies for tea, coffee, trucks and soap.

On 22 November 1943, Höss had left Auschwitz to take up the post of Deputy Inspector of Concentration Camps at WVHA headquarters.[38] Thereafter, Auschwitz was split into three administratively distinct camps. The main camp, Auschwitz I, was placed under the command of SS-Lieutenant Colonel Arthur Liebehenschel; Birkenau, which comprised the extermination camp and an agricultural sub-camp, was commanded by SS-Lieutenant Colonel Friedrich Hartjenstein; while the industrial sub-camps, which included the IG Farben Buna plant and a growing number of other concerns, became Auschwitz III under SS-Captain Heinrich Schwarz. Liebehenschel subsequently took command of the Majdanek concentration camp in May 1944; SS-Major Richard Baer took his place at Auschwitz. At the same time, Hartjenstein handed command of Birkenau to SS-Captain Josef Kramer.[39]

Two months later, the advancing Soviet armies were within 150 miles of the Auschwitz complex and the process of evacuating prisoner workers began. At this time, there were some 155,000 prisoners within Auschwitz, Birkenau and the industrial sub-camps; about half of them had been evacuated by the beginning of October. Nevertheless, in some respects, business carried on as usual within the camps. New buildings were erected and there were plans almost to double the size of the already vast Birkenau compound.

However, with the war clearly lost, both the SS and the remaining prisoners in the camp were becoming increasingly anxious about the future. In particular, the Jewish special units who worked within the gas chambers and crematoria knew that their days were numbered. Consequently, on 7 October, the special unit in Birkenau's Crematorium IV staged a revolt during which they attempted to destroy the crematorium and the gas chamber with explosives smuggled in from one of Auschwitz III's factories. The rebellion spread to several other crematoria, three SS men were killed and twelve wounded, and a number of special unit prisoners managed to break out of the camp and hide in the surrounding woodland. But any hopes that a general uprising would follow were soon dashed. Once the rebellion had been quelled, 425 members of the special units were killed, along with the women who had smuggled in the explosives. Crematorium IV was damaged beyond repair, but the remaining extermination facilities remained fully operational. Throughout October, some forty thousand people were murdered at Auschwitz–Birkenau.[40]

Himmler finally ordered the cessation of the extermination project the following month. The surviving members of the special units were now put to work eliminating all traces of the crimes that had been committed at Auschwitz. The ovens and the ventilation equipment from the gas chambers were dismantled and taken to other concentration camps; the corpse-burning pits were filled in and covered with turf; the chimneys and ducts in the gas chambers through which the Zyklon B had been introduced were blocked.[41]

On 12 January 1945, a sudden Soviet advance threatened the Auschwitz complex directly. Within a few days, the Red Army was so close that the prisoners could hear their artillery; and, on the 17th, the decision was taken to evacuate the camp rather than leave the remaining prisoners to be found by the Soviets. By this stage, there were 68,000 prisoners within the whole complex. The intention was to march the prisoners to railheads at Rybnik and Gleiwitz, from where they would be transported on trains to concentration camps in the 'old' Reich.[42]

The weather conditions were horrific and, of course, the prisoners were severely malnourished, weak and dressed only in their thin camp uniforms. Each was issued with just a small lump of bread for the march. Inevitably, many of the weaker prisoners could not keep up with the marching columns and were shot by the SS guards; many others died from exhaustion or exposure. Those who reached Gleiwitz were temporarily abandoned by the SS when a rumour circulated that the Soviets were in the area, and a few prisoners escaped into the countryside. However, most were too apathetic, scared or exhausted to make the break, and when the SS returned they were loaded into open wagons for the move westwards.[43]

Meanwhile, back within the Auschwitz complex, the remaining SS personnel attempted to cover their tracks. Much of the camp's archive was destroyed on bonfires, and the remaining gas chamber buildings were blown up with explosives. The last of the extermination facilities, Crematorium V, was destroyed on 25–26 January, and the storage area for the possessions of Birkenau's victims, known as 'Canada' in the camp vernacular, was torched by the SS. The resultant inferno also destroyed many of the camp's wooden huts.[44]

The Red Army arrived at Auschwitz on 27 January 1945. They found some six hundred corpses and around seven thousand living prisoners – those who had been too weak to take part in the evacuation. A significant number of them would die over the next few weeks.

The 43,000 surviving evacuees were now being distributed around other concentration camps. The regime in these camps was little different to that in Auschwitz: the prisoners continued to be worked to death, brutalised, starved and murdered by their new

SS gaolers. A typical example was the Bergen–Belsen camp.* Originally used as a holding camp for special Jewish prisoners, it was now a dumping ground for those evacuated from the East. The huge influx of prisoners completely overwhelmed existing supplies and medical provision, and the camp descended into chaos, with thousands dying from rampaging epidemics and starvation. Desperate prisoners both here and elsewhere were forced to resort to cannibalism in order to survive. In the last weeks of the war, Himmler finally allowed the Red Cross to distribute food and medicine within the camps; but this pathetic gesture, designed entirely to save his own skin, was far too little, far too late.

As the German military collapse continued in the spring of 1945, further evacuations from the camps took place, with marching columns of prisoners in their striped clothes becoming a common sight on Germany's roads. At the end of April, approximately ten thousand prisoners from Neuengamme, Stutthof and Dora-Mittelbau – many of them former Auschwitz inmates – were loaded aboard the former cruise liners *Cap Arcona* and *Deutschland* and the smaller vessels *Thielbek* and *Athen* off the port of Lübeck on the Baltic coast. The Regional Leader of Hamburg at the time later claimed that the ships were going to take the prisoners to neutral Sweden; the former Gestapo chief of Lübeck said that they were going to be scuttled in the sea to kill all the prisoners. We shall never know the truth, because the German authorities did not get the chance to display either their compassion or their brutality. On 3 May, three days after Hitler's suicide in Berlin, the ships were attacked by rocket-firing fighter-bombers of the RAF. The *Cap Arcona* and the *Thielbek* were severely damaged, set on fire and sunk. Between them, they had held approximately 6500 prisoners; no more than 500 survived.[45]

*

* Others were Buchenwald, Dachau, Mauthausen, Gross-Rosen and Sachsenhausen.

Since the liberation of Auschwitz, many estimates have been made regarding the total number of murders committed there. As early as May 1945, the Soviet Army released a press statement which suggested that four million prisoners had perished in the camp. This figure was reached by estimating the crematoria's full capacity and then assuming that the camp had operated flat out for more than two and a half years; but it was picked up and quoted in the world's media, as well as at the post-war Nuremberg trials. For many years, it was also the 'official' number quoted by the Auschwitz memorial.

Rudolf Höss, the former commandant, came up with an estimate of three million, with 500,000 prisoners dying from disease or malnutrition, rather than gassing. The latest scholarship suggests that around 1.1 million people were murdered at Auschwitz, with 960,000 of them Jewish, approximately 75,000 non-Jewish Poles, 21,000 gypsies, 15,000 Soviet prisoners of war, and between 10,000 and 15,000 from other nations. Up to 200,000 others died of disease or malnutrition.[46]

The Auschwitz extermination complex was a place of industrial savagery unparalleled in human history. It was also the inevitable consequence of SS ideology.

25

The Final Act

The SS ended with a whimper. By the summer of 1944, the Third Reich was beleaguered on all fronts and the vast military machine that Hitler and his generals had assembled was crumbling. The tide of the war had been decisively turned by the Soviet victory at Stalingrad in the winter of 1942–3, and ultimately by the failure of the German Kursk offensive in July 1943. Thereafter, despite the best efforts of ordinary German soldiers and airmen, as well as the workers on the home front who attempted to sustain them, the German armed forces could do little more than fight a series of increasingly futile holding actions against the overwhelming strength of the Red Army. In September 1943, Italy – Germany's principal European ally – surrendered. Nine months later, the Germans' inability to repulse the Allied landings in northern France merely confirmed that the war was already irretrievably lost.

This fact was not lost on Himmler and the senior officers of the SS. Walter Schellenberg had succeeded Heinz Jost as chief of Office VI of the RSHA in 1943,[1] and he had also become Himmler's closest professional confidant since the death of Heydrich. Through his access to foreign intelligence, Schellenberg was in no doubt that Germany was heading for defeat, and indeed had been so ever since the United States had joined the war in December 1941. By his own account, he had proposed seeking peace with the Western Allies to Himmler as early as the summer of 1942. Himmler was too nervous and indecisive to plot against Hitler at that time, but he had not dismissed the idea out of hand.[2]

Schellenberg knew that the West would not countenance an armistice while Hitler remained in control, and he hoped to convince Himmler of that reality, too. Throughout 1943, he used Office VI's network of contacts in neutral countries to float the idea of the removal of Hitler as a prelude to peace negotiations with a number of potential intermediaries. But all of this came to nothing: Schellenberg was unable to obtain any meaningful guidance or support from the Western Allies, who remained implacably committed to a policy of unconditional surrender. Without this, Himmler continued to lack the strength of will to act against Hitler.

While Himmler vacillated, he and the senior leadership of the RSHA were aware of several knots of political resistance within the German establishment. The most important of these was centred on the Abwehr, the German military intelligence service commanded by Wilhelm Canaris. His deputy, General Hans Oster – in the full knowledge of Canaris himself – had coordinated resistance within the military, and had liaised with rebels in the Foreign Office and other parts of the German establishment. The Gestapo learned something of this after arresting Wilhelm Schmidhuber, a currency speculator and smuggler whom Oster had used as an informant and to smuggle Jews out of Germany. Under interrogation, Schmidhuber revealed his links with the resistance, implicating Oster and others within the Abwehr, as well as General Beck, the retired chief of the General Staff, and Karl Goerdeler, a former mayor of Leipzig. Obviously, this evidence of a resistance network at the highest levels of the Abwehr meant that Canaris came under suspicion too, but at this stage no arrests were made. Instead, Oster and one of his associates were merely dismissed from the Abwehr while the Gestapo continued to investigate.[3]

Finally, in January and February 1944, a number of Abwehr personnel, including Canaris, were arrested, while the Abwehr itself was incorporated into the RSHA. (It became known as the Military Office.) However, none of the Gestapo's investigations unearthed an even more significant resistance cell within the headquarters of the Replacement Army, the German Army's home command. By June, these plotters, led by Colonel Claus von Stauffenberg, had decided that the only way to save Germany from total collapse was to stage a *coup d'état*.[4] Their interpretation was correct. On the Eastern Front, the *Wehrmacht* was being overwhelmed by the massive Red Army, which was pushing into Poland and South-East Europe. In the West, the Allies had established a firm beachhead in Normandy.[5]

Von Stauffenberg, who had been severely wounded in North Africa,* was chief of staff to the commander of the Replacement Army, which gave him access to Hitler's field headquarters at Rastenberg, East Prussia. On 20 July, after several earlier abortive attempts, he smuggled a small bomb – made from British plastic explosives – into Hitler's daily situation conference. Having set the fuse, he excused himself, saying he needed to make a telephone call. The bomb exploded and von Stauffenberg was convinced that Hitler must have been killed. He talked his way out of Rastenberg and flew back to Berlin to coordinate the rest of the coup from the Replacement Army headquarters in Bendlerstrasse.[6]

The rebels' plan was based on an existing contingency plan, codenamed Valkyrie, which had been developed to counter civil unrest in Germany. Hitler's assassination would have given the Replacement Army the perfect justification to implement this plan, impose martial law and oust any loyalists who insisted on prolonging the war. However, Hitler was not assassinated: he sustained only minor injuries in the explosion. Nevertheless, von Stauffenberg's group were determined to continue. They issued

---

* He lost his left eye, his right hand and two fingers from his left hand when his car was strafed by British aircraft in Tunisia in 1943.

orders to military district commanders in the name of the commander of the Replacement Army, claiming that an element within the party was attempting a coup and ordering the arrest of regional leaders, other senior party officials, senior SS and police leaders, senior Waffen-SS commanders and other SS and police officers. Some arrests were made in Vienna, while in Paris Senior SS and Police Leader Carl Oberg and other high officials were taken into military custody.[7]

Coincidentally, Himmler was at his own field headquarters near Rastenberg when the attack took place,* and he hurried to Hitler's side.[8] Like many others, he put his leader's survival down to providence and temporarily shelved any doubts he had about his conduct of the war. Instead, he attempted to exploit the situation for his own advantage. That very afternoon, he persuaded Hitler to appoint him Commander-in-Chief of the Replacement Army. In some respects, this represented the zenith of Himmler's power.

The situation throughout German-occupied Europe remained confused for some hours as contradictory orders were issued by the conspirators and by Hitler loyalists in Berlin and Rastenberg. But before long it was evident that the plot had failed. Members of the conspiracy could have cut communications from Rastenberg, but they failed to do so, which meant that Hitler and senior loyalists were able to countermand Valkyrie. After a struggle between conspirators and loyalists at Bendlerstrasse, von Stauffenberg and three other leaders of the plot were summarily executed in the courtyard of their headquarters.

The SS could never claim to have foiled the plot. The so-called 'state protection corps' had no knowledge of von Stauffenberg's group before the bomb exploded; and, perhaps even more damningly, they did virtually nothing to counter the coup once it had

---

* The conspirators had originally intended to kill both Himmler and Hitler in a single explosion, in the hope of paralysing the SS as well as the government, but this plan was abandoned because Himmler rarely attended the situation conferences.

been launched. Von Stauffenberg's rebellion was stopped in its tracks by members of the German Army acting at the behest of the regime's political leadership. The first SS personnel to arrive in Berlin were members of the Waffen-SS special forces from their base at Friedenthal, under the command of Otto Skorzeny, chief of sabotage within Office VI of the RSHA. But the crisis was already over by the time they showed up.

However, having failed to detect the conspiracy, the Gestapo now swung into action to exact revenge for it. Interrogations of existing resistance suspects were stepped up and around five thousand more people were arrested over the next few months. Many of these were not associated with the bomb plot, but they were still identified as potential opponents of the state. After a series of show trials, about two hundred alleged and genuine conspirators were executed between August 1944 and April 1945.[9]

On paper, Himmler was now the second most powerful man in Germany. As National Leader of the SS and Chief of the German Police, he controlled the nation's security and police apparatus, the intelligence service, and the Waffen-SS (which, by now, was notionally thirty-eight divisions strong). As Commander-in-Chief of the Replacement Army, he commanded all military units on home territory. But the reality was somewhat different. The vast majority of the Waffen-SS units were out of Himmler's reach, under the command of the OKW: his responsibility extended no further than supplying them with such men and materials as were still available. Meanwhile, by and large, the police were controlled by local party and civil authorities. Himmler occasionally attempted to transfer policemen into the Waffen-SS, but his efforts were invariably stymied by the party and regional leaders. Finally, his new command of the Replacement Army gave him authority over a vast pool of manpower, but there was little he could actually do with it: the Replacement Army was designed to supply units for combat, not to engage in combat itself.

Even more ominously for Himmler, his hold over the RSHA was slipping. During the course of the investigation into the bomb plot, Ernst Kaltenbrunner had started to forge an alliance with Martin Bormann, Hitler's secretary and head of the Party Chancellery. Like all senior figures in the National Socialist hierarchy, Bormann was highly experienced at the political in-fighting that earned power and prestige. He had also viewed Himmler's meteoric rise with some alarm and was determined to undermine him in order to increase his own influence. He did this by giving Kaltenbrunner direct access to Hitler, thus cutting Himmler out of the loop that controlled the RSHA. In practice, this meant that Himmler's orders – for example, those concerning the release of selected prisoners from concentration camps – could be ignored or even countermanded by Kaltenbrunner. In the RSHA, both Kaltenbrunner and his chief ally Müller loathed and distrusted Himmler's main confident, Schellenberg.

However, Himmler barely noticed any of these machinations against him. In November 1944, Hitler decided to create a new army group – Upper Rhine – for the area between Karlsruhe and the Swiss border. Early the following month, Bormann proposed Himmler as its commander, his argument being that, as head of the Replacement Army, Himmler would be able to muster the soldiers to man it.[10] Hitler agreed, and Himmler was duly appointed. It is not clear whether Bormann nominated Himmler in the genuine belief that he was the best man for the job or because he expected him to fail and consequently lose even more prestige. Either way, failure was inevitable because the formations under Himmler's command were weak and poorly trained. Nevertheless, Himmler was delighted finally to possess a high military command, and he was determined to launch an operation. It was decided that his new army group would combine with Army Group G to retake Strasbourg, which had recently been captured by the US 7th Army.

The assault began on 5 January 1945 and achieved some initial success, with Himmler's formations advancing to within a few kilometres of Strasbourg. However, the collapse of the Ardennes offensive to the north freed American troops to counter-attack. A few days after they did so, Himmler's forces were involved in a desperate fight just to cling on to the ground they had won.[11] On 24 January, Army Group Upper Rhine was deactivated and its formations – primarily the 19th Army and the various elements of the Replacement Army that had been assembled by Himmler – were subordinated to Army Group G. However, this was not quite the end of Himmler's military command career. The OKW had already decided to create a new army group – Vistula – in Pomerania, in order to coordinate the defence against the Soviet advance there. Field Marshal Maximilian von Weichs was just about to assume command when Hitler asserted his authority. In the teeth of opposition from the Army Chief of Staff, General Heinz Guderian, he handed the position to Himmler on 24 January.[12]

By now, Himmler had realised that he was not cut out for military command, but he was too intimidated to refuse. Army Group Vistula consisted of three armies – the 3rd Panzer Army, the 9th Army and the 21st Army, in total about 500,000 soldiers – but it was desperately short of vehicles and supplies, and so was barely operationally effective. In the first week of Himmler's command, several of his operations failed dismally. He subsequently retreated to the SS hospital at Hohenlychen, north of Berlin, claiming illness.

Throughout February, Guderian lobbied Hitler to replace Himmler with a competent, experienced general, but Hitler refused. Eventually, in mid-March, the Chief of Staff decided that he must press Himmler himself to resign. He arrived at Vistula's headquarters to learn that Himmler had been absent for more than a week, supposedly suffering from influenza. Guderian travelled on to Hohenlychen, found Himmler, and diplomatically suggested that he should relinquish his command 'on health grounds'. Himmler timidly agreed, and on 20 March General Gotthard Heinrici was appointed to succeed him.[13]

By now, Himmler seems to have been in a quandary about how to save his own skin. He remained terrified of challenging Hitler, yet was also desperate to improve his reputation with the Western Allies. On 19 February, he had met Count Folke Bernadotte, a member of the Swedish royal family and representative of the Red Cross, and had agreed to release some Scandinavian concentration camp prisoners.[14] Now, Schellenberg attempted to persuade him that he should make a peace offer to the Western Allies, via Bernadotte.[15] The two men met on 2 April, but Himmler remained indecisive. Later, Schellenberg attempted to persuade Bernadotte to act as a go-between with General Eisenhower, commander of the Western Allies, but the Swede said he would do so only if Himmler took power. When Schellenberg put this to Himmler, he continued to equivocate.

While Himmler vacillated in Germany, the Senior SS and Police Leader in Italy, SS-General Karl Wolff, was in an advanced stage of negotiations with Allen Dulles, the American representative in Switzerland, to surrender all German forces on the Italian front.[16] However, word of this leaked out in mid-April, and Wolff was summoned to Berlin to face the music. Himmler was furious with the former head of his personal staff for endangering his own position by opening negotiations behind his back, but Wolff countered that he was acting within his authority from Hitler. On 18 April, Wolff met Hitler and Kaltenbrunner and received permission to continue the negotiations.[17] He flew back to Italy and surrendered the German forces there on 29 April.[18]

Himmler's last meeting with Hitler occurred on 20 April, at a tea party held in what remained of the Reich Chancellery to celebrate the dictator's fifty-sixth birthday. The next day, he met Bernadotte again, but their discussions went nowhere. By now, though, Berlin was in the combat zone and Hitler would inevitably soon be trapped behind Russian lines. That fact seems to have finally emboldened Himmler. On the evening of 23 April, he and Schellenberg met Bernadotte at the Swedish Consulate in Lübeck, where Himmler made the following statement:

We Germans must declare ourselves as beaten by the Western
Allies. That is what I request you, through the Swedish government, to convey to General Eisenhower, so that any
further senseless fighting and unnecessary bloodshed might
be spared. To the Russians it is impossible for us Germans,
and above all for me, to capitulate. We will continue to fight
there until the Western Allied front has, so to speak, relieved
the German fighting front.[19]

This offer was put in writing and Bernadotte agreed to present it
to the Swedish government, who, in turn, would hand it on to the
Western Allies.

Neither Himmler nor Schellenberg seems to have appreciated
that this offer was meaningless. Himmler had no operational
authority over any combat troops, and he had received no autho-
risation from Hitler to seek peace. Moreover, it apparently did not
occur to Himmler that the Western Allies viewed him as a notorious war criminal and were not prepared to enter into any
negotiations with him.

Nevertheless, on 28 April, international press agencies carried
the story that Himmler had offered to surrender Germany to the
Western Allies. Obviously, this was picked up in Berlin, where
Hitler and his inner circle were sheltering in their bunker, now
completely surrounded by the Red Army.[20] Hitler was incensed by
what he regarded as treason from a man whose loyalty he had
never questioned. Of course, Himmler *had* remained loyal – at
least until Hitler's position had become literally hopeless – but that
was not enough for the dictator.

Hitler's first act of vengeance for this supposed treachery fell not
on Himmler, but on SS-General Hermann Fegelein. The dashing
cavalry commander had succeeded Wolff as liaison officer between
Himmler and Hitler in October 1943, and had cemented his place
in Hitler's inner circle by marrying Eva Braun's sister the following year. He had been living in and around the bunker as the
Soviets had tightened their noose around Berlin, but had suddenly

disappeared on 27 April. Members of Hitler's close protection detail, led by SS-Lieutenant Colonel Peter Högl,[21] were sent to find him, and Fegelein was discovered with his Hungarian mistress at his flat off the Kurfürstendamm,* drunk, dressed in civilian clothes, with a stash of cash and jewellery.[22] A court-martial was immediately convened under the presidency of SS-Brigadier Wilhem Möhnke, the commander of Hitler's SS military escort. However, Fegelein was too drunk to face this, so he was put in the custody of Heinrich Müller to sober up. News of Himmler's peace moves arrived while he was being interrogated the next day. A search of Fegelein's office revealed that he knew of Himmler's contacts with Bernadotte, and the enraged Hitler ordered him to be shot without further ado.[23] He was taken into the garden of the Reich Chancellery and executed by a firing squad from Hitler's close protection team.[24]

Himmler himself was stripped of all of his state and party roles on 29 April. Karl Hanke, the Regional Leader of Breslau, was appointed National Leader of the SS in his place.[25] However, this appointment was as meaningless as Himmler's peace offer: Hanke was still in Breslau, which was besieged by the Soviets.

The next day, Soviet soldiers advanced to within a few hundred metres of Hitler's bunker. A surprisingly large proportion of the defenders were of foreign origin, drawn from the Norwegian and Danish Panzer-Grenadier regiments of the *Nordland* Division, a few hundred French volunteers, and a company of Spanish fascists who had joined the Waffen-SS when the Blue Division was withdrawn from German service in 1943. As these soldiers were forced back by the Red Army, Hitler appointed Admiral Karl Dönitz, the chief of the German Navy, based in the north German town of Plön, his successor as head of state. Then the man who had ruled Germany for over twelve years committed suicide. To all intents and purposes, the National Socialist era was over.

---

* One of Berlin's most fashionable shopping streets, equivalent to Knightsbridge in London or Park Avenue in New York.

By this stage, Himmler had established his headquarters at Lübeck, and he immediately offered his services to the new administration when word arrived from Bormann that Hitler was dead and Dönitz was now in control of Germany and its armed forces. Dönitz later claimed that he turned Himmler down flat, but this seems unlikely, given the number of conversations the two men had around this time.[26] In fact, it seems that Himmler advised on the best way to conduct surrender negotiations until 5 May, when a provisional ceasefire came into effect on Dönitz's orders. At this point, Himmler gave a short speech to his remaining entourage – a disparate group of senior SS bureaucrats, Waffen-SS personnel, members of the Concentration Camp Inspectorate, and his personal staff, including SS-Colonel Rudi Brandt, his long-serving personal assistant – in which he effectively told them to make a run for it.

Himmler himself remained in and around Flensburg for a few days after the German surrender on 7 May, probably with his mistress.* Then he tried to escape, heading south towards Bavaria disguised as a Field Security Police NCO and wearing an eyepatch. He was accompanied by Werner Grothmann, one of his adjutants, and Heinz Macher, a young but highly decorated Waffen-SS captain, who were both dressed as army privates. They set out first by car and then, after reaching the River Elbe, on foot, posing as military refugees who were heading home. On 21 May, they were stopped at a British checkpoint between Hamburg and Bremen. Unfortunately for Himmler, he now discovered that Field Security Police NCOs were subject to automatic arrest, so all three men were detained and then moved to a holding camp at Westertimke. Nobody recognised Himmler, but he was sent on to

---

* Himmler is reputed to have had affairs with several women during his years as National Leader of the SS. The longest lasting of these was Hedwig Potthast, the daughter of a Cologne businessman, who had worked as Himmler's secretary and with whom he had two children (a son born in 1942 and a daughter born in 1944).

an interrogation centre at Barfeld, near Lüneberg, where he arrived on 23 May.[27] At that point, he decided to identify himself. In a meeting with the camp commandant, Captain Selvester, he removed his eye-patch, put on his distinctive spectacles and quietly said, 'Heinrich Himmler.' Selvester later recalled: 'His identity was at once obvious.'[28]

Military intelligence was immediately alerted, and Himmler was given a thorough body search. This revealed two brass tubes, similar to cartridge cases: one was empty, while the other contained a glass phial of a substance Selvester took to be poison. The commandant assumed that Himmler had concealed the other phial, possibly in his mouth. Selvester ordered food and tea for the prisoner and watched closely as he ate, but he noticed nothing unusual. A few hours later, Himmler was collected by Colonel Michael Murphy, from Montgomery's intelligence staff, and driven to a villa in Lüneburg.[29] The British were still convinced that he was concealing poison in his mouth; and they were right. As a military doctor prepared to give him an oral examination, he turned his head to one side, flicked the phial from a gap in his teeth with his tongue, and bit down on it.

Despite prolonged resuscitation attempts by the doctor, Heinrich Himmler was dead within a few minutes.[30]

Epilogue

It proved relatively easy to bury the SS in the aftermath of the war. Waffen-SS personnel were obliged to conform with the terms of the German surrender and turn themselves in to the Allied occupation forces as prisoners of war, and the great majority of them did so.[1] By 1945, the General-SS consisted of little more than a few offices manned by men too old or unfit to have been conscripted into the armed forces or Waffen-SS. For the most part, these remnants of a bygone age hung up their uniforms, went home and hoped that their connection to the organisation would not be noticed by the occupiers.

A few senior SS officers tried to go on the run, but none got very far. Globocnik hid in the Austrian Alps but was found by a British patrol after being denounced by an informer. He killed himself by taking poison on 31 May 1945.[2] Kaltenbrunner was arrested in the Bavarian Alps[3] and faced trial at Nuremberg, which made him the most senior member of the SS to face the International Military Tribunal. He was hanged after being found guilty of war crimes, as were Oswald Pohl and Kurt Daluege.* Heinrich Müller was probably killed – or committed suicide – in Berlin shortly after Hitler's death, although his body was never found.[4] Likewise,

---

* Daluege had suffered a massive heart attack in 1943 and had effectively retired. He had been replaced as head of the Order Police Main Office by General Alfred Wünnenberg.

Richard Glücks, the last Inspector of Concentration Camps, seems to have killed himself at Murwik Naval Base, Flensburg, on 10 May 1945,[5] but his death went unrecorded.

A few SS men who had committed war crimes and/or crimes against humanity managed to evade justice, for a time at least. The best known of these was Adolf Eichmann, who was captured by the US Army under the name 'Otto Eckmann' but managed to escape, via Italy, to Argentina. He lived and worked there – as 'Ricardo Klement' – for ten years before being captured by Israeli agents in 1960. Franz Stangl, the commandant of Treblinka, also escaped via Italy. He ended up in Brazil, where he lived under his own name for sixteen years before being extradited to West Germany. Aside from two months as a prisoner of war in 1945, Josef Mengele, the notorious Auschwitz medical officer, was never captured. He died in Brazil in 1979. None of these men benefited from any sort of conspiratorial SS underground network. Instead, they were assisted by a few naive or sympathetic individuals who were prepared to help them evade justice.[6]

Most former SS personnel faced nothing more than a spell in a prisoner of war camp, followed by a 'de-Nazification' hearing at the time of their release. This included the higher echelons of the organisation. In the view of Heinz Höhne, 'The majority of the SS leaders were treated with remarkable leniency.'[7]

Of course, history has not been so forgiving. When Himmler assumed control of the SS in 1929, he envisioned it becoming the *Staatschutzkorps* (state protection corps), an all-pervasive police and security body that would replace the existing police system. However, he saw its role as much more than simply engaging and defeating enemies of the state. As a wholehearted adherent to the racist doctrine of National Socialism, as well as a fiercely ambitious man, he wanted to place his organisation in the vanguard of the Third Reich as the principal protector of the German racial community. That necessitated total acceptance of Hitler's racist philosophy and determination to put it into practice by recruiting men with the ideological conviction to carry out whatever measures were deemed necessary. He achieved this by making the SS an 'elite order', vaguely modelled on medieval chivalric orders but imbued with National Socialist ideology. Talented and ambitious young men flocked to join, providing Himmler with the manpower to enforce Hitler's will. The central idea of National Socialism – that the German people were involved in a Darwinian struggle with the Jews for world supremacy – gave the SS its mission and transformed it from a repressive police force into an instrument of genocide.

Appendix: Table of Comparative Military Ranks

Waffen-SS	German Army	British Army	US Army	Command Responsibility
SS-Schütze, SS-Grenadier, SS-Pionier, SS-Kanonier, etc.	Grenadier, Pionier, Kanonier. etc.	Rifleman, Trooper, Gunner, Sapper. etc.	Private, Trooper, etc.	Normally none
SS-Sturmmann	Gefreiter	No rank equivalent but similar to a senior private	Private First Class	Usually none but may be section/squad 2ic
SS-Rottenführer	Obergefreiter	Lance corporal	Corporal	Section/squad 2ic
SS-Unterscharführer	Unteroffizier	Corporal	Sergeant	Section/squad commander
SS-Scharführer	Unterfeldwebel	No equivalent. The normal duties of a Scharführer were similar to those of a British staff sergeant but it was a lower rank	Sergeant	Usually associated with a clerical or administrative role at company level
SS-Oberscharführer	Feldwebel	Sergeant/staff sergeant	Staff sergeant	Platoon leader or 2ic. In the British Army, a platoon is usually led by an officer with a sergeant/senior staff sergeant as their 2ic
SS-Hauptscharführer	Oberfeldwebel	WO 2 (company sergeant major, etc.)	Technical sergeant	Normally the senior NCO within a company, with responsibility for administration, discipline, etc.
SS-Sturmscharführer	Hauptfeldwebel	WO 1 (regimental sergeant major, etc.)	Master sergeant	Normally the senior NCO within a battalion, with responsibilities for administration, discipline, etc.
SS-Untersturmführer	Leutnant	Second lieutenant	Second lieutenant	Platoon commander

SS rank	German Army	British Army	US Army	Command
SS-Obersturmführer	Oberleutnant	Lieutenant	Lieutenant	Platoon commander
SS-Hauptsturmführer	Hauptmann	Captain	Captain	Company commander. In the British Army, company-level sub-units are commanded by majors, while captains are typically company 2ics or battalion staff officers
SS-Sturmbannführer	Major	Major	Major	Battalion commander. In the British Army, majors command companies
SS-Obersturmbannführer	Oberstleutnant	Lieutenant colonel	Lieutenant colonel	Senior battalion or regimental commander. Battalion commander in the British Army
SS-Standartenführer/ SS-Oberführer	Oberst	Colonel. The rank of 'full' colonel in the British Army is not associated with a particular command function and is usually held by a senior staff officer, e.g. the chief of staff of a division	Colonel	Regimental commander
No equivalent	No equivalent	Brigadier	Brigadier general	Brigade commander
SS-Brigadeführer	Generalmajor	Major general	Major general	Normally a divisional commander
SS-Gruppenführer	Generalleutnant	Lieutenant general	Lieutenant general	Corps commander
SS-Obergruppenführer	General	General	General	Army commander
SS-Oberstgruppenführer	Generaloberst	No equivalent	No equivalent	
No equivalent	Generalfeld marschall	Field marshal	General of the army	In its short lifespan, the Waffen-SS produced no strategic-level commanders of note, although both Paul Hausser and Heinrich Himmler commanded army groups

Notes

Introduction
1   See, for example, Padfield, *Himmler*, or, for a more up-to-date picture, Longerich, *Heinrich Himmler*.
2   See Arad, *Belzec, Sobibor, Treblinka*.
3   Hathaway, *In Perfect Formation*, p. 11.

Chapter One: The Defeat of Wilhelmine Germany and the Origins of the National Socialist Party
1   Evans, *The Coming of the Third Reich*, p. 80.
2   Hitler, *Mein Kampf*, p. 192.
3   Kershaw, *Hitler: Hubris*, p.110.
4   Kershaw, *Hitler: Hubris*, p. 119.
5   Kershaw, *Hitler: Hubris*, p. 114.
6   Höhne, *The Order of the Death's Head*, p. 16.
7   Höhne, *The Order of the Death's Head*, p. 17.
8   Kershaw, *Hitler: Hubris*, p. 158.
9   Koehl, *The SS*, p. 20.
10 USNA BDC, SSO Personalakte Hewel.
11 Kershaw, *Hitler: Hubris*, p. 208.

Chapter Two: The Rebirth of National Socialism and the Creation of the SS
1   Kershaw, *Hitler: Hubris*, p. 211.
2   Kershaw, *Hilter: Hubris*, p. 211.
3   Kershaw, *Hitler: Hubris*, p. 213.
4   Evans, *The Coming of the Third Reich*, p. 195.
5   Evans, *The Coming of the Third Reich*, p. 195.
6   Kershaw, *Hitler: Hubris*, p. 217.
7   Evans, *The Coming of the Third Reich*, p. 196.
8   Evans, *The Coming of the Third Reich*, p. 196.
9   Quoted in Evans, *The Coming of the Third Reich*, p. 196.

10 Kershaw, *Hitler: Hubris*, p. 217.
11 Evans, *The Coming of the Third Reich*, p. 196.
12 Kershaw, *Hitler: Hubris*, p. 219.
13 Kershaw, *Hitler: Hubris*, p. 225.
14 Kershaw, *Hitler: Hubris*, p. 224.
15 Kershaw, *Hitler: Hubris*, p. 234.
16 Evans, *The Coming of the Third Reich*, p. 201.
17 Koehl, *The SS*, p. 24.
18 Koehl, *The SS*, p. 28.
19 Trevor-Roper, *Hitler's Table Talk*, p. 167.
20 Kershaw, *Hitler: Hubris*, p. 119.
21 BDC, SSO072B.
22 Koehl, *The SS*, p. 29.
23 Trevor-Roper, *Hitler's Table Talk*.
24 BDC, Personalakt Bednarek.
25 Bullock, *Hitler*, p. 128.
26 NARA, T-580/87.
27 Koehl, *The SS*, p. 30.
28 BDC, SSO100B.
29 BDC, SSO027A.
30 NARA, T-580/87.
31 NARA, T-580/87.
32 NARA, T-580/87.
33 NARA, T-580/87.
34 Evans, *The Coming of the Third Reich*, p. 206.
35 NARA, T-580/87.
36 Höhne, *The Order of the Death's Head*, p. 24.
37 Höhne, *The Order of the Death's Head*, p. 22.
38 Höhne, *The Order of the Death's Head*, p. 22.

Chapter Three: Heinrich Himmler
1   K. Himmler, *The Himmler Brothers*, p. 24.
2   Longerich, *Heinrich Himmler*, p. 18.
3   K. Himmler, *The Himmler Brothers*, p. 26.
4   Padfield, *Himmler*, p. 20.
5   George Hallgarten, a Jewish classmate of Himmler, quoted in Padfield, *Himmler*, p. 24.
6   Padfield, *Himmler*, p. 28.
7   Longerich, *Heinrich Himmler*, pp. 31–2.
8   Longerich, *Heinrich Himmler*, p. 32.
9   Padfield, *Himmler*, p. 37.
10 Höhne, *The Order of the Death's Head*, p. 31.
11 Padfield, *Himmler*, p. 38.
12 Höhne, *The Order of the Death's Head*, p. 34.

13 NARA BDC, SSO99A Personalakt Heinrich Himmler.
14 Padfield, *Himmler*, p. 67.
15 Padfield, *Himmler*, pp. 68–72.
16 Longerich, *Heinrich Himmler*, p. 88
17 Otto Strasser quoting his brother Gregor, quoted in Padfield, *Himmler*, p. 80.
18 NARA BDC, SSO99A, Personalakt Heinrich Himmler.
19 Karin Himmler, *The Himmler Brothers*, p. 118.
20 Quoted in Padfield, *Himmler*, p. 83.
21 NARA, T-580/87.
22 Koehl, *The SS*, p. 37.
23 Koehl, *The SS*, p. 38.

Chapter Four: A New Broom

1 NARA, T-580/87.
2 The best account of Dietrich's life, avoiding the 'fanboy' hagiography of much writing about him, is to be found in Messenger, *Hitler's Gladiator*.
3 Messenger, *Hitler's Gladiator*, p. 7
4 Messenger, *Hitler's Gladiator*, p. 209
5 NARA, T-580/87.
6 Koehl, *The SS*, p. 46.
7 Yerger, *Allgemeine-SS*, p. 53.
8 Kershaw, *Hitler: Hubris*, p. 334.
9 Kershaw, *Hitler: Hubris*, p. 326.
10 Kershaw, *Hitler: Hubris*, p. 327.
11 NARA BDC, SSO0134 Personalakt Kurt Daluege.
12 Höhne, *The Order of the Death's Head*, p. 55.
13 Höhne, *The Order of the Death's Head*, p. 57.
14 Höhne, *The Order of the Death's Head*, p. 58.
15 Koehl, *The SS*, p. 46.
16 Koehl, *The SS*, p. 47.
17 NARA, T-580/87.
18 Andrew and Mitrokhin, *The Sword and the Shield*, p. 124.
19 NARA BDC, SSO0134 Personalakt Kurt Daluege.
20 Koehl, *The SS*, p. 58.
21 Wistrich, *Who's Who in Nazi Germany*, p. 59.
22 Hathaway, *In Perfect Formation*, pp. 23ff. This is an excellent account of Darré's 'blood and soil' ideas.
23 This account of eugenics is based on Weale, *Science and the Swastika*, pp. 31ff.
24 Höhne, *The Order of the Death's Head*, p. 47.
25 NARA, T-580/87.
26 Koehl, *The SS*, p. 84.
27 H. Himmler, *Die SS*. This is a brief history of the SS and an explanation

of its ideology, originally published under Himmler's name in 1939 although drafted by the SS propagandist Gunther D'Alquen. It was widely reproduced, with revisions, until 1945, appearing in publications like SS pocket diaries and recruitment material.

28 Hathaway, *In Perfect Formation*, p. 47.
29 Neil Gregor, *How to Read Hitler*, p. 103 onwards.

Chapter Five: Taking Control

1 Kershaw, *Hitler: Hubris*, p. 363.
2 Bullock, *Hitler*, p. 253.
3 Höhne, *The Order of the Death's Head*, p. 156.
4 Höhne, *The Order of the Death's Head*, p. 153.
5 Quoted in Höhne, *The Order of the Death's Head*, p. 147.
6 Padfield, *Himmler*, p. 107. Padfield speculates on the motivation of many leading National Socialists, and he suggests quite strongly that Naval Intelligence infiltrated Heydrich into the SS.
7 Schellenberg, *The Memoirs of Hitler's Spymaster*, p. 31.
8 Padfield, *Himmler*, p. 155.
9 Quoted in Whiting, *Heydrich, Henchman of Death*, p. 35.
10 Browder, *Foundations of the Nazi Police State*, p. 26.
11 Himmler, 'Rede zur Officeseinführung von Ernst Kaltenbrunner als neuer RSHA-Chef am 30.1.43', quoted in Wildt, *Nachrichtendienst, politische Elite und Mordeinheit*, p. 9.
12 Browder, *Foundations of the Nazi Police State*, p. 28.
13 Browder, *Foundations of the Nazi Police State*, p. 27.
14 Bullock, *Hitler*, p. 261.
15 Kershaw, *Hitler: Hubris*, p. 456.
16 Evans, *The Third Reich in Power*, p. 11.
17 Kershaw, *Hitler: Hubris*, p. 459.
18 Browder, *Foundations of the Nazi Police State*, p. 54.
19 Evans, *The Third Reich in Power*, p. 11.
20 Kershaw, *Hitler: Hubris*, p. 461.
21 Kershaw, *Hitler: Hubris*, p. 468.
22 Höhne, *The Order of the Death's Head*, p. 70.
23 Browder, *Foundations of the Nazi Police State*, pp. 67–8.
24 Westermann, *Hitler's Police Battalions*, p. 39.
25 Browder, *Foundations of the Nazi Police State*, pp. 55–62. This is an excellent account of the early days of the Gestapo.
26 Westermann, *Hitler's Police Battalions*, pp. 39–40.

Chapter Six: Consolidation

1 Höhne, *The Order of the Death's Head*, p. 85.
2 Höhne, *The Order of the Death's Head*, p. 87.
3 Höhne, *The Order of the Death's Head*, p. 87.

4 Kershaw, *Hitler: Hubris*, p. 505.
5 Evans, *The Third Reich in Power*, p. 30 and Höhne, *The Order of the Death's Head*, pp. 90–2 for the machinations of Heydrich against Röhm and the SA.
6 Höhne, *The Order of the Death's Head*, p. 91.
7 Reportedly Hitler's words to von Blomberg, quoted in Höhne, *The Order of the Death's Head*, p. 96.
8 Kershaw, *Hitler: Hubris*, p. 511.
9 Höhne, *The Order of the Death's Head*, p. 102.
10 Kershaw, *Hitler: Hubris*, p. 513.
11 Messenger, *Hitler's Gladiator*, p. 61.
12 Höhne, *The Order of the Death's Head*, p. 116.
13 Koehl, *The SS*, p. 100.
14 Koehl, *The SS*, p. 98.
15 Koehl, *The SS*, p. 100.
16 Kershaw, *Hitler: Hubris*, p. 522.

Chapter Seven: Dachau and the Establishment of the Concentration Camps

1 NARA BDC, SSO Personalakte Eicke.
2 Sydnor, *Soldiers of Destruction*, p. 4.
3 Sydnor, *Soldiers of Destruction*, p. 5.
4 NARA BDC, SSO Personalakte Eicke.
5 NARA BDC, SSO Personalakte Eicke.
6 NARA BDC, SSO Personalakte Eicke.
7 Sydnor, *Soldiers of Destruction*, p. 8.
8 NARA BDC, SSO Personalakte Eicke.
9 Sydnor, *Soldiers of Destruction*, p. 9.
10 Sydnor, *Soldiers of Destruction*, pp. 10–11.
11 Höss, *Commandant of Auschwitz*, p. 65.
12 Sydnor, *Soldiers of Destruction*, p. 13.
13 Weale, *Science and the Swastika*, p. 126ff.
14 Quoted in Weale, *Science and the Swastika*, p. 127.
15 Quoted in Weale, *Science and the Swastika*, p. 132.
16 NARA BDC, SSO007B Personalakt Rascher.
17 Sydnor, *Soldiers of Destruction*, p. 10.
18 NARA BDC, SSO Personalakt Eicke.
19 Caplan and Wachsmann, *Concentration Camps in Nazi Germany*, p. 21.
20 Caplan and Wachsmann, *Concentration Camps in Nazi Germany*, p. 23.
21 For details of the concentration camps, see Sydnor, *Soldiers of Destruction*, Krausnick and Broszat, *Anatomy of the SS State* and Allen, *The Business of Genocide*.
22 Caplan and Wachsmann, *Concentration Camps in Nazi Germany*, p. 33.

Chapter Eight: The Central Organisation of the SS

1   The following organisational structures are derived primarily from Gelwick, *Evolution and Structure of the Waffen-SS* and 'Personnel Policies and Procedures of the Waffen-SS', Koehl, *The SS* and Yerger, *Allgemeine-SS*.
2   NARA BDC, SSO Personalakte Pohl.
3   Allen, *The Business of Genocide*, p. 26.
4   Goldensohn, *The Nuremberg Interviews*, p. 398.
5   Allen, *The Business of Genocide*, p. 24.
6   Goldensohn, *The Nuremberg Interviews*, p. 399.
7   Goldensohn, *The Nuremberg Interviews*, p. 400.
8   Allen, *The Business of Genocide*, pp. 27–29.
9   Allen, *The Business of Genocide*, pp. 31–33.
10 Allen, *The Business of Genocide*, pp. 33–35.
11 Allen, *The Business of Genocide*, p. 59.
12 Allen, *The Business of Genocide*, p. 85.
13 Gelwick, *Evolution and Structure of the Waffen-SS*, p. 70.
14 Gelwick, *Evolution and Structure of the Waffen-SS*, p. 72.
15 NARA BDC, SSO058 Personalakte Berger.
16 Höhne, *The Order of the Death's Head*, p. 417.
17 NARA BDC, SSO058 Personalakte Berger.
18 UKNA, KV2/172.
19 NARA BDC, SSO058 Personalakte Berger.

Chapter Nine: The Race and Settlement Office

1   Hathaway, *In Perfect Formation*, p. 26.
2   Evans, *The Third Reich in Power*, p. 27.
3   Yerger, *Allgemeine-SS*, p. 15.
4   Höhne, *The Order of the Death's Head*, pp. 271–72.
5   Höhne, *The Order of the Death's Head*, p. 145.
6   Koehl, *The SS*, p. 114.
7   NARA BDC, SSO Personalakt Himmler.
8   NARA BDC, SSO Personalakt Steiner.
9   Yerger, *Allgemeine-SS*, p. 15.
10 Gelwick, *Evolution and Structures of the Waffen-SS*, p. 90.
11 Koehl, *The SS*, p. 116.
12 Goodricke-Clarke, *The Occult Roots of Nazism*, p. 178.
13 Pringle, *The Master Plan*, p. 47.
14 Pringle, *The Master Plan*, p. 47.
15 Pringle, *The Master Plan*, p. 49.
16 Goodricke-Clarke, *The Occult Roots of Nazism*, p. 187.
17 Goodricke-Clarke, *The Occult Roots of Nazism*, p. 191.
18 Pringle, *The Master Plan*, p. 50.
19 Pringle, *The Master Plan*, pp. 57–62.

20 For a full account of the SS mission to Tibet, see Hale, *Himmler's Crusade*. The mission forms the backdrop to the Hollywood movie *Seven Years in Tibet* (1997).

21 Pringle, *The Master Plan*, p. 191.

22 Yerger, *Allgemeine-SS*, p. 15.

Chapter Ten: The SD – The Intelligence and Security Wing of the SS

1   In his monumental work on the leadership corps of the SD: Wildt, *Generation des Unbedingten*.

2   Wildt, *Generation des Unbedingten*, p. 10 (from a lecture given at the International Institute of Holocaust Research).

3   Höhne, *The Order of the Death's Head*, p. 162.

4   Kershaw, *Hitler: Hubris*, p. 365.

5   Westermann, *Hitler's Police Battalions*, p. 56.

6   Höhne, *The Order of the Death's Head*, p. 185.

7   NARA BDC, SSO Personalakt Six.

8   Browder, *Hitler's Enforcers*, p. 180.

9   Cesarani, *Eichmann*, p. 48.

10 NARA, T-175/265.

11 UKNA, KV2/2646.

12 UKNA, KV2/279.

13 UKNA, KV2/279.

14 UKNA, KV2/279.

15 UKNA, KV2/279.

16 UKNA, KV2/279.

17 UKNA, KV2/279.

18 Höhne, *The Order of the Death's Head*, p. 281.

19 Höhne, *The Order of the Death's Head*, p. 237.

20 UKNA, KV2/95.

21 Höhne, *The Order of the Death's Head*, p. 236.

22 Höhne, *The Order of the Death's Head*, p. 235.

23 Wildt, *Generation des Unbedingten*, p. 11.

24 Wildt, *Generation des Unbedingten*, p. 13.

25 Höhne, *The Order of the Death's Head*, p. 235.

26 UKNA, KV3/249.

27 UKNA, KV3/249.

28 UKNA, KV3/249.

29 UKNA, KV3/249.

30 Burleigh, *The Third Reich*, p. 671.

31 UKNA, KV2/397.

32 UKNA, KV2/397.

33 UKNA, KV2/397.

34 Fest, *Plotting Hitler's Death*, p. 199.

35 UKNA, KV2/95.

36 UKNA, KV2/95.
37 Hinsley and Simkins, *British Intelligence in the Second World War*, IV, p. 195.
38 Höhne, *The Order of the Death's Head*, pp. 456–57.
39 NARA BDC, SSO Personalakt Daluege.
40 This was revealed by Schellenberg during his post-war interrogation: see UKNA, KV2/95.

Chapter Eleven: The Path to Genocide
1 See, for example, Hilberg, *The Destruction of the European Jews*.
2 Hilberg, *The Destruction of the European Jews*, p. 28 (all references to Hilberg are from the single-volume, abridged version, unless a volume number is given).
3 Weale, *Science and the Swastika*, p. 40.
4 Weale, *Science and the Swastika*, p. 40.
5 Rigg, *Hitler's Jewish Soldiers*, p. 80.
6 Quoted in Gellately, *The Gestapo and German Society*, p. 109.
7 Browder, *Hitler's Enforcers*, p. 81.
8 Höhne, *The Order of the Death's Head*, p. 303.
9 NARA BDC, SSO Personalakt Eichmann.
10 Lang and Sibyll, *Eichmann Interrogated*, p. 14.
11 Lang and Sibyll, *Eichmann Interrogated*, p. 16.
12 Lang and Sibyll, *Eichmann Interrogated*, p. 23.
13 Lang and Sibyll, *Eichmann Interrogated*, p. 23.
14 Lozowick, *Hitler's Bureaucrats*, p. 26.
15 Lang and Sibyll, *Eichmann Interrogated*, pp. 32–33.
16 Höhne, *The Order of the Death's Head*, p. 309.
17 Lang and Sibyll, *Eichmann Interrogated*, p. 34.
18 Cesarani, *Eichmann*, p. 58.
19 Cesarani, *Eichmann*, p. 65.
20 Höhne, *The Order of the Death's Head*, p. 311.
21 Höhne, *The Order of the Death's Head*, p. 311.
22 Höhne, *The Order of the Death's Head*, p. 314.
23 Overy, *Goering*.
24 Höhne, *The Order of the Death's Head*, p. 319.

Chapter Twelve: Euthanasia and the Beginning of Mass Murder
1 Weale, *Science and the Swastika*, p. 44.
2 Weale, *Science and the Swastika*, p. 45.
3 Wolfgang Eckhardt, quoted in Weale, *Science and the Swastika*, p. 47.
4 Quoted in Weale, *Science and the Swastika*, p. 64.
5 Quoted in Weale, *Science and the Swastika*, p. 66.
6 Quoted in Burleigh, *The Third Reich*, p. 382.

7 Burleigh, *Death and Deliverance*, pp. 99–100. This is the best and most accessible discussion of the National Socialist euthanasia programme.
8 Burleigh, *Death and Deliverance*, p. 98.
9 Burleigh, *Death and Deliverance*, p. 98.
10 Burleigh, *Death and Deliverance*, p. 114.
11 Franz Stangl, quoted in Gitta Sereny, *Into that Darkness*, p. 50.
12 Burleigh, *Death and Deliverance*, p. 125.
13 Quoted in Weale, *Science and the Swastika*, p. 79.
14 Friedlander, *The Origins of Nazi Genocide*, p. 17.
15 Friedlander, *The Origins of Nazi Genocide*, p. 149.
16 Friedlander, *The Origins of Nazi Genocide*, p. 151.

Chapter Thirteen: Origins of the Waffen-SS
1 UKNA, KV2/172.
2 NARA BDC, SSO105a Personalakt Höss.
3 SS-Colonel Karl Heinz Bühler, letter to author, 3 March 1981.
4 UKNA, KV2/172.
5 UKNA, KV2/172.
6 NARA, T-354/194/3853322.
7 Stein, *The Waffen SS*, p. 6.
8 NARA, T-354/203/3865608.
9 Gelwick, *Evolution and Structure of the Waffen-SS*, p. 32.
10 NARA, T-580/87, directive dated 16 December 1934.
11 Gelwick, *Evolution and Structure of the Waffen-SS*, p. 31.
12 NARA, T-175/153/682779ff.
13 NARA, T-175/91/2613342.
14 NARA, T-175/153/682747.

Chapter Fourteen: Militarising the 'Political Soldiers'
1 Quoted in Hathaway, *In Perfect Formation*, p. 141.
2 UKNA, KV2/397.
3 Wegner, *The Waffen-SS*, p. 159.
4 Wegner, *The Waffen-SS*, p. 160.
5 Hathaway, *In Perfect Formation*, p. 103.
6 Wegner, *The Waffen-SS*, p. 154.
7 Wegner, *The Waffen-SS*, p. 271.
8 Quoted in Weale, *Renegades: Hitler's Englishmen*, p. 149.
9 USNA, SSO153B.
10 Stein, *The Waffen SS*, p. 14.
11 *Der Freiwillige*, May 1982.
12 NARA BDC, SSO152.
13 UKNA, KV2/172.
14 NARA BDC, SSO Personalakte Gille.
15 NARA BDC, SSO Personalakte Jüttner.

Chapter Fifteen: Expansion of the Militarised SS

1 Kershaw, *Hitler: Nemesis*, p. 53.
2 Kershaw, *Hitler: Nemesis*, p. 54.
3 Höhne, *The Order of the Death's Head*, p. 230.
4 Gelwick, *Evolution and Structure of the Waffen-SS*, p. 61.
5 Nuremberg Doc 467-PS.
6 NARA, T-580/87.
7 Mooney, *Dietrich's Warriors*, p. 30.
8 Höhne, *The Order of the Death's Head*, p. 416.

Chapter Sixteen: The Invasion of Poland and the Special Task Groups

1 Höhne, *The Order of the Death's Head*, p. 275.
2 Höhne, *The Order of the Death's Head*, p. 277.
3 Burleigh, *Death and Deliverance*, p. 129.
4 Burleigh, *Death and Deliverance*, p. 130.
5 Höhne, *The Order of the Death's Head*, p. 230.
6 Heydrich, letter to Special Task Force commanders, 21 September 1939, quoted in Aly, *'Final Solution'*, p. 14.
7 Aly, *'Final Solution'*, p. 15.
8 Rossino, *Hitler Strikes Poland*, pp. 90–91.
9 Westermann, *Hitler's Police Battalions*, p. 121.
10 Höhne, *The Order of the Death's Head*, p. 280.
11 Höhne, *The Order of the Death's Head*, p. 280.
12 Rossino, *Hitler Strikes Poland*, p.96.
13 Westermann, *Hitler's Police Battalions*, p. 144.
14 USNA, T-175/237/725997ff.

Chapter Seventeen: The SS and the Polish Jews

1 Cesarani, *Eichmann*, p. 78.
2 Cesarani, *Eichmann*, p. 79.
3 Cesarani, *Eichmann*, p. 79.
4 For a detailed discussion of the resettlement programme as it impacted on the Jews of Poland, see Aly, *'Final Solution'*.
5 Yerger, *Allgemeine-SS*, p. 20.
6 Aly, *'Final Solution'*, p. 107.
7 Cesarani *Eichmann*, p. 83.
8 Padfield, *Himmler*, p. 301.
9 Hilberg, *The Destruction of the European Jews*, p. 161.
10 Goldhagen, *Hitler's Willing Executioners*, p.146.
11 Hilberg, *The Destruction of the European Jews*, pp. 74ff.
12 Hilberg, *The Destruction of the European Jews*, pp. 80ff.
13 Hilberg, *The Destruction of the European Jews*, p. 90.
14 Browning, *The Path to Genocide*, p. 43.
15 Browning, *The Path to Genocide*, p.

16 Browning, *The Path to Genocide*, p. 44.
17 Hilberg, *The Destruction of the European Jews*, p. 338.

Chapter Eighteen: Gottlob Berger and the Creation of the Waffen-SS

1 UKNA, KV2/172.
2 Höhne, *The Order of the Death's Head*, p. 419.
3 Private Bob Brown, Royal Norfolk Regiment, quoted in 'Britannia and Castle', *Journal of the Royal Norfolk Regiment*, Number 104, December 2005.
4 NARA, SSO186A Personalakte Knöchlein.
5 Brunnegger, *Saat in dem Sturm*, p. 76.
6 Sydnor, *Soldiers of Destruction*, p. 106.
7 Sydnor, *Soldiers of Destruction*, p. 109.
8 Sydnor, *Soldiers of Destruction*, p. 109.
9 Brian Fahey, account on www.jazzprofessional.com, accessed 19 Feb 2006.
10 Mooney, *Dietrich's Warriors*, p. 40.
11 Höhne, *The Order of the Death's Head*, p. 420.
12 NARA, T-175/104/626381.

Chapter Nineteen: Making Up the Numbers: Foreign Volunteers and Criminals in the Waffen-SS

1 Gelwick, 'Personnel Policies and Procedures of the Waffen-SS', p. 537.
2 Gelwick, 'Personnel Policies and Procedures of the Waffen-SS', p. 539.
3 Eichmann, quoted in Lang and Sibyll, *Eichmann Interrogated*, pp. 16–17.
4 NARA BDC, SSO Personalakte Riedweg.
5 UKNA, KV2/376.
6 Sydnor, *Soldiers of Destruction*, p. 41.
7 Michaelis, *SS-Heimwehr Danzig*, p. 38.
8 UKNA, KV2/376.
9 USNA, T-175/50/2564266.
10 UKNA, HO336/2.
11 UKNA, HO45/25805.
12 UKNA, HO45/25805.
13 NARA, T-175/104/626381.
14 Höhne, *The Order of the Death's Head*, p. 422.
15 USNA, T-175/19/2523362-2523363.
16 Littlejohn, *Foreign Legions of the Third Reich*, I, p. 35.
17 USNA, T-175/19/2523346.
18 Quoted in Gelwick, 'Personnel Policies and Procedures of the Waffen-SS', p. 545.
19 Gelwick, 'Personnel Policies and Procedures of the Waffen-SS', p. 547.
20 USNA, T-175/103/2625971, quoted in Stein, *The Waffen SS*, p. 101.
21 BA, R 22/1007, Bl. 23, quoted in Klausch, *Antifaschisten in SS-Uniform*, p. 32.

22 IMT Nuremberg, testimony of Gottlob Berger.
23 IMT Nuremberg, testimony of Gottlob Berger.
24 BA, R22/1008, Bl. 25, quoted in Klausch, *Antifaschisten in SS-Uniform*, p. 32.
25 Klausch, *Antifaschisten in SS-Uniform*, p. 33.
26 Klausch, *Antifaschisten in SS-Uniform*, p. 35.
27 Klausch, *Antifaschisten in SS-Uniform*, p. 35.
28 NARA, SSO, Personalakt Dirlewanger.
29 NARA, SSO, Personalakt Dirlewanger.
30 NARA, SSO, Personalakt Dirlewanger.
31 BA, R 22/1007, Bl. 25, quoted in Klausch, *Antifaschisten in SS-Uniform* p. 33.
32 Klausch, *Antifaschisten in SS-Uniform*, p. 46.
33 Maclean, *The Cruel Hunters*, p. 58.
34 Klausch, *Antifaschisten in SS-Uniform*, p. 52.
35 Rubinstein, William D, 'The Secret of Leopold Amery', *History Today*, Volume 49, Issue 2, February 1999, pp. 17–23.
36 SS-*Hauptsturmführer* Alexander Dolezalek, letter to author, 1994.
37 UKNA, WO71/Wilson.
38 UK NA, WO71.
39 3./SS-Frw.-Panzer-Aufklärungs-Abteilung 11.
40 UKNA, KV2.
41 UKNA, KV2.
42 UKNA, HO45.
43 UKNA, KV2/631.
44 See, for example, SSO files on Dad Quan Allah and Gurbacan (*sic*) Singh Mangat: NARA BDC series.
45 Quoted in Stein, *The Waffen SS*, p. 195.
47 Bergmeier and Lotz, *Hitler's Airwaves*, pp. 79–80.
48 Du Vair family website: http://www.du-vair.nom.fr/index.htm.
49 Bergmeier and Lotz, *Hitler's Airwaves*, p. 81.
50 Bergmeier and Lotz, *Hitler's Airwaves*, p. 82.
51 USNA, SSO058, Personalakte Gottlob Berger, fr. 66178.
52 USNA, SSO058, Personalakte Gottlob Berger, fr. 66177.

Chapter Twenty: The Waffen-SS Heads East

1 Stein, *The Waffen SS*, p. 120.
2 Stein, *The Waffen SS*, pp. 130–32.
3 *Oxford Companion to the Second World War*, p. 113.
4 *Oxford Companion to the Second World War*, p. 437.
5 Stein, *The Waffen SS*, p. 152.
6 Buss and Mollo, *Hitler's Germanic Legions*, p. 17.
7 Stein, *The Waffen SS*, p. 155.
8 Stein, *The Waffen SS*, p. 162.

9   Stein, *The Waffen SS*, p. 170.

10 Stein, *The Waffen SS*, p. 180.

11 Stein, *The Waffen SS*, p. 181.

12 Lepre, *Himmler's Bosnian Division*, pp. 82–108 is the best account of the mutiny.

13 See Stein, *The Waffen SS*, pp. 184–88. Few of these formations either achieved divisional size or entered combat. Some confusion about this is caused by the German practice of 'battlegrouping' unconnected units with established formation headquarters.

14 Wegner, *The Waffen-SS*, p. 227.

Chapter Twenty-One: Operation Barbarossa and the First and Second Sweeps

1   Rhodes, *Masters of Death*, p. 14.

2   Hilberg, *The Destruction of the European Jews*, p. 103.

3   Höhne, *The Order of the Death's Head*, p. 328.

4   Höhne, *The Order of the Death's Head*, p. 329.

5   NARA, SSO076 Personalakte Blobel.

6   Rhodes, *Masters of Death*, p.11.

7   Evidence given at the Nuremberg Military Tribunal, *Einsatzgruppen* Trial.

8   Hilberg, *The Destruction of the European Jews*, p. 107.

9   Hilberg, *The Destruction of the European Jews*, p. 109.

10 *Einsatzgruppen* reports, quoted at Nuremberg Military Tribunal, *Einsatzgruppen* Trial.

11 *Einsatzgruppen* reports, quoted at Nuremberg Military Tribunal, *Einsatzgruppen* Trial.

12 *Einsatzgruppen* reports, quoted at Nuremberg Military Tribunal, *Einsatzgruppen* Trial.

13 *Einsatzgruppen* reports, quoted at Nuremberg Military Tribunal, *Einsatzgruppen* Trial.

14 Evidence given at Nuremberg Military Tribunal, *Einsatzgruppen* Trial.

15 *Einsatzgruppen* reports, quoted at Nuremberg Military Tribunal, *Einsatzgruppen* Trial.

16 Evidence given at Nuremberg Military Tribunal, *Einsatzgruppen* Trial.

17 Evidence given at Nuremberg Military Tribunal, *Einsatzgruppen* Trial.

18 Hilberg, *The Destruction of the European Jews*, p. 136.

19 Lang, *Top Nazi*, p. 180.

20 Burleigh, *Death and Deliverance*, p. 221.

21 Burleigh, *Death and Deliverance*, p. 221.

22 Hilberg, *The Destruction of the European Jews*, p. 138.

23 Browning, *Ordinary Men*.

24 NARA BDC, SSO Personalakte Fegelein.

25 Burleigh, *The Third Reich*, p. 563.

26 Yerger, *Riding East*, p. 104.
27 Yerger, *Riding East*, p. 104.

Chapter Twenty-Two: The Wannsee Conference
1 Quoted in Hilberg, *The Destruction of the European Jews*, p. 162.
2 Quoted in Klee, Dressen and Riess, *The Good Old Days*, pp. 219–20.
3 Minutes of the Wannsee Conference, International Military Tribunal Documents.
4 Minutes of the Wannsee Conference, International Military Tribunal Documents.
5 Minutes of the Wannsee Conference, International Military Tribunal Documents.
6 Minutes of the Wannsee Conference, International Military tribunal Documents.
7 Minutes of the Wannsee Conference, International Military Tribunal Documents.
8 Minutes of the Wannsee Conference, International Military Tribunal Documents.
9 Minutes of the Wannsee Conference, International Military Tribunal Documents.
10 Minutes of the Wannsee Conference, International Military Tribunal Documents.
11 Minutes of the Wannsee Conference, International Military Tribunal Documents.
12 Minutes of the Wannsee Conference, International Military Tribunal Documents.
13 Minutes of the Wannsee Conference, International Military Tribunal Documents.
14 Minutes of the Wannsee Conference, International Military Tribunal Documents.

Chapter Twenty-Three: The Extermination Camps
1 Poprzeczny, *Odilo Globocnik*, p. 32.
2 Poprzeczny, *Odilo Globocnik*, p. 208.
3 Arad, *Belzec, Sobibor, Treblinka*, p. 16.
4 TAL/ZStL, File No. 208 AR-Z 252/59: Case Against Josef Oberhauser et al.
5 IMT, Vol 6. PS-1553 on 30 January 1946.
6 Sereny, *Into That Darkness*, p. 36.
7 Arad, *Belzec, Sobibor, Treblinka*, p. 78.
8 Arad, *Belzec, Sobibor, Treblinka*, p. 76.
9 Arad, *Belzec, Sobibor, Treblinka*, p. 80.
10 Arad, *Belzec, Sobibor, Treblinka*, p. 87.
11 Arad, *Belzec, Sobibor, Treblinka*, p. 195.

12 *Oxford Companion to the Second World War*, p. 1260.
13 Arad, *Belzec, Sobibor, Treblinka*, p. 298.
14 Hilberg, *The Destruction of the European Jews*, III, p. 1219.
15 Arad, *Belzec, Sobibor, Treblinka*, p. 379.
16 This telegram was intercepted and decoded by the British signals intelligence service: UKNA, HW 16/23, decode GPDD 355a, distributed on 15 January 1943, radio telegrams nos. 12 and 13/15, transmitted on 11 January 1943.
17 USNA, SSO016a Personalakt Globocnik.
18 Hilberg, *The Destruction of the European Jews*, III, p. 951.

Chapter Twenty-Four: Auschwitz
1 Steinbacher, *Auschwitz, passim.*
2 Biographical information on Höss is from USNA BDC, SSO Personalakte Höss and Höss, *Commandant of Auschwitz.*
3 Höss, *Commandant of Auschwitz*, p. 82.
4 Steinbacher, *Auschwitz*, p. 29.
5 See, for example, USNA BDC, SSEM Personalakte Otto Moll.
6 Interview with Sam Pivnik, prisoner 135913, 3 October 2008.
7 Interview with Sam Pivnik, prisoner 135913, 3 October 2008.
8 Höss, *Commandant of Auschwitz,* p. 144.
9 Höss, *Commandant of Auschwitz*, p. 147.
10 Interview with Sam Pivnik, prisoner 135913, 3 October 2008.
11 Hilberg, *The Destruction of the European Jews*, p. 247.
12 Müller, *Eyewitness Auschwitz*, p. 71.
13 Höss, *Commandant of Auschwitz*, p. 198.
14 Interview with Sam Pivnik, prisoner 135913, 3 October 2008.
15 Interview with Sam Pivnik, prisoner 135913, 3 October 2008.
16 USNA BDC, SSO Personalakte Mengele.
17 Weale, *Science and the Swastika*, p. 148.
18 Steinbacher, *Auschwitz*, p. 58.
19 Interview with Sam Pivnik, prisoner 135913, 3 October 2008.
20 Hilberg, *The Destruction of the European Jews*, II, p. 611.
21 Hilberg, *The Destruction of the European Jews*, II, p. 609.
22 Hilberg, *The Destruction of the European Jews*, II, p. 657.
23 Hilberg, *The Destruction of the European Jews*, II, p. 594.
24 Hilberg, *The Destruction of the European Jews*, II, p. 608.
25 Hilberg, *The Destruction of the European Jews*, II, p. 568.
26 Hilberg, *The Destruction of the European Jews*, II, p. 672.
27 Hilberg, *The Destruction of the European Jews*, II, p. 674.
28 Hilberg, *The Destruction of the European Jews*, II, p. 679.
29 Hilberg, *The Destruction of the European Jews*, II, p. 688.
30 Hilberg, *The Destruction of the European Jews*, II, p. 692.
31 Hilberg, *The Destruction of the European Jews*, II, p. 698.

32 Hilberg, *The Destruction of the European Jews*, II, p. 708.
33 Hilberg, *The Destruction of the European Jews*, II, p. 801.
34 Hilberg, *The Destruction of the European Jews*, II, p. 824.
35 Hilberg, *The Destruction of the European Jews*, II, p. 844.
36 Hilberg, *The Destruction of the European Jews*, II, p. 845.
37 Hilberg, *The Destruction of the European Jews*, II, p. 855.
38 Höss, *Commandant of Auschwitz*, p. 158.
39 Steinbacher, *Auschwitz*, pp. 59–60.
40 Steinbacher, *Auschwitz*, p. 121.
41 Steinbacher, *Auschwitz*, p. 124.
42 Steinbacher, *Auschwitz*, p. 125.
43 Interview with Sam Pivnik, prisoner 135913, 3 October 2008.
44 Steinbacher, *Auschwitz*, p. 127.
45 Langer, *Cap Arcona*, p. 108.
46 Steinbacher, *Auschwitz*, pp. 134–36.

Chapter Twenty-Five: The Final Act

1   UKNA, KV2/97.
2   Schellenberg, *The Memoirs of Hitler's Spymaster*, p. 352.
3   Fest, *Plotting Hitler's Death*, p. 202.
4   Fest, *Plotting Hitler's Death*, p. 216.
5   Fest, *Plotting Hitler's Death*, p. 235.
6   Fest, *Plotting Hitler's Death*, pp. 258–60.
7   UKNA, KV2/1668.
8   Kershaw, *Hitler: Nemesis*, p. 675.
9   Fest, *Plotting Hitler's Death*, pp. 292ff.
10 Padfield, *Himmler*, p. 546.
11 Kershaw, *Hitler: Nemesis*, p. 745.
12 Kershaw, *Hitler: Nemesis*, p. 758.
13 Kershaw, *Hitler: Nemesis*, p. 759.
14 Padfield, *Himmler*, p. 565.
15 Schellenberg, *The Memoirs of Hitler's Spymaster*, pp. 434ff.
16 Padfield, *Himmler*, p. 573.
17 Lang, *Top Nazi*, p. 290.
18 Lang, *Top Nazi*, p. 296.
19 UKNA, KV2/97.
20 Kershaw, *Hitler: Nemesis*, p. 817.
21 Fest, *Inside Hitler's Bunker*, p. 99.
22 Padfield, *Himmler*, p. 596.
23 Fest, *Inside Hitler's Bunker*, p. 100.
24 Fest, *Inside Hitler's Bunker*, p. 100.
25 Padfield, *Himmler*, p. 598.
26 For a detailed account of the contacts between Himmler and Dönitz, see Padfield, *Himmler*, pp. 600–05.

27 Padfield, *Himmler*, p. 609.
28 Quoted in Padfield, *Himmler*, p. 609.
29 Padfield, *Himmler*, p. 610.
30 Padfield, *Himmler*, p. 611.

Epilogue

1 UKNA, FO1038/13.
2 Poprzeczny, *Odilo Globocnik*, p. 369.
3 UKNA, KV2/271.
4 Walters, *Hunting Evil*, p. 37.
5 Allen, *The Business of Genocide*, p. 270.
6 The most comprehensive and credible account of the escapes of Nazi war criminals and subsequent efforts to capture them is Walters, *Hunting Evil*.
7 Höhne, *The Order of the Death's Head*, p. 536.

Bibliography

Allen, M. T., *The Business of Genocide: The SS, Slave Labor and the Concentration Camps* (University of North Carolina Press, 2002)

Aly, G., *'Final Solution': Nazi Population Policy and the Murder of the European Jews* (Arnold, 1999)

Aly, G., *Hitler's Beneficiaries* (Verso, 2007)

Aly, G. and S. Heim, *Architects of Annihilation: Auschwitz and the Logic of Destruction* (Weidenfeld and Nicolson, 2002)

Andrew, Christopher and Vassili Mitrokhin, *The Sword and the Shield: The Mitrokhin Archive and the Secret History of the KGB* (Basic Books, 1999)

Annas, G. J. and M. A. Grodin, *The Nazi Doctors and the Nuremberg Code* (Oxford University Press, 1992)

Arad, Y., *Belzec, Sobibor, Treblinka: The Operation Reinhardt Death Camps* (Indiana University Press, 1999 edition)

Arad, Y., S. Krakowski and S. Spector (eds) *The Einsatzgruppen Reports* (US Holocaust Museum, 1990)

Arendt, H., *The Origins of Totalitarianism* (André Deutsch, 1951)

Arendt, H., *Eichmann in Jerusalem: A Report on the Banality of Evil* (Penguin, 1994)

Bankier, D., *The Germans and the Final Solution: Public Opinion under Nazism* (Blackwell, 1996)

Barnett, V., *Bystanders: Conscience and Complicity during the Holocaust* (Greenwood Press, 2000)

Bartov, O., *The Eastern Front 1941–45: German Troops and the Barbarization of War* (Palgrave Macmillan, 2001)

Bartov, O., *Germany's War and the Holocaust: Disputed Histories* (Cornell University Press, 2003)

Bauer, Y., *They Chose Life: Jewish Resistance in the Holocaust* (New York Institute of Human Relations, 1973)

Bauer, Y., *The Holocaust in Historical Perspective* (Seattle, 1978)

Bauer, Y., *A History of the Holocaust* (Franklin Watts, 1982)

Bauer, Y., *Rethinking the Holocaust* (Yale University Press, 2002)

Benz, W., *The Holocaust: A German Historian Examines the Holocaust* (Columbia University Press, 1999)

Bergmeier, H. J. P. and R. E. Lotz, *Hitler's Airwaves* (Yale University Press, 1997)

Berkley, G. E., *Hitler's Gift: The Story of Theresienstadt* (Branden, 2002)

Bernstein, R J., *Hannah Arendt and the Jewish Question* (Polity Press, 1996)

Biddiscombe, Perry, *The SS Hunter Battalions* (Tempus, 2006)

Black, E., *IBM and the Holocaust* (Little, Brown, 2001)

Blood, Philip W., *Hitler's Bandit Hunters* (Potomac Books, 2008)

Bloxham, D., *Genocide on Trial: War Crimes Trials and the Formation of Holocaust History and Memory* (Oxford University Press, 2001)

Borowski, T., *This Way for the Gas, Ladies and Gentlemen* (Penguin, 1976)

Bosworth, R. J. B., *Explaining Auschwitz and Hiroshima: History Writing and the Second World War 1945–90* (Routledge, 1993)

Bower, T., *Blind Eye to Murder* (André Deutsch, 1981)

Bracher, K. D., *The German Dictatorship: The Origins, Structures, and Effects of National Socialism* (Pelican University Books, 1973)

Breitman, Richard, *The Architect of Genocide: Himmler and the Final Solution* (Grafton, 1992)

Breitman, Richard, *Official Secrets: What the Nazis Planned,*

What the British and Americans Knew (Hill and Wang, 1998)

Broszat, Martin, *The Hitler State* (Longman, 1981)

Browder, George, *Hitler's Enforcers* (Oxford University Press, 1996)

Browder, George, *Foundations of the Nazi Police State* (University Press of Kentucky, 2004)

Browning, Christopher, *The Path to Genocide* (Cambridge University Press, 1995)

Browning, Christopher, *Nazi Policy, Jewish Workers, German Killers* (Cambridge University Press, 2000)

Browning, Christopher, *Ordinary Men: Reserve Police Battalion 101 and the Final Solution in Poland* (Penguin, 2001)

Browning, Christopher, *The Origins of the Final Solution: The Evolution of Nazi Jewish Policy 1939–1942* (Heinemann, 2004)

Brunnegger, Herbert, *Saat in dem Sturm* (Stocker Verlag, 2000)

Buergenthal, Thomas, *A Lucky Child* (Profile Books, 2009)

Bullock, Alan, *Hitler: A Study in Tyranny* (Penguin, 1990)

Burleigh, Michael, *Death and Deliverance: 'Euthanasia' in Germany 1900–1945* (Cambridge University Press, 1994)

Burleigh, Michael, *Ethics and Extermination: Reflections on Nazi Genocide* (Cambridge University Press, 1997)

Burleigh, Michael, *The Third Reich: A New History* (Macmillan, 2000)

Burleigh, Michael, *Germany Turns Eastwards: A Study of Ostforschung in the Third Reich* (Pan, 2002)

Buss, Philip H. and Andrew Mollo, *Hitler's Germanic Legions* (MacDonald and Jane's, 1978)

Cesarani, D. (ed.), *The Final Solution: Origins and Implementation* (Routledge, 1994)

Cesarani, D., *Eichmann: His Life and Crimes* (Heinemann, 2004)

Chêne le, E., *Mauthausen: The History of a Death Camp* (Methuen, 1971)

Cornwell, J., *Hitler's Pope: The Secret History of Pius XII* (Penguin, 1999)

Cornwell, J., *Hitler's Scientists: Science, War and the Devil's Pact* (Penguin/Viking, 2003)

Crankshaw, E., *Gestapo: Instrument of Tyranny* (Four Square, 1966)

Crew, D., *Nazism and German Society 1933–1945* (Routledge, 1994)

Dallin, A., *German Rule in Russia* (Macmillan, 1981 edition)

Davies, N., *Rising '44: The Battle for Warsaw* (Viking, 2004)

Dawidowicz, L., *The War against the Jews 1933–45* (Pelican, 1979)

Dean, M., *Collaboration in the Holocaust: Crimes of the Local Police in Belorussia and the Ukraine, 1941–1944* (Macmillan/ US Memorial Holocaust Museum, 2000)

Dederichs, M., *Heydrich: The Face of Evil* (Greenhill, 2006)

Engel, D., *The Holocaust: The Third Reich and the Jews* (Longman, 2000)

Evans, R. J., *Telling Lies about Hitler: The Holocaust, History and the David Irving Trial* (Verso, 2002)

Evans, R. J., *The Coming of the Third Reich* (Allen Lane, 2003)

Evans, R. J., *The Third Reich in Power* (Allen Lane, 2005)

Evans, R. J., *The Third Reich at War* (Allen Lane, 2008)

Fest, Joachim, *Plotting Hitler's Death* (Weidenfeld and Nicolson, 1996)

Fest, Joachim, *Inside Hitler's Bunker* (Pan, 2005)

Finkelstein, N. G., *The Holocaust Industry: Reflections on the Exploitation of Jewish Suffering* (Verso, 2001)

Finkelstein, N. G. and R. B. Birn, *A Nation on Trial: The Goldhagen Thesis and Historical Truth* (Holt and Co., 1998)

Fischer, K. P., *Nazi Germany: A New History* (Constable, 1995)

Friedlander, Henry, *The Origins of Nazi Genocide: From Euthanasia to the Final Solution* (University of North Carolina Press, 1995)

Friedländer, Saul, *Nazi Germany and the Jews: The Years of Persecution 1933–39*, Vol. I (HarperCollins, 1997)

Friedländer, Saul, *The Years of Extermination* (Weidenfeld and Nicolson, 2007)

Friedman, S., *A History of the Holocaust* (Vallentine Mitchell, 2002)

Gellately, Robert, *The Gestapo and German Society: Enforcing Racial Policy 1933–1945* (Clarendon Press, 1990)

Gellately, Robert, *Backing Hitler: Consent and Coercion in Nazi Germany* (Oxford University Press, 2001)

Gelwick, Robert S., 'Personnel Policies and Procedures of the Waffen-SS', unpublished Ph.D. dissertation, University of Nebraska, 1971

Gilbert, Martin, *Auschwitz and the Allies* (Michael Joseph, 1981)

Gilbert, Martin, *The Holocaust: The Jewish Tragedy* (Collins, 1986)

Goldensohn, Leon, *The Nuremberg Interviews* (Knopf, 2004)

Goldhagen, D. J., *Hitler's Willing Executioners: Ordinary Germans and the Holocaust* (Abacus, 1996)

Goodrick-Clarke, N., *The Occult Roots of Nazism* (I. B. Tauris, 1985)

Graber, G. S., *History of the SS* (Robert Hale, 1978)

Greenman, Leon, *An Englishman in Auschwitz* (Vallentine Mitchell, 2001)

Gregor, Neil, *How to Read Hitler* (Granta Books, 2005)

Gutman, I., *The Jews of Warsaw 1939–43: Ghetto, Underground, Revolt* (Indiana University Press, 1982)

Guttenplan, D. D., *The Holocaust on Trial: History, Justice and the David Irving Libel Case* (Granta Books, 2001)

Hale, Christopher, *Himmler's Crusade* (Castle, 2006)

Hartog, Rudolf, *The Sign of the Tiger* (Rupa and Co., 2001)

Hastings, Max, *Das Reich* (Michael Joseph, 1981)

Hathaway, J., *In Perfect Formation* (Schiffer, 1999)

HBSZ, *Der Dienstkalender Heinrich Himmlers 1941/42* (Christians Verlag,1999)

Headland, R., *Messages of Murder: The Study of the Reports of the Einsatzgruppen of the Security Police and Security Service 1941–43* (Fairleigh Dickinson University Press, 1992)

Herbert, Ulrich, *Best* (Dietz Verlag, 2001)

Hilberg, Raul, *The Destruction of the European Jews* (Holmes and Meier, 1985 three-volume, revised edition)

Hilberg, Raul, *The Destruction of the European Jews* (Holmes and Meier, 1986 single-volume, abridged edition)

Hilberg, Raul, *Perpetrators, Victims, Bystanders* (Harper, 1992)

Hillgruber, A., *Germany and the Two World Wars* (Harvard University Press, 1981)

Himmler, Heinrich, *Die SS* (1939)

Himmler, Katrin, *The Himmler Brothers* (Macmillan, 2007)

Hinsley, F. H. and C. A. G. Simkins, *British Intelligence in the Second World War* (HMSO Books, 1990)

Hitler, Adolf, *My Struggle* (Jaico Publishing House, 2007)

Höhne, H., *The Order of the Death's Head: The Story of Hitler's SS* (Penguin [1969] 2000)

Höss, Rudolf, *Commandant of Auschwitz* (Phoenix Press, 2001)

Hoffmann, Peter, *Hitler's Personal Security* (Da Capo Press, 1979)

Irving, David, *Hitler's War*, two volumes (Papermac, 1977)

Irving, David, *The War Path* (Michael Joseph, 1978)

Jäckel, E., *Hitler in History* (London, 1984)

Jacobs, Benjamin, *The Dentist of Auschwitz* (University Press of Kentucky, 2001)

Johnson, E. A., *The Nazi Terror: The Gestapo, Jews and Ordinary Germans* (John Murray, 1999)

Kahn, David, *Hitler's Spies* (Da Capo Press, 2000)

Kaienburg, Hermann, *Die Wiertschaft der SS* (Metropol, 2003)

Kaienburg, Hermann, *Der Militär- und Wirtschaftskomplex der SS im KZ-Standort Sachsenhausen-Oranienburg* (Metropol, 2006)

Kater, M. H., *Doctors under Hitler* (University of North Carolina Press, 1989)

Keneally, Thomas, *Schindler's Ark* (Sceptre, 1983)

Kershaw, Ian, *Popular Opinion and Political Dissent in the Third Reich: Bavaria 1933–1945* (Oxford University Press, 1983)

Kershaw, Ian, *The Hitler Myth: Image and Reality in the Third Reich* (Oxford University Press, 1987)

Kershaw, Ian, *Hitler: Hubris* (Allen Lane, 1998)

Kershaw, Ian, *Hitler: Nemesis* (Allen Lane, 2000)

Kershaw, Ian, *The Nazi Dictatorship: Problems and Perspectives of Interpretation* (Arnold, 2000 edition)

Kershaw, Ian, *Hitler, the Germans and the Final Solution* (Yale University Press, 2008)

Klausch, Hans-Peter, *Antifaschisten in SS-Uniform* (Edition Temmen, 1993)

Klee, E., W. Dressen and V. Reiss, *The Good Old Days: The Holocaust as Seen by its Perpetrators and Bystanders* (Free Press, 1991)

Koch, H. W. (ed.), *Aspects of the Third Reich* (Macmillan, 1987)

Koch, H. W., *In the Name of the Volk: Political Justice in Hitler's Germany* (I. B. Tauris, 1997)

Koehl, Robert Lewis, *The SS: A History 1919 to 1945* (Tempus, 2000)

Kogon, Eugen, *The Theory and Practice of Hell: The German Concentration Camps and the System behind Them* (Time Warner, 1998 edition)

Krausnick, Helmut and Martin Broszat, *Anatomy of the SS State* (Paladin, 1973)

Kumm, Otto, *Prinz Eugen* (J. J. Fedorowicz, 1995)

Lang, Jochen von, *Top Nazi* (Enigma Books, 2005)

Lang, Jochen von and Claus Sibyll, *Eichmann Interrogated: Transcripts from the Archives of the Israeli Police* (Da Capo Press, 1999)

Langer, L., *Holocaust Testimonies: The Ruins of Memory* (Yale University Press, 1991)

Langer, Wilhelm, *Cap Arcona* (Helmut Kaun, 1988)

Lepre, George, *Himmler's Bosnian Division* (Schiffer, 2000)

Levi, Primo, *If This is a Man* (Abacus, 1987)

Levi, Primo, *The Drowned and the Saved* (Abacus, 1989)

Levi, Primo, *Survival in Auschwitz: The Nazi Assault on Humanity* (Touchstone, 1996 edition)

Lifton, Robert Jay, *The Nazi Doctors: A Study of the Psychology of Evil* (Macmillan, 1986)

Lipstadt, D., *Denying the Holocaust: The Growing Assault on Truth and Memory* (Penguin, 1994)

Littlejohn, David, *Foreign Legions of the Third Reich* (R. James Bender, 1979)

Longerich, Peter, *The Unwritten Order: Hitler's Role in the Final Solution* (Tempus, 2003)

Longerich, Peter, *Heinrich Himmler, Biographie* (Siedler, 2008)

Lozowick, Yaacov, *Hitler's Bureaucrats: The Nazi Security Police and the Banality of Evil* (Continuum, 2000)

MacLean, French, *The Cruel Hunters: SS-Sonderkommando Dirlewanger, Hitler's Most Notorious Anti-Partisan Unit* (Schiffer, 1998)

MacLean, French, *The Field Men: The SS Officers Who Led the Einsatzkommandos – The Nazi Mobile Killing Units* (Schiffer, 1999)

Malkin, Lawrence, *Kruger's Men* (Back Bay Books, 2006)

Mangat, Captain G. S., *The Tiger Strikes* (Gagan, 1986)

Mayer, A., *Why Did the Heavens Not Darken? The Final Solution in History* (Pantheon, 1990)

Mazower, Mark, *Inside Hitler's Greece, 1941–1944* (Yale University Press, 1993)

Mazower, Mark, *Hitler's Empire* (Allen Lane, 2008)

Merkel, Peter H., *The Making of a Storm Trooper* (Princeton University Press, 1980)

Messenger, Charles, *Hitler's Gladiator* (Brassey's, 1988)

Michaelis, Rolf, *Das SS-Sonderkommando Dirlewanger* (Michaelis Verlag, 1998)

Michaelis, Rolf, *SS-Heimwehr Danzig in Poland 1939* (Schiffer, 2008)

Mommsen, Hans, *From Weimar to Auschwitz* (Oxford University Press, 1991)

Mommsen, Hans (ed.), *The Third Reich between Vision and Reality* (Berg, 2001)

Mommsen, Hans, *Germans against Hitler* (I. B. Tauris, 2009)

Mooney, Peter, *Dietrich's Warriors* (Schiffer, 2004)

Mueller-Hill, B., *Murderous Science: Elimination by Scientific Selection of Jews, Gypsies and Others in Germany 1933–45* (Oxford University Press,1997)

Müller, Filip, *Eyewitness Auschwitz: Three Years in the Gas Chambers* (Dee/The US Holocaust Museum, 1979)

Overy, Richard, *Goering* (Routledge and Kegan Paul, 1984)

Overy, Richard, *Interrogations* (Allen Lane, 2001)

Padfield, P., *Himmler: Reichsführer-SS* (Henry Holt, 1990)

Pelt, Robert Jan van, *The Case for Auschwitz* (Indiana University Press, 2002)

Pierik, Perry, *From Leningrad to Berlin* (Aspekt, 2001)

Poprzeczny, Joseph, *Odilo Globocnik* (McFarland and Co., 2004)

Posner, G. L. and M. Berenbaum, *Mengele: The Complete Story* (Cooper Square Press, 2000)

Pringle, Heather, *The Master Plan, Himmler's Scholars and the Holocaust* (Hyperion, 2006)

Proctor, R. N., *Racial Hygiene: Medicine under the Nazis* (Harvard University Press, 1988)

Ralhan, O. P., *Subhas Chandra Bose* (Raj Publications, 1996)

Read, Anthony, *The Devil's Disciples* (Jonathan Cape, 2003)

Reitlinger, G., *The Final Solution: The Attempt to Exterminate the Jews, 1939–1945* (Vallentine Mitchell, 1953)

Reitlinger, G., *The SS: Alibi of a Nation* (Arms and Arbour Press, 1981)

Reuth, Ralf Georg, *Goebbels* (Constable, 1993)

Rhodes, Richard, *Masters of Death: The SS Einsatzgruppen and the Invention of the Holocaust* (Perseus Press, 2002)

Rigg, Bryan M., *Hitler's Jewish Soldiers* (University Press of Kansas, 2004)

Roseman, M., *The Villa, the Lake, the Meeting: Wannsee and the Final Solution* (Allen Lane/Penguin Press, 2002)

Rossino, Alexander B., *Hitler Strikes Poland* (University Press of Kansas, 2003)

Russell, Lord, of Liverpool, *The Scourge of the Swastika* (Cassell and Co., 1954)

Schellenberg, Walter, *The Memoirs of Hitler's Spymaster* (André Deutsch, 2006)

Segev, Tom, *Soldiers of Evil* (McGraw-Hill, 1988)

Sereny, G., *Into That Darkness: From Mercy Killing to Mass Murder* (Pimlico, 1995 edition)

Sereny, G., *The German Trauma: Experiences and Reflections 1938–2000* (Allen Lane, 2000)

Shepherd, Ben, *War in the Wild East* (Harvard University Press, 2004)

Sofsky, W., *The Order of Terror: The Concentration Camp* (Princeton Press, 1993)

Spitzy, Reinhard, *How We Squandered the Reich* (Michael Russell, 1997)

Stein, George H., *The Waffen SS* (Cornell University Press, 1966)

Steinbacher, Sybille, *Auschwitz: A History* (Penguin, 2005)

Stroop, J., *The Stroop Report* (Secker and Warburg, 1980 edition)

Sydnor, Charles W., *Soldiers of Destruction* (Princeton University Press, 1977)

Toland, J., *Adolf Hitler* (Doubleday, 1976)

Trevor-Roper, Hugh, *Hitler's Table Talk 1941 to 1944* (Phoenix Press, 2000)

Volkner, Werner, *Many Rivers I Crossed* (W. Volkner, 2004)

Voss, Johann, *Black Edelweiss* (Aberjona Press, 2002)

Walters, Guy, *Hunting Evil* (Transworld, 2009)

Weale, Adrian, *Renegades: Hitler's Englishmen* (Weidenfeld and Nicolson, 1994)

Weale, Adrian, *Science and the Swastika* (Channel 4 Books, 2001)

Wegner, Bernd, *The Waffen-SS* (Blackwell, 1990)

Weingartner, James J., *Hitler's Guard* (Battery Press, n.d.)

Westermann, Edward B., *Hitler's Police Battalions* (University Press of Kansas, 2005)

Wetter, Wolfram, *The Wehrmacht* (Harvard University Press, 2006)

Whiting, Charles, *Heydrich: Henchman of Death* (Pen and Sword, 1999)

Wildt, Michael, *Generation des Unbedingten* (Hamburger Edition, 2003)

Wildt, Michael (ed.), *Nachrichtendienst, politische Elite und Mordeinheit: Der Sicherheitsdienst des Reichsführers SS* (Hamburger Edition, 2003)

Wistrich, Robert S., *Who's Who in Nazi Germany* (Henry Holt, 1982)

Yerger, Mark C., *Riding East: The SS Calvalry Brigade in Poland and Russia 1939–1942* (Schiffer, 1996)

Yerger, Mark C., *Allgemeine-SS: The Commands, Units and Leaders of the General SS* (Schiffer, 1997)

Index

About the Author

Adrian Weale was born in 1964 and educated at York University, the Royal Military Academy Sandhurst and the Joint Services Command and Staff College. After service in the regular army as a military intelligence officer, he has, since 1992, pursued twin careers as a writer and journalist, and active reserve officer. He has published eight works of non-fiction and written for most of the national newspapers, and broadcasts regularly on defence and historical topics on radio and television. As a soldier he has served in Britain, Europe, the Middle East, Africa and the Americas. He is married with three children and lives in London and the Welsh borders.